Gene Cartels

To my wife, Vanessa

Gene Cartels

Biotech Patents in the Age of Free Trade

Luigi Palombi

Regulatory Institutions Network, Australian National University, Australia

With a Foreword by Baruch S. Blumberg

Edward Elgar
Cheltenham, UK • Northampton, MA, USA

© Luigi Palombi 2009

Published by
Edward Elgar Publishing Limited
The Lypiatts
15 Lansdown Road
Cheltenham
Glos GL50 2JA
UK

Edward Elgar Publishing, Inc.
William Pratt House
9 Dewey Court
Northampton
Massachusetts 01060
USA

A catalogue record for this book
is available from the British Library

Library of Congress Control Number: 2008943832

PEFC
PEFC/16-33-111
CATG-PEFC-052
www.pefc.org

ISBN 978 1 84720 836 1

Printed and bound in Great Britain by MPG Books Ltd, Bodmin, Cornwall

Contents

Foreword

The patent system and its predecessors date back to the earliest period of the Common Law. British practices applied to their North American colonies and the US constitution of 1787 included a provision for the granting of patents. Benjamin Franklin was not only a politician, diplomat, soldier, and public official but also a very productive inventor and successful entrepreneur. He managed to franchise his printing business at an early age, giving him the time and the resources to pursue his interest in science and in national and world affairs. He was a member of the US Constitutional Convention and is believed to have encouraged the inclusion of the patent provision into the Constitution; he himself never patented his own many inventions. Thomas Jefferson, initially as Secretary of State, had responsibilities for the patent law. He was skeptical, but in time appreciated the potential value of linking the possibilities of personal profit with the introduction of new and applicable ideas that would benefit society in general. The system was open, relatively inexpensive, and available to all, no matter their social status.

When Franklin founded the American Philosophical Society ('Philosophical' in the 18th century sense of 'natural philosophy', that is, science) he emphasized the discovery of the new:

> All new-discovered Plants, herbs, Trees, Roots, etc. their Virtues, uses, etc; Methods of propagating them. . . .New Methods of Curing or Preventing Diseases. New and useful improvements in any Branch of Mathematics; New Discoveries in Chemistry, such as Improvements in Distillation, Brewing, Assaying of Ores. New mechanical Inventions for saving labour; as Mills, Carriages, etc., and for Raising and Conveying of Water, Draining of meadows, New Arts, Trades, manufactures, etc. that may be proposed or thought of; Surveys, maps and Charts of Particular Parts of the Sea-coasts or Inland Countries.

His list included discoveries about the natural world, ideas and abstract notions, but also the practical application this 'new' and 'useful knowledge' through the action of human ingenuity into inventions. It was the voice of the enlightenment on a new shore speaking to a new nation about the importance of science and scientific endeavor.

They wanted to foster discovery and invention and patents were seen as a possible aid to the process of invention.

How does a practicing scientist regard the patent system? My experience in science spans more than 50 years, primarily in medical biological science latterly including space-related biological science. Attitude towards patents and commercial application of research have changed radically over these years. In medical school in the late 1940s, commercial applications of medicine and biological discovery did not even enter our conversation. Recently, universities and research laboratories are focussed on extracting income from the products of their staff's research activities. The academic and science institutional model comes closer and closer to the business model. Patents – that embody and order valued 'intellectual property' – are considered an important part of the assets of a successful institution. As a consequence there is an increased emphasis on application (technology transfer, translational science) to produce patentable and marketable products to add to the institutions portfolio.

However, there is a downside to this approach that could have the effect of diminishing innovation. Research programs that are directed towards a particular product – develop a drug for a specified disease, design a vaccine for an identified microbial target, devise a machine to deliver a drug for a known purpose – are goal directed; you know where the path is leading. However many of the great advances in science and medicine have come from institutions that provide an environment of basic research, research that can produce totally new ideas that could not have been perceived at the beginning of the project. The path may be known but not where it will lead. This kind of research is done to understand fundamental natural phenomenon and is often generated by a driving curiosity that may be idiosyncratic and is often not in a popular research area. Historically, it is often research of this kind – not goal directed, not patent-bound, not previously defined research – that leads to the most exciting and useful results. If institutions are totally committed to generating application and patents there will be less funding for this essential discovery activity. A well-directed institution will know how to maintain a balance and not expend all its energies on immediately patentable products. It is reassuring that many scientists, even those involved in the most basic and even esoteric fields of research, are very happy to see their discoveries applied and generate wealth and do not require much urging to do so. Independent of any other reason for obtaining a patent, at a practical level, it is usually very difficult to have research converted to a widely used product unless a commercial company assumes the burden of development; they often will not do this without patent protection.

Gene Cartels: Biotech Patents in the Age of Free Trade is a valuable book for the scientist providing, in an elegantly scholarly style, deep insights into the origins, history, evolution, and current status of patent systems. It also discloses features that can lead, in effect, to a misuse of power. It focuses on the special case of the invention of 'naturally occurring biological materials that have been removed from their natural environment – that is isolated.' This raises profound questions including the ancient and ongoing question of 'What is life?'. It is particularly intriguing in the case of the patenting of genes. Rarely genes are totally deterministic, that is the presence of the gene in appropriate dose, is the equivalent of having the disease. There are many such genes, but the diseases they control are usually, but not always, rare. Most genes that are involved with common diseases – cardiovascular, cancer, infectious agents, etc. that impose the greatest burden on humanity are susceptibility genes. Their presence may increase the likelihood of a disease but other factors external to the gene – environmental agents, the internal environment, behavior, and other etiologic factors – are required before disease is manifest. And, there are usually many susceptibility gene loci that affect a particular disease. How does this effect invention and patentability?

Genes have many effects in addition to those initially ascribed to them and often reflected in their name. There is a remarkable amount of conservation in the human genome; that is, there are strong similarities (homologies) between the human genes and those of precedent species. It is remarkable that archaea, (bacteria-like organisms that usually live in extreme environments of temperature, pressure, pH, light, radiation, etc.) that are probably the most 'primitive' of life forms, share one third of their genome with mammals. Evolution uses existing genes, including the conserved genes, to respond to changes in the environment over generations. We, in effect, carry our biological history within our genome. It is likely that these homologous genes in humans still retain characteristics of earlier organisms that may be expressed in the human under some circumstances. Does the 'inventor' need to know what these are when a gene is used for a medical purpose?

It is likely that increasing awareness of the biology of living systems – not just of an isolated natural substance – will alter our views on the use of natural materials or life forms. It is essential for the scientists and those who apply their discoveries to understand how expanding biological knowledge engages with the long and changing history of patent systems.

Baruch S. Blumberg
Fox Chase Cancer Center

Preface

The word 'patent' does not appear in its title yet the Statute of Monopolies, passed by the English Parliament in 1623, is the mother of modern patent law in all common law countries. It became law in 1624 near the end of the reign of James I,[1] at a time when Parliament was asserting its political independence of the King and dealt with one of a number of issues that contributed to the growing tension between them and, ultimately, the King's heir, Charles I.[2]

When James I inherited the throne of England and Ireland in 1603 on the death of Elizabeth I,[3] he also inherited her dislike of Parliamentary interference. He considered himself divinely appointed and resented Parliament's claim that he was subject to its law; he dissolved it eight years later in 1611. Unfortunately for him, since Edward III had been forced to concede the royal prerogative power of taxation to Parliament in April 1341, his ability to replenish his treasury was restricted and so he, like his predecessor, sold monopolies, titles and other offices (including judicial offices) as a means of overcoming the fiscal consequences that came with this political independence. In time his excessive spending and the economic impact of the abusive monopolies, which his exercise of crown privileges created, led to his growing unpopularity, and with England in recession he begrudgingly recalled Parliament in 1621. This time however the parliamentarians were not in a forgiving mood; they realized that as long as the King had the power to finance his treasury without recourse to taxation, by bestowing monopolies as he saw fit, not only did he have the power to distort prices and the availability of commodities at will, but he could, as he had done for 10 years, rule without Parliament. This option was no longer acceptable to the Puritan parliamentarians, whose vision for England had no place for the powers expected by James I.

Regrettably the war of words begun between James I and Parliament was to end badly for Charles I, who, lacking his father's judgement, took the argument with Parliament into the battlefields of England. Having started a civil war against Parliamentary forces in 1642, when he lost in 1645 he refused to negotiate a power sharing agreement with Cromwell. Instead, during his captivity at Hampton Court Palace and, after a failed escape, at Carisbrooke Castle on the Isle of Wight, he preferred negotiating with the Scots, who promptly avenged him with a second civil war. This was to seal his fate. Failing to triumph in battle, in 1648 he was handed over to the Parliamentary army, placed in custody, charged with treason, tried, convicted and finally publicly executed at Whitehall on 30 January 1649 as a traitor. He died holding the firm belief that as King he was accountable to no man, no court and no Parliament and that, as a divinely anointed agent of God, he was answerable to no law other than His. Charles I's execution had a profound impact upon England, leading not only to the formation of a republic, albeit briefly, but to reforms in the law and the system of justice. With the Restoration of Charles II[4] to the throne in 1660, many of those reforms were disposed of, but never again would an English King raise his standard against an English Parliament.

* * *

With this brief glimpse into the political scene that existed around the time of the Statute of Monopolies, it is worth emphasizing that the modern Anglo-American patent systems that are its progeny are intimately connected to these events. Although the present politics and economics of the world are unquestionably unique, the history of the origins of the patent systems provides useful insights into their constructions, purposes, objectives and, most importantly, limitations. Modern proponents of patents will often refer to only one objective: a reward for those who have disclosed to the world an *invention*. They cite this as if all other objectives of these patent systems are irrelevant. They ignore or are ignorant of their history. They suggest that the term 'invention' even extends to naturally occurring biological materials that have been removed from their natural environments – that is, isolated. They claim 'anything under the sun made by man',[5] including a genetically modified organism, is an 'invention' – because in 1980 the US Supreme Court held in the famous case of *Diamond v Chakrabarty* that a genetically modified bacterium, a life form, was properly the subject of a patent under US patent law. They also argue that it is right to patent even isolated human genes or gene mutations, that is those genes which are linked to human illnesses such as cystic fibrosis and breast and ovarian cancer.[6] They say that without patents the risky and expensive research and development needed to compensate investors in the pharmaceutical and biotechnology industries would evaporate.[7] But are they right? Louis Pasteur, Joseph Lister, Alexander Fleming, Howard Florey, James Watson and Francis Crick, to name a few, are persons of science whose discoveries and work were risky and time-consuming, yet they did not patent the results of their humanitarian work (although Pasteur was awarded US patents for inventions relating to beer production). Pasteur discovered that bacteria transmitted infection and developed methods to kill them; he also developed vaccines for cholera, anthrax and rabies. Joseph Lister discovered that carbolic acid could be used to sterilize surgical equipment, wounds and surgeons' hands; Alexander Fleming observed that a fungal spore killed a bacterium and named this natural substance 'penicillin'; Howard Florey pursued Fleming's research to develop penicillin as a medicine; James Watson and Francis Crick produced a model of the molecular structure of DNA. Each have been revered for their breakthroughs in science, yet each of them was hardly motivated by the promise of a patent. In commenting on how the patent system has motivated inventors, Christine MacLeod and Alessandro Nuvolari noted that during the nineteenth century 'in Britain one could become a "great inventor" without obtaining a patent',[8] and speculated, 'it may owe something to the high esteem in which the British held public-spirited inventors who foreswore intellectual property rights, thereby enhancing their reputation as disinterested benefactors'.[9] Pasteur was buried in the Cathedral of Notre Dame, but his body now lies in the Institute Pasteur, a research institution established in his honour; Lister was made a Baron by Queen Victoria; Fleming was Knighted by King George VI and shared the Nobel Prize with Florey and Chain; Florey was made a Baron by Queen Elizabeth II; and Watson and Crick were awarded the Nobel Prize. Each of them made contributions to science and humanity, improving and saving the lives of millions. We, and future generations, owe a great deal to each of them, but had they faced the multitude of patents that face medical and scientific researchers today – patents over genes, non-genes, gene mutations, and other biological materials – would they have been free to undertake their work, to make their discoveries?

As the economic fortunes of countries and empires have waxed and waned, the walls of protection around each have gone up and down. Patents have long held a traditional role as a tool for sovereignties and governments to assist in the protection of economies; yet as the post-World War II world has firmly entered the era of free trade, the monopolies which patents create sit on the landscape like crumbling ruins of a bygone age. For many decades prior to this modern era, passionate legislative debate about the patent system was a colourful feature on both sides of the Atlantic, but this has quietened to an uneasy hum as a new patent paradigm has emerged – no longer seen as a protectionist tool, the monopoly has assumed the role of a legitimate reward for innovation, granted increasingly to multinational corporations which paradoxically hold no allegiance to any one country. And as new technologies enter the field these monopolies are now automatically granted, even when innovation is hard to discern. The once-limited monopoly of the traditional patent can now be manipulated to cover too widely and for periods many times longer than deemed appropriate. Yet there is disquiet among legislators, the judiciary, scientists and academics alike over the role that patents play in the free-trade world, and indeed they are torn over whether they should play any role at all, as the far-reaching consequences of patents are being felt.

This book seeks to trace how we have arrived at this situation, re-examining within their historical and economic contexts the legislative debates and key judicial arguments that the patent community now dismisses as historically quaint and irrelevant, convinced as it is of the patent's legitimacy and permanency while its eyes are firmly fixed to the future. But there are strong lessons to be gleaned from turning over the debates of the past, especially for the developing world that, too, is being swept along by the enthusiasm for patents, either willingly or forcibly through international treaty, and it is this fast-growing sector that the author hopes will also find salient truths.

NOTES

1. 1566–1625; reigned as James VI of Scotland from 1567 and as James I of Great Britain from 1603.
2. 1600–1649; King of England, Scotland and Ireland, 1625–1649.
3. 1533–1603; Queen of England and Ireland, 1588–1603.
4. 1630–1685; King of Scotland, 1649–1660; King of England, Scotland and Ireland, 1660–1685.
5. *Diamond, the Commissioner of Patents v Chakrabarty*, 447 US 303, 309 fn 6 (1980).
6. Crespi, S (1995), 'Biotechnology Patenting: The Wicked Animal Must Defend Itself', *European Intellectual Property Review*, **17** (9), 431–41.
7. Blackburn, RP (1999), 'Chiron's Licensing Policy', *Science*, New Series, **285** (5430), 1015.
8. MacLeod, C and A Nuvolari (2006), 'The Pitfalls of Prosopography: Inventors in the Dictionary of National Biography', *Technology and Culture*, **47**, 757–776, 776.
9. *Ibid.*

Table of cases

United States

PART I

Monopolies in the age of free trade

Lord Derby himself told us, that he considered Protection as quite gone. It is a pity they did not find this out a little sooner; it would have saved so much annoyance.

Queen Victoria, in a letter to her uncle, King Leopold I of Belgium in 1852

1. The early history of Anglo-American patent systems

The exercise of crown privileges, some of which created monopolies, was recorded on the Calendar of Patent Rolls as early as 1202, and 'letters patent' (that is, open letters instructing the public about a range of topics) were granted by English monarchs to create monopolies with respect to the provision of goods within their realm.

The Calendar records that one of these monopolies was awarded under the authority of Edward III[1] by his son, John of Gaunt 1st Duke of Lancaster,[2] to John Pecche, a former mayor of London. The monopoly to Pecche was arranged by Richard Lyons, a merchant and alderman of London, who was in the business of financing the Duke's rather extravagant lifestyle. In this case, the Duke, in flagrant disregard of a Parliamentary ban on its sale, arranged for Pecche to be granted letters patent over the sale of sweet wine in London, but on condition that Pecche pay the King a royalty based on the volume of sweet wine sold. Naturally the Duke pocketed the royalty; but by 1376, with Edward,[3] the Duke's eldest brother and heir to the throne, dead, the King gravely ill and Richard,[4] the 8-year-old heir apparent, under the influence of his uncle, Parliament had to demonstrate its authority. This it did by charging Lyons, who was alleged to have unfairly used his monopoly to extract exorbitant prices for sweet wine, with 'engrossing'[5] and Pecche, who was alleged to have failed to pay the King's royalty, with fraud. Perhaps in these circumstances Lyons and Pecche were simply scapegoats, but the fact that Parliament acted to close down this unlawful monopoly demonstrates that it was intent on establishing a precedent against the misuse of market power, regardless of the fact that it had been established under the authority of the King's letters patent.

Indeed it would appear that Parliament's stand had some effect because by the time of Henry VI[6], the Duke's great grandson, the types of monopolies that had been arranged for Pecche were not in vogue. In fact Henry VI's first grant of letters patent in 1449 was to a Flemish man for the manufacture of stained glass in England. The use of letters patent for this purpose possessed the elements of a bargain, in which the *quid pro quo* for the royal monopoly was the bringing into the realm of a new technology that would create employment and reduce imports. This bargain between the State and the individual recognized that prices for the commodities produced with this new technology would be higher, but balanced against this effect were the benefits that the introduction of new arts, crafts and trades brought to England's economy in other ways. Unfortunately this considered approach was not to last, and by the time of James I Parliament once again was forced to act – this time decisively.

SIR EDWARD COKE AND HIS STATUTE OF MONOPOLIES

The Statute of Monopolies of 1623[7] was drafted principally by Sir Edward Coke,[8] who served Elizabeth I as Solicitor General[9] and Attorney General[10] and James I as Chief Justice of the Court of Common Pleas,[11] Chief Justice of the Court of the King's Bench[12] and as a Privy Councillor.[13] As its title suggests it was a law about monopolies, but its principal objective was to outlaw abusive monopolies – particularly those granted under the authority of the King's letters patent. Coke was therefore no supporter of undeserving monopolies and his opposition to them came through in a number of his judgments,[14] which so annoyed James I that it led to his removal as the Chief Justice of the King's Bench in November 1616.[15]

In an attempt to neutralize Coke's judicial activism, James I appointed Coke as a Privy Councillor in 1618; but the King had not foreseen that Coke would eventually use this position to transform his ideas, developed through the common law, into statutory law. In his new role, when James I restored Parliament in 1621, Coke was able to pursue his law reform agenda by garnering the support of Puritan parliamentarians who were at odds with the King over their claim to speak freely about foreign policy, something which the King believed was exclusively his business. Once appointed to chair a Committee of Grievances, Coke investigated complaints about how the King's letters patent were adversely impacting upon the economy; and, having gathered sufficient evidence, ultimately used it to pressure James I into revoking 18 letters patent. Encouraged rather than appeased by the King's concession, Coke, now in his seventies, drafted and introduced into Parliament a 'Bill for Free Trade'. Insightfully relying on the common law precedence that he helped create as a judge, Coke used its repugnance of unreasonable restraints of trade to justify a statutory policy of 'free trade'. The idea was to outlaw all monopolies except those that Parliament deemed acceptable – a result that suited the Puritans because it reduced James I's financial independence of Parliament, and thus made it harder for the King to ignore it when formulating foreign policy.

Embroiled in the Puritan cause, Coke played a significant role in the drafting of the 'Great Protestation', a document which was used to challenge openly the King's independence of Parliament by proclaiming: 'the liberties, franchises, privileges and jurisdictions of Parliament are the ancient and undoubted birthright and inheritance of the subjects of England'. This was too much for James I, who reacted by tearing the page recording it from the Journal of the Commons, dissolving Parliament and having Coke imprisoned in the Tower of London. Fortunately for Coke, his nine-month taste of the King's displeasure was an experience that he survived, and its effects were mitigated by Parliament's impeachment of Sir Francis Bacon (his nemesis, who had been appointed over him in 1618 as Lord Chancellor) on charges of corruption.[16]

By the time Coke's 'Bill for Free Trade' was law it had become the Statute of Monopolies and, although the term 'free trade' suggests a liberal trading policy, in truth Coke was a protectionist. In fact Coke had argued in Parliament against the export of wool and the import of Spanish tobacco. At the time there were many English trading companies, such as the East India Company (which was licensed to transport bullion) and the Virginia Company (which was licensed to produce tobacco in North America), whose charters provided them with specifically assigned and exclusive territories and permitted them to control the trade in many types of goods; indeed it was unlawful for anyone to interfere with their trading monopolies. Furthermore there were many craft and trade guilds which had been formed hundreds of years earlier which ensured full employment, quality of production and the availability of locally manufactured goods. These craft and trade guilds were operated as monopolies, as membership was a prerequisite to work in a particular craft or trade. Coke generally saw no harm in these, as long as the guild by-laws were not unreasonable or unfair, because they regulated the behaviour of those trade guilds.

Ironically some 20 years earlier Coke, as Elizabeth I's Attorney General in the case of *Darcy v Allein* (*The Case of Monopolies*) (1602) 77 ER 1260, was obliged to defend a royal monopoly. In that case the court held invalid a monopoly for the making, importing and selling of playing cards for a period of 21 years in return for an annual payment to the Crown, established by letters patent granted by Elizabeth I to Edward Darcy, a member of her Court. In the court's opinion the monopoly unreasonably restrained skilled persons from practising their trade and resulted in higher prices for articles of manufacture with no assurance or guarantee as to their quality. Although Coke's advocacy failed to uphold the Queen's letters patent, when he came to writing his *Reports*[17] some 12 years later his reference to the 'freedom of trade and traffic extendth to all vendible things, notwithstanding any charter of franchise granted to the contrary'[18] and '[the] glorious preamble and pretence of this odious monopoly',[19] suggested that his defence of the royal prerogative was somewhat half-hearted. It also contributed to the myth that Coke was in favour of free trade, which he was not. Coke was in favour of controlled or regulated trade and full employment. His reference to the 'freedom of trade' was directed to the common law's distaste for restrictive and unfair trade practices that impeded employment, not to free trade in the modern sense.

Coke was also of the view that the common law was paramount, even over Parliament, and this he made clear in 1610 as Chief Justice of Common Pleas in *Dr Bonham's Case* (1611) 77 ER 638.[20] This was an action for false imprisonment brought by Dr Bonham against the president and the censors of the College of Physicians and two of their servants. The College had originally been established by letters patent issued by Henry VIII, but eventually an Act of Parliament in 1553 gave the College the sole right to license and regulate the practice of medicine in London. Bonham began his medical practice in 1606 and was examined by the College but, having failed to gain a license, he disregarded the College and continued practising. Eventually his actions were reported to the College, which then fined him and directed that he cease practice. Bonham refused to pay the fine, ignored the direction and was finally, on the order of the College, arrested and imprisoned for seven days. Bonham, who was a graduate of the University of Cambridge and a qualified physician, then sought the assistance of the Court of Common Pleas by entering a writ of habeus corpus. As Chief Justice Coke obliged and ordered his release from prison, much to the dismay of the College which now felt compromised by the challenge to its authority.

As the gauntlet was thrown down the College responded in May 1607 in the way in which persons of power and position did in those times, by seeking the intersession of the King's law officers. Accordingly the opinions of the Lord Chancellor, Sir Thomas Egerton (Lord Ellesmere); the Lord Chief Justice of the Court of the King's Bench, Sir John Popham; Chief Baron of the Exchequer, Sir Thomas Fleming; Justices Williams and Tamfield of the Court of the King's Bench and Justices Walmesley and Warburton of the Court of Common Pleas were sought. Having heard the College's complaint over Bonham's release by Coke, this august group came down in support of the College and confirmed that in its collective opinion the College was within its power to fine and imprison.[21]

Armed with this advice the College pursued Bonham, this time with evidence of a complaint of malpractice made against a Mrs Paine, who tried to deflect her prosecutors by claiming that she was the vicarious agent of Bonham. Bonham denied the charge, but it was to no avail; the College was determined to sue him in the Court of the King's Bench, which by that time had Fleming as its Chief Justice. The College's suit sought damages of £60 against Bonham; but, not to be outwitted Bonham, a tenacious litigant, retaliated by suing the College for false imprisonment in the Court of Common Pleas, seeking damages of £100.

As it turned out the Court of the King's Bench delivered its decision in 1609 nearly one year before the Court of Common Pleas and, consistent with the opinions of the group of which Fleming had been a member, held that Bonham was guilty of illicit practice and fined him the sum sought by the College. Eventually Coke delivered his decision.

The issue was whether the Act of Parliament that incorporated the College empowered the College to imprison Bonham for illicit practice. In answer Coke held that while it made good sense for the practice of medicine to be regulated, the power to imprison granted to the College under the statute was to protect the public against malpractice and not otherwise to restrain a qualified physician, which Bonham was, from practising his profession. Having seen that the College was trying unfairly to restrain Bonham by unreasonably withholding his licence to practise medicine, Coke distinguished between the act of practising without a licence and the act of malpractice and used this distinction to drive home the message that the common law would not tolerate capricious use of monopoly powers. He held that while the College had the power to fine in respect to the former, it could only imprison with respect to the latter, and that, as Bonham was not guilty of malpractice, in imprisoning him it had acted *ultra vires* (Latin: beyond the power). According to Coke Bonham had indeed been falsely imprisoned.

However Coke was not prepared to leave it there. He grasped the opportunity to develop the common law further and used it to send Parliament the message that the common law was not subservient to statutory law; and this he achieved by questioning the validity of the scheme which the Act of Parliament endorsed. In his opinion the scheme which permitted the College to act as 'judges, ministers, and parties' created a conflict of interest because it empowered the College to regulate those who competed with its members. Accordingly, as the scheme itself was tainted by this conflict it violated the common law and 'when a statute was against the common right and reason, or repugnant, or impossible to be performed, the Common Law will control it and adjudge such Act to be void'.[22]

Of course for Coke it followed that if an Act of Parliament was subject to the review of the common law so were the King's monopolies, and in *The Case of the Tailors of Habits &c. of Ipswich* (1614) 77 ER 1218, decided by the Court of the King's Bench in 1614 with Coke as its Chief Justice, James I was publicly rebuked. The case involved an action in debt brought by the Corporation of the Tailors of Ipswich against William Seninge, who had

moved to Ipswich to work as a tailor. The letters patent incorporating the
guild under charter were granted by James I and provided that the guild
could regulate its trade. A by-law of the guild restricted the right of anyone
to work as a tailor unless first vetted and approved by the guild, despite the
fact that, by effect of Statute passed under the reign of Elizabeth I, once an
apprentice in any trade had completed seven years of apprenticeship they
were lawfully qualified to work in that trade. The issue was whether that
by-law was lawful, and the King's Bench decided that it was not, because it
restrained, 'the Freedom and Liberty of the Subject, . . . [and was] a means
of Extortion in drawing moneys from them, either by delay, or some other
subtle device, or of oppression of young Tradesmen, by the old and rich of
the same Trade'.[23] In other words it was the kind of unreasonable restraint
of trade that Coke opposed – one that was arbitrary in nature and that
provided no real benefit to anyone but the King and the monopolists.

The decision was a landmark, both in Coke's relationship with the King
and in the development of patent law. In terms of the former, within two
years Coke was no longer Chief Justice of the Court of the King's Bench.
In terms of the latter it provided an inkling of what was soon to become
legislation. Section 1 of the Statute of Monopolies 1623 provided:

> All monopolies and all commissions, grants, licenses, charters and letters patent
> theretofore made or granted or heretofore to be made or granted to any person
> or persons, bodies politic or corporate whatsoever, of or for the sole buying,
> selling, making or using of anything within this realm . . . utterly void and of
> none effect.

However, as Coke was not of the opinion that all monopolies were
bad, a number of exceptions were made. The first of these was in section
6, which allowed the King to issue letters patent for 'any manner of new
manufactures' to 'the true and first inventor and inventors', provided that
the monopoly did not extend beyond 14 years and 'be not contrary to the
law nor mischievous to the state by raising prices of commodities at home,
or hurt of trade, or generally inconvenient'.

The remaining exceptions concerned activities that were considered
necessary for the defence of the realm, such as printing and the production
of saltpetre (section 7); the activities of the courts provided by 'warrant
or privy seal' (section 8); certain 'liberties' for the regulation of 'city,
borough or town'; trading companies, such as the Spanish, East India and
Virginia Companies; and guilds 'erected for the maintenance, enlargement,
or ordering of any trade or merchandise' as existed before the Statute
(section 9). It also provided in section 4 for triple damages for those who
were 'hindered, grieved, disturbed, or disquieted, or by means of having
his or their goods or chattels, seized, attached, distrained, taken, carried

away, or detained' in the attempted enforcement of a monopoly voided by section 1, and provided that the 'courts of kings bench, common pleas, and exchequer' were to have jurisdiction over the grant of any crown privilege, although it should be noted that the Privy Council did not actually cede this jurisdiction to the common law courts until 1753.

Plainly Coke believed that some monopolies were important to the economy of England, and this protectionist agenda was supported by the need for Parliament to be able to grant 'letters patent' as an economic tool that could be used to entice foreign artisans, craftsmen and tradesmen to come to England and bring with them their specialized knowledge to locals, so as to make the English economy more robust; and it is for this reason that for 250 years the phrase 'the true and first inventor' included the first to import a new technology to England.

LETTERS PATENT AND THE PILGRIMS

In September 1620 the Pilgrims sailed from Plymouth in England on the *Mayflower*. They were bound for a new colony on the east coast of North America and they took with them not only their puritan religious beliefs and their protestant work ethic, but also English law. The *Mayflower Compact*, signed by 41 of the adult men of the colony on 11 November 1620, was the instrument through which the colony acknowledged James I as its sovereign and received the laws of Great Britain, France and Ireland into the colony. Subsequently another 12 North American colonies were established on similar terms, and they remained loyal to the English monarchy until 4 July 1776 when, during the reign of George III,[24] they declared their independence, fought the War of Independence until 1783, won and ultimately established the United States of America under its own Constitution on 17 September 1787.

Under Article I, Section 8, Clause 8 of the US Constitution, Congress was given the power '[t]o promote the Progress of Science and useful Arts, by securing for limited Times to Authors and Inventors the exclusive Right to their respective Writings and Discoveries'. This power was used by the first Congress on 10 April 1790, when the first US Patents Act established a single patent system which on 31 July 1790 saw the grant of the first US patent to Samuel Hopkins for his invention entitled 'Making Pot and Pearl Ashes'.

Like the Statute of Monopolies 1623 which regularized and legalized the creation of limited monopolies for manners of new manufactures, the US Patents Act 1790 regularized and legalized the creation of limited monopolies for 'any useful art, manufacture, engine, machine, or device, or any improvement therein not before known or used'.

BOX 1.1   SECTION 1, US PATENTS ACT 1790

'That upon the petition of any person or persons to the Secretary of State, the Secretary for the department of war, and the Attorney General of the United States, setting forth, that he, she, or they, hath or have invented or discovered any useful art, manufacture, engine, machine, or device, or any improvement therein not before known or used, and praying that a patent may be granted therefor, it shall and may be lawful to and for the Secretary of State, the Secretary for the department of war, and the Attorney General, or any two of them, if they shall deem the invention or discovery sufficiently useful and important, to cause letters patent to be made out in the name of the United States, to bear teste by the President of the United States, reciting the allegations and suggestions of the said petition, and describing the said invention or discovery, clearly, truly and fully, and thereupon granting to such petitioner or petitioners, his, her or their heirs, administrators or assigns for any term not exceeding fourteen years, the sole and exclusive right and liberty of making, constructing, using and vending to others to be used, the said invention or discovery; which letters patent shall be delivered to the Attorney General of the United States to be examined, who shall, within fifteen days next after the delivery to him, if he shall find the same conformable to this act, certify it to be so at the foot thereof, and present the letters patent so certified to the President, who shall cause the seal of the United States to be thereto affixed, and the same shall be good and available to the grantee or grantees by force of this act, to all and every intent and purpose herein contained, and shall be recorded in a book to be kept for that purpose in the office of the Secretary of State, and delivered to the patentee or his agent, and the delivery thereof shall be entered on the record and endorsed on the patent by the said Secretary at the time of granting the same.'

So popular was this law that the mandated system of oral presentations of patent applications by inventors created such a huge backlog of applications that it became unworkable. Choked by this enthusiasm and desperate to overcome the build-up of applications, in 1793 Congress passed the second US Patents Act. The US Patents Act 1793 did away with the need for oral presentations of inventions and simply required written patent applications to be registered with the Office of the Secretary of State. The impact of this change was stunning. Between 1790 and 1793 only 55 patents were granted, but by 2 July 1836, when the third US Patents Act was passed, 9957 patents had been granted, highlighting the need for further reform, especially as the quality of those patents began to be questioned as the courts scrutinizing them began to question their validity. Clearly the unbridled enthusiasm by which American inventors embraced this new form of private property had to be tempered. Thus the US Patents Act 1836 established the US Patent Office and the Office of Commissioner of Patents. Borrowing from a Venetian idea, the US patent system now required all patent applications to undergo pre-grant examination – a step that would not be correspondingly undertaken in Britain until 1883, when the Office of the Comptroller of Patents and pre-grant examination were established.

Nonetheless, the first Congress of the United States of America clearly borrowed from the Statute of Monopolies 1623. Of course between 1623 and 1790 there were developments in the common law regarding letters patent for manners of new manufacture in England, and these developments were reflected in the US Patents Act 1790. The most important of these was the requirement for a written specification, that is a description of the nature of the invention provided by the inventor. This written specification became a regular feature of patents granted during the reign of Queen Anne;[25] although a written specification had been first provided by one Sturtevant in 1611 as part of his petition for the grant of letters patent over 'certain inventions in connexion with the application of coal for smelting iron'. It was however the precedent established by the inventor John Nasmeth, who filed a written description after his patent was granted in 1711, that cemented that practice. By 1778 it had become a formal requirement of the common law, as Lord Mansfield in *Liardet v Johnson* (1780) 62 ER 1000 explained:

> The law relative to patents requires as a price the individual should pay the people for his monopoly, that he should enrol, to the very best of his knowledge and judgment, the fullest and most sufficient description of all the particulars on which the effect depended, that he was at the time able to do.

This common law requirement provided the justification for the 'social contract' between the State and the Inventor, and was codified by section 2 of the US Patents Act 1790.

The Anglo-American laws concerning patents had several elements in common, the first being the grant to the inventor. The true and first inventor is a term found in the Statute of Monopolies 1623 and the Patents Act 1790. The second similarity was the term of 14 years. The third was the exclusive right to work or manufacture of the invention, which the

Patents Act 1790 defined as: 'devise, make, construct, use, employ, or vend'. The fourth was the subject matter which the Patents Act 1790 defined to mean 'any useful art, manufacture, engine, machine or device, or any improvement therein'.

Where they diverged was, first, in the absence of any proviso regarding the adverse economic impact of the grant of letters patent and, secondly, in the use of the words 'discovered' and 'discoverer'.

While the first Congress borrowed from both English statutory and common law, it also sought to define the scope of patentable subject matter in terms of specific things rather than by the use of the phrase 'manners of new manufactures', which the English Statute of Monopolies 1623 did not define. Moreover it introduced the idea that those who 'discovered' useful ways of doing or making those things could also apply for patents as inventors. However the US Congress, like the English Parliament, did not intend that the discovery of just anything useful was patentable subject matter. Whatever it was, whether it was invented or discovered, the thing that was the subject of the patent had to be a *useful art, manufacture, engine, machine or device*. In other words it had to be a practical example of one of these man-made things. Today section 101 of the US Patents Act 1952 uses slightly different language from section 1 US Patents Act 1790: patentable subject matter is defined as any 'new and useful process, machine, manufacture, or composition of matter, or any new and useful improvement thereof', but the central rationale in these two sections remains the same.

Even though the US patent legislation always allowed 'discoverers' to apply for patents, it never extended the grant of patents beyond that contemplated by the Statute of Monopolies 1623. The limitation in the language was explained by the US Supreme Court in a number of cases, but the most relevant in terms of biotechnology is *Diamond v Chakrabarty* (1980) 447 US 303, in which Chief Justice Burger held that section 101 was not boundless. He said:

> The laws of nature, physical phenomena, and abstract ideas have been held not patentable. . . . Thus, a new mineral discovered in the earth or a new plant found in the wild is not patentable subject matter. Likewise, Einstein could not patent his celebrated law that $E = mc^2$; nor could Newton have patented the law of gravity. Such discoveries are 'manifestations of . . . nature, free to all men and reserved exclusively to none.' *Funk, supra*, at 130.[26]

In terms of the other remaining point of diversion between the US Patents Act 1790 and the Statute of Monopolies 1623, namely the proviso against the grant of patents which were injurious to the economy, it needs to be recognized that under the scheme of patentability established by the US

Patents Act 1790, the Board which recommended the grant of US patents was made up of three senior members of the US Government. They were Thomas Jefferson, the Secretary of State; Henry Knox, the Secretary of War; and Edmund Randolph, the Attorney-General. Thus Congress built into the legislation a mechanism which ensured that they vetted all patent applications and relied on their judgement in deciding whether a patent application was 'sufficiently useful and important, to cause letters patent to be made out in the name of the United States' (section 1). Although this procedure was replaced by a simple registration system under the US Patents Act 1793, in doing so, and despite that fact that it took Congress another 100 years before it passed the Sherman Antitrust Act in 1890, it is unlikely that Congress thereby implied that undeserving or injurious monopolies would be lawful.

In this regard not only was the law of England influential on the framers of the US Constitution, the members of the first Congress and the drafters of the US Patents Act 1790, but so were the philosophies of Edward Coke and John Locke.[27] It was of paramount importance to Coke that lawful monopolies should benefit the economy by encouraging employment through new trade and technologies, and for Locke that the social contract between those elected to government and the electors required a legitimate civil government to preserve their rights to life, liberty, health and property. This meant that government not unreasonably interfere with the citizenry's right to make a living in practising their trade or profession. Locke's labour theory of property also provided the rationale for people to own property derived from their labour, and from this the Congress legislated for the creation of a *property right* in a patent (section 1, US Patents Act 1790, 'the sole and exclusive right and liberty').

The notion of a social contract also provided the rationale for the development of a written specification. In England this development came through the common law (*Liardet v Johnson, 1780 per* Lord Mansfield, 'the price the individual should pay the people for his monopoly') but in the United States it became part of the patent legislation (section 2, US Patents Act 1790: 'a specification in writing, containing a description . . . of the thing or things invented').

Although the issue of letters patent in England remained the exercise of a crown privilege and was not therefore strictly a property right as in the United States, influential writers and thinkers were beginning to speak of a patent as property. Adam Smith,[28] for instance, suggested in 1762 that the *property* an inventor had in a machine he had invented and patented was a form of personal property.

By the beginning of the nineteenth century the British and American patent models were established and, although there still remained differences between them, they shared a common history and objective, as Justice Storey acknowledged in *Pennock v Dialogue* (US Sup Ct, 1829):

> Many of the provisions of our patent acts are derived from the principles and practice which have prevailed in England . . . and although the known and settled construction of the English statute of Monopolies, by their courts of law, has not been received by our courts with all the weight of authority, yet the construction of that statute by the English courts, and the principals and practices which have regulated the grants of English patents afford materials to illustrate our statute.

Even so the economic objective that underscored the Constitutional imperative ('To promote the Progress of Science and useful Arts') was parochial and, like that in Coke's England, was designed to benefit the local economy. The US Patents Acts of 1790, 1793 and 1836 were all sculpted to secure US markets for US industry. For example, under the 1793 legislation, the right to a patent extended only to 'citizens of the United States' (section 1) and, although that changed under the 1836 legislation to 'any person' (section 6), if the inventor was an 'alien' at the date of grant of the US patent and 'failed and neglected for the space of eighteen months . . . to put and continue on sale to the public, on reasonable terms', this could be raised as a defence to a claim of infringement (section 15). There were also differences in patent application filing fees which for a US citizen (or 'an alien' who became a citizen with one year) were fixed at US$30, but for a 'subject of Great Britain' (which by the time of Queen Victoria covered a good section of the globe) it was US$500, and for the rest of the world it was US$300 (section 9). These were not trifling differences. Moreover only US citizens had the right to lodge 'caveats', which were statutory reservations filed confidentially with the US patent office over technology that was yet to be the subject of a US patent application (section 12). This mechanism gave US inventors the advantage over 'aliens', in that it gave them a one year head start as 'the first and true inventors' in a market which, even at that time, was already an attractive export market for European industry. It was clearly a proactive move designed to give US industry an edge over foreign industrial competition. Caveats thereby secretly secured the potential US inventor's technological patch well before a foreigner could file a patent application over the same technology.

The caveat was also useful in terms of another uniquely American patent procedure, the 'interference' (section 8). Under this procedure the Commissioner of Patents was duty bound to notify the applicant for a US patent (who may have been a foreigner) that a subsequent US patent application had been filed by another over an alleged invention which corresponded to, or overlapped with, the alleged invention in the prior US patent application. Given that caveats and US patent applications were both confidential documents, only the Commissioner of Patents could declare an interference, and if he did he would decide which US patent applicant had priority of invention after the respective patent applicants had provided evidence of how they arrived at their invention. The first 'to conceive and reduce to practice' the invention was the winner of this contest. In this situation the caveat, though not itself a patent application, would have provided evidence of invention if a US patent application had subsequently transpired and would have given US citizens the edge in interference proceedings.

Importantly the US Patents Act 1836 created the Office of the Commissioner of Patents and directed the Commissioner 'to superintend, execute and perform all such acts and things touching and respecting the granting and issuing of patents' (section 1) and these included, 'an examination of the alleged new invention' in order to determine whether that patent application was worthy of a patent (section 7).

Accordingly if the pre-grant examination satisfied the Commissioner that the 'alleged invention' had not, prior to the application, been 'invented . . . by any other person [in the United States]'; 'patented or described in any printed publication anywhere'; or 'in public use or on sale with the applicant's consent or allowance' and was deemed to be 'sufficiently useful and important', then it was 'his duty to issue a patent' (section 7). On the other hand if he found that the alleged invention lacked 'novelty' or 'the description [was] defective and insufficient', he was required to provide a report to the patent applicant explaining the nature of the deficiencies and inviting either a withdrawal of the application or the patentee to amend its application to 'embrace' only that part of the invention or discovery which was 'new'.

In the event that the patent applicant wished to proceed without amendment, he would be required to 'make oath or affirmation anew' and file an appeal to 'the board of examiners, to be composed of three disinterested persons . . . one of whom at least, to be selected, if practicable and convenient, for his knowledge and skill in the particular art, manufacture, or branch of science to which the alleged invention appertains'.

Once the Commissioner of Patents was satisfied that the patentability criteria had been satisfied, a US patent was granted, and along with that grant came a legal presumption of validity. Even so US courts were able to review the decision of the Commissioner of Patents after grant, and defendants to infringement actions were able to have US patents revoked in part or whole by order of the US courts. There were of course other grounds upon which the validity of a patent could be challenged, such as

priority of inventorship (see for example *Bedford v Hunt* (1817) 3 F Cas
37, which held that reducing the invention to practice (that is, making a
working prototype) was crucial to resolving inventorship priority); written
description (*Grant v Raymond* (1832) 31 US 218) and double patenting
(*Suffock Mfg Co v Hayden* (1866) 70 US 315).

THE FREE TRADE CHALLENGE TO THE BRITISH PATENT SYSTEM

Having become convinced of the benefits of free trade, between 1842
and 1846 the British Prime Minister, Sir Robert Peel,[29] reduced tariffs on
all commodities (with the exceptions of sugar, coffee, wines, spirits and
timber) consistent with a policy of tariff reduction which had started in
1825. By this time Great Britain had concluded bilateral trade agreements
with France, Prussia, Austria, Sweden, the Hanse towns, Denmark, the
United States and most South American republics, with the specific intent
of lowering tariffs. Between 1825 and 1860 the average tariff in Great
Britain as a percentage of import value fell from 65 per cent to 18 per
cent, and the average customs rate fell from 53.1 per cent to 8.9 per cent.[30]
Furthermore a significant victory for free traders within Great Britain
came with the repeal of the Corn Laws in 1845. These laws were designed to
protect corn farmers by limiting the import of corn when prices fell below
a certain point. By restricting corn imports in times of over-production a
floor price for corn was maintained. Opponents of this mechanism, such as
Richard Cobden,[31] one of the founders of the Manchester Anti-Corn Law
League in 1838, argued that this protective price mechanism subsidized
inefficient farmers by inflating the price of corn.

The main reason for the change in economic policy from protectionism
to free trade was Great Britain's growing reliance on overseas trade. As
its manufacturing capacity grew with the ability to transform imported
raw materials, such as timber, wool and cotton, into finished manufactured goods, so did its desire to grow its export markets, which were now
fuelling British profits, industry and employment. In this context the high
tariffs imposed on British manufactured goods by its trading partners were
increasingly seen as obstacles to this trade; but it was also thought that if
trade barriers were dismantled, not only would Great Britain benefit by
gaining easier access to its foreign markets, but through open international
trade and competition the price of goods would fall, and this would be
beneficial not only to Great Britain but to its trading partners.

In time attention soon turned to the impact that patent monopolies had
on the British economy. On 1 February 1851 *The Economist* wrote:

The privileges granted to inventors by patent laws are prohibitions on other men, and the history of inventions accordingly teems with accounts of trifling improvements patented, that have put a stop, for a long period, to other similar and much greater improvements. It teems also with accounts of improvements carried into effect the instant some patents had expired. The privileges have stifled more inventions than they promoted, and have cause more brilliant schemes to be put aside than they the want of them could ever have induced men to conceal. Every patent is a prohibition against improvements in a particular direction, except by the patentee, for a certain number of years; and, however beneficial that may be to him who receives the privilege, the community cannot be benefited by it. . . . On all inventors it is especially a prohibition to exercise their faculties; and in proportion as they are more numerous than one, it is an impediment to the general advancement, with which it is the duty of the Legislature not to interfere, and which the claimers of privileges pretend at least to have at heart.

Judging by this criticism it is unsurprising that the free traders sought the abolition of the British patent system. However despite this and other opposition, after a Parliamentary Select Committee Inquiry in 1851 in which the patent system was investigated, the Government responded with the Patent Law Amendment Act 1852. This was the first specific patents legislation passed by the Parliament since the Statute of Monopolies in 1623 and thereafter British patents were granted not under the Statute of Monopolies 1623 but under this legislation. The 1852 legislation established the British Patent Office, but it was not empowered to undertake pre-grant examinations of patent petitions which were still required to be made to 'the Commissioners'. The Commissioners consisted of the Lord Chancellor, the Master of the Rolls, the Attorneys-General of England and Ireland, and the Solicitor-General for Scotland. In effect the Patent Office was merely an administrative facility which recorded and housed patent applications and grants and 'was one of registration, not examination'; and furthermore it 'provided no quality control at the point of enrolment, so that the only time the sufficiency of a specification was tested was when and if there were court proceedings'.[32] Neither did the Commissioners undertake any pre-grant examination of any 'petitions for letters patent' but acted by delegation to a Law Officer, who then had the role of ensuring that the petition complied with the procedural requirements provided by the legislation. The Law Officer's cursory examination therefore lacked the rigour and particularity required by the US pre-grant examination.

Nevertheless the reforms introduced by the 1852 legislation were significant in other ways. First the patent systems of England and Wales, Scotland and Ireland, which until that time had been separate and which had required a British inventor to apply for patents in each jurisdiction, were united; what resulted was one patent application, one filing fee and one patent throughout Britain. Secondly, the cost of a patent application was reduced in two ways: by the unification of the patent systems into one and the reduction of the fee. Until 1852 the filing fee in England and Wales was £100 and £350 to include Scotland and Ireland. This was reduced to £25 for the provisional filing fee, and with the patent fees paid at end of the third year (£50) and seventh year (£100), whereby the total cost of a 14-year patent was reduced to £175. Third was the publication of patent specifications (that is the section of the patent in which the inventor disclosed the invention and how to make it) by the Patent Office, making it possible for there to be a repository of information about inventions granted in Great Britain. This work was undertaken under the direction of Bennet Woodcroft, the newly appointed Superintendent of Specifications, and resulted in the indexing, by name and subject, and publication of 14 360 patents granted between 1617 and 1857, when that work was completed. Fourth came the creation of the Abridgements of Specifications – a register which categorized and summarized patents granted from 1617. This led to the establishment of a system of classification of British patents, thereby simplifying the process involved in searching the register for prior granted patents, which was useful (although not a pre-grant examination requirement) in establishing the novelty of any patent application for an invention filed thereafter.

Having reformed the patent system, the question that then preoccupied British policy-makers was how best to bring the benefits of free trade to all of Great Britain's trading partners. By this time the consensus among free traders was that this was to be achieved by example and not by way of bilateralism, the policy which Great Britain had adopted with some success. A number of key countries, such as Spain and Portugal, had steadfastly refused to enter into bilateral trade agreements with Great Britain, so the Liberal Prime Minister, Lord Palmerston,[33] put it to Parliament in July 1859: 'when foreign countries . . . find that your policy has tended to the increase of your prosperity . . . they will in all probability be more likely to imitate your examples than if you were to ask them to surrender an advantage which they imagine they possess'.[34]

During the 1850s Richard Cobden's stature and influence within political circles had grown; so much that in October 1859, when he travelled to France in his private capacity to discuss the possibility of a treaty with his French counterpart, Michel Chevalier,[35] Palmerston was, in view of his publicly stated position, a little uneasy with the proposal that was to became known as the Cobden–Chevalier Treaty. That he overcame his feelings was indicative of how issues of trade policy became secondary when the threat of war was present and diplomacy demanded a way of ameliorating the chance of war. Such was the situation between France and England at that time. It was believed in Great Britain that France was capable of invading England and, in the context of a naval–military race, her fleet of iron-plated wooden ships was superior, both in number and technology, to those possessed by the British navy. As such Palmerston was wary of Naploeon III,[36] especially as the latter had done much to damage Austria's claim over northern Italy by placing 200 000 troops there in response to Austria's declaration of war against Piedmont in April 1859. During this brief conflict Britain and Prussia had remained neutral, thereby highlighting Austria's isolation over the 'Italian question'.[37] This tactical decision had further encouraged Napoleon III, destabilizing the fragile power structure in Europe at a time when the 'Italian question' remained unresolved; and the Conservative Smith-Stanley Government's accommodation of France led to its downfall in June 1859.[38] As tensions rose throughout 1859, and with it the threat of a European war intensifying, the idea of a commercial treaty between France and Great Britain began to be seen as politically useful, even if it was strictly inconsistent with the free trade purist ambition of achieving free trade without bilateralism.

It was in this context that Cobden wrote to Chevalier on 14 September 1859 that he saw 'no other hope but in such a policy for any permanent improvements in the political relations of France and England',[39] reinforcing his preference for diplomacy through free trade rather than through politics, writing, 'I utterly despair of finding peace and harmony in the efforts of Governments and diplomatists'.[40] In this regard Cobden's idea of peace through trade laid the foundation of Cordell Hull's[41] thinking. In 1916 Hull proclaimed, 'unhampered trade dovetailed with peace',[42] and his views persuaded President Roosevelt to support the Bretton Woods Conference held by the Allied Powers in 1944. In the words of Cobden, 'the people of the two Nations must be brought into mutual dependence by the supply of each other's wants. There is no other way of counteracting the antagonism of language and race. It is God's own method of producing an entente cordiale, and no other plan is worth a farthing.'[43]

By the time Cobden met with Napoleon III on 27 October 1859 this private audience had the secret, but official, support of William Gladstone,[44] then Chancellor of the Exchequer; John Russell,[45] then Foreign Secretary and, importantly, Palmerston. In France, as in England, during this and other meetings that Cobden was to have with French Minister for Foreign Affairs, Count Walewski, and his advisers, he found that political rather than commercial considerations were driving the French towards the view that Cobden firmly held. Cobden reported in his diaries that he had told the French:

. . . so far as I was acquainted with the state of public opinion in England, nothing would so instantaneously convince the people of the emperor's pacific

intentions as his entering boldly upon a policy of Commercial Reform, by which
he would enable those, who, like myself, took the unpopular side in opposing
the current of prejudice which was running against him in England, to turn the
table [*sic*] on his accusers and detractors.[46]

Despite the readiness of the French to listen to Cobden it took until 23
December 1859 before the official word was given to Russell that Napoleon
III was prepared to enter into formal discussions for the negotiation of
such a treaty. In supporting a free trade agreement with Great Britain
Napoleon III had to suffer the consequences of upsetting the protection-
ists, who held the predominant and popular view at that time in France,
especially in the manufacturing industries.

Accordingly in coming to the decision to go ahead with the Cobden–
Chevalier proposal, both the British and the French Governments were
taking steps that were unpalatable in their respective countries, but which
were seen diplomatically as essential to establishing political stability and a
lasting peace between them. In Great Britain, while free trade was preferred
to protectionism, the manner of achieving this was an issue and, in this
respect, bilateralism was not popular. In France protectionism was seen as
essential to protecting the livelihoods of the French people from the predatory ambitions of the English. Beyond these concerns, as the discussions
proceeded into 1860, the single most important issue upon which the success
of the entire agreement rested was concord between France and Great
Britain over how to deal with Italy. In a letter to Gladstone on 8 January
1860 Russell expressed the view, 'if England and France should be united
in the question of Italy, no war would be feared and the Commercial Treaty
might go on'.[47] In the end, even though no political alliance was forged
between France and Great Britain over the 'Italian question', the importance of easing the political tension between Great Britain and France out-
weighed all other considerations and so negotiations were concluded within
one month. The Cobden–Chevalier Treaty was signed on 23 January 1860.

The Treaty directly led to the mutual reduction of tariffs on a range
of goods including cotton, wool, sugar and coffee, but excepted brandy,
spirits and wine. In Britain, where popular opinion supported free trade,
The Times newspaper on 16 January 1860 applauded Napoleon III as
'no ordinary man' because, even though tariff reductions were achieved
through bilateralism, in supporting the Treaty, it reported, 'he shivers at
one blow the fetters of French commerce and defies the protectionist interest which has always supposed itself a match for any government, however
powerful'.

For free traders the patent system remained a source of irritation despite
the reforms made by the 1852 legislation; so, after a decade during which

constant criticism was levelled at the patent system the Government convened a Royal Commission, 'Into The Working Of The Law Relating To Letters Patent For Inventions'.

The Royal Commission was chaired by Lord Stanley[48] and included Sir William Page Wood, a Vice Chancellor, and Sir William Atherton, the Attorney General. It was a wide-ranging inquiry, conducted between 1862 and 1864, and took evidence in London, Bradford, Manchester, Halifax, Liverpool and Glasgow. Those who contributed to the inquiry or gave evidence included inventors, such as John Lister (the elder brother of Samuel Lister, the inventor of the Lister Nip Comb wool-combing machinery) and Sir Francis Crossley MP,[49] as well as barristers, officers of the Patent Office and the Patent Commissioners themselves. Among those who were critical of the patent system was, in fact, one of the Patent Commissioners and the Master of the Rolls, Sir John Romilly,[50] who wrote, 'great public inconvenience'[51] was caused by 'the multiplicity of Patents, and that many Patents taken out, which, if contested, would be found to be wholly invalid'.[52] He also explained in the same letter to the Commissioners that the post-grant challenge to the validity of patents through the writ of *scire facias* (Latin: made known, which was until then the only mechanism to seek the revocation of letters patent) was 'very unsatisfactory and should be discontinued',[53] for the reason that 'many persons now prefer paying a small sum of money for a licence to incurring the expense and anxiety of legal proceedings to contest the validity of the Patent'.[54] He expressed the view that 'greater facilities should be provided for the repeal of invalid Patents'.[55]

BOX 1.2   SCIRE FACIAS

Prior to 1883 the revocation of letters patent involved a procedure commenced in the Court of Chancery in which a writ of *scire facias* would be sought by the challenger to command the presence of the grantee of letters patent. The court would then hear the parties and, if it found that there was due cause, a trial before a jury in the King's Bench would ensue. The results of that trial would then be brought back before the Court of Chancery which in turn remitted its recommendations to the Lord Chancellor. The Lord Chancellor then made the decision whether or not to revoke.

Others, such as Bennet Woodcroft, the Superintendent of Specifications at the British Patent Office, were very much against any change to the British patent system that would require US-style pre-grant examination.

Woodcroft supported this opinion with several references to communications he had with his American counterpart, Mr Justice Mason: 'the
Americans pay about £23 000 a year for preliminary examination and they
are very much dissatisfied with it';[56] 'it was a very inadequate system, and
a very unfair one';[57] 'it was a very cumbrous, unsatisfactory, and unfair
mode';[58] and 'the system of preliminary examination has been tried and
found wanting . . . in France, Austria, Sardinia and Belgium . . . and abandoned in each country'.[59] He did however agree with Lord Romilly MR
that *scire facias* was 'a very expensive roundabout process',[60] and thought
a way of clearing the patent register of 'old inventions, as old as the hills',[61]
was by 'a simple application by motion'[62] which could be brought 'at the
insistence of anyone of the public'.[63] Despite these criticisms however, he
was in favour of the retention of the patent system and believed that it
made a worthwhile contribution to British industry.

One of the concerns which the Commissioners investigated was the
proliferation of patents of a 'trifling and frivolous nature',[64] to which the
idea of pre-grant examination was raised as a way of checking the worst
excesses of the patent system. Thomas Webster, a noted London barrister
and drafter of the original version of what became the 1852 legislation,
explained that pre-grant examination had indeed been prescribed but
was deleted as a feature of the system by the House of Lords during its
Parliamentary debate. He argued that without pre-grant examination the
patent system 'was not only useless, but positively mischievous', because it
gave encouragement to a 'large class of speculators' against which 'almost
all the objections'[65] which had been made about the patent system arose. He
pointed out that under the 1852 legislation, the two law officers who were
duty bound to 'examine' the petition for letters patent had 'granted within
a very short time, [patents] containing if not the same thing, so much of the
same thing that one Patent would vitiate the other',[66] and suggested that in
the absence of a 'community of information'[67] in regard to what was being
patented, the patent system was flawed in that it was impossible properly to
separate good from 'bad' patents. Clearly Webster was in favour of extensive pre-grant examination and referred the Commissioners to the fact that
in the original Bill, which he drafted in 1851, the Law Officer was required
to appoint a suitable expert to examine the patent application. In his view,
if inventors knew that such an examination would take place it would 'stop
a great number of Patents *in limine*'[68] (Latin: at the threshold).

Another concern was the cost of patent litigation. According to William
Carpmael,[69] a noted London patent agent with about 40 years' experience,
the *scire facias* procedure used to invalidate patents was 'a very expensive
remedy'.[70] He attributed the major cause of the increasing expense of patent
litigation to the lack of a requirement on the patent owner to 'state with

sufficient accuracy the precise point'[71] in which the patent was infringed, and explained that often 'the defendant has not the slightest notion',[72] until the opening of the case, what the precise point of the complaint for the infringement against him was. Thomas Webster agreed, arguing that the 'greatest expense' of the proceedings arose from the 'bush-fighting'[73] between the parties, where neither was compelled to disclose his case. In a related issue concerning the adequacy of the courts to deal with the factual and legal issues surrounding patent validity, Thomas Webster suggested that it would be better to 'get rid of the jury', and patent cases should be 'tried by one of the Judges of the superior courts'[74] with the aid of scientific assessors.

An American firm of patent attorneys, H & C Howson, who were observing the patent debate in Great Britain, agreed with Webster and Carpmael. They reported that the British patent system encouraged '[the] indiscriminate and uncontrolled issue of patents . . . [with] no check upon the repeated patenting of similar inventions'.[75] Worse still, the adjudication of the validity of British patents in the courts was 'so terrible an ordeal, that sooner than invite it, most ordinary mortals would be content to have their rights remain forever undefined and unrespected'.[76]

BOX 1.3   A NOTE ON THE COST OF PATENT LITIGATION IN THE NINETEENTH CENTURY

It is indeed ironic, given the extremely high costs of patent litigation in the United States today, that in promoting the US pre-grant examination system over the British as it was in 1870, Howson said, 'patent litigation [in the United States] is not so costly, nor so unsatisfactory, as in England, and this fact may very well largely be attributed to the effect of our examining system, in reducing and simplifying the questions before the court'.[77]

The British Admiralty also made submissions to the Commission that were critical of the patent system. The Duke of Somerset (the First Lord of the Admiralty) and Rear-Admiral Robinson gave evidence of 'the great inconvenience to the Admiralty . . . [caused by the] apparent facility with which persons can obtain Patents covering a very large number of different inventions under one Patent',[79] and gave the example of 'a Patent which one gentleman obtained some years ago, in building ships for a combination of wood and iron'.[80] The Duke elaborated:

BOX 1.4   US CONGRESSIONAL INQUIRY ON PATENT LAW REFORM 2007

'. . . litigation costs are escalating rapidly and proceedings are protracted. Surveys conducted periodically by the American Intellectual Property Law Association indicate that litigation costs, millions of dollars for each party in a case where the stakes are substantial, are increasing at double digit rates. At the same time the number of lawsuits in District Courts is increasing.'[78]

Dr Mark B. Myers, Sr Vice President, Xerox Corporation,
15 February 2007

. . . a Patent of that kind, where it is wide-spread, as it is in this case, brings us continually under difficulties with this Patentee . . . [in that] [w]henever we apply wood and iron he is watching to see whether or not his Patent is invaded, and he complains and says, that different improvements which we have made without any notion of his Patent have been infringements of his Patent rights.[81]

His evidence also suggested that the cost and inconvenience of litigation to challenge the validity of patents resulted in the Admiralty's lawyers often recommending that it 'pay the money'[82] demanded by patentees rather than 'enter into a lawsuit to defend ourselves'.[83] His dissatisfaction with patents also extended to the breadth of the monopolies claimed, pointing out, 'the Patents seem to be given too vaguely and too widely'.[84] Furthermore patentees were not obliged to work the inventions, but could wait until they caught 'somebody else in his hook'.[85] Rear-Admiral Robinson gave evidence of the extensive number of patents that related to the construction of ships, and explained that the Admiralty was 'stopped at every turn'[86] with respect to their improvement. He also gave the example of the patent discussed above, known as the 'Feather's patent', which the Admiralty was alleged to have infringed in the construction of *HMS Enterprise* because 'about one-third of the upper side . . . [was laid] with iron and the rest wood . . . [which was] the only method in which the Government vessel resembled the Patentee's vessel'.[87] In terms of the information disclosed by patents, Lord Overstone, one of the Commissioners, put it to Rear-Admiral Robinson that with respect to a 'patented article of war',[88] disclosure would 'necessarily communicate that secret immediately to any foreign government',[89] to which the Rear-Admiral replied:

> Not necessarily, because the terms of the Specification are so vague, and so much is often reserved, especially the making of a machine, which a gun may be called, as to the mode in which the material shall be put together, that the Specification does not always enable you to know it.[90]

In response to this answer Lord Overstone put the following question to him:

> Do you not think that that is a great defect with regard to the Specification, and that it does not answer the purpose which it was intended to answer, of putting the public so effectively in possession of the secret that they could themselves work it whenever the obstruction of the Letters patent was removed?[91]

The response from the Rear-Admiral was '[s]o far as I can understand it I think that there is a very great laxity in the way in which Specifications are drawn up – laxity both ways'.[92]

A Report was finally presented to the Government on 29 July 1864 by Lord Stanley.[93] It was critical of the patent system, particularly with respect to 'the protracted litigation and consequent expense',[94] and the 'multiplicity of patents'[95] enabling 'the existence of a number of Patents for alleged inventions of a trivial character . . . which are either old or practically useless, and are employed by the patentees only to embarrass rival manufacturers'.[96] The Report observed that rather than being 'the stimulus . . . to invention',[97] the patent system was criticized for obstructing 'the progress and improvement of arts and manufactures'.[98]

Despite these criticisms, it did not recommend the repeal of the patent system. Instead it recommended that 'importers of foreign inventions' not be granted patents,[99] and 'in no case' should the patent term exceed 14 years.[100] It also rejected calls for the preliminary examination of patent applications and for the appointment of a 'special Judge' to try patent cases,[101] but recommended that a judge and a scientific assessor (absent a jury) adjudicate the 'validity of Patents'.[102]

Unfortunately the Report's delivery came on the heels of the sudden death of Palmerston, the Prime Minister. His successor, John Russell,[103] was then replaced within a year by Edward Smith-Stanley[104] (Lord Stanley's father), who was in turn replaced by Benjamin Disraeli,[105] a Conservative, in early 1868. This frequent change in political leadership dissipated the Report's impact and produced more uncertainty, especially as Disraeli's appointment was short-lived and at the same time as the fragile peace between Prussia and France seemed doomed.

Nonetheless, with the appointment of the Liberal Gladstone Government, a Select Committee of Enquiry was appointed to reinvestigate the British patent system, taking evidence between 1869 and 1872. Once again the British patent attorney and legal professions, as well as inventors, came to its defence, emphasizing the favourable effects on British industry: William Grove, a patent lawyer, proposed that litigation by patent owners was beneficial to British enterprise because it would 'stimulate other manufacturers', and Thomas Webster, the same barrister who had given evidence in both the 1851 and 1864 enquiries, described the Crossley family (who controlled carpet manufacturing in Britain) as 'very beneficent despots'. On the other side of the floor however were the trade associations. Their evidence was that 'capitalists' were centralizing control over carpet manufacturing and wool-combing by using patents and the threat of litigation to extort high prices for their machines, thereby putting many tradesmen out of business. Unimpressed, the Select Committee's Report was so damning of the British patent system that it recommended: (a) a reduction in the patent term from 14 years to seven years; (b) a strict pre-grant examination of patent applications; (c) revocation of patents not worked within two years; and (d) the compulsory licensing of all patents.

Within months of the Report the Patents Reform Bill, 1872, which contained provisions consistent with the Committee's recommendations, was passed in the House of Lords. It was then sent down to the House of Commons for debate. There it languished, eventually being withdrawn in 1874 as Britain's manufacturing industry slowed as a result of a world recession and the Liberals were defeated at the election.[106] The failure of Gladstone's diplomacy to stop the Franco-Prussian War in 1870 eventually led to the complete breakdown of the Cobden–Chevalier Treaty.[107] Within a decade the tolerance of the free trade agenda among European policy-makers was gone as, one by one, France, Germany, Russia, Austria and Italy all raised tariffs and reinforced their protectionist trade barriers, of which one was their patent systems.

PATENT REFORM AND PROTECTIONISM

The UK Patents, Designs and Trade Marks Act 1883 was a significant piece of legislation; apart from placing the pillars of intellectual property under one roof, the legislation established the office of the Comptroller of Patents. Why the 'Comptroller' and not the 'Commissioner', as the US Patents Act 1836 styled the head of the Patent Office, is immaterial for the roles bore marked similarities.

It also abolished the ancient proceedings in *scire facias* and transferred the power to revoke to the courts (but using the grounds of invalidity available under *scire facias*), a procedure also more consistent with US patent law.

Until then the granted patent had consisted of two formal elements: the title of the invention and the provisional and/or complete specification, which contained a written description of the invention and how it was performed or made. Under this new legislation a third element was formally mandated – the claims. These were defined as 'a distinct statement of the invention claimed', and at least one such claim was to be made at the end of the complete specification. Thus the claim requirement that had previously been introduced into US patent law in 1836 (section 6, '. . . and shall particularly specify and point out the part, improvement, or combination, which he claims as his own invention or discovery') was also now part of UK patent law.[108]

BOX 1.5   THE CLAIMS

Today the claims are central to a patent, for these not only define the invention but they define the scope or legal boundaries of the patent monopoly. Whether it is a case of infringement or revocation, the courts look to the claims. Even though they are distinct from the complete specification they are related in the sense that the complete specification provides the information which support the claims, and in the case of ambiguity in the language of the claims may be referred to in resolving that ambiguity.

The difference between the invention as claimed and that as described in the specification need not be the same. While the specification provides information about the invention, the inventor can claim less than that described in the specification; but, importantly, if more is claimed than is described, the validity of the entire patent is jeopardized – although in the US the patentee was permitted to 'disclaim' that part of the invention which contravened this requirement in order to save the patent (section 7, 1836). The reason for this comes down to the fairness of the social contract or bargain, or, as Lord Mansfield in *Liardet v Johnson* (*1780*) put it, 'the price the individual should pay the people for his monopoly'.

Beyond these important reforms the 1883 legislation further reduced the cost of a patent application from £25 to £4; the renewal fees remained at £50, but the renewal dates were extended by one year to the end of the fourth and eighth years, effectively reducing the cost of a four-year patent

---

BOX 1.6   THE EFFECT OF BROAD CLAIMS

'That the law will permit an inventor to claim that which he has invented by means of successful experiments or otherwise, and which he has given to the public, but not that which is the mere subject of his speculation or imagination, or of his endeavouring to grasp more than he is entitled to. I think we are bound to give, as far as possible, the fullest effect to an invention; but, on the other hand, we are also bound to oppose the endeavours to make a patent grasp at, and embrace, a number of matters that were never in the head of the inventor.'

Per Pollock CB, *Tetley v Easton* (1853) 118 ER 1024.

'A patentee who claims broadly must prove broadly; he may not claim broadly, and recede as he later finds that the art unknown to him has limited his invention. That is the chance he must take in making broad claims; if he has claimed more than he was entitled to, the statute does give him a locus poenitentiae, but he must reasonably disclaim the broad claims in toto; He may not keep them by interpretative limitation; he must procure new claims by reissue.'

Per Learned Hand, Swan and Chase JJ, *Foxboro Co v Taylor Instrument Companies* (1846) 157 F 2d 226.

---

from £75 to £4; an eight-year patent from £125 to £104; and a 14-year patent from £175 to £154; and, like the US 1836 patent legislation, it introduced for the first time in Britain the formal requirement of pre-grant examination by an examiner of the Patent Office. Transacting business with the Patent Office was furthermore made easier by the ability of the inventor or his patent agent to file all patent documents by post, rather than requiring their personal attendance at the Patent Office.

The British patent examiners in turn were required to examine a patent application to see whether:

1. the nature of the invention had been 'fairly described' (section 6);
2. the application, specifications and any drawings had been prepared in the 'prescribed manner' (section 6);
3. the 'title' sufficiently indicated the subject matter of the invention (section 6) and

4.   the invention described in the provisional patent application was 'sub-
     stantially the same' as that in the complete specification (section 9).

Unlike in the US however there was not any requirement for them to
examine the *novelty* of the invention. The scrutiny regarding this requirement remained within the sole dominion of the courts, being an element
of a valid grant of Letters Patent (section 29). In this regard the legislation
addressed the criticisms made during the Royal Commission (1862–1864)
that the lack of particularity made it impossible for the parties to know
each other's case until the trial. Accordingly it was made a requirement of
the proceedings that sufficient particulars be given, as to both allegations
of infringement and invalidity. With regard to an allegation of the lack of
novelty of the invention, it was specifically mandated that 'the time and
place of the previous publication or use' be particularized (section 29(3)).

The legislation also continued the pre-grant procedure first established
under the 1852 legislation (section 12), namely the 'opposition' (section
11), but confined the scope of the opposition to three grounds. Under this
amended opposition procedure 'any person' (although it was subsequently
held in *Reg. v Comptroller, ex parte Tomlinson* (1899) 16 RPC 233 that
only a person having a real interest in a prior patent or some substantial
interest had standing) could, within two months of the publication by the
Patent Office of the acceptance of the patent application, file an opposition to the proposed grant of a patent on the grounds that: (a) the named
inventor had misappropriated the invention from the person opposing; (b)
the invention had already been patented in Great Britain; or (c) an examiner had reported that it was the same invention as had been comprised
in a specification that bore the same or similar title. The opposition was
handled by a Law Officer who could employ 'the assistance of an expert'
to determine whether the grounds of opposition were satisfied. If so the
Patent Office's acceptance of the patent application was reversed and the
patent application refused. The decision of the Law Officer was final, but
a finding in favour of the patent applicant did not act as a bar to an action
for revocation in the courts once the patent had been granted.

Despite the passing of some 20 years since he gave his evidence before the
Royal Commission, the Duke of Somerset's evidence did not go unheeded.
While a patent was as binding upon 'Her Majesty the Queen her heirs and
successors' as it was upon a 'subject' (section 27(1)), the Crown, as the
British State was called in legislation, could legitimately 'use the invention
for the services of the Crown' without the authority of the patent owner
on terms 'as agreed' or, in the absence of any agreement on terms, as
'settled by the Treasury' (section 27(2)). This was exceptionally broad in
its effect, since the term, 'services of the Crown', could encompass literally

any governmental activity. The legislation went even further: in addition to the Crown itself, the legislation also quarantined 'the agents, contractors or others' of the Crown from the threat of infringement proceedings. Thereafter the Crown was able to call the shots in any negotiation with a patent owner over the use of a patented invention, whether it be used for military or other governmental purposes.

The 1883 legislation also introduced the ability for any interested person to petition the Board of Trade for a compulsory licence of a British patent (section 22). Once the Board of Trade was satisfied that a ground for the grant of a compulsory licence was established, it could issue a compulsory licence and there was no appeal available to the patent owner. The grounds for such a licence were: the patent was worked or the patented article was manufactured 'exclusively or mainly outside the United Kingdom'; 'the reasonable requirements of the public' were not supplied; or 'any person' was prevented from working or using 'to the best advantage' his invention. Without doubt the policy behind this amendment was the encouragement of foreign patent owners to work their patents in the UK and not use them to suppress British industry and, consequently, employment.

According to Edward Daniel, a patent law commentator of the day, this amendment was 'quite new and marked a considerable change in the law',[109] and its inclusion demonstrated that while British policy-makers were content to retain the patent system, they were not prepared to allow foreigners to obtain British patents and frustrate British industry's participation in the exploitation of that patent. That Great Britain was an attractive and mature market for foreigners to exploit perhaps made British policy-makers somewhat circumspect, especially given that German industry had already started nipping the lion's heel, and so the compulsory licence and the Board of Trade provided a mechanism in which to keep control.

MEANWHILE, ACROSS THE ATLANTIC . . .

The first major amendment made to American patent law after the 1836 legislation was in 1839, and it provided that an application for a foreign patent by another party over the same invention that had been made less than six months prior to a US patent application could not act as a bar to the grant of the US patent (section 6). This was to give US patent applicants a six-month grace period to counter the otherwise novelty-destroying effect of the grant of a foreign patent over the corresponding invention. The next was not until just before the outbreak of the Civil War in 1861, when the patent term was increased from 14 years to 17 years as compensation to patent owners for the removal of the right created by section 18 US Patents Act 1836 to apply to the Commissioner of Patents for an extension of the term beyond 14 years.

However while the US Congress was increasing its patent term, in Great Britain (as well as in France and Germany) there was considerable debate as to the merits of the patent system altogether. No doubt because of the political situation between the Union and Southern states and the ensuing Civil War between 1861 and 1865, while Great Britain and Europe were reflecting upon the merits of their respective patent systems, policy-makers in the United States were distracted. Nonetheless after the Civil War the US patent system was scrutinized, and according to one commentator, Chauncey Smith, writing in *The Quarterly Journal of Patent Law* in 1890, 'a member of Congress from Massachusetts'[110] had told him that in the past 'a large number of the members of the House of Representatives were ready . . . to vote for the repeal of the patent law'.[111] According to Smith opposition to the US patent system had come from farmers in the West and Southern planters over the 'enforcement of Whitney's rights under his patent for the cotton gin',[112] but such opposition eventually dissipated.

In 1870 inventors were granted a grace period of two years in which to use the invention publicly where previously such action had barred them from applying for a US patent: the rationale here was that inventors often needed time in which to undertake experiments, and unless extended this liberty they would be less inclined to disclose their inventions and take advantage of the US patent system. Given that in the United States the key date for a US patent application in terms of establishing the priority of the patent application against all other inventors was the date of invention, not the date of disclosure as it was in Britain and Europe, it mattered little to a US inventor if the invention was publicly displayed in the US prior to the making of a US patent application (section 24), providing that such use did not destroy the novelty of the invention. The same grace period was notably extended to foreign inventors who had been granted a foreign patent and who were applying for a US patent over the same invention, provided that such public use was confined to the United States (section 25).

In terms of specifying the requirements of disclosure of the invention, once again the American patent system set the pace across the Atlantic. Under the 1870 legislation the manner and process of making, constructing, compounding and using the invention had to be described in:

> . . . full, clear, concise, and exact terms as to enable any person skilled in the art or science to which it appertains . . . to make, construct, compound, and use the same; and in case of a machine, [should] explain the principle thereof, and

the best mode in which he has contemplated applying that principle so as to distinguish it from other inventions. [section 26]

These specific requirements were not incorporated into British patent legislation until 1949. Furthermore the patent application filing fee went from US$30 under the 1836 legislation to US$15, and the same fee was made applicable to foreigners – which was significant; in the case of British inventors it brought the cost down from US$500 and for other foreign inventors down from US$300.

Another important amendment concerned actions for infringement and the defences available. Under the 1836 legislation (section 15) it was a defence to infringement if the foreign patent owner had 'failed and neglected' over the space of 18 months from the date of the patent to allow the sale of the patented 'invention or discovery' to the public, 'on reasonable terms', in the United States. Although not a ground of revocation, clearly the object of this defence was to encourage the working of the patented invention in the United States. However in the 1870 amendments this defence was removed: its deletion was to have a significant and painful impact upon the United States when World War I arrived.

In 1893, two years after the creation of the Federal Courts of Appeal, appeals from the decision of the Commissioner of Patents were transferred to the Federal Court of Appeal for the District of Columbia. In 1897 the US patent system was again modified slightly through the reduction of the grace period (sections 24 and 25) from two years to one; and foreigners who had been granted a foreign patent could apply for a US patent over the same invention provided the foreign patent did not predate the US application by more than seven months (section 3).

The US patent system, established by the US Patents Act 1836 and refined by its subsequent amendment, was well accepted by inventors. By 4 July 1890 441 498 US patents had been granted. While Chauncey Smith acknowledged in 1890 that many important inventions were made without a patent system, such as 'the invention of gunpowder and firearms . . . the mariner's compass . . . [and] the telescope', and accepted that 'even now the highest efforts of the human mind' were directed to scientific discovery 'without thought of pecuniary reward', he believed: 'it [was] fair to conclude that the recognition of the value of the patent law to [the United States] has had its influence in leading other countries to the belief that it was wise to invest inventors with a right to their inventions'.[113]

Smith's positive assessment of the US patent system was echoed by the US Commissioner of Patents, who wrote in his 1890 Report, 'the triumphs of American invention have attracted universal admiration, and the conspicuous demonstrations of their importance and usefulness has turned distrust to confidence'. He went further and said he believed 'no law or legal system in any age or any land has ever wrought so much wealth, furnished so much labour for human hands, or bestowed so much material blessing in every way as the American patent system'.[114]

Perhaps the confident perspectives were appropriate in the 1890s, but by 1915 the German dyestuffs, chemical and pharmaceuticals industries and the actions of the German Government would provide Americans with another, more sobering, perspective.

NOTES

1. 1312–77; Edward III, King of England, 1327–77.
2. 1340–99; Duke of Lancaster, 1362–99.
3. 1330–76; Edward of Woodstock, Prince of Wales (subsequently known as the Black Prince) and father of Richard II.
4. 1367–1400; Richard II, King of England, 1377–99.
5. The offence of engrossing was directed to the unfair exercise of market power over essential commodities (usually food), resulting in inflated prices – although the word 'monopoly' was not to become part of the English lexicon for another 100 years, evidently Parliament had already formed the view that predatory commercial conduct was unacceptable.
6. 1421–71; King of France, 1422–53.
7. Passed in 1623 and became law in 1624.
8. 1552–1634.
9. Appointed 1592.
10. Appointed 1593.
11. Appointed 1606.
12. Appointed 1613.
13. Appointed 1621.
14. Subsequently described in his *Reports*. See Sheppard, S (ed.) (2003), *The Selected Writings and Speeches of Sir Edward Coke* (Liberty Fund: Indianapolis).
15. While it was a blow to his ambitions, Coke quickly recovered by arranging the marriage of his 14-year-old daughter to Sir John Villiers, the elder brother of the 1st Duke of Buckingham and one of the King's favourites.
16. In 1621 Bacon was fined and sent to the Tower of London, albeit for only a few days. He was also banned from sitting in Parliament and from holding any office for life. There are some modern historians who argue that Bacon was innocent and that his confession was obtained under extreme duress.
17. Coke (1615), Part 11. Above n 14, 394–404.
18. Ibid, 404.
19. Ibid.
20. *Dr Bonham's Case* (1611) 77 ER 638, 645–6.
21. Cook, HJ (1985), 'Against Common Right and Reason: The College of Physicians Versus Dr. Thomas Bonham', *American Journal of Legal History*, **29**, 301.
22. Coke (1611), Part 8. Above n 14, 275.
23. Coke (1615), Part 11. Above n 14, 394.
24. 1738–1820; King of Great Britain and Ireland 1760–1801; King of the United Kingdom, 1801–20.
25. 1665–1714; Queen of England, Scotland and Ireland, 1702–14.
26. *Diamond v Chakrabarty* (1980) 447 US 303, 309.

27. 1632–1704.
28. 1722–90; author of *An Inquiry into the Nature and Causes of the Wealth of Nations* (1776).
29. 1788–1850.
30. Nye, JV (1991), 'The Myth of Free-Trade Britain and Fortress France: Tariffs and Trade in the Nineteenth Century', *The Journal of Economic History*, **51** (1), 23–46, 26.
31. 1804–65.
32. MacLeod, C (1992), 'Strategies for Innovation: The Diffusion of New Technology in Nineteenth-Century British Industry', *The Economic History Review*, New Series, **45** (2), 285–307, 288.
33. 1784–1865; Prime Minister 1855–58 and 1859–65.
34. Iliasu, AA (1971), 'The Cobden-Chevalier Commercial Treaty of 1860', *The Historical Journal*, **14** (1), 67–98, 71.
35. 1806–79.
36. 1808–87; First President of the French Republic, 1848–52; Emperor of the Second French Empire, 1852–70.
37. Iliasu, above n 34, 72; Parry, JP (2001), 'The Impact of Napoleon III on British Politics, 1851–1880', *Transactions of the Royal Historical Society*, 6th Ser, 147–75, 159.
38. Ibid, Parry.
39. Iliasu, above n 34, 75.
40. Ibid.
41. 1871–1955; US Secretary of State 1933–44; Nobel Peace Prize, 1945.
42. Hull, C (1948), *The Memoirs of Cordell Hull* (New York, Macmillan Co), Vol 1, 81. See also Schatz, AW (1970), 'The Anglo-American Trade Agreement and Cordell Hull's Search for Peace 1936–1938', *The Journal of American History*, **57** (1), 85–103.
43. Iliasu, above n 34, 75–76.
44. 1809–98; Prime Minister 1868–74, 1880–85, 1886, 1892–94.
45. 1792–78; Prime Minister 1846–52; 1865–66.
46. Iliasu, above n 34, 78–9.
47. Ibid, 86.
48. 1826–93; 15th Earl of Derby (son of Lord Edward Smith-Stanley, Prime Minister of England: 1852, 1858–59 and 1866–68).
49. 1st Baronet of Halifax; his father, John Crossley (1772–1837), invented power looms for carpet weaving and made a fortune in carpet manufacturing.
50. 1802–74; MR 1851–73, 1st Baron Romilly.
51. UK Royal Commission (1865), *Report of The Commissioners, Working of the Law Relating to Letters Patent for Inventions*: Appendix No II to the Report, 178 (4).
52. Ibid, 178 (4).
53. Ibid, 178 (5).
54. Ibid, 178 (4).
55. Ibid, 178 (6–7).
56. Ibid, 3 (90).
57. Ibid, 4 (122).
58. Ibid, 5 (130).
59. Ibid, 4 (122).
60. Ibid, 5 (131).
61. Ibid, 5 (146).
62. Ibid, 5 (143).
63. Ibid, 5 (144).
64. Ibid, Minutes of Evidence, p xxiv, Question 5: 'Do you consider that Patents ought to be refused on the ground of the trifling and frivolous nature of the inventions for which they are claimed?'
65. Ibid, 96 (1670).
66. Ibid.
67. Ibid.
68. Ibid, 98 (1686).

69.   1804–67; a founding partner of the London patent agent firm Carpmael & Rainsford.
70.   Ibid, 15 (346).
71.   Ibid, 17 (366) – a question by Lord Stanley.
72.   Ibid, 17 (366).
73.   Ibid, 125 (2062).
74.   Ibid.
75.   Howson, H and C (1872), *A Brief Inquiry into the Principles, Effect, and Present State of the American Patent System* (Philadelphia, Penn: Sherman & Co), 37.
76.   Ibid, 43.
77.   Ibid, 42.
78.   US House of Representatives Subcommittee on Courts, the Internet, and Intellectual Property Committee on the Judiciary, Intellectual Property Rights in the Knowledge-Based Economy, *A Patent System for the 21st Century*, 15 February 2007.
79.   UK Royal Commission, above n 51, 127 (2083).
80.   Ibid, 127 (2083).
81.   Ibid.
82.   Ibid, 128 (2086).
83.   Ibid.
84.   Ibid, 128 (2088).
85.   Ibid.
86.   Ibid, 130 (2109).
87.   Ibid, 130 (2117–2118).
88.   Ibid, 130 (2123).
89.   Ibid.
90.   Ibid.
91.   Ibid, 130 (2125).
92.   Ibid.
93.   UK Royal Commission, above n 51, Report, pp v–xiv.
94.   Ibid, p v.
95.   Ibid.
96.   Ibid.
97.   Ibid.
98.   Ibid, p v.
99.   Ibid, p xiii.
100. Ibid.
101. Ibid.
102. Ibid.
103. 1792–1878; Prime Minister 1865–66; peerage, 1st Earl Russell.
104. 1799–1869; Prime Minister 1852, 1858–9 and 1866–8; peerage, 14th Earl of Derby.
105. 1804–81; Prime Minister 1868; 1874–80; peerage, 1st Earl of Beaconsfield.
106. Parry, above n 37, 171.
107. Zebel, SH (1940), 'Fair Trade: An English Reaction to the Breakdown of the Cobden Treaty System', *The Journal of Modern History*, **12** (2), 161–185.
108. The actual practice of including 'claims' commenced in England prior to 1836 (*Kay v Marshall* (1836) 2 Webs Pat Cas 39 per Lord Cottenham, '[t]he claim is introduced . . . not to aid the description, but to ascertain the extent of what is claimed as new').
109. Daniel, EM (1884), *A Complete Treatise upon The New Law of Patents, Designs and Trade Marks Act, 1883* (London UK: Steven & Hayes),143.
110. Smith, C (1890), 'A Century of Patent Law', *The Quarterly Journal of Economics*, **5** (1), 44–69, 58.
111. Ibid, 58–9.
112. Ibid, 61.
113. Ibid, 63.
114. Ibid, 69.

2. Patents and their use in economic warfare

> It is nonsense to talk about 'crushing' Germany. . . . The best thing that could happen would be that when the two sides are seen to be evenly matched America should step in and impose terms on both.
>
> Lloyd George, British Minister of Munitions to CP Scott Editor,
> *The Manchester Guardian*, December 1915

Between 1850 and 1874 the British Empire so clearly dominated world trade that it even toyed with the idea of removing the patent system altogether. With no obvious contenders for her position British policy-makers could afford to be magnanimous and proposed lowering British tariffs, opening Britain's borders to its trading partners, and seeking easier access to the markets of its trading partners on the basis that free trade promoted domestic prosperity. However that policy began to change in the wake of the declaration of the German Empire, on 18 January 1871, where Wilhelm I,[1] the King of Prussia, was proclaimed the first German Emperor and Otto von Bismarck[2] its first Chancellor.

The first cracks in the British Empire's industrial fortunes started to appear as the world went into recession in early 1873 – a recession brought on by the disruption to world capital markets caused by the Franco-Prussian War of 1870 and widened with Germany's industrial ascendancy during that decade with her imperialist foreign policies of *Weltpolitik* (German: world policy) and *Mitteleuropa* (German: Central Europe). The latter in particular posed a direct threat to the British Empire's hegemony.

It was Germany's capacity for industrial innovation that really marked her with distinction. A stellar example was the dye manufacturing partnership established in 1863 by Friedrich Bayer, a dye salesman, and Johann Weskott, a textile dyer, which by 1881 had become Farbenfabriken Bayer, Vormals Friedrich Bayer & Co (Bayer Germany) and which later produced phenacetin, a medicine that was administered for the treatment of influenza during the world epidemic of 1889–92. By 1896 Bayer Germany had established Elberfeld Farbenfabriken Co Ltd, a fully owned British subsidiary, which in 1898 changed its name to Bayer Co Ltd. By 1898 Bayer Germany had also developed diacetylmorphine sold under the trade mark Heroin, and acetylsalicylic acid sold under the trade mark Aspirin. More important was the kind of innovation practised by Bayer and other German chemical manufacturers which saw the price of dyes fall dramatically. For example the price per kilo of alizarine fell from about 200Marks in the early 1870s to 9Marks by 1886. As AD Chandler illustrated:

> By the 1890s, these firms concentrated their production in one or two giant works on the Rhine in which raw materials brought by water and rail were transformed into a variety of intermediate chemicals which in turn were processed into hundreds of different finished dyes and pharmaceuticals. The addition of each new dye or pharmaceutical added little to the overall production costs and thus permitted the reduction of the unit costs of each individual dye and pharmaceutical far below those of their smaller competitors.[3]

The comparative trading advantage which massive price reductions of this kind produced, coupled with the large production capacity of chemical factories, necessitated the search for new overseas markets for Germany's industrial output and, like the UK, new colonies for the provision of raw materials. A policy of *Weltpolitik* (or imperialism), in which Germany established colonies, made perfect sense. Complementing this policy was the concept of an expanded form of the *Zollverein* (German: customs union) which had existed between the various Prussian States prior to Germany's unification, but now covered Germany and its central European neighbours to form a European trading bloc providing preferential trading terms to its members. German policy-makers called this policy *Mitteleuropa*. The objective was to protect the German Empire's growing economy from the British Empire, Russia and the United States.

These manoeuvrings unsettled British industry and policy-makers alike and encouraged them to retreat from free trade and back towards protectionism. The decision to retain and amend the British patent system in 1883 signalled the first move, but by 1902 the British Empire needed further reinforcement.

In 1902 the British Parliament passed important amendments to the UK Patents, Designs and Trade Marks Act 1883. These were the first significant amendments in nearly 20 years and the first of many between 1902 and 1977 designed to protect the British economy. Under these amendments the limited pre-grant examination of patent applications was broadened to include *novelty*, thereby enabling the British Patent Office, as the London patent barrister Thomas Webster had suggested during the 1864 Royal Commission into the patent system, to halt *in limine* patent applications which claimed, as inventions, technologies that had already been the subject of a British patent or patent application within 50 years of the date of the patent application.[4] From now on pre-grant examination would, in addition to the criteria provided in the 1883 legislation,[5] include that the invention claimed had not already been fully or partly claimed or described in any British specification published before the date of the application, and 'deposited' within 50 years before the date of the application (section 7a(1)).[6]

While the amendments in 1902 brought the UK pre-grant examination closer to that of the US, it was still not quite the same, since in the US *any* document which was published at *any time* prior to the date of the patent application *anywhere* in the world was relevant to the issue of novelty. Restricting the parameters of novelty examination to British patent specifications published or accepted within 50 years of the application date did not mean that the invention in a British patent was 'new' as against worldwide publications, only as against this class of British documents. What this meant was that it remained possible for a British citizen to learn of a new technology, either directly or through communication from abroad, and then import it back to the UK as an 'invention', permitting him to apply for patents as the 'first to invent' in the UK. It had long been accepted by the common law, which had been codified in section 10 of the 1852 legislation, that even if a British patent was obtained without the authority or knowledge of the foreign inventor the British inventor was protected, 'since from a very early period in the history of patents, the first introducer of an invention into this country was always held to be the first inventor thereof within these realms – *Edgeberry v Stephens (2 Salkeld, 447); Carpenter v Smith (9 M and W, 300)*'.[7]

The Paris Convention for the Protection of Industrial Property of 1883, which the UK signed on 7 July 1884, had however provided foreign patent applicants with a one-year priority period within which to apply for a British patent over the same invention. If the foreign inventor did not avail himself of that priority period any British patent application over the same invention would proceed without reference to the prior dated foreign patent application. So it still remained possible after 1883 for a British inventor to import new foreign technology into the UK and thus retain an advantage over foreign inventors. This advantage was never available under the US patent system because the scope of the novelty examination extended to publication or use of the invention beyond the US, and even though by 1883 the US patent system had been amended so that public display of the invention within two years of the filing of a US patent application was overlooked for the purposes of novelty, that display had to have occurred in the United States. Nonetheless the US patent system had other mechanisms that gave US inventors the edge over foreign inventors and, as previously discussed, the caveat was one such mechanism.

British pre-grant examination was also different from the US pre-grant examination in another important respect. Whereas in the US a granted patent was presumed to be valid, in the UK this was not the case. In fact the pre-grant assessment for novelty expressly provided no 'guarantee [of the] validity of any patent', and 'no liability' was accepted 'by reason of [or] in connection with any such investigation . . . or any proceeding consequent thereon' (section 7(9)). This meant that in rejecting a patent application which for instance may well have been novel, the British Patent Office was absolved of any responsibility and no disgruntled patent applicant could threaten to sue or recover damages in respect of error, omission or negligence on the part of the British Patent Office in the performance of its novelty assessment. Likewise if a granted British patent was subsequently revoked by a court on the grounds of novelty, the British Patent Office was immune. In other words the British Patent Office was unaccountable for its actions. Furthermore, in terms of the pre-grant opposition procedure, the grounds of opposition were not amended to include a novelty objection. The British Parliament was intent on leaving novelty disputes regarding granted patents to revocation proceedings exclusively in the courts (section 26).

In 1907 the British Empire's economic shield was significantly strengthened with the repeal of the 1883 legislation and its replacement with a new UK Patents and Designs Act 1907. Unlike the 1883 legislation, which gave the power to revoke exclusively to the courts, for the first time the Comptroller of Patents was provided with the power to revoke, after a four-year threshold, on the grounds that the patented article or process was 'manufactured or carried on exclusively or mainly outside the UK' (section 27). This was in addition to petitions to the Board of Trade for compulsory licences and revocation (sections 24 and 25). The new legislation provided a twofold defence for domestic industry. While the working of a patent by a patent owner exclusively outside the UK was retained as a ground upon which to seek relief, under section 27 the place of contest was transferred from the Board of Trade to the Comptroller of Patents and the applicable relief was not a compulsory licence but revocation. Moreover, while the ability to petition for a compulsory licence or revocation was carried over from the 1883 legislation, under the new section 24 the Board of Trade was obliged to refer a *prima facie* case to a court, which would then decide whether to grant a compulsory licence or revoke the patent (section 24(3)).

The rationale for this escalation in protectionism was, according to Fulton, a patent law commentator of the day, to restore the 'original intention of the Statute of Monopolies'.[8] Fulton wrote:

It is indisputable that, under the Statute of Monopolies patents were not granted to inventors as a reward for being ingenious, but for the purpose of introducing new manufactures into the country and to create increased employment for the working classes. It is equally indisputable that, under the conditions existing before the coming into force of the present Act, many a patent granted to a foreigner, so far from being an encouragement to native industry, was a positive fetter upon the wrists of those who would otherwise have found profitable employment had working in this country been made compulsory.[9]

David Fulton was not the only person to have held this opinion. David Lloyd George MP[10] (who was the British Prime Minister between 1916 and 1922) introduced the Bill (which became the UK Patents & Designs Act 1907) into Parliament while he was President of the Board of Trade, in order to 'combat the evil'[11] created by the 'abuse'[12] of the British patent system. In giving the Comptroller of Patents the power to revoke patents (previously only courts could revoke), the British Parliament had strengthened compulsory licensing by making the petition for revocation (the ultimate penalty for uncooperative patentees) more administrative, less formal and less expensive than proceedings before a court. It was a measure clearly aimed at encouraging local industry to seek relief against the German dyestuffs, chemical and pharmaceutical industries which, according to Lloyd George, had 'practically a monopoly' in the UK.[13] Describing them as 'powerful foreign syndicates'[14] that had been awarded 'wide patents covering all possible combinations'[15] of chemical inventions 'that had not been tried in practice at all',[16] Lloyd George believed that they discouraged 'the ingenuity of the poor British inventor'.[17] Fulton added, 'the commercial working of the invention within the realm had fallen into abeyance during the latter half of the eighteenth century',[18] with the result that 'foreigners could obtain patents in this country with no intention of working them here, but merely for the purpose of preventing competition by tying the hands of British manufacturers and enabling the patentees to manufacture abroad and import to England at prices which were often exorbitant'.[19]

The concerns expressed by Lloyd George, a politician, and Fulton, a patent lawyer, were by no means isolated. They repeated a view which then had echoed through the halls of the British business community as well as the British legal community. Another patent lawyer, Kenneth R Swan (who, as already discussed, would eventually chair a UK Parliamentary Select Committee into the British patent system conducted between 1945 and 1947), had warned in his 1908 treatise on British patent law:

Latter-day commercial methods have . . . shown that in the hands of unscrupulous [patent] proprietors a British patent can be turned to great profit for the patentee without a corresponding benefit to the public. Patents have occasionally been acquired not for the purpose of establishing a new manufacture 'within the realm', but . . . as a means of suppressing the manufacture in this country, whilst the invention is being worked abroad and the patented article imported into England and sold at exorbitant prices.[20]

Swan was particularly incisive and accurately foresaw another danger posed to the British economy by allowing a patent system to operate without adequate safeguards against what he described as 'unscrupulous tactics'.[21] Swan noted:

Taking advantage of their monopoly simply to prevent manufacture in this country, powerful foreign companies built up their businesses on that Continent and in America on such a gigantic scale that *even after the expiration of the British patents, they continued to monopolise our markets*, owing to the impossibility of creating and fostering these industries at home in the face of such formidable competition from well-established industries abroad.[22]

Swan's point is as true today as it was in 1908 – the patent systems of the world are being carefully manipulated by the pharmaceutical and biotech industries in order to suppress the production of generic medicines after the original patents have expired.

As a politician, Lloyd George was focused on his constituency and on his re-election. In a speech made at the Manchester Corn Exchange on 22 April 1908 he predicted, to the warm cheers of British workers, 'in the course of the next few years [the UK Patents & Designs Act 1907] would [result in] employment to thousands, and in the course of the next ten years it would bring employment to scores of thousands of people in this country'.[23] Unfortunately, World War I was to intervene and so his prediction remained unfulfilled.

Notwithstanding the simplified form of revocation provided by section 27 the new law did not quite achieve its objective of increasing manufacturing in Britain. A specialist patent judge had been appointed to hear appeals from the Comptroller's decisions, to adjudicate upon patent cases, to hear patent term extension applications and to order the revocation of patents by way of cross-claim (as a defence to a patent infringement action) rather than by way of separate revocation action. While this improved the efficiency of the courts, for they could now deal with patent infringement and validity in the one action, the first specialist patents judge, Parker J, decided to interpret section 27 strictly.[24]

In *In re Hatschek's Patent* [1909] 2 Ch 68 Parker J provided a convoluted comparison as the test for determining whether there had been 'adequate' manufacturing in the UK. According to this test a comparison was required between 'the extent to which' the article or process was 'manufactured or carried on' in Britain and the extent to which it was manufactured or carried on abroad, and whether the 'articles so manufactured or resulting from the process so carried on abroad' were imported into Britain or not. Only if the patent owner gave foreigners 'preferential terms in the grant of licences' or exercised his 'rights' so as to give other countries a four-year advantage over production in Britain was the relief provided by section 27 available. Parker J's interpretation of section 27 as a comparative assessment made it understandably difficult for the Comptroller to decide whether the patented article or process was being manufactured 'exclusively or mainly' outside Britain.

Despite Parker's judicial torpedo directed towards Lloyd George's policy of protectionism,[25] Lloyd George also increased tariffs on imported goods; and, as he had predicted, foreign industry (mainly American and German) finally responded to both the intent of section 27 and these other instruments by restructuring their existing businesses and investing more in their British subsidiaries. In 1910 Bayer & Co Ltd, the British subsidiary of Bayer Germany, ceased being merely an agent for Bayer Germany and took over the UK operations. In 1911 the Ford Motor Company (US motor vehicles) established an assembly plant in Manchester, and by 1914 Mannesmann (German electrical), Hoechst (German chemicals and pharmaceuticals), Hoffmann-La Roche (Swiss pharmaceuticals), Ciba (Swiss chemical and pharmaceuticals), Jönköping-Vulcan (Swedish matches), and Pirelli (Italian rubber) in a joint venture with General Electric Company (British submarine telephone cables and electrical equipment), had all built factories and established themselves in the UK.

This 'distinctly British contribution'[26] to patent law, as PJ Federico,[27] an American patent law academic, described section 27, was never incorporated into the US patent system; although between 1836 and 1870 it had been a defence in an action for patent infringement that for 18 months after the grant of a US patent the foreign patent owner 'had failed and neglected . . . to put and continue to put on sale to the public, on reasonable terms, the invention or discovery for which the patent issued' in the United States (US Patents Act 1836, section 15). So as Germany's economic fortunes rose from the 1870s the US, unlike the UK, had no legal mechanism in place to ameliorate the economic consequences of the patenting strategy employed by the powerful and wealthy German chemical and pharmaceutical companies. As such, and in the mistaken belief that America's patent law brought only significant economic benefits to its economy, American policy-makers overlooked the subterfuge – one that effectively blinded them to the actions of German patentees who endeavoured to suppress rather than encourage innovation, industry and employment in the US.

THE PATENT MONOPOLY AS AN ECONOMIC WEAPON

Having witnessed how the British Empire had used international trade to become the world's superpower, Bismarck was determined that the German Empire would follow suit. One of the first things that Bismarck did was to overhaul Germany's education system by centralizing the curriculum in secondary schools. He anticipated that German industry would need a steady supply of science and engineering graduates to fuel technological development in chemical and engineering industries that would give it a comparative advantage in world markets. Bismarck's determination to complete the industrialization of Germany came on the heels of its unification, but with a reputation for being a producer of 'cheap and bad products'[28] it was critical that its reputation for quality improved.

Bismarck understood that the patent system together with high tariffs would provide Germany with a duality of protection. He was influenced by Friedrich List,[29] a German economist, who had written in 1841, 'free competition between two nations which are highly civilised can only be mutually beneficial in case both of them are in a nearly equal position of industrial development'.[30] Bismarck knew that the German Empire was no match for the British Empire and he was ambitious to change that, but List cautioned him against falling for the free trade deception. Having industrialized by using high tariffs and protective instruments, such as patents, Britain, argued List, 'can do nothing wiser than to throw away . . . [the] ladders of her greatness, to preach to other nations the benefits of free trade, and to declare in penitent tones that she has hitherto wandered in the paths of error, and has now for the first time succeeded in discovering the truth'.[31]

Bismarck was a patriot and a protectionist who believed that Germany needed to protect her fledgling industries from foreign competition; and while high tariffs were the blunt instrument of protectionism, the patent system was much more subtle. The idea was simple enough: at home encourage German industry to use the patent monopoly to protect its home market, and abroad encourage German industry to use the patent monopoly in the foreign market to suppress the host country's local manufacturing. Of course Germany had to develop industries that gave them competitive advantages in those foreign markets, but having made the decision to centralize education and focus on producing scientists and engineers, Bismarck steered Germany in the right direction.

By May 1877 Bismarck had also centralized Germany's fragmented patent systems into one national patent system. The new German patent law provided a maximum patent term of 15 years and contained an important limitation that was not present in either the British or American patent system, namely a prohibition on the patenting of chemical substances per se. Indeed, in a pioneering move, the German patent system directed the German inventor's mind toward the development of new chemical processes, rather than focusing on the protection of the end product (which is what the American and British patent systems did), thereby creating a sort of *innovative competition* in manufacturing and engineering processes. By ensuring that a German patent owner could not simply gain a patent monopoly that blocked production of chemical substances no matter how they were produced, Bismarck's patent law encouraged German inventors to invent around the patented chemical processes so that the same chemical substances could be produced using new and, hopefully, more efficient and cheaper chemical processes. Thus the German patent owner had to work harder than his equal in America or Britain – the idea was ultimately to bring the price of chemicals and products down (giving Germany a competitive edge) through the use of novel and more efficient and cheaper processes.

Dovetailing this innovative competition was the formation of industry-wide associations. Neither Bismarck nor German policy-makers were actually concerned by this development, despite the fact that industrial collusion generally tended to reduce competition, because cartelization encouraged German industry to focus its economic strengths on capturing overseas markets *en masse*. Bismarck finally completed putting the pieces of his strategy in place in 1879 by massively increasing tariffs on imported goods.

Bismarck's successor, Count George Leo of Caprivi,[32] further enhanced the German patent system in 1891 (and the economic protections of the German domestic market) so that new chemical products – although themselves still not patentable inventions – could nevertheless be protected in Germany through the chemical process inventions used to produce them. This *product-by-process* protection provided *de facto* patent protection for new chemicals (being manufactured cheaply in Switzerland) and further encouraged German inventors to invent around patented chemical processes, while hindering Swiss chemical manufacturers.

Bismarck's strategy was brilliant. By 1900 the markets of the United Kingdom, the United States, Russia and France for dyestuffs, chemicals and pharmaceuticals belonged to Germany. The value of US imports of German dyestuffs alone, in 1900, was US$3 822 162 out of total of US$4 890 072. By comparison, in the same year, the total value of dyestuffs manufactured within the United States was US$52 648, a little over 1 per cent of the total value of dyestuff imports. Naturally as the success of this strategy became more apparent it became intolerable to Germany that its neighbour, Switzerland, which had finally adopted a patent system in 1887, would still not allow patents with respect to chemical processes and their products. Germany urged Switzerland to change its patent policy, and by 1907 Switzerland had relented. By 1913 global production of dyes stood at 160 000 tons. Of that Germany produced 140 000, Switzerland 10 000 and the UK 4100. According to Chandler, 'the story was much the same for pharmaceuticals, films, agricultural chemicals and electro-chemicals'.[33]

The significance of these data cannot be underestimated in the context of the argument that proponents of the patent system often use, namely that patent systems provide an incentive for research, development and invention by rewarding inventors. Certainly this evidence shows that the German patent system played a role in Germany's economic growth by stimulating innovation, but this stimulus did not by itself explain Germany's economic success story. By contrast during the same period the British patent system seems not to have provided any inventive stimulus to the British chemical industry despite the fact that synthetic dyes are a by-product of coal and, at that time, the UK had the world's largest known reserves of high quality coal, and William Perkin, an Englishman, invented the first synthetic dye made from coal. Yet British dyestuff manufacturers were unable to come anywhere near their German rivals in terms of quality, quantity or price. There were three reasons for this. The first was Germany's own plentiful coal reserves. The second was Germany's innovative use of large manufacturing plants built on the banks of the Rhine River which enabled her industries to produce dyes, both in quantities and prices, unmatched by British dye manufacturers. This had the effect of boosting German production, giving German factories the cost benefits that come with large-scale manufacture and which in turn gave them a significant edge over local chemical manufacturers in those host markets. The third was Germany's exploitation of foreign patent systems. In Germany the domestic patent system was a powerful tool, not only because it provided a reward for innovation within Germany but, critically, because it protected its industries from foreign competition in the German market. However in the hands of German inventors foreign patent systems were turned into economic weapons: by providing them with patent monopolies within their host markets, these foreign patent monopolies enabled German owners of foreign patents to suppress local competition in their export markets. This patent strategy was further enhanced by the ability of German inventors to obtain British and American patents over chemical substances per se, not simply the processes of their manufacture. This was a significant advantage, and one that was not available in Germany, because a patent over the chemical substance created a monopoly over any process of its manufacture, not simply the product as manufactured by a specific process.

Without doubt section 27's requirement to have the working of German patented technology enforced in the UK was introduced into the 1907 legislation to counteract this unfortunate outcome (and German patent law too was amended in 1911 in a tit-for-tat response to section 27),[34] and while the post-1907 statistics suggest that German industry responded by investing more heavily in the UK, it is certainly not the case that German industry then used its British subsidiaries or factories to maximize its potential production capacities for the benefit of the British economy. In essence German manufacturers were able to meet the intention of section 27 by substituting exports to the UK for production in the UK. While this substitution did increase foreign investment and domestic employment in the UK, unfortunately profits on UK sales and royalty earnings levied on the use of German-owned inventions in the UK were nevertheless repatriated to Germany. At the same time, while German industry lost some of its productive capacity to the UK, it was able to retain the bulk of its productive capacity in Germany, particularly as the 1870 amendments to the US patent legislation no longer required the working of German-owned US patented inventions in the United States.

In the meantime two major chemical cartels had formed in Germany. At the suggestion of Carl Duisberg (1861–1935; Head of Bayer Germany, 1900–1925) in 1904 Bayer Germany, Griesheim Electron, Aktiengesellschaft für Anilin-Fabrikation (AGFA) and Badische Anilin- und Sodafabrik (BASF) formed the *Dreibund* (German: three way alliance). In response, between 1904 and 1907, Farbwerke Meister Lucius & Bruning Hoechst (Hoechst), Cassella Farbwerke and Kalle & Co AG formed the *Dreiverband* (German: three way association). These two cartels then competed with each other; this outcome was not exactly what Duisberg had in mind, as his suggestion envisaged one cartel and no competition. Nonetheless he had sown the seeds for the creation of a single organization that went beyond a mere association of independent chemical companies cooperating with each other. His vision involved the formation of a centralized administration which brought its members together more in the sense of a merger. In 1916, with Germany fighting in World War I and under pressure, his vision came a step closer with the formation, by *Dreibund* and *Dreiverband*, of *Interessengemeinschaft der deutschen Teerfarbenindustrie* (German: community interest group of the German tar-colour industry), but even this was not quite what he had in mind. Eventually his vision was realized, but not until the 1920s.

THE IMPACT OF WORLD WAR I

The United States soon began to experience first-hand the consequences of a patent policy that failed to insist on the local manufacture or use of patent technology, and it was the American Pharmaceuticals Association, and not the American Patent Law Association, which raised the alarm to US policy-makers. In February 1917 Dr FE Stewart, a noted pharmacist, wrote:

It becomes evident that [US] patent law as now interpreted and applied does not promote progress in the arts of chemistry, pharmacy and drug therapeutics as carried on in the United States; in fact it is a very serious hindrance . . . to science . . . because it does not stimulate original research on the part of would-be inventors in this country. Neither does it build up United States industries.[35]

His comments came after a report prepared by the American Medical Association's Council of Pharmacy and Chemistry expressed concern over the safety of patented medicines which the German-owned pharmaceutical companies produced. At that time there was no Federal Food and Drug Administration (FDA) to regulate and control the manufacture and sale of pharmaceuticals in the United States. The report noted:

The council has continued its study of the United States patent law as it applies to medicine, and has become convinced that in many instances the patent law or its enforcement is contrary to the best interests of the public, both as concerns health and prosperity. The council feels it is a duty at this time to protest against provisions of our patent law, or the methods of its enforcement, which permit the granting of patents without thorough and scientific investigation of the claims advanced by such letters patent.[36]

Calvin De Witt Paige,[37] a Republican first elected to the US House of Representatives in 1913, heard the call. He responded with a Bill (HB 11967) to amend the US patent legislation. The main objective of his Bill was to limit the patenting of chemicals by prohibiting patents on chemical products. Patent protection would be restricted to processes for their manufacture. His Bill, like section 27 of the UK Patents & Designs Act 1907, also sought to introduce a 'patent working' provision where, unless foreign patentees manufactured the patented products in the United States within two years of the granting of their US patent, that patent was subject to revocation.[38]

Unfortunately the Paige Bill was never passed into law and eventually lapsed, for the simple reason that the retaliative measures that were soon employed against Germany proved much more effective and longer lasting.

In addressing the 65th Congress on 2 April 1917, four days before the United States officially declared war on Germany, President Woodrow Wilson[39] justified America's pending entry into World War I by proclaiming that America's motives would not be 'revenge or the victorious assertion of the physical might of the nation, but only the vindication of right, of human right', maintaining that Americans 'have no quarrel with the German people [and] . . . no feeling towards them but one of sympathy and friendship'.[40] Those sentiments however did not extend to US assets owned by German individuals and companies.

Under the Trading with the Enemy Act, 1917 the Office of Alien Property Custodian was established and empowered to 'receive, hold, administer, and account for all money and property in the United States due or belonging to an enemy, or ally of [an] enemy' (section 6). The Alien Property Custodian appointed by Wilson, Mitchell Palmer,[41] wasted no time. Within two years 32 296 trusts had been created to administer enemy assets to the value of US$502 945 724.75.[42] Considerably more however was sold to Americans.

As American participation in World War I progressed and, with American soldiers dying in European trenches, the mood against Germany intensified, prompting Palmer on 7 March 1918 to ask Congress for an extension of his powers to include patents, trade marks and copyrights. He asked that he be allowed to sell these assets, rather than hold them and their accumulating royalties in trust for German industrialists, who were already profiting from the war while 'killing American soldiers'. On 28 March 1918 the Congress passed amendments permitting Palmer to sell enemy property to Americans by public auction, and on 4 November 1918 it expanded the class of assets to include patents, trade marks, copyrights and related applications. However in December 1918, within a month of the cessation of military hostilities, the President modified the requirement for public sale, thereby enabling Palmer, with the authority of the Acting Secretary of State, Frank L Polk,[43] to sell to whomever he wanted, however he wanted, so long as the purchaser was American.

Despite the fact that World War I had ended, during 1919 some 10 000 patents were seized under the Trading with the Enemy Act 1917, including about 100 patents which related to radio technologies. While the confiscated radio patents were sold to the US Navy Department for next to nothing, by far the largest single sale of enemy intellectual property was to The Chemical Foundation, Inc.

CONFISCATED US PATENTS AND THE CHEMICAL FOUNDATION

The Chemical Foundation, Inc was established in Delaware on 16 February 1919, and with the assistance of Polk, Palmer and Francis Garvan[44] on 26 February 1919 it acquired 4764 German-owned US chemical and pharmaceutical patents and 288 patent applications, paying US$271 850, an average price of US$41.98.[45] In addition it acquired 874 trade marks and 492 copyrights. The principal objective of the Foundation was to gain ownership and control of German-owned US patented technology for the express purpose of using it, through non-exclusive licensing to American companies, to springboard the US chemical and pharmaceutical industry into local and international markets previously dominated by the German manufacturers. The fact that German manufacturers had established US subsidiaries, built factories, established distribution channels and employed US labour was irrelevant. The United States was a major market for German industry for dyestuffs, chemicals and pharmaceuticals and supplied 90 per cent of the dyes used by US industries (in 1914 Bayer Germany earned 84 000 000 Marks in sales solely from the United States). The opportunity to advance US economic interests at a time when popular opinion against Germany was running high was one not to be missed. As Floyd Vaughan, a commentator at the time, wrote, it was 'anticipated that nearly every important American manufacturer' would become 'a stockholder in this concern', and the Foundation did indeed become the US chemical and pharmaceutical industry's chief benefactor.[46]

In a study conducted by Vaughan in 1919, entitled 'Suppression and Non-Working of Patents, With Special Reference to the Dye and Chemical Industries',[47] he found that 'the extent to which United States patents may be suppressed by foreigners' was suggested by the large number of patents in both absolute and relative terms which were 'granted to foreigners' by the US, and provided statistics which showed that between 1910 and 1915 'the United States granted 21 073 patents to citizens of foreign countries, 11.43 per cent of the total number of patents granted during this period' and that, of those, England received 22 per cent and Germany 33 per cent.[48] In terms of the patents granted to German citizens he pointed out that the vast majority were directed to dyes and chemicals, and that of this class of patents the 'German inventor' was granted 90 per cent of all US patents. His study concluded that this dominance, together with the non-working of such patents in the United States, largely accounted for the 'lack of development of these industries' in the US prior to World War I.[49]

Vaughan's study provided academic support for the US Government's actions. Having already experienced the economic and social disruption caused by severe shortages of chemicals and pharmaceuticals brought on by the outbreak of war in Europe, coupled with the inability of US industry to respond and make up the shortfall to satisfy domestic demand – due directly to the German-controlled US patents and the lack of mature domestic chemical and pharmaceutical industries – US policy-makers became painfully aware of just how foreign-owned US patents could be used to suppress

---

BOX 2.1   THE PRESIDENT OF THE UNITED
           STATES' MESSAGE TO CONGRESS,
           20 MAY 1919

'The experiences of the war have made it plain that in some
cases too great reliance on foreign supply is dangerous, and
that in determining certain parts of our tariff policy domestic
considerations must be borne in mind which are political as well
as economic. Among the industries to which special consideration should be given is that of the manufacture of dyestuffs and
related chemicals. Our complete dependence upon German
supplies before the war made the interruption of trade a cause
of exceptional economic disturbance. The close relation between
the manufacturer of dyestuffs, on the one hand, and of explosives and poisonous gases, on the other, moreover, has given
the industry an exceptional significance and value. Although the
United States will gladly and unhesitatingly join in the program
of international disarmament, it will, nevertheless, be a policy of
obvious prudence to make certain of the successful maintenance
of many strong and well-equipped chemical plants. The German
chemical industry, with which we will be brought into competition, was and may well be again, a thoroughly knit monopoly
capable of exercising a competition of a peculiarly insidious and
dangerous kind.'

---

rather than encourage domestic innovation and industrialization in the
United States.

The confiscation of German-owned US patents was only the start.
Production of chemicals and pharmaceuticals required plant and equipment
and technical expertise. The former were simple to secure: in 1917 the Alien
Property Custodian confiscated the shares which Bayer Germany owned in
Bayer Co Inc (Bayer America), its fully owned American subsidiary, and in
December 1918 sold them to Sterling Products, Inc (Sterling), an American
company. Through that share acquisition Sterling gained effective ownership of the Bayer factory at Rensselaer, New York and Bayer's US business, which extended to Latin America. The US patents and trade marks
owned by Bayer Germany were also sold to Sterling. In total Sterling paid
US$5 310 000. However that and similar early sales raised some concerns.
It was thought that if this ad hoc approach were to continue then perhaps
the incentive for the development of the necessary technical expertise for

synthetic organic chemistry across the United States would be absent, and so with the 'impartial' counsel of Charles H Henty, the president of the American Chemical Society, the Government decided that The Chemical Foundation, Inc would be the beneficiary of any remaining chemical and pharmaceutical patents, and so the Foundation became the US public trustee of this technology. The idea was to share the patented technology around so as to encourage the establishment of a wider organic chemistry knowledge base. The Foundation subsequently licensed the patented technology on a non-exclusive basis to 103 American manufacturers, earning the Foundation about US$700 000 in royalties between 1919 and 1922.

The Foundation then used this income to fund its educational activities which, amongst other things, promoted the broadening of the chemical knowledge basis and kept politicians and policy-makers informed of the benefits which the US chemical and pharmaceutical industries derived from the Foundation's stewardship of these patents. In essence the Foundation had become a political lobbyist for the US chemical and pharmaceutical industries.

AND OTHER ALLIED POWERS HELP THEMSELVES

While the British did not compulsorily acquire the assets of German companies, they did put German-owned companies into the hands of administrators. On 2 June 1916 the Board of Trade made an order under the UK Trading with the Enemy (Amendment) Act 1916 directing that the business of Bayer Co Ltd be wound up. Once under government administration those assets could be dealt with in accordance with the existing laws and the emergency wartime powers, and on 18 March 1920 the administrator, with the sanction of the UK High Court, allowed Bayer America to acquire the remaining assets, which included the UK registered Bayer trade marks and the goodwill of the UK business.

In this instance Australia pre-empted the UK, and on 17 September 1915 the Prime Minister, William (Billy) M Hughes,[50] announced that the Commonwealth of Australia had licensed Henry W Shmith and George RR Nicholas to manufacture and sell Aspirin. According to Hughes the Australian-made version of Aspirin was 'purer' than the German and the 'conditions of the license' ensured that the drug should, 'comply strictly with the requirements of the British *Pharmacopœia*', and that the conditions of manufacture and the price at which Aspirin would be sold should be 'satisfactory to the Attorney-General'.[51] The Australian version used the trade mark Aspro, and through the marketing of this medicine by Alfred Nicholas sales of Aspro were eventually made to the UK, South Africa,

Belgium, Egypt and, by 1935, to France. This move by Hughes established one of Australia's most important pharmaceutical companies and went on to provide hundreds of jobs to Australians and made the Nicholas family extremely wealthy. The objective of the war between the British and German Empires, as he said during a speech reported in *The Times* which he gave to the Empire Parliamentary Association in London on 10 March 1916, was 'to destroy German control of British trade'.

THE TREATY OF VERSAILLES AND ENEMY PATENTS

The Treaty of Versailles came into effect on 20 December 1920, officially concluding hostilities with Germany (although military hostilities had ended on 11 November 1918), and contained clauses which ratified the war-time measures taken by the Allied Powers against Germany, its allies and their nationals between the time that war was declared and the time that the treaty came into effect, including the Allied confiscation of German-owned patents (Section VII, Article 306). The Allied Powers were now in a position of considerable strength and, as the victors, were determined to hang on to as much of the economic advantage which flowed from the application of emergency wartime measures as they possibly could. Of paramount importance was the development of their own capacities for the production of chemicals and pharmaceuticals, and they expected that in suppressing Germany's chemical and pharmaceutical industries in the post-war world considerable competitive advantages would be given to their own fledgling industries. The longer it took for Germany to rebuild these industries the better; and, for the Allies, what better way to extend this time than through the use of the very same patent monopolies that German industry had once aimed at them.

According to Article 306 of the Treaty the Allies were reserved:

> . . . the right to impose such limitations, conditions or restrictions on rights of industrial, literary or artistic property (with the exception of trade-marks) acquired before or during the war . . . [and] as regards rights of industrial, literary and artistic property acquired after . . . the present Treaty, the right so reserved by the Allied and Associated Powers shall only be exercised in cases where these limitations, conditions or restrictions may be considered necessary for national defence or in the public interest.

For the Allied Powers it was in the 'public interest' that key industries, such as chemical and pharmaceuticals, be developed so that their economies would never again be as vulnerable as they were shown to be at the outbreak of the war.

PEACETIME POLITICS COMPLICATES THE WORK OF THE CHEMICAL FOUNDATION

Peace however complicated the work of the Chemical Foundation. With a change in the presidential administration in 1921 the incoming US government, rather surprisingly, sought to overrule the previous US government's transfer of German-owned US patents to the Foundation and encouraged the Department of Justice to sue the Foundation for allegedly conducting illegal activities during the war. The new President, Warren Harding,[52] and his Republican colleagues were determined to embarrass the Democratic presidential administration of Woodrow Wilson and, in spite of the depth of popular animosity against Germany, the Department of Justice set about investigating allegations against the Foundation at a time when about 60 lawsuits were brought against the Foundation by German nationals to recover their US patents. The Department of Justice's principal allegation was fraud and its key evidence was the below-market price which the Foundation had paid the Alien Property Custodian for the patents. At less than US$50 per patent this seemed a credible allegation, especially given that in 1916 the patents for Salvarsan and Neosalvarsan alone earned the US importer, Herman Metz, revenues of US$970 000 and profits of US$430 000. Both of these drugs were used in the treatment of syphilis and tryanosomiasis (sleeping sickness), and Metz estimated that in 1919, when the transfers to the Foundation were effected, the market value of these two US patents was over US$1 000 000.

USA v THE CHEMICAL FOUNDATION

Despite this and other similar evidence presented by the Department of Justice during the District Court trial in *USA v The Chemical Foundation, Inc* (1924) 294 F 300, the trial judge, Judge Morris, dismissed the case against the Foundation. The subsequent appeal upheld his decision. Ultimately the case reached the US Supreme Court in 1926 ((1926) 47 S Ct 1). It too found in favour of the Foundation. The District Court, Federal Appeals Court and the Supreme Court all held that the Government had the power to confiscate 'alien' property in wartime and, as the absolute owner of that property, was able to dispose of it as it saw fit, even if the price was below market value. Furthermore the Supreme Court found that when taking the national interest and the role which the Foundation played in relation to it into account, 'the arrangement was intended to amount to a public trust for those whom the patents will benefit and for the promotion of American industries'. The beneficiaries of this 'public trust' were, of course, the American chemical and pharmaceutical companies which were given 'the right to have on equal and reasonable terms licenses to make, use and sell the inventions covered by the patents'. Accordingly as the Foundation was 'an instrumentality created under the direction of the President to effect that disposition and subsequent control of the patents which he determined to be in the public interest', the transfer of the German-owned US patents to the Foundation for the benefit of the nation 'did not involve any of the evils aimed at by section 41'[53] of the US Criminal Code, even though the Foundation earned licence fees and its officers were thereby remunerated.

Apart from the unsurprising judgments, one of the arguments that was made during the trial, and the evidence called both in support and in answer to it, are worth exploring; the same argument, albeit with regard to biotechnology, is equally applicable today.

This argument concerns the practical value of the information disclosed by the patent. The Foundation alleged that for the most part this information was either deliberately misleading or insufficiently detailed, so that local manufacturers were unable to produce the chemicals and pharmaceuticals in the quantities and to the qualities necessary for the purposes of large-scale production, distribution and sale. They alleged that substantial and significant modifications were required to the inventions described in the German-owned US patents and that the patents were not worth anywhere near what the Department of Justice claimed was the market price. The Foundation produced witness after witness, all well respected chemists from academia, who testified to this effect. The Foundation also had at its disposal companies such as Du Pont and Abbott Laboratories which corroborated this evidence with anecdotal evidence from their employed scientists and production engineers. Related to this issue were the problems associated with identifying the patents that produced the dyes, the poor yields that were produced and evidence that the patents did not have 'any practical value without the know-how'.[54]

THE DISCOVERY THAT COMMERCIAL-SCALE KNOW-HOW WAS NOT DISCLOSED BY GERMAN INVENTORS

The lack of know-how was a significant issue; while the Foundation argued that this was essential information that was missing from the specifications of the German-owned US patents, the Government countered that the exclusion of this information did not render the patents invalid, as the problems which the local manufacturers were encountering in working the patented inventions were caused by their lack of expertise and experience in organic chemistry, not by a lack of information in the patents. The Government maintained that the disclosure requirement of US patent law was satisfied if a person of *ordinary skill* in the relevant art understood the information disclosed in the patent. It was not necessary for the patent to explain to such a person how to make the invention on a commercial scale. The US Patent Office had vetted and granted these patents and, naturally, as they had satisfied the thresholds provided by US patent law, passed the pre-grant examination process and were presumed to be valid, the government lawyers were bound to defend them by defending the system that created them.

The Foundation produced some star witnesses. One was Dr Julius Stieglitz,[55] an organic chemist from the University of Chicago, who had received his doctorate from the University of Berlin. Stieglitz was born in New Jersey to German immigrants and in 1905 was appointed a professor of chemistry. In 1915 he was appointed chair of the chemistry department, a position he was to retain until he retired in 1933. His research was in organic chemistry, and by the time he gave evidence at the trial he had served as president of the American Chemical Society in 1917 and was the recipient of the prestigious Willard Gibbs Medal.[56] Although his expertise was well above the minimum required by patent law (that is, a person of ordinary skill in the art), his testimony showed that while the United States had the necessary expertise to assess the quality of the information contained in these patents, it did not have the necessary know-how needed usefully to employ the patents on a commercial scale.

His evidence, along with the many other experts, highlighted how the disclosure requirement under US patent law did not enable commercial-scale production of the German inventions. It was one thing for an inventor to disclose in a patent what was done in a laboratory or in the development of a prototype product, but unless the know-how for commercial production was also disclosed the information contained in the patent lacked practical value. What this evidence also highlighted was a flaw in the US patent system itself. Given that the original function of patents under the Statute of Monopolies 1623 was to increase local employment by encouraging the transfer of new arts, crafts and trades into England, if the disclosure of the invention in the written specification was not capable of achieving this then clearly the threshold value implied by the social contract, which Lord Mansfield emphasized in *Liardet v Johnson* in 1780 and which was incorporated into US patent law by section 2 US Patents Act 1790, was not being reached.

With this kind of evidence it is unsurprising that Morris blamed Germany for the US's economic vulnerability, finding, 'by her patent monopoly, by bribery and by dumping, Germany had prevented the building up of an organic chemical industry in the United States'. Suddenly the US patent system was seen not just as a mechanism that encouraged innovation and industry; it was a foreign protectionist bullet which had hit the United States right between the eyes. Morris went on to add, 'the technical skill and equipment provided by an active chemical industry furnishes the means, and almost the sole means, to which the nation must look, in war and in peace, for advances in the application of chemical science to practical undertakings'. In other words, merely relying on the written description of the invention in a patent did not create a secure basis for a robust and productive industry; more was needed in the form of hands-on experience and know-how, and a patent system which handed out monopolies to foreign patentees without requiring them to work those patents in the granting country undermined economic growth, not encouraged it.

In effect the US patent system had made the US economically and strategically vulnerable to Germany, a country which was technologically superior to the US with regard to the production of dyestuffs, chemicals and pharmaceuticals, simply as a result of the fact that the disclosure of the invention in the written specification of these patents was confined to experimental or workbench examples of the invention. Importantly, once the patents were granted by the US Patent Office, these patents came with a *presumption of validity*, which the German owners of these US patents deliberately used legitimately and legally to control their US markets for their German-manufactured dyes, chemicals and pharmaceuticals.

To make matters worse the Foundation produced evidence which showed that in some cases the information contained in German-owned patents was more than misleading and was actually dangerous, arguing that this confirmed their 'bad reputation'. Morris was sympathetic to this argument as well, noting:

> In a book published in 1917 – Seward's Science and the Nation, Defendant's Exhibit 50, p. 18 – Sir William Pope was quoted as saying: 'In fact, some German patents are drawn up for the purpose of discouraging investigation by more practical methods; thus, any one who attempted to repeat the method for manufacturing a dyestuff protected by Salzmann & Krueger in the German patent No. 12,096 would be pretty certain to kill himself during the operation.'[57]

To reinforce this crucial point and neutralize the Department's main argument, the Foundation zeroed in on the most valuable patent in its portfolio, the patent for the drug Salvarsan.[58] This drug was developed in the laboratory of Paul Ehrlich[59] at the German National Institute for Experimental Therapeutics after one of his students, Sahachiro Hata,[60] who was there to study chemotherapy, discovered that it also had anti-syphilitic properties. Until then Ehrlich had focused his research on its use for the treatment of sleeping sickness. Hata and Ehrlich's work represented a major breakthrough in the treatment of syphilis, which beforehand was treated with mercury compounds. With the outbreak of war sales of the new anti-syphilitic drug exploded, but like all drugs it affected patients in different ways and in some instances fatally. The efficacy of the drug produced using only the information disclosed in the patent was the subject of considerable debate and the evidence from Stieglitz that it had taken his laboratory five months of experiments to produce Salvarsan which could be safely administered was not at all helpful to the Department's case. On the basis of this and other evidence, Morris held:

> These and other obvious risks and hazards incident to the purchase of enemy patents make it clear that from a business point of view they constituted an investment of a most highly speculative character.... Any ability to practice the process of the patents or to make the products thereof that might become apparent after sale as a result of long periods of costly experiments, or otherwise, is without practical evidential value in determining what an American citizen would have been justified in paying for the patents or would pay for them before such ability became apparent. Nor could any knowledge, howsoever acquired by an American citizen, prior to sale, of how to use an enemy patent, be properly considered in estimating the value to an American citizen of the naked patent, unless that information was disclosed by the patent itself, or was known to the man skilled in the art of the patent.[61]

PATENT MONOPOLIES ARE NEVERTHELESS USED IN SUPPRESSING FOREIGN COMPETITION

The Foundation never challenged the validity of any of these patents, despite the fact that it used the lack of practical information contained in them to support its argument that they were worth a great deal less than the Department had alleged. The Foundation understood that it was not in the best interests of the fledgling US chemical and pharmaceutical industries to open the market to all, which would be the result of the revocation of these patent monopolies. Having acquired the patents it reasoned that, by retaining and using them, it could control the US market for the exclusive benefit of the United States. As the new owners they could now use patent monopolies to suppress German and other foreign competition in the US market, just as the German dye, chemical and pharmaceutical industries had used them to suppress the development of American industries.

While the United States confiscated German-owned US patents the British pursued a somewhat less draconian strategy, but nevertheless with the same objective. Apart from suspending the rights of German patent owners to sue for infringement during World War I, after the war it preferred to continue to use a policy of compulsory licensing, adding a twist: subject matter exclusion. The effect of this policy, while not as radical as confiscation, was more or less aimed at giving British industries (especially in chemicals, pharmaceuticals and food) an opportunity to develop without a foreign power or industry being able to affect the terms of trade within the UK. So German patent owners retained their ownership of the British patented technology, but with the expectation that they might be made subject to compulsory licensing. In addition, by excluding chemicals and food substances per se from patentability, British researchers and manufacturers in these industries were able to work with these substances without themselves being subject to any legal impediments. These were significant advantages but, unlike the US which simply acquired the technologies and then subjugated them, the British deprived its agencies and industries from exerting exclusive control over the use of the patented technology in the UK.

In the US the local manufacturers could produce under licence while the Chemical Foundation controlled the patent monopolies once owned by German industry, thereby ensuring that foreign competition was in check. In the UK however the resulting level playing field was nowhere near as useful to British industry because German industry remained free to compete with British industry and, while restricting patentable subject matter did reduce the patent monopoly advantage that the German chemical industry once had over British industry, it did not prevent the German chemical industry from using its pre-war distribution channels nor its production know-how from asserting their technical and marketing advantages over British competitors.

THE BRITISH RAISE THE PATENT BARRIERS

In 1919 the British Parliament passed amendments to the Patents & Designs Act 1907. Some of the amendments were in anticipation of the Treaty of Versailles, the terms of which were in the process of being settled. In addition to these other amendments were enacted:

- *Scope of pre-grant examination*: the novelty assessment was extended to ascertain whether the invention has been wholly or partially claimed (that is defined in the claims, as distinct from described in the complete specification) in a specification published at *any time* in the UK prior to the patent application (section 8(1));

- *Grounds of opposition*: the grounds were extended to include a lack of novelty (section 11(b), 11(bb));
- *Patent term*: British patent terms were extended from 14 to 16 years (section 17(1));
- *Licences of right*: patent owners could voluntarily elect to endorse patents with the words 'licences of right' so that the Comptroller of Patents could grant licences to any person who applies as a licensee (section 24);
- *Prevention of abuse of monopoly rights*: under this amendment patent owners who did not work their patent in the UK for any reason came within the scope of this provision. Previously this remedy applied if the invention was being worked exclusively outside the UK. With regard to determining the threshold for monopoly abuse the legislation provided that it should be taken that patents for new inventions were granted, 'not only to encourage invention', but to ensure that new inventions be worked on a commercial scale in the UK, 'without undue delay' (section 27(2)). Furthermore if the reason for this so-called abuse, that is the prevention or hindrance in working the invention in the UK on a commercial scale, was due to the importation of the patented article, then the normal four-year waiting period for a compulsory licence under this section was waived (section 27(2) (b)). If the Comptroller was satisfied that there was an abuse of monopoly rights the following remedies were available: (a) endorse the patent as 'licences of right' (section 24), which was in effect the same as a non-exclusive compulsory licence (section 27(3)(a)); (b) order the grant of a licence on such terms as the Comptroller 'may think expedient' (section 27(3)(b)); (c) in the absence of the patentee having the capital necessary to work the invention on a commercial scale in the UK, (i) grant an exclusive licence to the applicant (section 27(3)(c)), or (ii) revoke the patent (section 27(3)(d));
- *Inventions of military or strategic significance*: any patent concerning 'any improvement in instruments or munitions of war' could be assigned to the Secretary of War or the Admiralty 'with or without consideration' to the patentee (section 30);
- *Subject matter*: chemical products and substances intended for food or medicine per se could no longer be patented, 'except when prepared or produced by their special methods or processes of manufacture described and claimed or by their obvious chemical equivalents' (section 38A(1)) and
- *Licences for patents to processes for chemical products and substances intended for food or medicine*: the Comptroller of Patents was mandated, unless he saw 'good reasons to the contrary', to grant to any

person a licence which was limited to the use of the invention for the purposes of the preparation or production of food or medicine and, in settling the terms of such a licence, the Comptroller was directed to take into account 'the desirability of making the food or medicine available to the public at the lowest possible price consistent with giving to the inventor due reward for the research leading to the invention' (section 38A(2)).

THE INTER-WAR YEARS AND THE CONFISCATION OF BAYER'S US ASSETS

By the end of World War I, as William Reeves pointed out, the United States 'was the world's greatest creditor nation; it entered the war as a debtor nation'.[62] Reeves reasoned, '[t]his transformation was due very largely to the repatriation of foreign funds in the United States under the requisition of their dollar values by the respective governments for war purchases of American goods'.[63] There was however another important contribution: the confiscation of German-owned assets, including patents and trade marks, and their transfer to Americans. Apart from the dollar value of those assets, which was not insignificant, the transfer of ownership terminated royalty payments and profits to German owners during the war, and in many instances permanently. World War I therefore provided the United States with a windfall that enabled it to usurp the sponsors of war and, in grasping that opportunity, that is precisely what she did.

In 1917 Bayer America came under American control after the Custodian of Alien Property seized its shares from Bayer Germany. In December 1918 Sterling acquired those shares from the Custodian of Alien Property. Soon afterwards, Sterling sold part of the Bayer America factory at Rensselaer, NY, to the Grasselli Chemical Co, Inc for about US$2.5 million, nearly half as much as Sterling had paid to acquire Bayer America and Bayer Germany's patents and trade marks. It simultaneously established the Winthrop Chemical Co, Inc into which it transferred all of the former Bayer Germany patents and trade marks. In 1920 Sterling acquired the British trade marks and business of Bayer Co Ltd, the former British subsidiary of Bayer Germany, from the company administrator appointed by the British Board of Trade. The UK assets included Bayer's UK trade marks, which since 1914 had been in the name of the British subsidiary. One of the trade marks so acquired was the Bayer Cross trade mark consisting, in part, of the word Bayer written both horizontally and vertically, intersecting at the letter Y. It was a world famous trade mark and Aspirin, one of the many products sold under that trade mark, was a world famous pain-killing medicine.

In the meantime Sterling went on to acquire, using a route similar to that which it employed in the UK, the Bayer trade marks and businesses in Australia, Canada, Cuba, New Zealand and South Africa. By 1921 Sterling had become the owner of assets, both in the US and in these countries, once owned by Bayer Germany and its subsidiaries.

BAYER SUED FOR USING THE BAYER TRADE MARKS

In 1922, after it had recommenced exports of its pharmaceuticals from Germany, Bayer Germany found itself on the receiving end of actions filed by Sterling in the US, UK, Canada, Cuba, Australia, New Zealand and South Africa. Sterling alleged that Bayer Germany had infringed its Bayer trade marks. So the situation that faced Bayer Germany, a company which prior to World War I had not only developed these pharmaceuticals but patented and trade marked them since the 1880s, was that through Bayer America, a former subsidiary, Sterling not only controlled its trade marks, but could bring legal proceedings to prevent it from asserting its rights in those trade marks in practically all English-speaking countries throughout the world.

Despite the acquisition of Bayer Germany's patents however Sterling (as well as other American companies in Sterling's position) discovered that working the patents into commercial production required considerable know-how; know-how which it lacked and which Bayer Germany possessed. It would seem that both parties had much to gain and little to lose by cooperating with each other and so, as can be expected, these actions were eventually settled during meetings held in New York, the headquarters of Sterling.

One of the agreements from that settlement, signed in April 1923, catalogued Bayer Germany's loss of its intellectual property and businesses in the subject countries and also contained the concession not to sell or export certain 'defined products' into those countries other than through Bayer America or through another Sterling subsidiary, Winthrop Chemical Co. That same agreement also led, in May 1923, to the incorporation of Bayer Products Ltd (Bayer UK) as a fully owned subsidiary of Winthrop. Once incorporated Bayer UK acquired from Sterling all of the goodwill, patents and trade marks relating to the business formerly owned by Bayer Co Ltd, Bayer Germany's former British subsidiary.

In accordance with the April agreement in September 1923 Bayer Germany signed a separate agreement with Bayer UK in which it acknowledged that Bayer UK had been incorporated 'to carry on business in the

United Kingdom of Great Britain and Ireland including the British West Indies, the Commonwealth of Australia, New Zealand and the Australasian Islands and the Union of South Africa', and with respect to which it had 'the exclusive right to use on or in connection with . . . the word Bayer and the Bayer Cross mark . . . and also various patents . . . covering various processes or products.'[64] Clause 1 of the September agreement read:

> [Bayer Germany] agrees not to contest or in any way directly or indirectly put in issue the title of [Bayer UK] to the business property and rights including the said trade marks and patents or any of them owned by [Bayer UK] in respect of any of the said products.[65]

Beyond this concession Bayer Germany also agreed to transfer to Bayer UK all patents owned and 'any new inventions or discovery' by Bayer Germany 'covering the said products' in any of the named countries to Bayer UK without any payment; and further that Bayer Germany 'would use its best endeavours' to obtain patents, and transfer those patents to Bayer UK at no cost.[66]

Through this series of events Sterling went from being a small American company to being the new owner of Bayer Germany's business in the US, the UK, Canada, Cuba, Australia, New Zealand and South Africa. However during these negotiations Bayer Germany managed to gain a modest and, as it turned out, important concession from Sterling. In return for its know-how on all present and future pharmaceutical patents it would receive a 50 per cent share of Winthrop's profits. This at least enabled Bayer Germany to regain some of its lost market and cash flow, but quarantined from that deal were the profits of Aspirin sales in the US. This part of Sterling's business remained securely with Bayer America.

BRITISH TARIFFS GO HAND IN HAND

In 1925 the American percolation into British industry continued as General Motors went on to acquire Vauxhall, a British motor vehicle manufacturer. In 1928 the General Electric Company of America acquired the British- and American-owned Metropolitan Vickers Electrical Company and merged with British Thomson Houston (the British part owner of Vickers) to form Associated Electrical Industries (AEI) and the Ford Motor Company expanded its British operations by building a new factory at Dagenham.

The credit for the increase in foreign capital investment could not of course be attributed solely to the impact of the amendments to Britain's patent law. Significant increases in tariffs were introduced in 1915 which, for instance, placed a 33 per cent customs duty on all 'non-essential' commodities. Motor cars, tyres, chemicals and electrical equipment were all so defined, thereby creating a further incentive to manufacture in Britain. Other tariff measures were introduced in 1921 (Safeguarding of Industry Act), in 1923 over silk, and in 1927 over cinematographic art. Moreover Government departments and instrumentalities gave preference to awarding contracts to British companies.

THE CHANGING ECONOMIC LANDSCAPE

Despite the economic prosperity which the post-war 1920s brought to the United States and the increase in foreign capital investments which flowed from the United States into Britain, the economic benefits for ordinary Britons were mostly elusive, and for those who were employed in the coal mining industry it was a time of uncertainty, falling incomes and unemployment. The coal mining industry was in a state of decline, with productivity falling from 310 tons per man in the 1880s to less than 200 tons per man in 1924. The falling international price of coal, caused by the export of coal by Germany to France and Italy as part of the war reparations imposed upon it by the Treaty of Versailles, together with a revaluation of the British currency (as a result of the UK's re-adoption of the Gold Standard), further reduced coal export income to British mining companies, leading to cost-cutting measures in coal mines throughout the country. The easiest and simplest cost reduction was in wages. This in turn led to Britain's first general trade union strike on 4 May 1926, with an estimated 1 500 000 workers refusing to work until the strike was called off by the Trade Union Council on 12 May. The strike was an abject failure in that the union movement was unable to conclude a deal with either the Government or the mining companies that prevented wages from continuing to fall. Many miners were simply unable to afford the loss of income caused by the strike, forcing them to return to work, although for many unemployment was the only alternative.

For Germany, and particularly its dyestuff, chemical and pharmaceutical companies, the retaliation inflicted by the Allied Powers through the confiscation, acquisition and gratuitous use of German-owned patents and trade marks during and after World War I made it extremely difficult for them to recapture their foreign markets. These markets were not only important to the reconstruction of Germany's chemical and pharmaceutical industries, but were essential to Germany in terms of its ability to make the war reparations demanded by the Allied Powers. However the German industrialists had a plan, and ironically it would be the American banks and some of America's wealthiest families that would help them back on their feet.

In the meantime the international community realized that the effects of the terms of the Treaty of Versailles needed to be eased, and so during October 1925 a series of agreements between Belgium, the UK, Czechoslovakia, France, Italy and Poland were negotiated with Germany at Locarno in Switzerland. The Locarno Treaties, signed in London on 1 December 1925, paved the way for Germany's admission into the League of Nations in 1926. Although these treaties were strictly political in the sense that they settled questions about Germany's borders with Belgium and France, among other issues, they also engendered a spirit of international cooperation in the hope that a long and lasting peace could be achieved. This in turn filtered through into business and facilitated the kind of alliances that American companies were already starting to forge with German industry.

PATENTS, KNOW-HOW, CARTELS AND THE GERMAN INFILTRATION OF US AND UK COMPANIES

In the United States the US chemical and pharmaceutical companies had now appreciated that owning German patented technology and acquiring their factories was only the start of an indigenous chemical and pharmaceutical industry. After World War I many of the US companies that were the beneficiaries of confiscated German technology soon began employing German scientists and engineers and became involved, through joint research and development projects, with German companies. This process increased the storehouse of practical and innovative knowledge of a scientific and engineering nature in the US; a process that German industrialists readily cooperated with, as this provided them with access to much needed capital as they rebuilt their businesses. For instance, as already mentioned, in 1923 Sterling entered into an arrangement with Bayer Germany giving it a 50 per cent profit share in Winthrop in return for much needed German pharmaceutical production know-how; and by 1926 Standard Oil had commenced joint research into the establishment of synthetic fuel production in the United States with IG Farben, using German catalytic hydrogenation research.

Simultaneously German chemical industrialists at home were busy reorganizing themselves and had formed IG Farbenindustrie AG (IG Farben) on 1 December 1925. IG Farben was the culmination of Duisberg's vision and its formation was made easier with the encouragement of American bankers who were now working with German industrialists in the reconstruction of the German economy, devastated by the loss of its corporate property in its key markets and the impact of the Treaty of Versailles. Accordingly IG Farben, with Duisberg as the chairman of its *Vorstand* (its 50-member Board of Management), absorbed the assets, businesses and, importantly, the debts of the members of Interessengemeinschaft der deutschen Teerfarbenindustrie, or 'Little IG', as it had become known. In this form as a chemical conglomerate IG Farben went on to produce a wide variety of products such as synthetic rubber, methanol, nickel, plastics, explosives, gunpowder, sulphuric acid, dyes, dye accessories, pharmaceuticals, photographic supplies, artificial silk, perfumes, metals, nitrogen compounds, gasoline, bituminous and anthracite coal and other chemical compounds.[67]

Across the Channel Sir Harry McGowan, the chairman of Nobel Industries Ltd (Nobel), had already given some thought to the establishment of a British chemical conglomerate company. His suggestion involved the merger of Nobel with a number of smaller British chemical companies such as The British Dyestuffs Co, Brunner, Mond & Co, Castner-Kellner Alkali Co and Chance & Hunt; and, if it could be pulled off, this would not only ensure that essential know-how and chemical production was resident in a British company, but it would be world competitive against German and American chemical companies. So with the UK Government's support in December 1926 Imperial Chemical Industries Ltd (ICI) was formed. By the late 1920s its annual turnover was nearly £80 million and it employed 40 000.

The creation of IG Farben required amendments to the agreements that were signed between Bayer Germany and Sterling and Bayer UK during 1923, and on 25 November 1926 a new agreement was signed by IG Farben in which it ratified those earlier agreements. Crucially however the relationship between Sterling and IG Farben also changed at this time. By way of a separate agreement IG Farben converted its 50 per cent profit share of Winthrop into 50 per cent equity. Under this agreement IG Farben was to appoint half of Bayer UK's board of directors, including its chairman, with the other half appointed by Winthrop. The shares in Winthrop were not immediately transferred to IG Farben, as first other pieces in what was to become a very complex corporate jigsaw puzzle needed to be put in place:

First, in 1928 IG Farben purchased from Grasselli Chemical Co, Inc its remaining interest in the Grasselli Dyestuff Corporation (Grasselli Dyestuffs) for US$5.82 million. Grasselli Dyestuffs was formed in 1924 between Grasselli Chemical (51 per cent) and Bayer Germany (49 per cent).

As part of its capitalization Grasselli Chemical had transferred to Grasselli Dyestuffs the former Bayer America factory at Rensselaer, New York (which Grasselli Chemical had acquired from Sterling in 1920), and one of its own factories at Linden, New Jersey. The end result not only gave IG Farben full ownership of Grasselli Dyestuffs but returned the original Bayer America factory to German ownership. It also gave IG Farben ownership of the Linden factory and Herman Metz's businesses, which Grasselli Dyestuff had acquired prior to IG Farben's acquisition of the remaining shares.

Then later in 1928 IG Farben established (through a Swiss bank intermediary, Greutert et Cie) a Swiss holding company which was ultimately called Société Internationale pour Participations Industrielles et Commerciales SA (IG Chemie). Its shareholders were Dutch companies, Chemmo and Vooindu (both subsidiaries of IG Farben), a Norwegian company, Norsk Hydro (a partly owned subsidiary of IG Farben) and Swiss firms, Mithras and Osman. While IG Farben was not a shareholder it provided certain financial inducements and comforts to the Swiss shareholders in order to secure their cooperation. These inducements came in the form of a minimum ten-year dividend guarantee equal to that paid by IG Farben to its preference shareholders and an option to exchange IG Chemie shares for IG Farben shares within five years of the cancellation of the dividend guarantee agreement, but which upon execution gave IG Farben the right to claim ownership of any IG Chemie subsidiaries. In effect the Swiss shareholders were being paid by IG Farben to own shares in IG Chemie. The 400 000 'A' class preference shares were controlled by Greutert et Cie, IG Farben's Swiss banker.

Also in 1928 American IG Chemical Corporation (IG America) was established in Delaware by Herman Metz (the same person who gave evidence in *USA v The Chemical Foundation* in 1923 and who sold his dye businesses to Grasselli Dyestuffs in 1925). Then in early 1929 Grasselli Dyestuffs changed its name to the General Aniline Works (GAW).

Next IG Farben transferred the assets of GAW and the Agfa-Ansco Corporation (being a merger of the Ansco Corporation and AGFA) into IG America and, as per the April 1923 agreement between Sterling and IG Farben, Sterling transferred 50 per cent of Winthrop shares to IG America. This capitalized IG America which then enabled the law firm of Sullivan & Cromwell, of which John Foster Dulles[68] was a partner, together with bankers Brown Brothers and Harriman Bank to facilitate a bond offering of convertible debentures (with 5.5 per cent interest) on 1 April 1929 which raised US$30 million from American investors. IG America was now not only extremely liquid but also the owner of substantial US factories, patents, trade marks and businesses.

Then in late 1929 75 per cent of 'A' class shares in IG America were transferred to IG Chemie with the balance going to IG Farben's Swiss banker and members of IG America's board.

Finally in 1930 some 3 000 000 'B' class shares were transferred to IG Farben's Swiss banker, IG Chemie, Chemmo and Vooindu and Standard Oil (16.67 per cent).

Without doubt the object was to mask the true owner of IG Farben's American assets and to make IG Chemie, a Swiss corporation, an intermediary that could be used to protect against the possibility of a future policy of US confiscation. Having being bitten once the German industrialists were not prepared to risk losing their US assets (valued in 1930 at around US$60 million) a second time.

Unfortunately on Black Thursday, 24 October 1929, the Dow Jones collapsed, sending a ripple throughout the world which tipped over the fragile economies of Europe. It highlighted how unregulated capital could, without strict legal and economic guidelines, lead to poverty and not prosperity. Although not the sole cause of the coming world depression there is no doubt that the massive collapse in the share bubble epitomized by this event was a step in that direction, and it is now a matter of fact that the Dow Jones did not return to the heady levels of the 1920s until 1954, some 30 years later – prompting the economist Richard Salsman to note, 'anyone who bought stocks in mid-1920 and held on to them saw most of his adult life pass by without getting back to even'.[69] Despite the general economic malaise that followed, investors in IG America never went without a dividend payment.

Watching the corporate machinations of IG America the Alien Property Custodian, Garvan, remained unimpressed, unforgiving and sceptical. On 10 February 1930 he held a press conference during which he warned the American people that the intent of IG America was:

> . . . to deceive the America public into the belief that the proceeds of these bonds were to be used to foster and finance the development of chemical and allied industries in the US . . . whereas the real purpose and intent was to obtain $30,000,000 from American citizens with which to strengthen the IG Farbenindustrie Akiengesellschaft in Germany in competition with and in the destruction of the American chemical industry.[70]

Herman Metz, who had now become the vice-president and treasurer of IG America, ridiculed Garvan's attack; he described him as a man who 'was talking through his hat' and who did not know that 'the War' was over.[71] Metz countered by claiming that 95 per cent of dye production needed for US industry was now US-based and that US companies were in direct competition with IG Farben. In fact, as was reported at the time, Garvan's work as Alien Property Custodian and as president of the Chemical Foundation meant that 'the US chemical industry [had] flourished . . . [and] in sales and profits US chemical companies lead the world . . . [and the] export of chemicals exceeded $200,000,000'. *Time Magazine* suggested that with 'Du Pont, Allied Chemical & Dye and Union Carbide & Carbon . . . [having] total assets of $585,718,000 [and being] . . . twice the size of the Garvan-feared IG Farbenindustrie',[72] the US economy was well positioned to compete.

However the growth in exports which US chemical manufacturers had enjoyed had not gone unnoticed in Europe. In response to the growing competition from the US IG Farben, the silent partner of IG America, entered into an agreement with Swiss and French chemical companies. In April 1929 IG Farben and the Swiss chemical companies Ciba Ltd, RJ Geigy AG and Chemische Fabrik vorm. Sandoz, which already operated as a cartel within Switzerland, came together to form an international chemical cartel with a French chemical company, Centrale des Matières Colorantes (CMC). This cartel then controlled 80 per cent of the world's trade in dyestuffs and redistributed sales among themselves: 71.67 per cent to Germany, 19 per cent to Switzerland and 9.33 per cent to France. To signify their cooperation the cartel members even used the same letterhead.

BRITISH PATENT LAW DURING THE GREAT DEPRESSION

As the effects of the Depression started to bite the response of the British government was to raise economic protections. In 1931 the Abnormal Importations Act, which created a comprehensive system of tariffs, became law and in February 1932 Imperial Chemical Industries Ltd (ICI) became the fifth member of the international chemical cartel. This Anglo-German-Swiss-French super-cartel now controlled 90 per cent of the world's trade in dyestuffs and adjusted the redistribution of sales among its partners as to 66 per cent to Germany, 17 per cent to Switzerland, 8.55 per cent to France and 8.45 per cent to Britain. The cartel went on to conclude agreements with chemical manufacturers in Italy, Poland, Czechoslovakia, the Netherlands and others. Effectively the world market for dyestuffs had been divided three ways: the United States, Japan, and the rest of the world.

Moving closer towards protectionism the members of the British Empire formed the Imperial preference system, a trading bloc, by an agreement reached in Ottawa, Canada, on 20 August 1932. This brought down the final curtain on the UK's so-called official free trade policy first adopted in the 1830s; although the UK had started moving back towards protectionism from 1883, when tariffs were substantially increased in 1915 there was no going back to free trade. Pursuant to the Ottawa agreement the Gold Standard was once again abandoned, causing the Sterling Area countries to benefit from a 25 per cent devaluation of their currencies. This devaluation, coupled with massive increases in tariffs while guaranteeing preferential tariffs for its members, provided an enormous trading benefit to its members. It was markedly similar to the German policy of *Mitteleuropa*, a policy which the British had viewed with suspicion in the 1890s. The creation of an Imperial preference trading system alarmed United States policy-makers, especially Cordell Hull,[73] and from that moment it was an issue of contention between the UK and the US. Keynesian economic theory, now given great credibility by the UK and Sterling Area governments as providing the economic blueprint for curing the ills of the Depression (especially after John Maynard Keynes' polemic and almost prophetic book about the social and economic consequences of the Treaty of Versailles, *The Economic Consequences of Peace,* published in 1919), bore witness to an evangelical-like movement away from *laissez-faire* and back towards government intervention.

PATENTS – THE SUBTLE TRADE BARRIER

Patents also had their role to play in this latest defence of the British economy. In response to the Sargant Committee's recommendation[74] in 1931 the MacDonald Government[75] amended the UK Patents & Designs Act 1907 in 1932. One of the amendments (section 25) directed the codification of the grounds of revocation – a logical progression, given the decision first made in 1883 to abolish *scire facias* as a court procedure, especially given that 'other countries'[76] had already sought to enumerate these grounds in their respective patent laws. Often portrayed by patent law commentators as some minor development in aid of the internationalization of UK patent law, section 25 finally severed all ties to *scire facias* because it abolished the use of the common law to attack the validity of letters patent. For the first time the UK Parliament codified the grounds upon which a British patent could be revoked; and although some of these were merely adaptations of the common law, some were not. For instance section 25(2)(l) of the 1932 amendments provided that it was a ground of revocation '[if] the invention claimed in the complete specification [was] not the same as that for which protection [had] been applied for in the foreign state'. Although this provision resembled the requirement which grew out of the common law that there be conformity between the title of an invention and its description in the specification, and a lack of conformity between these two parts of a British patent was a ground of revocation, in reality section 25(2)(l), or the ground of *disconformity* as it became technically known, was quite different and significantly more dangerous for the foreign patent owner.

First, section 25(2)(l) was concerned with more than the mere conformity between the title of an invention and its description in the specification of a British patent. It was concerned with maintaining perfect symmetry between a foreign patent and the invention which it claimed with the corresponding British patent and the invention which *it* claimed. The idea was to ensure that a foreign inventor did not use the 12-month priority period provided by the Paris Convention 1883[77] to file a patent application for a British patent which was greater in scope than that granted overseas. Therefore in terms of the assessment of conformity it was much broader than provided by the common law.

Secondly it discriminated against Convention patent applications, in that it did not extend the flexibility to develop the invention in the same way that was open through British patent applications. For some time a British patent application could be commenced with the filing of a provisional specification. The provisional was a general description of the nature of the invention, and within 12 months the inventor was required to file a complete specification, which was not only specific but also contained claims which defined the scope of the patent monopoly. In the intervening period the inventor was entitled to use the doctrine of *legitimate development,* which enabled the inventor to make adjustments and improvements to the invention before having to craft the patent in very specific terms. However the doctrine of legitimate development was not available to the Convention applicant.

Accordingly under section 25(2)(l) any disparity between the foreign patent application upon which the Convention patent application was based and the corresponding British patent was fatal to the validity of the British patent.

An illustration of the impact that this provision had on the validity of a British patent which started life as a Convention application can be seen in the case of *Electric & Musical Industries Ltd v Lissen Ltd* [1938] 4 All ER 221. This case concerned an American invention of what was then a leading edge technology: a radio valve. At issue was whether the British patent monopoly extended to any use of the radio valve for the amplification of a radio signal irrespective of its strength or whether it captured only its use relative to the received signal strength. This distinction was relevant not only to the breadth of the patent monopoly, but to its very validity, because the British patent was being challenged on the ground of *anticipation*: that is the radio valve itself had already been published in the UK and therefore the invention lacked novelty. Accordingly while the broader interpretation of the main claim defined the invention as the radio valve, thereby casting a wide shadow, lurking in this shadow were prior publications that would destroy its very patentability. To overcome this the principal strategy of the American inventor was to cast a smaller shadow, thereby avoiding the prior publications. This was to be achieved by seeking a narrower construction of the main claim: namely by arguing that the British invention was the method of using the radio valve, not to the radio valve itself. The British challenger's rebuttal unfortunately put the American inventor, as Lord Russell described it, 'on the horns of the dilemma' – namely, *disconformity*: the American invention claimed in the American patent application was arguably different from the invention claimed in the British patent. Nevertheless such were the stakes that the American inventor pursued the matter by trying to skirt round both lines of attack and, after 23 days in the Patents Court before Luxmoore J, his arguments prevailed. Luxmoore held that the narrower interpretation applied, but failed to consider disconformity on the basis that it was not pressed during the trial. That success was short-lived.

By the time the Court of Appeal had finished Luxmoore's decision had been overturned. The British patent was held to be invalid on the ground that the British invention, which was the radio valve, had been anticipated by the prior publications and lacked novelty; again the issue of disconformity was not addressed. Dissatisfied with the decision the American inventor appealed to the House of Lords, obviously in the hope that Luxmoore's decision would be reinstated.

However after an appeal hearing which lasted 21 days the House of Lords affirmed the decision of the Court of Appeal. In doing so, and unlike the Court of Appeal which avoided the issue of disconformity, Lord Wright, who wrote the majority decision, made it clear that disconformity was 'a dilemma on one horn of which [the American inventor] must be impaled'. And impale the American inventor they did, for the House of Lords was in no mood to allow this American inventor to claim what he thought was an invention in America and then use the Paris Convention to maintain a patent monopoly in the UK with respect to an invention that was, in their opinion, invalid. Despite having found that the broader construction of the claimed invention applied to the British patent, the House of Lords was not going to leave it there and was determined to apply the law of disconformity. It found that although the British invention was to a radio valve – the same as the American invention – that did not mean that it was an identical invention to the American invention.

In first dealing with anticipation Lord Russell confirmed that the function of the claims, as distinct from the specification, was 'to define clearly and with precision the monopoly claimed, so that others may know the exact boundaries of the area within which they will be trespassers'. In this regard, he held '[their] primary object [was] to limit, and not to extend, the monopoly', so 'what [was] not claimed [was] disclaimed', and that the meaning of the claims was to be found 'in the language of the claims, and not elsewhere'. While the specification therefore formed part of the patent, it was not relevant in defining the scope of the patent monopoly, because a patentee who describes an invention in the body of a specification 'obtains no monopoly' unless it was claimed in the claims. Applying this reasoning Lords Russell, Wright and Macmillan held that the invention defined in the claims of the British patent was a radio valve and that it had been anticipated by the prior publications.

Lord Wright then went on to say that even if the British invention was a radio valve, it was nonetheless a different invention from the American invention; that is, they were both radio valves but not in terms of their purpose. In coming to this view he compared the language not only of the respective claims but also of the respective specifications. Specifically, he held that although '90 per cent of the [British] patent in suit [was] taken from [the American patent]' and that in both cases the invention as claimed was a radio valve, 'the [British] patent in suit [showed] a very different . . . purpose', namely, 'not to show the working of a novel construction of the radio valve', which is what the American patent did, but to claim 'a method of using the specified construction of tube with other elements, all of which [the American patent] treated as merely descriptive of the obvious or preferred mode of using [the] invention'. On this basis Lord Wright concluded that while the American patent made it 'clear' that it was claiming a 'particular construction' of the radio valve, the British patent on the other hand dealt with the use of the radio valve in an amplifier in which the radio valve was only 'one element', and for which 'no claim' was made.

Despite the caveat Lord Russell had put on the use of the specification in terms of claim construction, for the purposes of disconformity it was permissible to refer to the language in the foreign specification in order to ascertain the 'purpose' of the foreign invention. Disconformity required that respective inventions be identical, taking not only the claims but the totality of the respective patents into account. Their Lordships justified this apparent contradiction on the grounds that not all foreign patents used claims, as was the practice in the UK and the US, and that therefore it was necessary to look to the complete body of the foreign specification in order to ascertain the boundaries of the invention for the purposes of disconformity.

A further illustration of the impact of the revocation ground of disconformity was provided by *In The Matter Of A Petition For The Revocation*

Of Letters Patent No. 533,495 Granted To May & Baker Limited and Ciba Limited (1948) 65 RPC 255. The British patent in this case was the end product of what started out as four Convention patent applications filed in Switzerland by Ciba Limited. These four Swiss patent applications, filed between January and December 1938, were entitled 'Manufacture of New Benzene-Sulphonamido-Derivatives' and described a process for the manufacture of some 97 million chemical substances of the sulphanilamide group, more specifically known as para-amino-benzene-sulphonamido-thiazoles (thiazoles). There was no issue over the fact that all of these chemical substances were new.

The four Convention patent applications were eventually consolidated into one British patent application which by May 1946, when the patent was sealed, had become, through an agreement made in 1944, the joint property of Ciba and May & Baker Limited, a British pharmaceutical company.[78]

At the time of the case section 38A of the UK Patents & Designs Act 1907 prohibited the grant of a patent for chemical substances themselves unless the processes for their production were 'special'. According to the British patent specification these new sulphanilamide substances were chemotherapeutic and had therapeutic value in the treatment of some types of bacterial infections in humans.

The discovery that sulphanilamides were chemotherapeutic was however first made in 1933 when it was observed that a dyestuff called proptosil red, a sulphanilamide, killed streptococcal bacteria but not pneumococcal bacteria. It was also observed that proptosil red was highly toxic to humans. It followed that a sulphanilamide which was non-toxic to humans and which had wider bacterial toxicity would be an extremely valuable medicine. In fact by 1937 scientists at Ciba had modified the sulphanilamide molecule by the inclusion of heterocyclic groups and produced such a medicine. By 1937 however the manipulation of molecules involving the substitution of certain atomic constituents was well known to chemists. In May 1938 Sir Lionel Whitby, an authority on chemotherapy, published a paper in the *Lancet* which disclosed the chemotherapeutic value of pyridine, a different sulphanilamide group, but one closely related to the thiazoles group claimed in the British patent.

After the British patent was granted Boots Pure Drug Company Limited, a British generic pharmaceutical company which also operated retail pharmacies throughout the UK, sought to revoke it, prompting the patent owners to file an application to amend it; their object being to narrow the scope of the claimed invention from a class of thiazoles which claimed some 97 million kinds, to *only two* specific kinds of thiazoles, namely sulphathiazole and sulpha-methylthiazole.

Although this proposed amendment appeared to be a significant narrowing in the scope of the invention, it in fact had no commercial consequence because, as it turned out, the desired therapeutic value of this group of sulphanilamides was confined solely to sulphathiazole and sulphamethylthiazole. In other words although the patent specification suggested that all of the thiazoles were therapeutically valuable as anti-bacterials in humans, *there were no scientific data to support that statement.*

When the case came before Jenkins J in the Patents Court he was faced with considering the validity of the British patent both in the granted, but unamended, form as well as in the potentially amended form. The patent owners were clearly desperate to maintain the British patent because it provided a very valuable patent monopoly over the manufacture of what was the first sulpha-based anti-bacterial medicine. The amendment application was therefore a critical strategic move aimed at achieving that objective.

Jenkins held that the inventions claimed in the British patent as granted were neither anticipated nor obvious, despite what was known by 1938 about the therapeutic value of sulphanilamides and the chemical manipulation of molecules. It was however invalid because the breadth of the monopoly extended to cover all kinds of thiazoles when there was no scientific or medical evidence to support this claim. So the patent had over-reached, and on this basis Jenkins did not hesitate to find the patent invalid on the grounds of inutility, false suggestion and not being a manner of new manufacture.

Having done so he also found that although the invention in the proposed amendment had merit, there was a problem. Regrettably for the patent owners had he granted permission to amend, the invention as claimed in the amended patent would, according to Jenkins, have been different and this meant that there was no point in granting the amendment because of disconformity. Consequently the British patent was ordered to be revoked.

Ciba and May & Baker appealed to the Court of Appeal. The only ground concerned Jenkins' refusal to allow the application to amend the British patent. Lord Greene, the Master of the Rolls, noted, in his judgment in *Re May & Baker Ltd and Ciba's Patent* (1949) 66 RPC 8, 'it was accepted by the Appellants that the patent was obtained by the false representation or suggestion in the specification that all the substances included in the claims (said to number at least 97 000 000) had specially favourable chemo-therapeutic activity'. This rather late act of contrition was not able to save the British patent. The Court of Appeal showed no mercy and unanimously confirmed Jenkins' decision.

Again Ciba and Mayer & Baker appealed, this time to the House of Lords. Again they failed. On a 3:2 decision reported at (1950) 67 RPC

23, the House of Lords found that Jenkins and the Court of Appeal were correct. The two inventions were different and so there was no point in allowing the amendment.

As a result any pharmaceutical company could manufacture and supply sulpha medicines in the UK at normal competitive prices rather than at prices dictated by Ciba and Mayer & Baker.

MEANWHILE, BACK ON THE FARM . . .

In 1930 Congress passed the Plant Patent Act. It was not an amendment to the US Patents Act 1836 but a separate legislative measure designed to give plant breeders a limited form of intellectual property protection for new plant varieties (excluding tuber-propagated plants) which were produced asexually, that is by using reproductive techniques such as budding, grafting, cutting, root clippings and bulb division.

The fact that this legislation was passed at the beginning of the Great Depression was more of a coincidence than a deliberate response to it. Calls for some form of intellectual property protection for plant breeders had been made as far back as the 1880s, mainly because it had become accepted by farmers and plant breeders, through the initiative of the US Department of Agriculture, that the development of new varieties of crops could promote the export of American-grown agricultural produce, such as wheat. The problem was that asexual reproductive techniques were well known and practised and could, just as easily as sexual reproduction, be employed to reproduce a new plant variety, whether it be a fruit tree, vine, flower or shrub. Once a sample of the new plant variety was obtained it was relatively simple for a farmer or plant breeder to grow the new plant variety without reference to the original breeder. While attempts were made by plant breeders to impose conditions upon buyers of their new plant varieties through the use of contract law, thereby restricting their ability to pass on biological samples to third parties, for the most part these attempts failed because the cost of enforcement was high and risk of detection was low.

A further blow to plant breeders was the decision of the US Commissioner of Patents in *Ex parte Latimer* (1889) Dec. Com. Pat. 123 concerning an application for a US patent over a fibre which was derived from the needle of a type of conifer tree, *Pinus australis*. The idea behind the patent was to claim as an invention a product that would be a suitable substitute for jute. While the Commissioner acknowledged in his decision that it was 'unquestionably very valuable' and that the fibre was stronger, more durable and less expensive to produce than jute, he held that as it was identical to that

found in the *Pinus australis* needle, as '[a] natural product . . . [it could]
no more be the subject of a patent in its natural state when freed from its
surroundings than wheat which has been cut by a reaper or by some new
method of reaping can be patented as wheat cut by such a process'.

Between 1890 and 1930 persistence on the part of plant breeders,
together with the new scientific knowledge about plant genetics and the
realization that plant breeders could be more systematic in their attempts
to develop new plant varieties, made an impact upon Congress. By the late
1920s plant breeders had a voice through which to lobby Congress in the
American Association of Nurserymen. In 1929 its newly elected president,
Paul Stark, drafted the Bill (of what was to become the Plant Patent Act)
and Senator John Townsend (Delaware), himself the owner of an apple
orchard of some 130 000 acres being the country's second largest orchard,
argued that America had been 'wasting [the] dormant talent [of nursery-
men] that needs only to be awakened by the hope of ultimate reward to
bring into being marvels of plant life comparable in value to anything that
the industrial genius has given to our civilisation'.[79] Support for the Bill
came from other horticultural quarters throughout the United States, and
from other inventors such as Thomas Edison, who argued that the time
had come 'to give the plant breeder the same status as the mechanical and
chemical inventors'. Congressional hearings were conducted throughout
the remainder of 1929, and on 11 February 1930 the Bill was introduced
into Congress. At the time it was felt that encouragement should be given
to private enterprise to forge new and dynamic industries, and thereby
make the American economy more robust in the face of any collapse of
the industrial and manufacturing sectors; so the Hoover administration
supported the Bill and it was passed on 13 May 1930.[80]

Although not all horticultural breeders were happy with the exclusion
of sexual reproduction from the legislation, Stark, its driver, attempted
to reassure the American Seed Trade Association that for the time being
their exclusion was necessary to ward off any greater opposition to the
Bill, especially from farmers, who saved and used seed to grow food crops,
and from the public, who would be averse to the idea of giving control of
food production to anyone but farmers. In making this concession Stark
ensured that 'Congress recognised the rights of the plant breeder and
originator'[81] and predicted that, with time, attitudes would change, and
that eventually even seed producers would be given the same protections.
Stark's prediction has come to pass.

This idea was not taken up by the British, and beyond this significant
development in patent law in the United States the call for patent law
reform took a back seat until 1938, when attention turned to 'corporate
concentration' and the growing nationalism in Germany, Italy and Japan.

LASSOING THE GRECIAN HORSE: THE ROLE OF ANTITRUST LAWS IN REGULATING PATENT MONOPOLIES

With the smell of war in the air and the experience of the Allied treatment of the assets of 'enemy' corporations still very much a part of the living memory of German industrialists, it is not surprising that they attempted to isolate their American assets through corporate vehicles and trusts in countries like Switzerland. Garvan, ever suspicious of Germany, called IG America 'the Grecian Horse'.

As the Nazi government in Germany began to be seen as a real threat to peace in Europe, in 1935 IG America came to the attention of the Security and Exchange Commission (SEC). The SEC was curious about the identity of the beneficial owners of IG America, which had investments in various US companies which suggested that it was a holding company. The SEC was entitled to a written sworn declaration disclosing the identity of its beneficial owners, but as its unmet demands for this information grew, that curiosity turned into a full-scale investigation. By 1937 the SEC specifically asked IG America, 'did I.G. Farben or any corporation or individual or group of corporations or individuals through stock ownership, contract or agreement, elect the directors or dictate the policies of American I.G.?' A negative answer was given, but that was merely the trigger for the SEC to demand that IG America's principal office holders, Walter Duisberg (Carl Duisberg's son), Dietrich Schmitz and Walter Teagle (who was then also the chairman of Standard Oil and a director of the Federal Reserve Bank of New York), face the scrutiny of cross-examination at public hearings conducted in Washington, DC. Ultimately the SEC never got a satisfactory answer. However in 1937 IG Farben ceased appointing directors to Bayer UK.

Clearly informed of the SEC and FBI reports into the impact that US and German corporate collaboration was having on the national security of the United States, President Franklin D Roosevelt[82] and Congress ordered that the Temporary National Economic Committee investigate the impact of 'corporate collectivism' on the US economy. Prior to the establishment of the Committee, on 29 April 1938 Roosevelt sent a message to Congress stating, 'today a concentration of private power without equal in history is growing'. Referring to the Internal Revenue statistics of 1935, he made several points: 'of all corporations . . . less than 5% owned 87% of all the assets of all of them' and 'of all manufacturing corporations, less then 4% of them earned 84% of all of the net profits of all of them'. The US patent system was to come under the Committee's scrutiny. Roosevelt's concerns included the concentration of power in patent portfolios, recommending to Congress that it amend the patent law 'to prevent their use to suppress inventions and to create industrial monopolies', so that patented inventions would 'be made available for use by anyone upon payment of appropriate royalties'. His proposal, aimed at diminishing the impact of the patent monopoly, struck out at the ultimate power of the inventor – the right to exclude all others through the inherent potential for the patent system to be used to suppress innovation and *economic growth*.

This committee was popularly called the 'Monopoly Committee'. Between 1 December 1938 and 26 April 1941 it heard 552 witnesses give evidence over 192 sitting days, and despite the fact that within a year of its commencement Germany and the UK were at war, and that by its conclusion the UK was losing the war in Europe, many of the Americans who testified were more concerned with the American spirit of invention and references to the 'wild frontier' than with how the patent system could be used as a weapon against their own country. During this time some of America's wealthiest families were in business with or associated with businesses which were closely connected to the Nazi government. In the final analysis the Committee achieved nothing of any significance because corporate America and its industrialists could not recognize that they, whether they liked it or not, were about to become embroiled in World War II. According to Larry Owens, 'the political actors who might have forged the consensus necessary for legislation were befuddled by the inability to mobilize symbolic resources in a winning fashion . . . and they failed to modernise the patent system . . . because political discourse did not permit its change'.[83]

Soon after the UK declared war on Germany on 3 September 1939 IG America changed its name to General Aniline & Film Corporation (GAFC). By June 1940 IG Chemie was restructured, severing its ties to IG Farben although, strictly speaking, it was never a shareholder. This severance involved the cancellation of an options contract and a series of dividend guarantees given by IG Farben to IG Chemie's Swiss shareholders in 1928, and the payment of 25 million Swiss francs by Swiss shareholders to IG Farben. This shuffle supposedly gave IG Chemie a clean bill of health, at least as far as the Swiss Government was concerned; but the SEC, the FBI, the Alien Property Custodian and the US government saw it differently. The Swiss shareholders then put GAFC on the market with a US$62 million price tag and, naturally, the identity of any potential buyer was of interest not only to the Americans but to the British, who had placed IG Farben on their 'black list' of enemy collaborators. Even if IG Farben was not a shareholder of nor had contractual links to IG Chemie, it was obvious that its management could still influence IG Chemie and ultimately direct the use of the money obtained through the sale of GAFC for the benefit of the German war effort. On 28 July 1941 a *Time Magazine* article entitled 'Who Owns Aniline?' described the situation:

General Aniline's outward characteristics remained not Swiss but German. Its president, Dietrich A. Schmitz, is a brother of the chairman of the board of I.G. Farben, Hermann Schmitz. Walter H. von Rath, Aniline's secretary, is the son of a Schmitz predecessor as chairman of the Farben. General Aniline had some distinguished American directors when the Germans set it up in '27. But Walter Clark Teagle, chairman of Standard Oil of N.J. (with which the Farben used to share patents) resigned from the Aniline board last year, and Edgar M. Clark (a Standard Oil man) and Edsel Ford followed suit early this month. As the U.S. got less & less neutral, the Nazi cloud over Aniline looked thicker every day.

CONFISCATION AGAIN, PATENTS AND ANTITRUST LAW

The work of the Alien Property Custodian, Leo T Crowley, who replaced Garvan on his death in 1937, had recommenced in earnest on 10 April 1940. Within 19 months the United States would be at war with Japan, Germany and Italy. Although the Japanese air raid on Pearl Harbour on 7 December 1941 caught the American forces napping on that Sunday morning, in reality the United States had been in a state of preparedness for war since 1938. The actions of the SEC, the Department of Justice Antitrust Division and the Alien Property Custodian were its first strike at its enemy, Germany. The second strike – the military action – removed the camouflage of its neutrality and gave the United States *carte blanche* to, as Roosevelt said on 8 December in his speech to the joint sitting of Congress, 'gain the inevitable triumph – so help us God'.

In the meantime the attention of US regulators had also turned towards other American companies which had links to IG Farben. Under the watchful eye of Thurman Arnold,[84] a man who coordinated 'seasoned attacks on sinister Nazi influences on U.S. business' (as he was described by *Time Magazine* on 15 September 1941), Sterling Products, Inc, the 'No. 1 U.S. drugmaker', and its management were investigated. As a result of his investigation Sterling, three of its subsidiaries and two of its most senior directors agreed to pay fines totalling US$26 000 and undertook to break 'all contractual obligations with I.G. Farben' and 'agreed never again to promise any other drug manufacturer not to compete in foreign markets'.

Over in the UK Sterling and its British patent agent, Arthur Carpmael (a descendent of William Carpmael who gave evidence to the 1864 Royal Commission into the British patent system), had made an attempt through Bayer UK, its British subsidiary, to gain ownership of British patents which were in the name of IG Farben but which, since the outbreak of World War II, had been the subject of a vesting order made under the

UK Trading With The Enemy Act 1939. Accordingly the British patents were under the control of a British trustee. Bayer UK claimed that it was the beneficial owner of these patents because of a number of agreements made between Bayer UK and Bayer Germany on 1 September 1923, and between IG Farben and Bayer America and IG Farben and Bayer UK on 26 November 1926. However in November 1940 when Bayer UK brought the application before the British courts in *In Re I.G. Farbenindustrie Aktiengesellschaft's Agreement* [1941] Ch 147, hidden behind the façade of what, by then, were British-American companies was the alliance between Sterling, the parent of these British-American subsidiaries, and IG Farben formed through IG America's ownership of shares in Winthrop, another of Sterling's American subsidiaries. Obviously Bayer UK's attempt to gain ownership of these British patents was no longer just the innocent act of a British company seeking what was its property but, because of the state of war which existed between the UK and Germany, had more sinister implications. This point was not lost on ICI which, though not a party to the relevant agreements and not a claimant to the British patents, was nonetheless taking more than a casual interest in the proceedings and had retained W Trevor Watson KC and Lloyd-Jacob, at that time two of the UK's most well respected barristers in patent law. They, with the court's leave, argued that no decision should be made at that time and that the British patents ought to remain in the hands of the British trustee. The court nevertheless concluded that war should not inhibit an application and elected to permit Sterling and Carpmael to pursue their claim.

By January 1942 the time had come to strike out at GAFC. Five German-born naturalized-American directors of GAFC were removed from their positions on the orders of Henry Morgenthau,[85] and 50 other employees were sacked. Then on 16 February 1942 Treasury officials raided the offices of GAFC, seized records and commenced an investigation. Soon Morgenthau had evidence that the tentacles of the enemy had extended their influence to allied, neutral and US nationals. Within a month, on 11 March 1942, Roosevelt signed Executive Order 9095 empowering the Alien Property Custodian to seize 'any property, or interest, of any foreign country or a national'. While this Presidential Order did not extend to the property of a US national, the job of dealing with US 'conspirators' was left in the capable hands of Arnold (as an example see *United States v General Dyestuffs Corporation et al* (1944) 57 F Supp 642) and Morgenthau. Acting on this new power on 24 April 1942 Morgenthau ordered the US Treasury to seize all of the GAFC shares which were owned by IG Chemie (90 per cent) and to freeze GAFC's six New York bank accounts. IG Chemie, its Swiss shareholders and the Swiss Government protested and set in train litigation which was not resolved for decades.[86]

GARVAN VINDICATED – US PATENT CONFISCATION ACCELERATES

With the criminal prosecution of Sterling settled and the required undertakings given, the way was paved for Crowley to transfer the Winthrop shares, acquired by IG Farben under the terms of the November 1926 agreement, back to Sterling. In effect Sterling paid a mere US$26 000 (namely the fines) for the return of a half share of its former fully owned subsidiary. Winthrop was now back as a fully owned subsidiary of Sterling, but this time Sterling not only owned the intellectual property but possessed the chemical and pharmaceutical expertise and know-how that it needed. For a second time, and within only 14 years, the former Bayer Germany's assets in the US and the British Empire were back in American hands.

Arnold's investigations were relentless, as the Department of Justice's Antitrust Division sought to purge US companies of their involvement in 'Nazi controlled cartels'. Another company in his sights was Jasco Company. It was jointly owned by Standard Oil and IG Farben. Under an arrangement made in 1939 Jasco became the owner of all patents in the US, French and British territories and IG Farben the owner in the rest of the world. The objective was to avoid confiscation of patent rights, and it displayed a deliberate and premeditated attempt by both US and German company executives to neutralize 'the interference of any government as regards the processes in question'.[87] While being cross-examined in 1945 Dr Oskar Loehr, an IG Farben executive, gave the US War Department evidence of how Jasco had conspired with IG Farben to suppress the development of a synthetic rubber industry in the US. Of course the patent system aided and abetted that objective. It would seem that Garvan had been vindicated.

On 6 July 1942 the scope of Crowley's powers was further extended to include patents. By Presidential Executive Order 9193, 'any patent, patent application, or right related thereto, in which any foreign country or national thereof had any interest' vested in the Alien Property Custodian, 'to hold, use, administer, or otherwise deal with the vested patents in the interest and for the benefit of the United States'. The idea was to 'safeguard the rights of the residents of occupied countries' and 'to make the inventions an active part of the war machinery of the United States'.[88]

Crowley in turn pledged to hand these patented inventions over 'for the benefit of American industry, American labor, and the consuming public', and to take 'all necessary steps to make certain that the vested enemy were made available forever to American industry'.[89] Where exclusive licences to these patented inventions were not already held by American companies, Crowley issued revocable, non-exclusive, non-assignable, royalty-free licences to any 'reputable' American company or individual. The same terms applied with respect to the patents of enemy-occupied countries, except that the royalty-free period would expire six months after the war was over, and thereafter 'reasonable royalties' would be payable. In the case where American companies had already entered into exclusive licences with enemy aliens or those occupied by the enemy the licences continued, with the proviso that, as the new owner of the patented inventions to which the licenses pertained, all royalties were paid to the Alien Property Custodian. The Smaller War Plants Corporation was then established by the American government in order to facilitate the exploitation of enemy patents by small American manufacturers.

While the US government's policy of confiscation of enemy assets, including patents, continued during World War II, what distinguished it from its actions during World War I was the exercise of control extended over US patented inventions owned by the nationals of any country, Allied and neutral.[90] The extent of these powers enabled Crowley effectively to ignore the patent owner's right to exclude all others by licensing American companies to work the patented inventions on such terms as he found satisfactory. While not interfering with any exclusive licences already in place with American companies, in all other instances Crowley was the sole arbiter of how best to use any US patented invention. This may not have amounted to confiscation, in the sense that ownership was vested in him and then transferred to an American company, but it was nevertheless an expropriation because it effectively deprived the foreign patent owner of the ability to exercise the exclusive right to exclude all others – a right which defines patent law by effect of the state-sanctioned monopoly granted to inventors.

With World War II over, on 14 October 1946 President Truman[91] signed Executive Order 9788 transferring the duties performed by the Alien Property Custodian to the Department of Justice.

On 3 July 1948 the US Trading with the Enemy Act 1917 was amended to provide: 'no vested property or interest therein of Germany, Japan or any national of either such country shall be returned to the former owners thereof, or their successors in interest, and that the United States shall not pay compensation for any such property or interest therein' (section 39). This avoided the possibility of a repetition of the Chemical Foundation case, but by 1954 it was not a policy that reflected universal approval. In a paper which Otto Sommerich delivered as President of the American Foreign Law Association at the Fifth International Conference of the Legal Profession, held in the relative comfort of Monte Carlo in July 1954,[92] he questioned the benefit of such a policy since, as Edwin Borchard[93] had acutely observed in 1943, the United States and its citizens had 'more to lose by confiscation than any other country'.[94]

By the time of America's entry into World War II US foreign investment amounted to some US$11 billion. The staggering size of this investment had ultimately brought it home to the United States, as the world's new military and economic superpower, that its banks, industries and people were economically vulnerable to fascism, communism, nationalization and confiscation. Borchard's advice, in this instance, was for America to 'exert its influence to prevent the further corrosion of the institutions of private property' by using international law and not 'the preponderance of force'.[95]

SIFTING THROUGH THE RUBBLE

IG Farben, as it functioned from 1925, ceased operations in 1945 but continued as a corporate entity until it was finally de-listed from the Frankfurt Stock Exchange in 2003. In 1952 a new company, Bayer AG, inherited from IG Farben (now under the control of the Allied Powers) what were the original Bayer factories at Leverkusen and Elberfield and the Agfa photographic business from the remnants of IG Farben. Bayer AG eventually reacquired some of its US trade marks (but not for pharmaceuticals) in 1986 when it paid Sterling Drug, Inc US$25 million. In 1988 Eastman Kodak acquired Sterling Drug, Inc for US$5.1 billion and changed the name to Sterling-Winthrop, Inc. In 1994 Elf Sanofi, a French pharmaceutical company now called Sanofi-Aventis, acquired the prescription drug operations of Sterling-Winthrop, Inc from Eastman Kodak for US$1.675 billion. In the same year SmithKline Beecham acquired Stirling-Winthrop Inc's over-the-counter drug business from Eastman Kodak and sold it on to Miles, Inc (formerly called Bayer USA Inc), which had since 1978 been a fully owned subsidiary of Bayer AG. In this roundabout fashion Bayer AG reacquired ownership of all of the US Bayer trade marks confiscated by the US Alien Property Custodian during World War I and again during World War II. In 1995 Miles, Inc changed its name to Bayer Corporation.

Following Morgenthau's raid on GAFC and the seizure of its US assets in April 1942 the US government took over the administration of the company as a matter of national security. Having sacked its senior management Morgenthau appointed four American businessmen to run the company on the Government's behalf. GAFC was simply too valuable and strategic to allow the Swiss to sell or run it, and so the battle to keep control commenced through the courts. The new managers were Robert E McConnell, president; George Moffett, vice-president; and Robert E Wilson and Albert E Marshall, directors. Under US government administration GAFC continued supplying the US military with dyes for uniforms and camouflage cloth as well as dyes for smoke bombs throughout the war. During 1943 the factory at Linden, New Jersey (originally a Grasselli chemical factory) produced about 7 000 000 kilogrammes of dyes just for the military. GAFC was more valuable to the military than merely as a supplier of dyes. As a result of its association with IG Farben the company had acquired inventions and know-how to produce vinyalation and carbonyl iron powder among other things.

GAFC had a portfolio of nearly 4000 US patents and, despite the work of the Chemical Foundation since World War I, there remained a lack of technical capacity to make full use of them. Consequently GAFC established the Central Research Laboratory (CRL) in 1942 in Easton, Pennsylvania, in a disused silk mill. The first CRL director was William E Hanford.[96] By the end of World War II CRL employed 67 researchers with PhDs. Its research budget exceeded US$5 million by 1950, and GAFC continued in general business after the war, making a range of products including 16mm colour film under the trade mark Ansco.

In the meantime litigation between the Swiss government, the US government and the Swiss shareholders over the assets of IG Chemie (which had changed its name to Interhandel AG in 1945) proceeded through the US courts all the way to the US Supreme Court twice, and separately to the International Court of Justice. Despite numerous attempts to settle the dispute diplomatically, neither government was prepared to retreat from its respective position concerning the effect of the company's restructure in June 1940. The Swiss were convinced that the restructure was effective in expunging IG Farben's influence; the Americans were not.

By 1957 the US government was intent on proceeding to sell its interest in GAFC. The US advised the Swiss that a sale was 'desirable in the national interest of the United States, based in part upon considerations of national defence. Only the courts of the United States have jurisdiction to stay such a sale of property located in the United States; such jurisdiction is sovereign and exclusive.'

By this time the original claim for the return of the assets, filed by Interhandel in 1948 under the Trading With The Enemy Act 1917, had been dismissed by the US courts because it had failed to comply with an order of the US District Court requiring the parties to produce all relevant documents for inspection. Having been summarily dismissed on a technicality, not on substance, and with the US Supreme Court refusing to review the appeal court's confirmation of the dismissal, the US government was justified, under US law, in proceeding with its proposed divestiture of GAFC. However the Swiss had other ideas.

Switzerland filed an action against the United States in the International Court of Justice (ICJ) at the Hague on 2 October 1957 (*Switzerland v*

United States of America).[97] President Truman had signed a declaration on 14 August 1946 confirming the US's recognition of the jurisdiction of the ICJ to determine 'all legal disputes . . . concerning . . . any question of international law', making this action possible. The Swiss government had done the same with effect from 28 July 1948. The US declaration had specifically excluded the ICJ's jurisdiction with respect to 'disputes . . . essentially within the domestic jurisdiction of the US'; clearly what the US Government did with property confiscated under US domestic law was not strictly a matter for the ICJ. Nonetheless on 25 May 1946 the United States, as one of the three Allied Powers, came to an agreement with Switzerland regarding the liquidation and disposal of 'German property in Switzerland'. The Washington Accord, as this agreement was called, required Switzerland to pursue investigations that it had already commenced under the terms of a provisional agreement with the US, the UK and France made on 16 February 1945. The Washington Accord also contained an undertaking by the United States to 'unblock Swiss assets in the United States . . . without delay'. According to the Swiss government, having thoroughly investigated the events leading to and involving the reorganization of Interhandel in June 1940, it concluded that Interhandel was Swiss and not German, and on 4 May 1948 a diplomatic note was sent by the Swiss legation at Washington, DC, to the US government invoking the Washington Accord and requesting that Interhandel's shares in GAFC be released. The US government was unimpressed. On 26 July 1948 it rejected the Swiss request on the basis that the decision of the reviewing authority established by the Swiss government was 'inapplicable to property in the US'. The point of difference between the two governments regarding the Washington Accord was over the meaning of: 'German property in Switzerland'. The US government argued that the shares in GAFC were in the United States, not in Switzerland, and, in any event, were 'enemy assets', not Swiss.

For the Swiss it was important to force the United States into arbitration, which was the agreed path under the Washington Accord. For the United States it was important to keep the ICJ from even considering the argument. Nonetheless on 21 March 1959 the ICJ handed down its decision[98] in favour of the US position. Crucial to its decision was the fact that the US Supreme Court had reinstated Interhandel as a party to US proceedings, and accordingly at the 'present stage of the proceedings' it was not necessary for the ICJ to express an opinion on the matter; neither was it 'practicable, before the final decision of the domestic courts, to anticipate what basis they may adopt for their judgment'. Interhandel had previously sought to persuade the Supreme Court to intervene a second time, renewing its application to have it readmitted to the dismissed proceedings after a second Appeals Court had rejected its plan, which involved the use of a neutral investigator to inspect the Swiss documents for relevance. On 14 October 1957, during the second day of argument before the ICJ, it was announced to the ICJ that the US Supreme Court had ordered the reinstatement of Interhandel. According to the Supreme Court, having done all within their power to comply with the District Court's original order for the production of documents, Interhandel's failure to comply did not warrant summary dismissal because the Swiss secrecy laws which had prevented Interhandel from producing the relevant documents were not something that was within their control. Justice Harlan of the US Supreme Court[99] was sympathetic:

> The findings below, and what has been shown as to petitioner's extensive efforts at compliance, compel the conclusion on this record that petitioner's failure to satisfy fully the requirements of this production order was due to inability fostered neither by its own conduct nor by circumstances within its control. It is hardly debatable that fear of criminal prosecution constitutes a weighty excuse for nonproduction, and this excuse is not weakened because the laws preventing compliance are those of a foreign sovereign.

Having staved off the sale the litigation continued, but in March 1963, after nearly 20 years, the dispute was brought to a conclusion by Robert Kennedy[100] and Alfred Schäfer.[101] As a result GAFC was sold by public offering. The US government made US$328 million. Interhandel's only remaining shareholder, now the Union Bank of Switzerland (which absorbed the insolvent Basler Handelsbank and Eidgenössische Bank, formerly two of Switzerland's major banks, in 1945), made US$122 million. GAFC continued in business.

NOTES

1. 1797–1888; King of Prussia, 1861–88; First German Emperor, 1871–88.
2. 1815–98; Minister-President of Prussia, 1862–90; First Chancellor of Germany, 1871–90.
3. Chandler, AD (1992), 'Organizational Capabilities and the Economic History of the Industrial Enterprise', *The Journal of Economic Perspectives*, **6** (3), 79–100, 82.
4. For more detail see Chapter 1, n 68.
5. For more detail see Chapter 1, p 16.
6. By Order of the Board of Trade this section of the Act of 1902 came into operation on 1 January 1905. See also Fulton, D (1905), *The Law and Practice Relating To Patents, Trade Marks and Designs* (3rd edn, London: Jordan & Sons, Limited).
7. Daniel, EM (1884), *A Complete Treatise upon The New Law of Patents, Designs and Trade Marks Act, 1883* (London: Steven & Hayes), 120.
8. Fulton, D (1910), *The Law and Practice Relating To Patents, Trade Marks and Designs* (4th edn, London: Jordan & Sons, Limited), 10.
9. Ibid.

10. 1863–1945; MP, 1905–45; British Prime Minister, 1916–22.
11. Schuster, G (1909), 'The Patents and Designs Act, 1907', *The Economic Journal*, **19** (76), 538–51.
12. Ibid, 538.
13. Ibid, 551.
14. Ibid, 538.
15. Ibid, 538.
16. Ibid, 538.
17. Ibid, 538.
18. Fulton, above n 8, 11.
19. Ibid, 11.
20. Swan, KR (1908), *The Law and Commercial Usage of Patents, Designs and Trade Marks* (London: Archibald Constable & Co Ltd), 4.
21. Ibid, 4.
22. Ibid (my italics).
23. Schuster, above n 11, 67.
24. This subject was considered by the Stanley Committee's Report in 1865. Indeed the Committee explained: '[t]he objections to a special Court are various and strong. In the first place, the want of sufficient business to occupy its time fully. Secondly, that on trials of patent cases, questions are frequently arising which require an extended knowledge of other branches of the law; and that a Judge selected for his special acquaintance with mechanical and scientific topics, and one who in his judicial capacity was principally engaged in the consideration of such questions, would not be so competent to deal with the whole subject-matter of the case by whom all branches of our law were in turn handled. Thirdly, that such a constitution of the Court would render it extremely difficult, if not impossible, to secure an effectual appeal.' Nonetheless the Committee recommended that a judge be rotated from one of the 'Judges of the Courts of Law and Equity' with the aid of a scientific assessor or assessors and without a jury, should be the approach taken. See UK Royal Commission (1865), *Report of The Commissioners, Working of the Law Relating to Letters Patent for Inventions*, pp xi–xii.
25. This is a classic example of how a specialized patent judge, whose focus was on furthering the patent system without understanding that it was a protectionist tool, attempted deliberately to undermine the economic policy of the elected government of the day. It also demonstrated that there was a degree of tension building between British patent attorneys and lawyers who were being instructed, in many instances, by overseas associates in Germany and America. Indeed the British patent professions became the instruments of economic sabotage by using various strategies to overcome many of the protectionist barriers that were being imposed on foreign corporations which were using British patents to suppress production and employment in Britain. Swan, above n 19, and Fulton, above n 7, were particularly alert to the motives of foreign patent holders, but H Fletcher Moulton and JH Evans-Jackson in their treatise (1920), *The Patents, Designs, and Trade Marks Acts* (London: Butterworth & Co.), actually instructed the British profession on how to overcome section 38A(1), deliberately introduced in the 1919 amendments to the 1907 legislation to prohibit the patenting of chemical substances and so encourage the development of a British pharmaceutical production capacity.
26. Federico, PJ (1948), 'Compulsory Licensing in Other Countries', *Law and Contemporary Problems*, **13** (2), 295–319.
27. He was an American academic famous for explaining to a US Congressional Committee in 1951 which was considering the Bill for what was to become the Patents Act 1952 that an invention in section 101 was 'anything under the sun that is made by man'.
28. So described in 1876 by the German Commissioner for the World Exposition held in Philadelphia, USA: Kronstein, H (1942), 'The Dynamics of German Cartels and Patents. I', *The University of Chicago Law Review*, **9** (4), 643–71.

29. 1789–1846.
30. List, F (1841), *The National System of Political Economy* (transl by Sampson S Lloyd MP, 1885 edn), (London: Longmans, Green and Company), p xxvi.
31. Ibid, Chapter 33 'The Politics'.
32. 1831–99.
33. Chandler, above n 3, 92.
34. Schuster, EJ (1913), 'Germany', *Journal of the Society of Comparative Legislation,* New Series, **13** (2), 302–3, 303.
35. Sayre, LE (1919), 'Patent Laws in Regard to the Protection of Chemical Industry', *Transactions of the Kansas Academy of Science,* **30**, 39–44, 43.
36. Ibid, 41.
37. 1849–1930; US Congressman 1913–25 (Mass. R).
38. Sayre, above n 35, 42.
39. 1856–1924; President of the United States, 1913–21.
40. President Woodrow Wilson's Address to Congress, 2 April 1917, at 8.30pm., available at http://us.history.wisc.edu/hist102/pdocs/wilson_address.pdf.
41. 1872–1936; Alien Property Custodian, 1917–19; US Attorney-General, 1919–21.
42. US Alien Property Custodian (1919), US Government Printing Office; reprinted 1977, *Alien Property Custodian Report: A Detailed Report by the Alien Property Custodian* (New York: Arno Press). Mitchell Palmer's Report to President Wilson is dated 23 February 1919. In it he states: 'I think I am now able to say that practically all known enemy property in the United States has been taken over by me and is being administered according to the provisions of the trading with the enemy act', at 3.
43. 1871–1943; partner of the NY law firm Davis Polk.
44. 1875–1937; President of the Chemical Foundation 1919–37; Alien Property Custodian, March 1919–37.
45. Sommerich, OC (1955), 'Treatment by United States of World War I and II Enemy-owned Patents and Copyrights', *The American Journal of Comparative Law,* **4**, 587–600, 587.
46. Vaughan, FW (1919), 'Suppression and Non-working of Patents, With Special Reference to the Dye and Chemical Industries', *The American Economic Review,* **9** (4), 693–700, 699.
47. Ibid.
48. Ibid, 697.
49. Ibid, 698.
50. 1862–1952; Federal MP, 1901–52; Prime Minister of Australia, 1915–23.
51. *The Australian,* 17 September 1915 (Australian newspaper).
52. 1865–1921; President of the United States, 1921–23.
53. 'No officer or agent of any corporation . . . and no . . . person directly or indirectly interested in the pecuniary profits or contracts of such corporation . . . shall be employed or shall act as an officer or agent of the United States for the transaction of business with such corporation'.
54. Steen, K (2001), 'Patents, Patriotism, and "Skilled in the Art": USA v The Chemical Foundation, 1923–1926', *Isis,* **92**, 91–122, 112, n 48.
55. 1867–1937.
56. Also awarded to Marie Curie in 1921 and Linus Pauling in 1946.
57. *USA v The Chemical Foundation, Inc* (1924) 294 F 300, 318.
58. The trade mark for the drug Arsphenamine
59. 1854–1915; Nobel Prize in Physiology or Medicine, 1908.
60. 1873–1938.
61. *USA v The Chemical Foundation, Inc,* above n 57, 319.
62. Reeves, WH (1954), 'Is Confiscation of Enemy Assets in the National Interest of the United States?', *Virginia Law Review,* **40**, (8), 1029–60.
63. Ibid, 1039.
64. The agreements are described in detail in the judgment of the High Court of Ireland in *Sterling-Winthrop Group Limited v Farbenfabriken Bayer AG* [1976] RPC 469.

65. Ibid.
66. Ibid.
67. Feldenkirchen, W (1987), 'Big Business in Interwar Germany: Organizational Innovation at Vereinigte Stahlwerke, IG Farben, and Siemens', *The Business History Review*, **61** (3), 417–51. See also Feldenkirchen, W (1999), 'Germany: The Invention of Intervention' in J Foreman-Peck and G Federico (eds), *European Industrial Policy The Twentieth-Century Experience* (Oxford: Oxford University Press).
68. 1888–1959; US Secretary of State 1953–9.
69. Salsman, RM (2004), 'The Cause and Consequences of the Great Depression, Part 1: What Made the Roaring '20s Roar', *The Intellectual Activist*, **18** (4), 16.
70. *Time Magazine*, 10 February 1930.
71. Ibid.
72. Ibid.
73. 1871–1955; US Secretary of State, 1933–44; Nobel Prize, 1945.
74. UK Board of Trade, CH Sargant, (1931), *Report of the Departmental Committee on the Patents and Designs Acts and Practice of the Patent Office*, 1930–31 [Cmd 3829], 28 (122–124).
75. James Ramsey MacDonald (1866–1937); Labour Prime Minister, 1924, 1929–31; National Prime Minister, 1931–5.
76. UK Board of Trade (1931), above n 74, 28 (123).
77. For more detail about the Paris Convention see Chapter 5: Internationalism, Vienna, 1873 – The Road to the Paris Convention and The Paris Convention, 1883.
78. Until that agreement was reached Ciba and May & Baker had previously locked horns in a dispute over their respective patent applications, with Ciba claiming a process for manufacturing thiazoles and May & Baker claiming a process for manufacturing para-amino-benzene-sulphonamido-pyridines (pyridines).
79. 'The Importance of Plant Patents to Agriculture: A Statement by Hon. John G Townsend, Jr', *National Nurseryman*, 1 April 1930, **38**, 5. Also cited in Kelves, DJ (2002), 'A History of Patenting Life in the United States with Comparative Attention to Europe and Canada', *A Report to the European Group on Ethics in Science and New Technologies*, 5.
80. Cong. Rec., 71st Cong., 2nd sess., 5, 12 and 13 May 1930, 8391, 8751 and 8866.
81. Kloppenburg, JR Jr. (1988), *First the Seed: The Political Economy of Plant Biotechnology: 1492–2000* (New York: Cambridge University Press).
82. 1882–1945; President of the United States, 1933–45.
83. Owens, L (1991), 'Patents, the "Frontiers" of American Invention, and the Monopoly Committee of 1939: Anatomy of a Discourse', *Technology and Culture*, **32** (4), 1076–93, 1077.
84. 1891–1969; US Assistant Attorney-General (Antitrust Division US Department of Justice) 1938–43.
85. 1891–1967; US Secretary of the Treasury, 1934–45.
86. Re, ED (1953), 'United States: Dismissal of Suit for Failure to Produce Records; The "I.G. Chemie" Case', *The American Journal of Comparative Law*, **2** (4), 536–41 and Simmonds, KR (1961), 'The Interhandel Case', *The International and Comparative Law Quarterly*, **10** (3), 495–547.
87. Standard Oil Executive in evidence before The Committee on Patents, 77th Cong., 2nd Sess. (1942), part 6, 2921.
88. Sommerich, above n 45, 593.
89. Ibid.
90. Eisner, FW (1945), 'Administrative Machinery and Steps for the Lawyer', *Law and Contemporary Problems*, **11** (1), 61–75.
91. 1884–1972; President of the United States, 1945–53.
92. Sommerich, above n 45.
93. 1884–1951; Professor of Law, Yale University.
94. Borchard, E (1943), 'Nationalization of Enemy Patents', *The American Journal of International Law*, **37**, 92–7.

95. Ibid.
96. 1908–96; GAFC, 1942–57; co-inventor of a polyurethane process in 1942 US Patent 2,284,896.
97. Available at http://www.icj-cij.org/docket/files/34/10823.pdf.
98. Available at http://www.law.nyu.edu/kingsburyb/fall01/intl_law/unit2/interhandel. html.
99. *Société Internationale pour Participations Industrielles et Commerciales, SA v Rogers* (1958) 357 US 197.
100. 1925–68; US Attorney General, 1961–4.
101. 1905–86; President of UBS, 1953–64; Chairman of UBS, 1964–76.

3. Patent monopolies versus free trade

Even . . . Cordell Hull, great exponent of Good Neighbour policy and collaboration, is at pains to remind the American electorate that 'The foreign policy of every country must be expressive of that country's fundamental national interests'.

RJF Boyer, December 1944

At the Monetary and Financial Conference held at Bretton Woods, New Hampshire, in July 1944 the draft articles of the International Bank for Reconstruction and Development (now known as the World Bank) and the International Monetary Fund (IMF) were completed. Absent from consideration however was the role that the confiscation and use of enemy patents, trade marks and copyrights had played in the reconstruction or reshaping of the UK and US economies during, and between, both world wars. At Bretton Woods free trade and multilateralism did not extend to intellectual property. It was not until 1 January 1995 when the World Trade Organization (WTO) was established and the Agreement on Trade Related Aspects of Intellectual Property (TRIPS) became operational that intellectual property came together with the trade and tariff negotiations which had, until then, taken place under the terms of a provisional agreement, the General Agreement on Tariffs and Trade (the GATT).

That it took nearly 50 years to achieve this fusion is no accident. Protectionism at the time of Bretton Woods was a controversial issue, particularly after the British Empire's Imperial Preference system was agreed upon at Ottawa in August 1932 – a system which, by the outbreak of World War II, accounted for 40 per cent of all international trade. Cordell Hull and the US Department of State, which he headed, were determined to break what was, in their minds, an aberration. As far as the United States was concerned the British Empire's trading bloc had to go, and the outbreak of World War II presented Hull with the opportunity to press his point – that protectionism contributed to war.

Hull's perspective about the cause of war was not unique; but he, probably more than any other statesman of his time, is credited with doggedly pursuing a plan in which nations and people would work together to create a level playing field. In Hull's opinion a level playing field would encourage nations to act selflessly regardless of political borders and economic imbalances and, importantly, through the spirit of free enterprise and democracy not only would it reduce the misunderstandings and jealousies between nations and their peoples, but would eliminate the need for the use of 'violent force'. Peace, not war, was his *raison d'être*.

As US Secretary of State in the Roosevelt administration he was in a unique position to turn the ideas which he had vocalized since World War I into reality. As a visionary he captured the attention not only of Roosevelt but of other world leaders, and if there was any single event that made his vision worthy of serious consideration it was World War II. The combination of this man, his vision and the tragedy of World War II concentrated goodwill and generated consensus which led to the establishment of the many international organizations which today are in many respects taken for granted.

Unfortunately Hull did not seem to appreciate how the confiscation of about US$9 billion of German and 'enemy' assets during World Wars I and II put American industry,[1] the American economy and the American people in an enviable economic position – one which they arguably would not have otherwise attained. No matter how these actions were justified and explained away to fellow Americans, as Edwin Borchard had warned in 1943, if these actions were applied against American assets as Americans applied them against 'enemy' assets, they would have the most to lose.[2]

THE PRICE OF WAR AND PEACE

The Mutual Aid Agreement was negotiated between May 1941 and February 1942 and was signed in Washington, DC, on 23 February 1942 by Sumner Wells[3] on behalf of the United States and Viscount Halifax[4] on behalf of the UK. In its recital the Agreement declared that the US and UK were 'engaged in a cooperative undertaking' for the lofty purpose of ensuring a 'just and enduring world peace . . . to themselves and all nations'. It acknowledged that 'the defense of the United Kingdom against aggression [was] vital to the defense of the United States of America'. Both statements confirmed not only the closeness of their relationship, but that they were in an almighty battle to retain economic control of global markets. Once again Germany had threatened victory, but this time it was the United States, not the British Empire, which had the most to lose. In the intervening 20 years the United States' power and position had grown in terms of her capacity for both trade and war. She had done well from World War I and she was determined to do well again from World War II. The immediate economic objective was to provide the UK with the benefit of her arms, her factories and her farms. The immediate military objective was to defeat Germany. Clearly the 'provision of defense aid' to the UK was vital to the achievement of these objectives, but the long-term issue was: on what basis? The Agreement provided that 'certain considerations' should be taken into account. It was within this detail that Hull made his move.

The Agreement was a rather short document of only eight articles. Given the sentiments expressed in its recital one would have thought that the negotiations would move rapidly to a conclusion, but in fact the seventh article delayed consensus for ten months. The obstacle was a handful of words: '[the parties should] provide against discrimination . . . of the importation of any product originating in either country'.

The chief British negotiator, John Maynard Keynes,[5] was spectacularly unimpressed with the American proposal, describing it as 'lunatic'.[6] He was deeply concerned by Hull's attack on the bilateralism which underpinned the system of Imperial Preferences. The idea that the UK, which had finally and completely rejected free trade as an economic policy at Ottawa in 1932, would be thrust back into the nineteenth century by Hull was, for Keynes, full of 'unpleasant economic realities'.[7] As an economist for whom free trade and the Depression went hand-in-hand, *laissez-faire* economic policy was the antithesis of his 'General Theory of Employment, Interest and Money' – a theory which called for active fiscal management of the economy to restore and maintain equilibrium and full employment. Free trade meant reducing tariffs, eliminating quotas, open markets and low government intervention. Hull's demands irritated Keynes; yet he knew that compromise he must, for without American economic aid the UK was in a perilous situation. Even Roosevelt, a supporter of his General Theory with the New Deal as testament, knew by 1942 that the American economy was out of the Depression, not because of his New Deal, but because the UK's extraordinary wartime demand for US manufactured and agricultural goods had put the US economy into overdrive.

Yet war came at a price, and even as the UK's immediate material needs were met, both sides were contemplating the political and strategic shape of a post-war world. The Americans placed an IOU on the negotiating table: *multilateralism*. It was a condition that forced the UK, then the world's most powerful economic nation, to agree to enter into a dialogue with 'all other countries of like mind, directed to the expansion, by appropriate international and domestic measures, of production, employment, and the exchange and consumption of goods, which are the material foundations of the liberty and welfare of all peoples'. It was an audacious plan, for it assumed that every other Allied country would want to participate in this Anglo-American dalliance – which, by 1944, tired of war and desperate for peace, they did.

Hull counselled that 'trade retaliation and discrimination in its more vicious forms have been productive of bitter economic wars which in many cases have developed into wars of force'.[8] Therefore the removal of trade barriers, the encouragement of open markets and the deregulation of capital were essential objectives if a peaceful and productive world was to result. Nonetheless the Agreement foreshadowed a new world order in which America expected to play the most significant role and within which there was no place for Imperial Preferences or the British Empire. Despite its lofty sentiments this was an insurance policy which ensured that America's economic largesse during war was not its downfall during peace.

Tension developed between the State Department and Treasury, as Hull was convinced but Morgenthau more circumspect. In the end, after a fireside chat between Winston Churchill[9] and Roosevelt, the final text was agreed, and so Article VII read:

> In . . . return for aid furnished [to the UK] . . . the terms and conditions . . . shall include provision for agreed action by the United States of America and the United Kingdom, open to participation by all other countries of like mind, directed . . . *to the elimination of all forms of discriminatory treatment in international commerce, and to the reduction of tariffs and other trade barriers.*[10]

This result particularly suited the United States, given that it had also become embroiled in a war which by December 1941 included the Asia-Pacific region, and thus directly threatened its national security. Nonetheless the dialogue which Article VII envisaged was painful. It commenced in May 1942, the chief US negotiator being Harry Dexter White,[11] and by June 1943 it involved 37 countries and the consideration of two papers: one authored by White and the other by Keynes. Needless to say these papers were not the result of a collaborative effort and, as chairman, White took every opportunity to frustrate Keynes. This was not just an ideological battle between two brilliant economists – the Americans wanted control. In September 1943 a meeting of experts was held, but the British distaste remained evident. According to a memorandum from the Secretary of State for India to the UK War Cabinet on 20 December 1943, White's plan was seen to be 'a deliberate attempt to restore the mid-nineteenth century world of capitalist-individualist-internationalism'.[12]

Nonetheless the start of 1944 saw an optimistic mood swing among the Allies and encouraged them to establish institutions which would engender a long and sustained world peace when it came, so the ideological differences between White and Keynes had to be put aside. In July 1944, only a month after the D-Day landings, the Articles for the IMF and the World Bank were drafted at Bretton Woods[13] under the presidency of Morgenthau, but ironically it was Keynes who closed the meeting.

Speaking of 'the great intellectual and technical difficulty' which was sur-mounted by delegates who 'had to perform at one and the same time the tasks appropriate to the economist, to the financier, to the politician, to the journalist, to the propagandist, to the lawyer, and to the statesman – even, I think, to the prophet and to the soothsayer', Keynes emphasised, 'this was just the beginning'. He knew that the real job of selling multilateralism had only just begun. Moreover, the work towards the drafting of the charter of the International Trade Organization (ITO), the next step towards Hull's trade utopia, had yet to be started.

Before long Hull was awarded the Nobel Prize for Peace, a Conference had been held in San Francisco for the drawing up of the UN Charter and the UN's First General Assembly had been convened in London on 10 January 1946. During his Nobel Prize acceptance speech, delivered two months earlier by Lithgow Osborne, the US Ambassador to Norway, Hull repeated his hope for 'the creation of an international agency through which the nations of the world can, if they so desire, make peace a living reality'. The United Nations, though not yet inaugurated, was about to be. With his health failing and knowing that he would not live to see its full potential he pleaded to his august audience:

> With all its imperfections, the United Nations Organization offers the peace-loving nations of the world . . . a fully workable mechanism which will give them peace, if they want peace. . . . The crucial test for men and for nations today is whether or not they have suffered enough, and have learned enough, to put aside suspicion, prejudice and short-run and narrowly conceived interests and to unite in furtherance of their greatest common interest.

However by the time of the Havana Conference in March 1948, during which the charter for the ITO was drafted, the euphoria of Bretton Woods had been replaced by a hangover. Keynes was dead, having died on 21 April 1946, and Hull had retired. The irresolvable tension between free trade and protectionism began to expose a deep schism between and within countries which shared Hull's vision and those which feared that the ITO Charter would expose their markets to the precariousness of international competition.[14]

Incredibly, without Hull's guidance and Roosevelt's determination, the American strategic objective which lay behind Article VII, and which had been fully embraced by the Department of State throughout World War II, began to unravel. The United States simply backed away because the policy of free trade Hull had advocated since World War I, providing the rationale for Bretton Woods, no longer met the economic objectives of the Republican-controlled US Senate. The UK was no longer the most power-ful nation in the world, America was. No longer did the US need to sacrifice protectionism while pursuing a 'free trade' agenda because instead it could use the rhetoric of free trade to mask its protectionist agenda. In the end the General Agreement on Tariffs and Trade (the GATT), a provisional agreement which had been separately negotiated and concluded in Geneva on 30 October 1947, became the conduit through which the world's multilateral trade and tariff negotiations would be undertaken for the next 48 years.

BOX 3.1   ANOTHER PERSPECTIVE OF THE ITO

'The ITO went beyond trade. The Havana Charter was an ambitious effort to create an international institution comparable to the International Monetary Fund and the World Bank. Indeed, it went well beyond trade negotiations to include a full range of economic chapters ranging from commodity agreements to economic development and even to employment. When one considers the socialist thinking, nationalizations and central planning that were so much the vogue in the late 1940s in Paris and London and other major capitals, we are perhaps fortunate that it failed and thus those ideas did not become part of official international trade doctrine through the ITO. But a caveat is worth considering. One reason it failed was the trade provisions; organized opposition by protectionist forces persuaded President Truman to draw back from asking the Senate to ratify.'

Kenneth W Dam, Max Pam Professor Emeritus of American and Foreign Law, University of Chicago.

BRITISH PATENT LAW REFORM AFTER BRETTON WOODS – THE PATENT LOOPHOLE

In 1949 a new UK Patents Act 1949 replaced the Patents & Designs Act 1907. However, in spite of free trade aspirations which led to Bretton Woods, many of the protectionist features of the British patent system which underpinned the 1883 (and as amended in 1902), 1907 (and as amended in 1919 and 1932) Acts were retained in the 1949 legislation: for instance compulsory licensing by the Comptroller (sections 37–39), revocation by the Comptroller (section 42) and Crown use (section 46). The UK's national interests demanded protection, but there were some refinements, or perhaps reinforcements, incorporated into this legislation.

The first of these was the express limitation contained in section 4(7) that an invention did not extend to 'that substance when found in nature'. This seemed a curious amendment, given that ordinarily one would have thought that products of nature were not 'manners of new manufacture'. This exclusion had become necessary due to the fact that the previous prohibition on the patenting of chemicals as substances first introduced into the 1907 legislation in 1919, namely as section 38A(1), had been weakened. So in order to make it clear that products of nature, which were also chemicals, remained beyond the realm of patent protection, section 4(7) was introduced into the 1949 legislation. Policy-makers were adamant 'a claim for a new substance should always be deemed to exclude the same substance when found in nature'.[15]

This insertion of section 38A(1), a key protectionist measure, into the UK Patents & Designs Act 1907 had been designed to exclude from patentability 'any substances prepared or produced by chemical processes or intended for food or medicine', unless they were 'prepared or produced by special methods or processes of manufacture described and claimed'. The intent then was to place the British patent system on an equal footing with the German patent system, which had never permitted the patenting of chemical substances and which had permitted the patenting of processes for their manufacture only since 1891. Indeed Sir William Pearce, a Liberal in the House of Commons and himself a chemical manufacturer, believed that section 38A(1) was a 'great improvement' because patentability depended 'upon the process rather than the actual substance itself'.[16] Clearly the shortages of essential medicines and chemicals during World War I had exposed England's dependence on Germany for its supply of chemical and pharmaceutical products,[17] and the post-war government was determined to see that this never happened again. Essentially it was felt that by preventing German chemical manufacturers from gaining a patent monopoly in England which was unavailable to them in Germany, generic pharmaceutical production in England would be encouraged.

The government of the day had, unfortunately, underestimated the unpopularity of this policy among the British patent profession, particularly since many of them had acquired American clients as a consequence of the confiscation by the US Government[18] of 'enemy' patents, trade marks and chemical factories (among other assets). The consequential 'Americanization' of the pharmaceutical industry highlighted how American patent lawyers, used to American legal standards, were unsympathetic to the Lloyd George Government's policy that Britain maintain a domestic capacity for pharmaceutical production. In an effort to comply with the instructions received from American lawyers, British lawyers like Fletcher Mouton QC, a barrister practising at the patent bar in London, advised British patent attorneys to 'claim all practical modes of preparing' chemicals, including 'the best practicable method known'; even proposing that they 'take out one or more patents of addition for the alternative processes . . . preferably . . . before the publication of the first specification'.[19]

THE SWAN COMMITTEE 1945–47

So effective was this advice in fact that in 1946 a committee chaired by Kenneth R Swan QC, a senior patent law barrister, found that section 38A(1) had been easily circumvented[20] by 'the drafting . . . [of claims] to cover all conceivable methods of manufacture', so that 'the substance itself and not the process of manufacture'[21] was patented. Indeed contrary to the thinking in 1919 that the invention lay in 'the process' the Swan Committee received a submission from the Association of the British Pharmaceutical Industry (ABPI) to the effect that 'the real invention lies in the discovery of a new substance, with new and useful properties'[22] – a view that was more or less consistent with American patent law and practice.

Rather than completely capitulate to the pharmaceutical industry however, the Swan Committee observed that the policy protections inherent in section 38A(1) could be served by compulsory licensing, noting that under its proposed amended version of section 27 (the compulsory licensing provision under the 1907 legislation), 'neither the patentee nor the public would be deprived of the full benefit of the later invention, or hindered from using it'.[23] In other words, even if foreign pharmaceutical companies could patent chemical substances per se, the social and economic need of maintaining a British production capacity would be satisfied by the grant of compulsory licences to British manufacturers. Accordingly the Committee hoped to ease the tension between the demands of the ABPI for patents over chemical substances on the one hand and the political expectation for readily available and affordable medicines, by recommending that the Comptroller be obliged to grant compulsory licences, 'unless he sees good reason not to'.

Swan personally believed that it was important for the British Government to maintain some semblance of control over the commercial activities of pharmaceutical companies. Forty years earlier he had observed the relationship between trade marks and patented medicines, and had concluded in his 1908 treatise that the effective term of patent protection could be extended beyond the 16 years prescribed by the patent legislation by the effective use of trade marks.[24] This was to be achieved, he reasoned, not by the effect of a patent monopoly, but by the strong association between the patented medicine and its trade mark created in the mind of the consumer during the period of patent protection. Thus this association permitted the trade mark owner to maintain a marketing edge over generic medicine manufacturers even after the expiry of the patent monopoly. Since a trade mark could be extended in perpetuity Swan believed that a trade-marked medicine would insulate the patent owner from generic competition once the patent had expired. As it transpired Swan's hypothesis was confirmed by evidence. The Committee found (even with the benefit of the compulsory licensing provisions in the 1907 Act and the 1919 amendments to it) that prior to World War II, '[a] British manufacturer which obtained a compulsory license to manufacture a particular patented drug would find himself seriously handicapped through his inability to offer the drug of his manufacture to the medical profession and the public under the name by which they were accustomed to identify it'.[25] Indeed the Committee was so mistrustful of the pharmaceutical industry that it countenanced the repeal of section 38A(1) only on the condition that compulsory licensing provisions be reinforced. The Committee expressed the view that 'taken together, . . . [the compulsory licensing provisions as they were under the 1907 legislation were] not adequate to prevent patents being used to the prejudice of the public interest'.[26] When the Patents Act 1949 finally emerged, the results were fairly pragmatic.

THE UK PATENTS ACT 1949

The first refinement prohibited patents with respect to substances used in food or medicine which were produced by 'mere admixture' (section 10(1) (c)).

The second refinement enabled the compulsory licensing of medicines or food or surgical and curative devices for the purpose of ensuring that they should be 'available to the public at the lowest prices consistent with the patentees' deriving a reasonable advantage from their patent rights' (section 41(2)). With regard to these kinds of inventions, unlike the normal compulsory licensing provisions contained in sections 37–39, there were no prerequisite 'local working' thresholds. Price was the only relevant consideration, and once the Comptroller was satisfied that it was in the public interest to issue a licence under section 41, irrespective of the availability of the medicine or its production in the UK, a licence was issued entitling 'the licensee to make, use, exercise and vend the invention as a food or medicine, or for the purposes of the production of food or medicine or as or as part of a surgical or curative device' (section 41(3)). The policy behind this provision was to encourage generic pharmaceutical and medical device production within the UK so as to keep the price of medicines and food at affordable levels. The UK Government took heed of the Swan Committee's recommendations. This went much further than the original compulsory licensing provision first introduced in the 1883 legislation (section 22) and then strengthened in the 1907 legislation (section 24) and which made revocation another option to compulsory licensing. It also went further than the 1919 amendments (section 27), although it was similar to section 38A(3), which empowered and required the Comptroller to grant a compulsory licence with respect to a pharmaceutical unless he saw good reason not to.

The third refinement involved broadening pre-grant examination to include an assessment of frivolous inventions (that is those claiming 'anything obviously contrary to well-established natural laws') (section 10(1) (a)); inventions that were 'contrary to law or morality' (section 10(1)(b)); and inventions for 'a substance capable of being used as food or medicine' or 'a process producing such a substance' which was 'a mixture of known ingredients possessing only the aggregate of the known properties of the ingredients'(section 10(1)(c)). The last two were aimed at reinforcing the policy behind section 41 by halting these kinds of patent applications at the earliest possible stage in the application process.

The fourth refinement involved fine-tuning the grounds of pre-grant examination and the grounds of opposition (both introduced in the 1883 legislation) and revocation (first codified in section 25(2) of the 1932 amendments to the 1907 legislation). Under the Patents Act 1949 the patentability thresholds were enumerated in section 14 (the grounds of pre-grant opposition through the Comptroller) and section 32 (the grounds of post-grant revocation through the courts). Of the 20 grounds only four were found in both sections 14 and 32, while five were exclusive to an opposition (section 14), with the majority being exclusive to a revocation action (section 32). This distinction between opposition and revocation reflected the original idea when oppositions were first introduced in 1883, namely to keep the opposition administrative and relatively uncomplicated without the need for any oral examination of evidence. Revocation, on the other hand, permitted a more rigorous procedure permitting the greater scrutiny available in the courts. However Swan believed that justification for this distinction was no longer appropriate.

For instance the patentability threshold of 'obviousness' or 'lack of inventive step' had been codified in 1932 only as a ground of revocation (section 25(2)(f)), but in the 1949 legislation it was made a ground of opposition (section 14(1)(e)) as well as being retained as ground of revocation (section 32(1)(f)). In essence this meant that the Comptroller was required to assess the competing evidence of scientific and technical experts in order to come to a conclusion as to whether the invention was obvious to a person of ordinary skill in the relevant art, and although cross-examination was not part of that process, that being exclusively a matter for the courts, the inquiry as to obviousness was certainly not one that could be described as 'administrative'.

This doubling up was in effect a further protective measure. Not only did it permit the thorough scrutiny of patents by the Comptroller, but it enabled challenges to foreign patents, most of which were likely to be brought by British manufacturers.

In discussing obviousness the Swan Committee described something which 'obviously lacked inventive merit' to lack 'subject-matter'; that is it was not a 'manner of new manufacture' within the meaning of section 6 of the Statute of Monopolies 1623. Examples of such things included a discovery, a mathematical formula, a scientific observation, abstract ideas or products of nature. Prior to the codification of the grounds of revocation in 1932, section 6 of the Statute of Monopolies bundled all of the requirements of patentable subject matter into one generalized requirement: that it be a manner of new manufacture. An attack on the validity of a patent then did not require the challenger to plead specific grounds of invalidity, although there was a requirement to provide particulars as to how the alleged invention failed to meet the requirements of section 6.

However with the codification of the grounds of revocation that all changed. Finally there existed a distinction between something that was an *invention* and something that was a *patentable invention*. An invention was something capable of being the proper subject matter of the grant of letters patent, while a patentable invention was something that was an invention but also satisfied all other patentability criteria, namely that the invention was novel, involved an inventive step and was industrially applicable or useful. In practice what this meant was that if a patent application or patent was found to lack 'subject matter', in the sense that it was not an invention, it was invalid because it was not a 'manner of new manufacture' and there was no need further to consider the subsidiary 'patentability criteria', whereas if it was assumed or found to be an invention then its validity depended on it meeting the subsidiary patentability thresholds pertaining to those criteria. Consequently something was deemed to lack 'subject matter' if it was not considered to be something that had the potential for being a *patentable invention*. One example, specifically excluded by section 4(7) of the 1949 legislation, was a product of nature.[27]

The final refinement aided the bringing of revocation proceedings by removing the requirement that existed under section 25 of the 1907 legislation whereby a person was required 'to show that the patent he is seeking to revoke was obtained by fraud of his rights, or that he is otherwise injuriously affected by the patent in question'.[28] The Swan Committee recommended then that, rather than having to require such a person first to seek the 'fiat of the Attorney-General', 'any person' who felt aggrieved by the existence of a patent could present a petition for its revocation; and the legislation provided for just that.

The British Government thus continued the protectionist policies first built into the 1883 legislation and significantly strengthened by the 1907 legislation, and the amendments to that legislation in 1919 and 1932. However while obviousness was made a ground of opposition and a ground of revocation in 1949 legislation, the UK Parliament did not make it the subject of pre-grant examination. Once again the British patent profession was there to ameliorate the effect of these protections for the benefit of its foreign clients.

Obviousness however involved a contentious question which caused two members of the Swan Committee to dissent.[29] The point at issue was the ability of the Comptroller actually to carry out an obviousness assessment, given that unlike novelty, which involved only a review of documents which had been published in the UK prior to the filing of the patent application and which contained information relevant to its novelty, an obviousness assessment involved much more. Indeed obviousness demanded an appreciation not only of the kind of information that a person of ordinary skill in the relevant technology would have been appraised of at the time of the patent application, but required an assessment of how that person would have used that information to arrive at the alleged invention. This was a much more complex process of deduction, and one that the dissenters believed was simply not appropriate for the Comptroller at the pre-grant examination stage. Of particular concern to them was that a determination of subject-matter before grant necessitated an enquiry which involved taking oral evidence, and this was not only an expensive procedure but was not suited to a pre-grant examination.[30]

In spite of this dissent and the absence of obviousness as an area of inquiry under pre-grant examination, the underlying policy of economic protection remained firm; this was especially reinforced with regard to the ability of the Crown to make use of patented inventions (section 29). In this respect the original 1907 legislation, which followed the model provided by the 1883 legislation, had been amended in 1919 so that: (a) when the Crown made use of a patented invention, in the absence of an agreement as to terms the patent owner could seek the intervention of the court, which itself had the power to refer the dispute to an 'official referee' or 'arbitrator' (section 29(2)), and (b) although Crown use was no longer a ground of revocation, government departments could insist on requiring the patent owner to assign the ownership of the patent to the Crown (section 30).

Ultimately however the Swan Committee noted in its final report that there was a 'widely expressed desire for revision and amendment to section 29'.[31] This desire unsurprisingly came from the British Government's own departments, which sought to widen the Crown use powers to cover circumstances beyond merely 'the services of the Crown'. Having become accustomed to the flexibility provided through the exercise of emergency wartime powers, government departments were keen to continue that advantage during peacetime. The principal purpose, as they submitted, was to circumvent the delays associated with obtaining permission from the patent owner or a compulsory licence from the Comptroller. The Swan Committee remained circumspect and rejected these submissions; it recommended instead, 'in times of war' or 'emergency', the 'special measures' that were passed into law as a result of World War II, 'should form a permanent sub-section of s.29'.[32] The Attlee Government[33] concurred; but in section 46(5) of the 1949 legislation it provided a safety net which effectively ensured that government departments could, if it appeared to such departments to be 'contrary to the public interest', make whatever use of a patented invention they deemed appropriate. Effectively this provision enabled the Crown to intervene quite readily, as the phrase 'contrary to the public interest' was capable of being broadly interpreted. The legislation also introduced the ability to revoke a British patent in respect of Crown use by providing in section 32(3) for revocation if the patent owner had 'without reasonable cause failed to comply with a [British] government request to make, use or exercise the invention for services to the government on reasonable terms'. This gave the British Government some considerable ammunition in negotiating with obstinate patent owners and, reasonably, would have been used if and when government officials perceived that there was a need to press the point during negotiations.

Furthermore in the event of a declared emergency any patent could be used on such terms as the British Government deemed 'necessary and appropriate' to meet the specific purposes of the emergency. The prescribed emergencies were not however confined to war, and included 'the maintenance of supplies and services essential to the life of the community'; 'securing a sufficiency of supplies and services essential to the well-being of the community'; 'promoting the productivity of industry, commerce and agriculture'; 'fostering and directing exports and reducing imports, or imports of any classes, from all or any countries and for redressing the balance of trade'; and 'ensuring that the whole resources of the community are available for use, and are used, in a manner best calculated to serve the interests of the community' (section 49(1)). The 'period of emergency' in operation at the time of the legislation was stipulated to end on 10 December 1950, but could be extended, for any of the stated emergencies, at any time 'by Order in Council' (section 49(2)). Clearly the categories of emergency above had little to do with a military war, and in fact were obviously directed to economic events which were broad enough to cover situations which were beyond what would normally be considered 'an emergency'.

The ability to seek a compulsory licence on various grounds was seen by the Swan Committee and the UK Government to be an important mechanism through which the interests of the patent owner could be balanced with the protection of the British economy. Moreover the socio-economic protections incorporated into the Patents Act 1949 were a political acknowledgement that patents should not be allowed to interfere with Britain's economic development. Policies for the growth of British enterprise and the employment that they provided were central planks in the platform of Britain's economic development, and by effect of these legislative safety valves the message was reinforced that the unbridled enthusiasm which patent attorneys, inventors and industry had for the patent system was not shared by either British policy-makers or the UK Parliament.

However as with most legislative changes the full implications of the amendments were not necessarily foreseeable at the time, and certainly not in 1932 when the grounds of opposition and revocation were first introduced into the patents legislation. For instance the kinds of technological advances made in the field of bioscience during and after World War II were not; and in 1970 it was the House of Lords in *American Cyanamid Co v Upjohn Co* [1970] 3 All ER 785 which had to deal with the consequences.

This appeal concerned a UK patent granted over the antibiotic porfiromycin and, particularly, whether the obligation to make a proper disclosure of the claimed invention was satisfied. At issue was the value of the social contract, established as a principle of common law in 1780 in *Liardet v Johnson,* and whether the patent owner, American Cyanamid, had paid a sufficient price to justify the grant of a British patent.

Cyanamid had deposited three strains of *streptomyces verticillatus* with the American Type Culture Collection (ATCC). These strains were described as 'new' because they concerned human-induced mutations of the naturally occurring bacterium *streptomyces verticillatus* which produced what was claimed to be a new antibiotic. The issue arose because a condition of the deposit imposed upon the ATCC by Cyanamid was that the micro-organisms not be made publicly available until the grant of a US patent, eventually made in September 1965. In the meantime in August 1963 a British patent was granted, but when in September 1963 Upjohn's request for access was refused it sought to have the British patent revoked.

In his majority decision Lord Reid made this observation:

> If the present problem had arisen [before 1949] I am very much inclined to think that the court would have held that it was contrary to the general intendment

of the Statute of Monopolies 1623 and subsequent legislation that a patentee should be entitled to have the advantage of his patent and yet be able to preserve his monopoly after the expiry of his patent by refusing to take such steps as were necessary to enable others to carry out his invention when his patent had expired. If this could only be done by making his strain of micro-organism available to others and could not be done by giving information in his specification, then I think that the patentee would have been required to choose between making his organism available and having his patent repealed. The law was still sufficiently flexible for the court to be able to formulate a new ground of repeal or revocation to meet a new situation. *But the law was altered by the Patents Act 1949.*[34]

While the substance of Lord Reid's statement is not disputed, the law that he was referring to was changed, not in 1949, but in 1932 when the grounds of revocation were codified. It was that change which caused the loss of judicial 'flexibility'; and unfortunately what was neither foreseeable at that time nor in 1949 when the new patents legislation was passed was how the codification of the grounds of revocation would narrow the ability of the courts to scrutinize the value of that consideration as technologies evolved through the latter half of the twentieth century. It is likely that this was not the intention of the UK Parliament in 1932, especially given the protectionist agenda which was built into the 1907 legislation and the prevailing economic circumstances of the time, just as it was not likely in 1949 that the UK Parliament would allow the price of medicines, food and surgical devices to be subject to the whims of industrialists. The potential for technology to unravel these protections was obviously not anticipated by the Swan Committee either, and given that it was not until the mid-1960s that these kinds of patents materialized this oversight was completely understandable. Nonetheless by watering down section 38A while continuing to constrain the judicial scrutiny of the value of the social contract, the Committee unwittingly made the British economy vulnerable to patent abuse.

Consequently the ability of the common law to adjust to changing circumstances while tailoring the statutory language to maintain the protectionist policy inherent in the patent legislation was undermined. This was the reason his Lordship felt compelled to make this statement; he wanted British politicians and policy-makers to appreciate the need to keep abreast of issues and changes as and when they arise.

By the mid-1960s it was obvious that patent law was not coping well with bioscience. British policy-makers were under the influence of the powerful pharmaceutical lobby which was determined to increase the stable of patent monopolies, critical to achieving high prices for pharmaceuticals, and an addendum to the industry's paradigm was developing – patent law should be flexible enough to cover all technological development.

However if British patent law was being stretched by biosciences, within a decade of Lord Reid's decision internationalism was to come to its aid in the form of an international treaty specifically formulated to deal with the patenting of micro-organisms. The Budapest Treaty (as it is commonly known) dealt with the recognition of the deposit of micro-organisms into accredited depositories and patents over micro-organisms.

Nonetheless Lord Wilberforce, also in the majority in *Cyanamid*, expressed the modern view that patent law was no longer a mechanism of economic protection. He said, 'the nature of this "consideration" has been evolutionary'; and while its objective in the seventeenth century 'was found in the introduction of a new trade into the country', in the twentieth century 'the benefit has been seen rather in the general advantage of improved techniques coupled with the assurance that at the end of the monopoly period these improvements would pass into the public domain'. In the end the House of Lords held that the statutory requirements under the 1949 legislation had been met and the patent was held to be valid – only because there was no specific threshold requirement in the Patents Act 1949 for the deposit of and unconditional public access to a micro-organism at an accredited depository.

Unfortunately what Lords Wilberforce and Reid's historical reconstruction of patent law had failed satisfactorily to address was that, without access to the micro-organism, no one could make the antibiotic – which, after all, was what the patent monopoly was about. Whether or not there was a specific patent threshold requiring the deposit of a micro-organism was not the point. When the British patent was granted there was incomplete disclosure.

Beyond this issue the appeal also highlighted how patent litigants could steer the court's scrutiny away from issues which were commercially and legally unpalatable to patent owners. The attack was limited to three grounds out of a possible 12. One of the grounds available to Upjohn but not alleged was that the invention was not a manner of new manufacture (section 32(1)(d)). Lord Diplock, who disagreed with Lords Wilberforce and Reid, held the patent invalid, but he observed:

> Both parties to this appeal are members of the pharmaceutical industry and engage in this kind of research. Both are the owners of patents for new antibiotics in many countries throughout the world. The specifications for those granted in the United Kingdom are substantially in the form of the specification which is now in suit. *It is not in the interest of either party that any shadow of doubt should be cast on the eligibility of this type of discovery to protection as an 'invention' under the Patents Act 1949, or on the validity of the form of the specification.* This has been common ground and your Lordships have been deprived of the advantage of any critical analysis of a concept of invention which is wide enough to embrace the kind of discovery with which this appeal is concerned or of the consequences of applying that concept to the requirements of the Act as to the kind of information to be disclosed in the specification itself.[35]

His observation is as true today as the day he made it. Although present day controversy rages over the patentability of stem cells and genes, contemporary patent litigants have carefully avoided challenging each other's patents on the grounds that these things are not 'inventions', for the same reason that the antibiotic manufacturers in this case did not raise this argument to challenge the patent.

THE NATIONAL HEALTH SERVICE, THE PHARMACEUTICAL INDUSTRY AND THE EEC

In 1931 the Sargant Committee noted, '[d]uring the War it became apparent that Great Britain was suffering from a lack of medicine and drugs, many of which were the subject of patent rights in this country'.[36] This was also true in the United States. The Committee observed that the ability of German pharmaceutical and chemical companies to control the production of medicines through British patents made the British economy vulnerable. The Committee also observed, 'in many European countries (e.g., France and Germany, Switzerland) such substances were not capable of protection under the patent laws of those countries'. This did two things. First it directed innovation towards chemical processes, and secondly it prevented domestic and foreign inventors from obtaining monopolies on chemical substances as products. As a result the Committee noted that in 1919 'it was considered expedient to modify to some extent the monopoly consequent on the existence of patent rights in regard to such substances'.[37]

Accordingly the Committee felt comfortable, in the context of its review of the 1907 patents legislation, in recommending the retention of both the ban on the patenting of chemical substances and the Comptroller's power to revoke patents (section 38A, 1919). The Committee believed that foreign pharmaceutical patent owners were, as a result, more likely to grant licences in the UK on reasonable commercial terms.

The subsequent Great Depression and World War II not only reinforced this thinking but also led to the establishment of a universal system of social security which would protect all British citizens. The *Social Insurance and Allied Services Report* was presented to the British government in November 1942. The committee responsible was chaired by William Beveridge.[38] Not only was the scheme it proposed revolutionary, it was also very popular. Within days of its public release in December 1942 some 70 000 copies of the Report were sold, and in 1948 the National Health Service (NHS) was established. Among other things the NHS provided prescription medicines free of charge, so from that moment the price of public medicines became a fiscal issue for the British Government and the availability of medicines was germane to the Swan Committee's enquiry into the British patent system.

Now that the availability of medicines at reasonable prices was a national priority, the Comptroller was required to grant a compulsory licence (unless it was apparent to him that there were 'good reasons for refusing the application') to any applicant on such terms as he thought fit (section 41(1)(c)). This made it difficult for the Comptroller to reject an application for a compulsory licence. Moreover section 41(2) specified that food, medicines and surgical and curative devices were to be made 'available to the public at the lowest prices consistent with the patentees deriving a reasonable advantage from their patent rights'. This required a balancing act, but British policy-makers recognized that without this kind of mechanism they would not be able to keep a lid on the price of food or medicines. Indeed without it they expected the opposite, given that patent monopolies generally encouraged higher than normal prices.

However the Swan Committee's recommendation that compulsory licensing, not revocation, be the only mechanism under which this balancing act was to be performed was to have significant ramifications for the British health budget. What was not obvious at the time was how the cost of medicines would skyrocket, despite the British Government's attempt to control rising prices through compulsory licensing of British patents over medicines and surgical devices. British policy-makers understood the tension between competition and the positive benefits which this provided to the British economy in the form of lower prices, and patent monopolies which constrained competition and gave patent owners the ability to charge higher prices for their patented medicines.

BOX 3.2   THE PHARMACEUTICAL PRICE REGULATION SCHEME

'In total, we estimate that the NHS spent about £11 billion in 2005 on pharmaceuticals across the UK, reflecting both reimbursement of pharmacies for dispensing drugs in primary care and direct expenditure by hospitals. This is between 12 and 18 per cent of NHS expenditure on services in all four countries of the UK. Of this total, we estimate that about £8 billion was spent on branded drugs and £3 billion on generics.' (p16)

UK Office of Fair Trading, February 2007.

Pharmaceutical companies responded by skilfully employing trade marked medicines to neutralize the policy behind section 41. Although Swan himself was well aware of the potential for this kind of sabotage, given that he had written about it in 1908, his Committee had completely underestimated the creativity of pharmaceutical companies in using trade marks to thwart the effect of compulsory licensing. The problem which quickly confronted the British Government was the association between quality and trade-marked medicines. Doctors preferred prescribing the higher priced trade-marked medicines even though lower priced generic forms of these medicines were available.[39] Through the use of advertising, marketing and the persuasiveness of its travelling salespeople, the British Government found that the medical profession was influenced to prescribe the 'safer' and more 'efficacious' trade-marked medicines.[40] Soon the relationship between the doctor and pharmaceutical companies became much more entrenched as pharmaceutical companies began providing their clients with innocuous gifts such as pens, notepads and paperweights suitably inscribed with the name of the pharmaceutical company and one of its trade-marked medicines. Although it was considered unethical for doctors to receive financial gifts, their participation in the clinical trials and the sponsorship of medical meetings and conferences by pharmaceutical companies were convenient ways of sidestepping the ethical dilemma. It also meant that even when patents had expired trade-marked medicines could still attract patent-like prices.

Medicines which were tailored to deal with specific illnesses were another unforeseen headache. These 'magic bullets', first available in 1914 with Salvarsan (used to treat syphilis), had become available for a wider range of ailments. Antibiotics for instance, the new miracle drugs of the time, were both a blessing and a curse because they provided an unprecedented ability to treat illness, but their understandable popularity among doctors meant that they were often over-prescribed.

BOX 3.3   UK STANDING MEDICAL ADVISORY COMMITTEE REPORT, 'THE PATH OF LEAST RESISTANCE', 1997

'GPs, hospital physicians, surgeons, paediatricians or obstetricians continue to prescribe antibiotics, sometimes for inappropriate indications, in inappropriate doses, for inappropriate lengths of time [so that] . . . rates of resistance to penicillin and erythromycin had increased'.

So within a decade the NHS had become a serious financial burden for the British Government on two fronts: first, a prescribing bias of doctors in favour of trade-marked medicines and, secondly, the general increase in the prescribing of medicines to treat bacterial and viral infections.

Judy Slinn's study of the regulation of prescription pharmaceuticals in the UK between 1948 and 1967[41] confirmed that 'the total cost of running the NHS was considerably higher than had been anticipated and proved to be something of a shock to ministers and civil servants'. According to her, while '6.8 million prescriptions were dispensed by chemists' in June 1948, the month before the start of the NHS, 'by September . . . the monthly figure had doubled to 13.6 million'.[42] Needless to say the cost of the NHS led to a series of Parliamentary inquiries the principal objective of which was to investigate and recommend ways of containing the ballooning health budget. However by the mid-1950s the price of medicines was not the only issue.

Although penicillin was discovered in 1927 by Alexander Fleming,[43] a doctor at St Mary's Hospital in London, and a medicinal version developed for human use in 1941 by Howard Florey,[44] Ernst Chain[45] and Norman Heatley,[46] scientists at Oxford University, it was an American government scientist with the US Department of Agriculture, Andrew Moyer,[47] who was the first to patent a method of its commercial-scale production in 1948. So although scientists at British institutions had discovered penicillin and proved its efficacy as a human medicine, by the 1950s the antibiotic patent race was being convincingly won by American pharmaceutical companies which went on to find different and more potent antibiotics, such as streptomycin, aureomycin, chlormeycetin, terramycin and tetracycline, and patented them.

In what was portrayed as a lost business opportunity by the British pharmaceutical industry, British policy-makers and politicians were told that to regain the lead or, at least, to neutralize the impact that a liberal American patenting policy and the aggressive marketing tactics employed by American pharmaceutical companies were having on the NHS, a new approach to patents over pharmaceuticals was required. Indeed if they were to achieve the social objectives of providing universal health care and a social service net, they would need, like the United States, to encourage local pharmaceutical companies to produce new and patentable medicines. In this way the benefit of the higher prices paid for patented medicines would filter back into the British Treasury through the profits made by British pharmaceutical companies on potential sales made, not only within the UK, but throughout the world, and particularly on sales made in the United States. Suddenly it was thought expedient that the purchase of British patented and trade-marked medicines by other countries could off-set the burden that the NHS had become.

What was also apparent was how investment in research and development (R&D) in pharmaceuticals was a vital element of the strategy to maintain local pharmaceutical manufacturing capacity. To create economies of scale in terms of R&D some British pharmaceutical companies began acquiring smaller companies. Glaxo Laboratories for instance did just that under the chairmanship of Harry Jephcott,[48] swallowing up Allen & Hanburys, Evans Medical and British Drug Houses during the 1950s.

THE BIRTH OF THE GREAT LIE – THE PHARMACEUTICAL-PATENT PARADIGM

During the 1950s Glaxo also embarked upon an investment drive focused on finding foreign markets for its production. Together with Michael Perrin,[49] chairman of Wellcome from 1953, and Leslie Lazell,[50] chairman of Beecham, they guided the development of government policies. Their careful persuasion slowly softened the resolve of British policy-makers who were, at the time, more inclined to impose price control on pharmaceuticals than to grant British pharmaceutical companies any pricing latitude. As Slinn found, eventually British policy-makers accepted 'the dominant paradigm of the pharmaceutical industry', which was '[c]ompetition in the industry . . . depended on innovation rather than on price'.[51]

Achieving this paradigm shift was not straightforward. Throughout the 1950s the UK Treasury had remained antagonistic towards the Association of the British Pharmaceutical Industry (ABPI) which, as the mouthpiece of the British pharmaceutical industry, advocated a more liberal pricing structure. Moreover the UK Department of Health began investigating the phenomenon which had led to a massive increase in the prescription by doctors of patented medicines. The immediate target of its inquiry focused on the British medical profession which, it was alleged, had no real concern about the cost of the medicines it was prescribing. Such an allegation simply raised the hackles of the medical profession who retaliated by accusing Treasury of interfering with their Hippocratic oath – the subsequent inquiry was inconclusive on this point. Jephcott and Glaxo Laboratories also played important roles before the Guillebaud Committee, charged in 1953 with finding a solution to the cost of the NHS, and they criticized all and any pharmaceutical pricing proposals. To the ABPI and Jephcott price control was deplorable.

According to his biographer, Richard Davonport-Hines, Jephcott 'was receptive to all new scientific ideas, keenly interested in sales of pharmaceutical products and an astute business strategist who understood every aspect of company administration'.[52] He had served as an advisor to the

Ministry of Food between 1941 and 1943 and was appointed chairman of the Therapeutic Research Corporation (TRC), established in 1941 by Boots, British Drug Houses, Wellcome, Glaxo (which was itself established by Jephcott in 1935) and joined by May & Baker and ICI in 1942. Its function was to consolidate R&D for the war effort, particularly ensuring that the British government's production targets for penicillin were met. In this respect the British Government had provided £2 million during World War II for the construction of six factories for penicillin production, with the result that by the end of World War II British production of penicillin exceeded US production.

After World War II and with American investment in pharmaceutical production in Europe increasing significantly during the 1950s, the British Government was on the horns of a dilemma. On the one hand it was a matter of national security that the UK maintain a domestic pharmaceutical manufacturing capacity that produced medicines at a low price for the NHS, but on the other hand R&D had to be funded, and for this Jephcott argued that it was essential that British pharmaceutical companies remain profitable by being able to charge higher prices for patented medicines. In effect the higher price was needed in order to compensate or induce pharmaceutical companies to make the necessary investment needed to off-set the high risks inherent in the development of new medicines.

That Jephcott influenced British policy development is clear when one notes the role that he played as an advisor to the government during World War II, the adjustments that were made to pricing for the NHS under the Voluntary Price Regulation Scheme and, according to Davenport-Hines, 'his appreciation of the importance of patent law in pharmaceuticals'. Under these circumstances it is not surprising that UK policy-makers finally capitulated. The result was the Voluntary Price Regulation Scheme (VPRS). As TAB Corley observed in his study on the British pharmaceutical industry, the VPRS 'fixed drug prices at levels to allow manufacturers a reasonable return on investment'.[53] This was also consistent with the compulsory licensing powers under section 41 (which required the Comptroller to consider 'the patentees' deriving a reasonable advantage from their patent rights'). According to Corley, '[i]ts formula encouraged expenditure on innovative R&D that promised to yield good returns, and large exporters received added incentives', but 'it also penalised firms that were merely followers'.[54]

Of course a government rationale had to be adopted to justify the fact that under this scheme – which as its name suggests was 'voluntary' – pharmaceutical manufacturers were given three years' grace from any price control. The rationale provided by the ABPI was that this grace period contributed to the recoupment of very risky R&D. Under the VPRS the

British taxpayer in essence was to subsidize the R&D of patented medicines which would then be purchased by the NHS at monopoly prices for three years. The electorate required an explanation, and thus the pharmaceutical patent paradigm was born.

SCIENCE GIVES CREDENCE TO THE PHARMACEUTICAL-PATENT PARADIGM

The rationale for this paradigm shift was subsequently reinforced by scientists. One was Ernst Chain, who shared the Nobel Prize in 1945 with Howard Florey and Alexander Fleming for the discovery and development of penicillin as a medicine, and with respect to which no patent was sought. In fact Chain and Florey had argued bitterly over whether to patent the process for the production of penicillin. Florey had raised the issue with his superiors, but it was considered unethical. This attitude not only infuriated Chain, who had studied and worked in Germany and was familiar with the German tradition of patenting pharmaceutical processes, but it remained a sore point among people like Jephcott, especially after a US scientist was granted a US patent in 1948 for a process for the production of penicillin.

After spending nearly 20 years in self-imposed exile at the Istituto Superiore di Sanità in Rome, Chain returned to the UK in 1963 having accepted the influential Chair of Biochemistry at Imperial College in London. In June 1963 he was invited by the Royal Society of Arts to deliver a paper. That paper was entitled 'Academic and Industrial Contributions to Drug Research' and he used the occasion to broadcast his opinion: 'drugs are one of the greatest blessings – perhaps *the* greatest blessing – of our time'.[55]

Rebuffed 20 years earlier by a British ethic that Chain abhorred,[56] Chain, now holding an important professorial chair in England, was not about to miss the opportunity of driving the message home that it was certainly no longer true that the 'lion's share'[57] in chemical and biological scientific research was being undertaken by academic laboratories. The British reluctance to commercialize research through the collaboration between academic science and pharmaceutical companies could no longer be justified, and Chain stressed to his influential audience that only 'by the closest collaboration between academic and industrial research laboratories'[58] would the British national interest be best served. The painful history over penicillin was re-emphasized. He spelt out how a substance which had 'remarkable curative powers in severe bacterial infections'[59] was perfected in under-funded academic laboratories which did not have the resources to turn this important discovery into a commercially available medicine.

As 'dramatic'[60] as their research findings were, neither they nor the British or American Government could convince British pharmaceutical companies to commit to commercial-scale production. According to Chain, 'though they showed polite interest in what was undoubtedly a remarkable experimental result',[61] the British pharmaceutical industry believed 'the idea of developing the biological production process of penicillin to the stage where the substance could be a drug of practical value as completely unrealistic and Utopian'.[62] Chain could see the time had come for the UK Government to make it attractive for the British pharmaceutical industry to invest in the research undertaken in academic or governmental laboratories. The pharmaceutical industry, he believed, was 'essentially productive, and not parasitic, in nature',[63] being 'one of the most positive assets to our form of society'.[64] He chastised his audience, warning them that 'no pharmaceutical industry – no new drugs'.[65] He was not, he said, 'naïve enough to claim that everything is of a pure white within the pharmaceutical industry',[66] but he made it clear that '[he preferred] to have an active pharmaceutical industry and life-saving drugs, accepting in the bargain a few abuses, than to have a system in which theoretically no abuses are possible, but which produce no drugs'.[67]

Chain's recounting of the penicillin history was deliberately designed to rub salt into British wounds. Not only was it an American who ultimately claimed to have perfected the mass production of penicillin, but it was America, a country that allowed the patenting of chemical substances, which took first prize – the patent. That a British pharmaceutical industry, even with the research presented to it on a silver platter by one of Britain's leading academic institutions, Oxford, was reluctant to manufacture penicillin in commercial quantities demonstrated, according to Chain, how much of an incentive was needed before this industry would risk its capital.

PHARMACEUTICAL PRICE CONTROL (LORD SAINSBURY) v PHARMACEUTICAL PATENTS (SIR MAURICE BANKS)

The arguments that businessmen like Jephcott, Perrin and Lazell had made in the 1950s and that scientists like Chain were now making in 1960s were ultimately considered by two separate inquiries which had different purposes: An *Enquiry into the Relationship of the Pharmaceutical Industry with the National Health Service,* conducted between June 1965 and September 1967,[68] and an *Enquiry to Examine the Patent System and Patent Law,* conducted between May 1967 and May 1970.[69]

The first was chaired by Alan Sainsbury[70] and the second by Maurice Banks.[71] Both were highly respected men with significant business experience. Sainsbury became chairman of his family business, the grocer and food giant J Sainsbury, in 1956 and Banks rose through the ranks of British Petroleum to retire as a deputy chairman in 1967, after 43 years' service.

Although it was not apparent when the Sainsbury Committee commenced its enquiry into the NHS, these two enquiries would eventually confront each other. Partly due to their timing and partly because those responsible for their establishment failed to foresee the UK joining the EEC, both committees were frustrated by their terms of reference: the Sainsbury Committee in its ability to deal with patent law and the Banks Committee in its ability to deal with drugs and medicines.

The Sainsbury Committee expressed its frustration in rather diplomatic language, acknowledging 'that any analysis or proposals we might make may have wider implications' and, in terms of the relationship between patents and the pharmaceutical industry, stressed that without the ability to enquire into that relationship, 'we cannot assume (and we must emphasise this) that the pharmaceutical industry is necessarily a case apart, to be treated differently from all other industries'.[72] Indeed the Committee appreciated that the problem of recommending changes to the patent system to meet the particular exigencies of the NHS could apply generally to all industries. Accordingly it believed that '[a]ny changes proposed would clearly be difficult to implement without a careful consideration of their wider implications for the patent law generally and might involve some general modifications of it'.[73]

The Banks Committee, on the other hand, did not reciprocate that diplomacy. Rather it believed that while 'it is in the public interest that supplies of drugs should be freely available at reasonable prices, . . . it is equally in the public interest that new and better drugs should be discovered'.[74] This was not a surprising attitude, especially as Banks, coming from BP, was more sympathetic to the business imperative. His Committee believed:

> we should have in this country a soundly-based pharmaceutical industry able to make a contribution to the national economy, not only by providing the drugs we need but also by undertaking the research necessary for the discovery of new remedies and by using the results of this to maintain and expand the industry's export market.[75]

So, while Sainsbury's Committee was concerned to control the price of medicines and saw the pharmaceutical industry's use of the British patent system as the problem, the Bank's Committee had embraced Chain's message. The tension between these Committees was apparent, particularly by 1970 when the UK Government's desire to join the EEC meant that

Banks' approach was more compatible. The Government needed to be seen as conforming to the EEC's single patent policy – a policy that was to apply throughout the EEC, which had also embraced the new pharmaceutical patent paradigm.[76]

FOREIGN DOMINATION OF BRITISH PHARMACEUTICALS

In reality by 1965 the British pharmaceutical market was supplied mainly by foreign-owned companies. According to data presented to the Sainsbury Committee, American pharmaceutical companies supplied 49 per cent, the Swiss supplied 14 per cent and other European countries supplied 10 per cent. Only 25 per cent was supplied by British manufacturers, with the vast majority of these being generic medicines.[77] These data suggested that the ABPI was representing the interests of foreign-owned pharmaceutical companies – mainly Swiss and American. Motivated by the desire to reduce the patenting costs caused by differences in national patent systems and annoyed by the differing levels of patent protection afforded to pharmaceutical products across the globe, the pharmaceutical industry began to mobilize on a united front. Already able to patent pharmaceutical substances in a substantial market like the United States, American pharmaceutical companies wanted the world's patent systems to be brought into line with that of the United States. Having successfully persuaded the Swan Committee to recommend the removal of the subject matter restriction on the patenting of chemical substances, 11 years later the ABPI remained dissatisfied with the retention of compulsory licensing. It 'strongly opposed'[78] the continuing discriminatory treatment of pharmaceuticals brought about by the compulsory licensing regime under section 41 and proposed that medicines not be 'treated differently from other products'.[79] The Committee noted the ABPI's proposed reforms of the British patent system included permitting 'the patenting of new uses for known compounds',[80] and the extension of the patent term to 20 years.[81] According to the ABPI, 'only by the grant of "more effective protection . . . [could] the pharmaceutical industry continue its contribution to the advancement of medical science and to the national economy"'.[82]

Unfortunately for the ABPI, the Sainsbury Committee was unsympathetic. Apart from having to keep the price of medicines low (an economic priority for the Government, especially as the National Health Service provided prescription medicines free of charge), the Committee was suspicious of an organization that it believed was no longer British. Therefore not only did it reject the ABPI's submission regarding the extension of the British patent term from 16 to 20 years, but expressed the view that the existing term was: 'too long, and that the position could be met by a shorter period of complete protection'.[83] With regard to the need to 'induce adequate research and development and innovation in the pharmaceutical industry',[84] the Committee preferred the idea of 'a shorter period of monopoly for the patentee followed by a right to receive royalties under a licence of right'.[85] Moreover it rejected the ABPI's criticism that the main compulsory licensing provision, section 41, had been 'little used'[86] by explaining that this was due to the 'inefficient'[87] administration by the Comptroller of Patents which 'seemed to have discouraged or delayed potential licensees'.[88] Rather than recommending the repeal of compulsory licensing, the Committee expressed the view that through the 'considerable simplification and hastening of existing procedures'[89] compulsory licensing applications would be encouraged.

BOX 3.4   IBM'S EUROPEAN PATENT PROPOSAL

In July 2007 IBM proposed that a pan-European patent should not permit the patent owner to restrain anyone from exploiting the invention, but that the patents be endorsed 'licenses of right'. This would enable use of the invention on the payment of a reasonable royalty to the patent owner. IBM saw this as a 'positive approach'. However, there is nothing new in this idea. In fact President Roosevelt suggested to Congress on 29 April 1938: 'future patents might be made available for use by any one upon payment of appropriate royalties'. Roosevelt was particularly concerned to ensure that patent laws not be used to 'suppress inventions' and 'create industrial monopolies'. Indeed he was confident: 'once it is realized that business monopoly in America paralyzes the system of free enterprise on which it is grafted, and is as fatal to those who manipulate it as to the people who suffer beneath its impositions, action by the government to eliminate these artificial restraints will be welcomed by industry throughout the nation'. Furthermore under the British patent system prior to 1949 'Licences of Right' could be granted by the Comptroller of Patents and the Sargant Committee Report (1931).[90]

The result was a complete rejection of the pharmaceutical-patent paradigm. The Committee believed that a system of non-exclusive patent licensing would not only provide an adequate incentive for pharmaceutical

R&D, but would also mitigate against high prices for medicines. The ABPI had failed to bring a convincing case before the Sainsbury Committee; but even before its Report was presented to the British Government in September 1967, the Banks Committee had commenced its enquiry, and before this committee the ABPI was determined not to fail. Seizing upon the Sainsbury Committee's concession that it was unable to deal with the patent system in general terms because its terms of reference were limited to the NHS,[91] the Banks Committee, having terms of reference directly dealing with the patent system, with the encouragement of the ABPI proceeded to sanitize any adverse comment that the Sainsbury Committee had expressed about the relationship between the pharmaceutical industry and the patent system. In its Report presented to the Government in July 1970 the Bank's Committee did three things.

First it portrayed the British patent system as being out of step with the rest of the world with regard to 'the treatment accorded to drugs',[92] by pointing out that the patent laws of 'the United States and most of Western European countries do not distinguish between drugs and other chemical substances'.[93] This was quite misleading, since Germany's amendment to its patent law to allow for the protection of chemical substances had taken place only in September 1967 and most other European countries continued expressly to prohibit patents over pharmaceutical products.

Next it dismissed the Sainsbury Committee's recommendations for streamlining the administrative processes to improve the effectiveness of compulsory licensing, by arguing that whatever were the reasons behind section 41 (as recommended by the Swan Committee in 1947), it had 'not generally worked in the way in which it was intended'.[94]

Finally it redirected attention to the Crown use provisions of section 46, a provision which enabled the Government (as opposed to third parties) to use 'any patented medicine for the services of the Crown', and to sections 40 and 32(3), which respectively covered the Government's permission for the endorsement of patents as 'licenses of right' and the Government's ability to revoke a patent on the ground that the patentee has failed to make the patented invention available for government service upon reasonable terms. It suggested that instead of using section 41 the NHS, as a government service, could counter the price impact of a patented medicine by using section 46 to create a 'license of right', thereby permitting generic medicines to be legally supplied to the NHS at a lower price.[95]

While it was true however that the Sainsbury Committee had found section 41 underutilized, it also believed that it was beneficial to retain non-government compulsory licensing because it was important for generic drug producers or suppliers to be able to use the threat of an application to seek commercial licences to manufacture and supply generic patented medicines on reasonable commercial terms. Generic manufacturers, which made up the bulk of British-owned pharmaceutical companies, had successfully applied for 21 compulsory licences for medicines between 1960 and 1965.[96] Hence section 41 had not only encouraged 'extensive cross-licensing',[97] but had produced 'noticeable [downward] effects on certain price levels'.[98] The Committee found that while prescription medicines were a matter between the doctor and the NHS, many over-the-counter medicines were purchased directly by the public, and these medicines could not be brought within section 46.[99] Therefore the repeal of section 41 would have raised the price of trade-marked over-the-counter medicines.

GOVERNMENTS GIVE CREDENCE TO THE PHARMACEUTICAL-PATENT PARADIGM

By the time of the Banks Committee's Report in 1970 British politicians were ripe for manipulation by the ABPI. The steps towards patent law harmonization that had taken place in Europe during the 1960s, starting with the Strasbourg Convention in 1963 and continuing with the Draft European Patent Convention[100] circulated later that year by Kurt Haertel, President of the German Patent Office, required the complete obliteration of nationalistic-protectionist agendas. Furthermore the ABPI believed that once the British Government had joined the EEC, it would be only a matter of time before it could, through the patent law harmonization process, seek to constrain the conditions upon which EEC members could employ government compulsory licensing. This, as it turned out, is precisely what was to transpire.

Having laid the groundwork for change the Banks Committee ultimately made recommendations that suited both the ABPI and a thankful British Government – a government which was at pains to join the EEC.[101] These were that section 41 be repealed;[102] 'pharmaceutical substances . . . continue to be patentable';[103] and the term of a British patent be extended from 16 to 20 years.[104] In what was indeed a remarkable turnaround in fortunes for the ABPI, within three years the Sainsbury Committee Report had been thrown into the Parliamentary dustbin.

This was a remarkable achievement by Banks (who was then knighted for his services), especially as the running cost of the NHS had blown out beyond all expectation.[105] In fact the Sainsbury Committee's enquiry was one of a number that had been commissioned by successive British Governments since the NHS had started operation, all desperate to find ways of slowing the growth in prescriptions. So in spite of the fact that the Banks Committee's recommendations roughly translated into higher prices for medicines, the British Government was ultimately persuaded to adopt a patent model which was consistent with the 'dominant paradigm of the pharmaceutical industry . . . competition in the industry, therefore, depended on innovation rather than on price'.[106]

AMERICAN PATENT LAW REFORM AFTER WORLD WAR II

The US Congress waited until 1952 to pass new patent legislation.[107] Since intellectual property was not an item on the Bretton Woods agenda nor relevant to the GATT, nor was it something that the US Congress believed should change very much, the United States continued with a protectionist agenda despite the free trade rhetoric. Nonetheless while it was the most extensive legislative revision of the US patent system since the US Patents Act 1836, only a few of the revisions were substantive. Indeed the real changes in the intervening period were made by the courts. A statement by Justice Jackson, a US Supreme Court judge, in 1949 saying 'the only patent that is valid is one which this Court has not been able to get its hands on'[108] exemplified the Court's attitude towards patents – a view which had been encouraged by Roosevelt's preoccupation with the antitrust effect of patents.[109] Jackson was frustrated that his colleagues on the bench were not getting the message that a new world order required a new approach to patents. What needed to change was not the written law so much as the attitude towards that law.[110]

The new definition of patentable subject matter in 1952 was: 'any new and useful process, machine, manufacture, or composition of matter, or any new and useful improvement thereof' (section 101). Under the old law it was any 'new and useful *art* . . .'. This new word, process, was defined to mean '[any] process, art or method, and includes a new use of a known process, machine, manufacture, composition of matter, or material' (section 100(b)).

A more significant change was made with respect to the obviousness condition of patentability, first established nearly a century earlier in the case of *Hotchkiss v Greenwood* (1850) 11 How. 248. In *Hotchkiss* the US Supreme Court held that obviousness was a barrier to patentability unless the inventor could show 'more ingenuity and skill . . . than were possessed by an ordinary mechanic acquainted with the business'. This squared with the generally held notion of what the act of invention required at the time. Over time however, in a seesaw of court decisions, the obviousness standard moved back and forth, creating enormous scope for academic debate and disagreement, and so the legislators believed that by codifying the law in section 103 of the 1952 legislation some stability could be brought to the law.

Karl Lutz, a practising US patent attorney, wrote in 1953 that the 'less than benevolent attitude towards patents' was contrary to the intent of Article I, Section 8, Clause 8 of the US Constitution, which expressly gave Congress the power '[t]o promote the Progress of Science and useful Arts, by securing for limited Times to Authors and Inventors the exclusive Right to their respective Writings and Discoveries'. In his opinion the intent had been 'mis-read' by a US Supreme Court which had limited patents 'only for such startling innovations as [those that] "push back the frontiers of chemistry, physics, and the like" and "make a distinctive contribution to scientific knowledge" '.[111] Like many in the patent profession Lutz believed that the threshold of invention was too high. John Powell, a US patent lawyer, explained in 1959 that the legal gyration over the obviousness standard was due to 'the statutory presumption of validity', which had become meaningless because of 'a judicial feeling that the Patent Office was applying a standard of invention lower than that which the courts were bound to observe and that, therefore, little if any weight could legitimately be given the presumption'.[112]

According to section 103 an invention was obvious and not patentable if 'the differences between the subject matter sought to be patented and the prior art are such that the subject matter as a whole would have been obvious at the time the invention was made to a person having ordinary skill in the art to which said subject matter pertains'. That test was in many ways a mere restatement of *Hotchkiss*, but by 1980 Lutz's hope had became a narrow 5-to-4 reality.

The issue before the US Supreme Court in *Diamond v Diehr* (1980) 101 S Ct 1048 was whether the invention of a method of operating a rubber-moulding press for precession moulded compounds with the aid of a digital computer, where the total cure time was calculated using the 'Arrhenius equation', was a process that was patentable subject matter. Clearly it was a process, given that it produced vulcanized rubber, but because the only distinguishing feature of this process over existing processes was a *computer program* the USPTO had rejected the patent application. According to the USPTO this incremental 'advance' was nothing more than 'an abstract idea' involving the application of a mathematical formula to regulate the timing in an otherwise old process which produced an old product. As abstract ideas were not considered patentable subject matter, the examiner reasoned that the distinguishing feature (a computer program) was not enough to make the entire process a patentable invention within section 101.

Finally the US Supreme Court understood that patents were needed to grow the American economy, and so the majority rejected this reasoning,[113] holding that the invention was to 'the process as a whole', and although the Arrhenius equation itself was 'not patentable in isolation', a process which incorporated the equation in 'a more efficient solution' was a process which was 'not barred at the threshold by § 101'. In effect they transformed an old process (vulcanization) which produced an old product (vulcanized rubber) into an invention because of the contribution of one new element which was (a) 'an abstract idea' and (b) an obvious step. Frankly the idea of computerizing an old process was, by the 1970s, hardly an ingenious one.

Indeed this point had not escaped the dissenting judges who believed that there was nothing new in the subject process or in the vulcanized rubber that it produced. The only thing that was new was the use of a mathematical formula in a computer program which, in the absence of any 'other inventive concept disclosed in the patent application' meant that the process was not an invention but an 'abstract idea'. According to them, 'the essence of the claimed discovery . . . was an algorithm that could be programmed on a digital computer'. The minority criticized the majority because they had failed 'to understand . . . the distinction between the subject matter of what the inventor claims to have discovered . . . and the question whether that claimed discovery is in fact novel'. But their real complaint was directed towards 'the spokesmen for the organized patent bar', who they believed had 'uniformly favored patentability' and for 'industry representatives' who had 'taken positions properly motivated by their economic self-interest'.

Clearly the minority had rejected the notion 'that patent protection is essential for the growth of the software industry'. Almost harkening back to the frustrations of Jackson some 30 years earlier they had 'doubts that the present patent system can provide the needed protection'. The real momentum for changing the judicial attitude was to come with a new patent appeal court established by President Ronald Reagan[114] in 1982. The US Court of Appeals for the Federal Circuit (CAFC) was the result of a merger between the United States Court of Customs and Appeals and the appellate division of the United States Court of Claims and was given exclusive jurisdiction over appeals concerning patents, among many other areas of federal law, and within a decade it had transformed the judicial landscape.

In *In re Bell* (1993) 991 F 2d 781 the USPTO and the Board of Patent Appeals had both rejected a patent application for an invention over isolated nucleic acid molecules containing human DNA which coded for human insulin-like growth factors. The issue that confronted the CAFC was 'whether the . . . amino acid sequence of a protein in conjunction with a reference indicating a general method of cloning renders the gene prima facie obvious'. In reversing the Board's decision the CAFC held that neither 'the prior art references, either alone or in combination, teach or suggest the claimed invention', because of 'the degeneracy of the genetic code'. The CAFC reasoned that the 'vast number of nucleotide sequences that might code for a specific protein' made the predictability between the genetic structure of genes and protein structure impossible, and therefore not obvious. In order to provide patent protection for the biotechnology industry the CAFC accordingly moved the goal posts of 'invention' away from the techniques used to identify the human genes and towards the actual protein sequence and the gene that coded for it; and since the genetic sequence of the relevant gene had not been published, but only the partial amino acid (protein sequence) of the insulin-like growth factors, it was an invention to identify and isolate the gene. Two years later the CAFC applied this reasoning in *In re Deuel* (1995) 51 F 3d 1552 holding that the invention to isolated and purified DNA and cDNA (copy DNA) molecules (nucleotides) encoding heparin-binding growth factors (amino acids) was not obvious.

Predictably both decisions were scrutinized and justly criticized. Arti Rai, then Associate Professor of Law at San Diego University, in a paper entitled 'Addressing the Patent Gold Rush: The Role of Deference to PTO Patent Denials',[115] argued that the CAFC's 'treatment of DNA-based inventions as just another species of chemical compound' to be a gross oversimplification of the science because, 'as the PTO has pointed out . . . the informational link between proteins, amino acids, and DNA, knowledge of the protein's complete or partial amino acid sequence can be used to obtain the desired DNA sequence'. More pointedly she blamed 'the CAFC's reversal of PTO decisions denying patent protection to certain biotechnology and computer program inventions . . . for the recent proliferation of patents'. Consequently the CAFC's reductionism had 'substantially diminished the balance between property rights and the public domain achieved by various patentability requirements – most importantly the requirement of nonobviousness'.

In retrospect these two decisions probably marked the pinnacle of the CAFC's expansionist patent agenda in terms of biotechnology; but because patent litigant after patent litigant failed to appeal and question its reasoning in the US Supreme Court, the CAFC's position became understandably entrenched. Widely accepted throughout the biotechnology industry and by patent attorneys around the globe, patent challengers on both sides of the Atlantic stayed clear of the patentable subject matter threshold until finally, in 2006, Laboratory Corporation of America (LabCorp), one of America's largest human diagnostic companies, broke ranks.

In *Laboratory Corporation of America v Metabolite Laboratories* (2006) 126 S Ct 2921 the US Supreme Court finally was given the opportunity to correct the misapplication of the law. The argument was over an invention for a process which enabled the diagnosis of vitamin deficiencies in humans through the measurement of a human protein, homocysteine, in the body. According to the patent specification, if the level of this protein was elevated above the norm there was a vitamin deficiency, but the problem, according to LabCorp, was that this simply involved a doctor making a deduction once the results of a blood test that measured human protein were known. The process therefore was not an invention because any doctor was capable of making the association between elevated levels of homocysteine and a vitamin deficiency. LabCorp argued that what the patent sought to protect, under the guise of being an 'invention', was the correlation between two naturally occurring events – the elevated protein and the vitamin deficiency in a patient.

Unfortunately at no time during the trial or on appeal to the CAFC did LabCorp challenge the validity of this patent on this basis, but only before the US Supreme Court. This enabled Metabolite and the US Attorney General (in an amicus curiae brief, that is as a friend of the court) to criticize LabCorp. In fact, although the Court ignored this criticism at first and granted certiorari, after hearing oral argument it reconsidered and took the unusual step of withdrawing certiorari. Nevertheless three of the eight justices wrote a powerful dissent on the merits of the appeal. Justices Breyer, Stephens and Souter confirmed that as 'a principle of law', the exclusion of 'laws of nature, natural phenomena and abstract ideas finds it roots in both English and American law', arguing that its 'justification . . . does not lie in any claim that "laws of nature" are obvious, or that their discovery is easy, or that they are not useful'. Indeed they said, 'research into such matters may be costly and time consuming; monetary incentives may matter; and the fruits of those incentives and that research may prove of great benefit to the human race'. Nonetheless they explained, 'the reason for the exclusion is that sometimes too much patent protection can impede rather than "promote the Progress of Science and useful Arts" '. The fundamental problem created by overreaching patent monopolies arose, they said, 'from the fact that patents do not only encourage research by providing monetary incentives', but 'sometimes their presence can discourage research by impeding the free exchange of information'. Indeed they gave examples: 'by forcing researchers to avoid the use of potentially patented ideas, by leading them to conduct costly and time-consuming searches of existing or pending patents, by requiring complex licensing arrangements, and by raising the costs of using the patented information, sometime prohibitively so'.

Their dissent argued that there is a balance that must be maintained between the rights of the patent owner (not necessarily the inventor) and the rights of the society which grants such privileges, and it is the courts that bear the principle burden of maintaining that balance. In this respect, Justices Breyer, Stephens and Souter confirmed:

> Patent law seeks to avoid the dangers of overprotection just as surely as it seeks to avoid the diminished incentive to invent that underprotection can threaten. One way in which patent law seeks to sail between these opposing and risky shoals is through rules that bring certain types of invention and discovery within the scope of patentability while excluding others. . . . Thus the Court has recognised that 'phenomena of nature, though just discovered, mental processes and abstract intellectual concepts are . . . the basic tools of scientific and technological work' *Gottschalk v Benson* 409 US 63, 67 (1972)' and so the Court 'has treated fundamental scientific principles as 'parts of the storehouse of knowledge' and manifestations of laws of nature as 'free to all men and reserved exclusively to none' *Funk Bros*, supra at 130. And its doing so reflects a basic judgment that protection in such cases, despite its potentially positive incentives effects, would too often severely interfere with, or discourage, development and the further spread of useful knowledge itself.

However in 2007 the issue of obviousness (section 103) returned to the US Supreme Court. In *KSR International Co v Teleflex Inc* (2007) 127 S Ct 1727 the point in issue was over the CAFC's lowering of the obviousness threshold. The CAFC had held that unless a person of ordinary skill in the art was 'motivated to look at relevant prior art references', the prior art references were irrelevant in determining obviousness. The invention at the centre of this case was a mechanism that caused adjustments to motor vehicle accelerator pedals so that, irrespective of where in the car the driver was seated and the length of his leg, the driver's foot reached the pedal. In what was a close replay of *Diehr* KSR had developed an adjustable pedal system for cars with cable-actuated throttles. The idea of having adjustable pedals was old and there were plenty of examples in the prior art, but KSR had modified its system by adding a modular sensor for trucks using computer-controlled throttles (like adding a computer on an old process to make an old product). Unfortunately this modification came within the scope of a patent owned by Teleflex (which had been granted on the basis of CAFC precedence in *Diehr*), and when KSR was sued for patent infringement the validity of Teleflex's patent was challenged on the ground that the invention was obvious in light of a number of prior patents which concerned adjustable motor vehicle pedal systems.

At the trial before the District Court the evidence satisfied the trial judge that the obviousness standard had been breached, and as a result Teleflex's patent was held invalid, but on appeal the CAFC reversed by ignoring two prior patents on the basis of their *motivation* test – that is that the skilled person would not have been motivated to read them. The CAFC held that even though the patents were about adjustable motor vehicle pedal systems, they were addressing technical problems which were different from those which Teleflex's patent addressed. In what was a classic case of shifting the goal posts, the CAFC then cited its decision in *Deuel* to support its holding in that case that 'obvious to try' was not an indicia of obviousness.

The US Supreme Court however rejected this reasoning, and in doing so sent a strong message, not only to the CAFC but to dash the hopes of US patent attorneys who believed that the US Supreme Court ought to display a more 'benevolent attitude towards patents'. Justice Kennedy made that clear in preferring 'the "functional approach" of *Hotchkiss*' over 'the rigid approach of the Court of Appeals'. Indeed not only did this strike the right balance but he reinforced the fact that the 'combination of familiar elements according to known methods is likely to be obvious when it does no more than yield predictable results'.

For the biotechnology industry *KSR* marked the end of the patenting gold rush. In May 2007 the US Board of Patent Appeals and Interferences in *ex parte Kubin & Goodwin* upheld the USPTO's rejection of a patent application which claimed an invention for polynucleotides (nucleic acids) encoding Natural Killer Cell Activation Inducing Ligand polypeptides (NAIL) (amino acids) on the ground of obviousness. The appellants relied on the CAFC's decision in *Deuel* as authority against the USPTO's rejection. The Board however held that *Deuel* was 'not controlling', and thus '[did] not stand in the way of our conclusion'. In what was a clear rebuff to the CAFC's precedence, 'to the extent that *Deuel* [was] considered relevant to this case', the Board held, 'we note[d] that the Supreme Court [had] recently cast doubt on the viability of *Deuel* to the extent the Federal Circuit rejected an "obvious to try" test. Under KSR, [it was] now apparent "obvious to try" may be an appropriate test in more situations than we previously contemplated'.

The fallacy in the CAFC's reasoning in *Bell* and *Deuel* had finally been exposed, and now judicially denounced. Applying *KSR* the Board in *Kubin* explained that the '"problem" facing those in the art' was the limited number of methodologies available to isolate NAIL cDNA, meaning that the 'skilled artisan would have had reason to try these methodologies with the reasonable expectation that at least one would be successful. Thus isolating NAIL cDNA was "the product not of innovation but of ordinary skill and common sense"', and led them to conclude, 'NAIL cDNA [was] not patentable as it would have been obvious to isolate it.'

There still remained the issue of patentable subject matter. The US Patents Act 1952 made no change to the term 'composition of matter' in section 101 – a term which first appeared in the patent lexicon in 1793. Without doubt the significance of this term has changed since then, but it is doubtful whether it embraces isolated biological materials which are identical or substantially identical to products of nature. Fundamentally, 'laws of nature, natural phenomena and abstract ideas' do not come within the US constitutional mandate of Article I, Section 8, Clause 8.

As the Danish Council of Bioethics confirmed in its *Patenting Human Genes and Stem Cells* Report published in 2004: 'it cannot be said with any reasonableness that a sequence or partial sequence of a gene ceases to be part of the human body merely because an identical copy of the sequence is isolated from or produced outside of the human body.'

The recent decisions in *KSR* (majority) and *Labcorp* (minority) indicate that the US Supreme Court is in no mood for patent law which seeks to create monopolies in areas which have been excluded from patent protection principles established hundreds of years ago. The Statute of Monopolies 1623 – the legislative source of the Anglo-American patent systems – was the statutory instrument which placed a limit on the creation of monopolies, and the US Supreme Court has always acknowledged that the patent clause in the American Constitution must be interpreted with that limitation in mind. As Keith Maskus, an American economics professor, explained in his paper 'Reforming US Patent Policy: Getting the Incentive Right':[116]

America's robust economic competitiveness is due in no small part to a large capacity for innovation. That capacity is imperilled, however, by an increasingly overprotective patent system. Over the past twenty-five years, American legislators and judges have operated on the principle that stronger patent protection engenders more innovation. This principle is misguided. Although intellectual property rights (IPR) play an important role in innovation, the recent increase in patent protection has not spurred innovation so much as it has impeded the development and use of new technologies.

NOTES

1. Sommerich, OC (1945), 'A Brief against Confiscation', *Law and Contemporary Problems*, **11**, 152–65, 165. For a general discussion concerning the confiscation of intellectual property assets see Sommerich, OC (1955), 'Treatment by United States of World War I and II Enemy-owned Patents and Copyrights', *The American Journal of Comparative Law*, **4** (4), 587–600 and Berman, HA (1945), 'Cartels and Enemy Property', *Law and Contemporary Problems*, **11** (1), 109–17.
2. Borchard, E (1943), 'Nationalization of Enemy Patents', *The American Journal of International Law*, **37**, 92–7.
3. 1892–1961; Assistant Secretary of State, 1933–45.
4. 1881–1959; UK Ambassador to Washington, 1942–46.
5. 1883–1946; 1st Baron Keynes, 1942.
6. Opie, R (1957), 'Anglo-American Economic Relations in War-Time', *Oxford Economic Papers*, New Series, **9** (2), 138.

7. Ibid, 138.
8. Hull, C (1948), *The Memoirs of Cordell Hull* (New York: Macmillan Co). For a general discussion of events prior to WWII see Schatz, AW (1970), 'The Anglo-American Trade Agreement and Cordell Hull's Search for Peace 1936–1938', *The Journal of American History*, **57** (1), 85–103.
9. 1874–1965; Prime Minister of the UK, 1940–5, 1951–5.
10. My italics.
11. 1882–1948; US Assistant Secretary of Treasury, 1941–6. On 23 November 1953 his photograph appeared on the cover of *Time Magazine*. Below it the caption read: 'How much did President Truman know?' In a top secret memorandum dated 16 October 1950 to the Director of the FBI, White was posthumously identified as a Soviet spy with the code name 'Jurist'. It had been alleged that Dexter had passed top secret US Treasury information to the Soviet Union and once these allegations had surfaced he resigned the IMF position that had been preordained for him by President Truman. He died after a series of heart attacks on 16 August 1948 having only three days earlier testified to the Congressional House Committee on Un-American Activities that he was not a Soviet spy. Recently James Broughton has argued that White was an internationalist and that the evidence produced by the FBI to inculpate him was ambiguous, particularly since his contact with Soviet officials was consistent with his US Treasury duties. In Broughton's view the fact that White had a Soviet code name was also inconclusive as it was common practice for US officials mentioned in clandestine Soviet communications to be referred to by their codenames. See Broughton, J (2001), 'The Case against Harry Dexter White: Still Not Proven', *History of Political Economy*, **33** (2), 219–39.
12. Bell, R (1982), 'Testing the Open Door Thesis in Australia, 1941–1946', *The Pacific Historical Review*, **51** (3), 283–311.
13. Beckhart, BH (1944), 'The Bretton Woods Proposal for an International Monetary Fund', *Political Science Quarterly*, **59** (4), 489–528. This article provides a contemporaneous recount of the drafting of the charters for the IMF and World Bank, concluding that America should not participate in the IMF.
14. Henderson, H (1949), 'A Criticism of the Havana Charter', *The American Economic Review*, **39** (3), 605–17 and for the rejoinder see Ellsworth, PT (1949), ' The Havana Charter: Comment', *The American Economic Review*, **39** (6), 1268–73. Also see Dam, KW (2004), 'Cordell Hull, The Reciprocal Trade Agreement Act, and the WTO', Draft Paper, 10 October 2004.
15. UK Board of Trade, KR Swan (1947), *Patents and Designs Acts, Final Report of the Departmental Committee*, 1946-47 [Cmd 7206], 22 (95).
16. HC Debs 1919, Vol 118, Col 1, 860.
17. In 1931 the Sargant Committee noted: '[d]uring the War it became apparent that Great Britain was suffering from a lack of medicine and drugs, many of which were the subject of patent rights in this country': UK Board of Trade, CH Sargant, (1931), *Report of the Departmental Committee on the Patents and Designs Acts and Practice of the Patent Office*, 1930-31 [Cmd 3829], 43 (186).
18. Sommerich, OC (1955), 'Treatment by United States of World War I and II Enemy-Owned Patents and Copyrights', *The American Journal of Comparative Law*, **4** (4), 587–600.
19. Fletcher Moulton, H and JH Evans-Jackson (1920), *The Patents, Designs, and Trade Marks Acts* (London: Butterworth & Co.), 71.
20. UK Board of Trade, KR Swan, (1946), *Patents and Designs Acts, Second Interim Report of the Departmental Committee*, 1945–46 [Cmd 6789], 10 (35)
21. Swan Committee (1947), above n 15, 21 (para. 93).
22. Ibid, 21 (93).
23. Ibid, 22 (96).
24. Swan, KR (1908), *The Law and Commercial Usage of Patents, Designs and Trade Marks* (London: Archibald Constable & Co Ltd), 4.
25. Swan Committee (1946), above n 20, 10 (39). In fact this effect was well understood by

Carl Duisberg who was chairman of Bayer Germany (before it became part IG Farben) in 1919 when the company lost control of the 'Bayer' trade marks, including Aspirin. Effectively Bayer Germany had been locked out of its former US and South American markets even though the patent for Aspirin had expired.

26. Ibid, 10 (41).
27. Swan Committee (1947), above n 15, 22 (95): 'We also consider that a claim for a new substance should always be deemed to exclude the same substance when found in nature'.
28. Ibid, 46 (227).
29. Swan Committee (1946), above n 20, 32–3.
30. Ibid, 32: 'the Examiner cannot have cognisance of all matters relevant to a proper assessment of the advance described and claimed'.
31. Swan Committee (1947), above n 15, 15 (56).
32. Ibid, 17 (65).
33. Prime Minister Clement Attlee (1883–1967); Deputy Prime Minister 1942–5; Prime Minister 1945–51; 1st Earl Attlee, 1955. His Labour government was responsible for the nationalization of the coal and steel industries and for utilities such as electricity, gas, telephones, railways, road haulage and canal transport. The Beveridge Report was also implemented by his government, with the establishment of the National Health Service in 1945.
34. My italics.
35. My italics.
36. Sargant Committee (1931), above n 17, 43 (186).
37. Ibid.
38. 1879–1963; knighted KCB, 1919; life peer, 1946.
39. Coscelli, A (2000), 'The Importance of Doctors' and Patients' Preferences in the Prescription Decision', *The Journal of Industrial Economics*, **48** (3), 349–69.
40. See for instance a 2007 report by Consumers International, a not-for-profit organization, entitled 'Drugs, Doctors and Dinners, How Drug Companies Influence Health in the Developing World'. Although this report focuses on the decisions made by doctors in developing countries, there is evidence that the tactics employed by pharmaceutical companies were perfected by their use in developed countries (like England) after WWII.
41. Slinn, J (2005), 'Prescription Pharmaceuticals in the UK', *Business History*, **47** (3), 352–66.
42. Ibid, 353.
43. 1881–1955; knighted, 1944; Nobel Prize, 1945.
44. 1898–1968; knighted, 1944; Nobel Prize, 1945; Lord Florey, 1965.
45. 1906–79; Nobel Prize, 1945.
46. 1911–2004.
47. 1899–1959.
48. 1891–1978; knighted, 1946; 1st Baronet Jephcott, 1962.
49. 1905–88; knighted, 1967.
50. 1903–82.
51. Slinn, above n 41, 355.
52. Davonport-Hines, R (2007), 'Jephcott, Sir Harry', *Oxford Dictionary of National Biography*, available at http://www.oxforddnb.com.virtual.anu.edu.au/view/printable/31286.
53. Corley, TAB (1999) 'The British Pharmaceutical Industry Since 1851', Centre for International History, Working Paper Series, University of Reading, available at http://www.rdg.ac.uk/Econ/Econ/workingpapers/emdp404.pdf, 18; also reproduced in L Richmond, J Stevenson and A Turton (2003), *The Pharmaceutical Industry: a Guide to Historical Records* (Aldershot: Ashgate Publishing Limited; Burlington: Ashgate Publishing Company).
54. Corley, above n 53, 18–19.
55. Chain, EB (1963), 'Academic and Industrial Contributions to Drug Research', *Nature*, **200** (4905), 441–51.

56. Chain however did not share his colleague Florey's disinterest in the commerciality of their work and, although there is nothing to suggest that Chain's primary motivation was a patent, once they had managed to prove experimentally the medicinal application of penicillin, he raised the prospect with Florey. Florey in turn raised the subject with Sir Edward Mellenby, Secretary of the Medical Research Council, but Mellenby's reaction was predictable – the very idea that British scientists would profit by their work was repugnant; it was unethical. See Liebenau, J (1987), 'The British Success with Penicillin', *Social Studies of Science*, **17** (1), 69–86, 81.
57. Chain, above n 55, 441.
58. Ibid, 442.
59. Ibid, 448.
60. Ibid, 449.
61. Ibid.
62. Ibid.
63. Ibid, 450.
64. Ibid.
65. Ibid.
66. Ibid, 451.
67. Ibid.
68. UK Committee of Inquiry, Lord Sainsbury (1967), *Relationship of the Pharmaceutical Industry with the National Health Services*, [Cmd 3410].
69. UK Committee of Inquiry, MAL Banks (1970), *The British Patent System* [Cmd 4407].
70. 1902–98; life peer, 1962.
71. 1901–91; knighted, 1971.
72. Sainsbury Committee, above n 68, 42 (139).
73. Ibid, 42–3 (139).
74. Banks Committee, above n 69, 112 (394).
75. Ibid, 112–3 (395).
76. See Hansard, 1971–2 (HC Debs). Vol 826, Col 265, 22 November 1971.
77. Sainsbury Committee, above n 68, 9 (22).
78. Ibid, 43 (142).
79. Ibid.
80. Ibid, 43 (143).
81. Ibid.
82. Ibid, 44 (143).
83. Ibid, 45 (150).
84. Ibid, 76 (265).
85. Ibid.
86. Ibid, 45 (150).
87. Ibid.
88. Ibid.
89. Ibid.
90. UK Board of Trade, CH Sargant, (1931), *Report of the Departmental Committee on the Patents and Designs Acts and Practice of the Patent Office*, 1930-31 [Cmd 3829], 27 (114) to 28 (121).
91. Ibid, 42 (139).
92. Banks Committee, above n 69, 115 (401–3).
93. Ibid.
94. Ibid, 114 (398).
95. Ibid, 114 (399–400).
96. Sainsbury Committee, above n 68, 36 (118).
97. Ibid, 35 (118).
98. Ibid, 36 (118).
99. Ibid, 33 (105)–35 (113).

100. Oudemans, G (1963), *The Draft European Patent Convention* (London: Stevens & Sons Ltd; New York: Mathew Bender & Co. Inc.).
101. In fact had it not been for the veto exercised by French President Charles de Gaulle, the British application to join the EEC would have been successful in 1961.
102. Banks Committee, above n 69, 118 (410).
103. Ibid, 119 (410).
104. Ibid, 99 (348).
105. Slinn, above n 41, 353
106. Ibid, 355.
107. Federico, PJ (1993), 'Commentary on the New Patent Act', *Journal of the Patent Office Society*, **75**, 162–231.
108. *Jungersen v Ostby & Barton* (1949) 335 US 560, 572.
109. Waller, SW (2004), 'The Antitrust Legacy of Thurman Arnold', *St. John's Law Review*, **78**, 569–613.
110. Powell, JF (1959), 'Patents: Standard of Invention: Effects of Sections 103 and 282 of Patent Act of 1952', *Michigan Law Review*, **57** (3), 426–9, particularly at 429 where the author makes the case: 'the anticipated stabilization of the standard of inventions . . . [would help] the courts . . . towards achieving the congressional goal of uniformity and more favourable attitude towards patents'.
111. Lutz, KB (1953), 'The New 1952 Patent Statute', *Journal of the Patent Office Society*, **35** (3), 155–62, 157 quoting Douglas and Black JJ in *Great A & P Tea Co. v Supermarket Co.*, 71 Sup Ct 127.
112. Powell, above n 110, 429.
113. In fact the decision was soon to have a flow-on effect to the new biotechnology industry. Even though *Diehr* was a case about something completely artificial, in that every integer of the invention was 'made by man', the reasoning was subsequently applied to permit the patenting of biological processes which used isolated biological materials to manufacture other biological materials which were identical to those existing in nature. While the processes were artificial constructs, the end products of those processes were biologically, genetically and efficaciously identical to products of nature.
114. 1911–2004; President of the United States, 1981–89.
115. Rai, A (2000), 'Addressing the Patent Gold Rush: The Role of Deference to PTO Patent Denials', USD School of Law, Public Working Paper No 5 and Law and Economics Research Paper 2, *SSRN*, 223758.
116. Maskus, KE (2006), 'Reforming US Patent Policy: Getting the Incentive Right', *Innovations*, **1** (4), 127–53.

4. The patent systems of Continental Europe

When the Germans think of the future, its neighbours inevitably remember the past.

Michael Stürmer, 'Deutchlands Rolle in Europa', *Frankfurter Allgemeine Zeitung*, 28 November 1991

By the thirteenth century the practice of bestowing exclusive trading privileges, or *privilegi* as they were known in Italy, upon artisans, craftsmen and tradesmen and their representative guilds was well established. These *privilegi*, granted by royal prerogative or by the rulers of city-state Republics, gave their holders the exclusive right to work their art, craft and trade within the confines of these city-states, thereby harbouring them from competition.[1] These monopolies nurtured a symbiosis of protectionism. The ruling classes had come to understand that by bestowing *privilegi*, not only with respect to the importation of raw materials such as silk, cotton and wool into their realms, but also with respect to the kinds of work performed by the people who held the secrets of how to use those materials and the tools and machinery which they employed in the production of finished goods such as sail cloth and brocade, they and their territories and kingdoms were wealthier as a result.

It followed that those who held the trade secrets of the State were jealously protected, and criminal and financial penalties were imposed to encourage them not to emigrate. The Piedmontese for instance passed laws that made industrial espionage punishable by death. John Lombe,[2] who started the silk milling industry in England in the eighteenth century after spending two years in Piedmont learning all he could, literally risked his life for King and country. He did this despite Vittorio Zonica publishing a book in Padua in 1607 entitled *Nuovo Teatro di Machine et Edificii* which disclosed the intricate details of a silk milling machine. This was not enough for Lombe, who lived at a time when literacy was not commonplace. Rather, as Carlo Cipolla acknowledged, in the sixteenth century real-life human knowledge and experience was the main route of technology transfer, and so the movement of labour, not the transfer of know how through the written word, was strenuously regulated.[3] The Republic of Venice imposed prison sentences on anyone who tried to leave who was skilled in any technology that was important to the State. The governments of neighbouring Italian city-states likewise jealously guarded their state secrets by restricting the movement of labour. In the sixteenth century the Duke of Florence issued a decree demanding the return to Florence of brocade workers who had earlier emigrated; those who refused to return were sentenced to death *in absentia* and a bounty of 200 *scudi*, dead or alive, was placed upon their heads.[4] It had in fact been the neighbouring Duke of Milan who in the fifteenth century had enticed Florentines to bring their silk manufacturing knowledge to Milan in return for a monthly subsidy and tax incentives.

Despite the *privilegi* and the trade laws, famine, disease and war disrupted and unsettled the power of the ruling classes, and from time to time power vacuums emerged, economies faltered and emigration was the inevitable consequence. Religious persecution also played a role. The resulting exodus of Catholics from Belgium to Sweden in the sixteenth and seventeenth centuries brought new techniques of casting iron cannons; while that of the Huguenots from France to England during the seventeenth century brought the know-how of clockmaking to London.[5] Industrial espionage, such as Lombe had undertaken, was not unheard of and was often rewarded by the State. On his return to England Lombe petitioned Parliament and in 1718 was granted letters patent[6] as a reward, not for his ingenuity, but for his courage in bringing the closely guarded Italian secrets of silk milling to England (which included bringing two skilled Italian silk workers with him). John Lombe actually paid the ultimate price for his treachery in 1722, allegedly poisoned by an Italian female spy, but his brother and partner, Thomas, was knighted in 1727 by a grateful George II[7] on his accession to the throne. Thus a system of punishment and rewards was used to manipulate the movement of labour, and those rewards included not just the promise of the types of monopolies granted by letters patent, but money, land, position and tax incentives.

These *privilegi* were subject to the same kinds of abuses as occurred in England and for similar reasons were not always considered appropriate.[8] The Florentines too discovered that *privilegi* tended to encourage predatory commercial behaviour, and while the trade guilds in Florence were mostly tolerated and their practices supported by the State there was no consistency in the application of an anti-monopoly law which attempted to temper the worst excesses of this practice. Its interpretation, as Prager pointed out, 'lay in the hands of a government controlled by the leaders of the cartels', and so 'strict compliance was enforced only against the unorganised workers, and against lesser guilds, whose performance and price levels affected the cost of living and minimum wages, such as bakers, butchers, and Masters of Stone and Wood'.[9] Hence the Florentines were happy to grant Filippo Brunelleschi,[10] the architect of the dome of the Cathedral of Florence, a three-year patent in 1421 over the use 'on the river Arno or on any other river, stagnant water or swamp, or water running or existing in the territory of Florence' any 'machine or ship or other instrument, be it newly invented or made in new form' which was 'designed to import or ship or transport on water any merchandise or any things or goods'. The only condition imposed was that it had to be new – emphasized by the exception that applied to 'such ship or machine or instrument as they may have used until now for similar operations'.[11]

However this approach changed with the return of a more feudalist rule over the Florentine Republic under Cosimo di Giovanni de' Medici.[12] In 1447 a state decree was proclaimed which empowered a commissioner to 'investigate about any art and trade of which there is no artisan known in the city of Florence', and other monopolistic misconduct, even outlawing the grant of patents of the kind enjoyed by Brunelleschi. Perhaps the ebb and flow of protectionism exemplified by the Florentine State merely reflected its changing fortunes, but their example was not followed by the government of the Venetian Republic which decided instead to codify the *privilegi*.

THE VENETIAN PATENT STATUTE

In 1474 the government of the Venetian Republic created the first known statutory alternative to the *ad hoc* practice surrounding the grant of *privilegi*. This was the world's first patent system regulated by specific legislation. The preamble to the Venetian statute explained that the city had, 'by its excellence and greatness', attracted 'many men of diverse origins, having most subtle minds and able to devise and discover various ingenious artifices'. The Venetian government recognized that having attracted such men it had to keep them. Creating a formal system of *privilegi* which rewarded them with attribution for their ingenuity and which gave them legal control over their 'works and devices' was seen as an answer. According to the Venetian patent system the statutory privilege was available for 'any new and ingenious device not previously made' within the Venetian Republic, and it was designed to offer advantages over the existing and continuing practice of the *privilegi*.[13]

The Venetian patent system did five things. First it acknowledged that those who devised and discovered 'new and ingenious artifices' within the Venetian State were 'the authors' and that they were entitled to attribution for their ingenuity. In so doing it removed the arbitrariness and subjectivity associated with the *privilegi* and provided greater certainty to those who were the holders of the statutory privilege. Quite unlike the *privilegi,* which were granted for all manner of skilled or trade activities such as stonemasonry, dyeing, cloth making – which, while requiring skill, were not necessarily ingenious – this exclusive right provided 'authors' with uniform economic protections across all industries and throughout the Venetian State as a reward for the achievement of a specific task, namely the provision of an invention.

Secondly it established a central registration authority, the office of the *Provveditori di Comun,* enabling 'authors' to register their 'new and ingenious artifices'. This created a technological library or resource which then enabled independent assessment, not only of the invention but of how the invention could be used for other purposes perhaps not envisaged by the author or perhaps be further improved upon by the author. Furthermore in mandating registration it not only provided a standardized and centralized registration system, but importantly it gave to the Venetian Government a source of information about technological developments within its borders, enabling it to fine-tune the movement of skilled labour by being able to assess leading-edge technological developments.

Thirdly it gave 'authors' the exclusive right 'within any territories to make the device or instrument' for a period of 10 years. This reward was specifically defined as being the exclusive right to reproduce and work their 'new and ingenious artifices' within the borders of the Venetian State and did not involve the grant of other emoluments or rewards.

Fourthly it made it a crime for 'anyone else within any territories to make any other device in the form or likeness of that one without the author's consent or licence', subject to a fine of 100 *ducats* and the immediate destruction of the infringing device.

Finally it exempted the Venetian Government from the operation of the law and reserved to itself, 'at its total pleasure', the appropriation and use of 'any of the said devices or instruments'.

The Venetian patent system was unprecedented; at a time when the grant of *privilegi* was practised in neighbouring cities in northern Italy the system acknowledged that knowledge was power and that those who turned that knowledge into new and ingenious devices contributed to the State's power.

Naturally such a reward could not be granted to everyone who claimed to have 'devised and discovered' a 'new and ingenious artifice'. A system of examination, although not unique to the Venetian patent system because examination was sometimes also a feature of the *privilegi,* was essential to its operation. Magistrates were assigned to this task, and the constitution of the group differed depending on the nature of the technology involved or the intended use of the artifice. Giulio Mandich, a former Professor at the Istituto Superiore d'Architettura in Venice, explained that this process of examination was often no more than a 'preliminary examination' which was conducted on the basis of a model, description or statement and that there was 'no direct assessment of novelty'.[14]

Once the petitioning author satisfied the examining magistrates they would make a recommendation to the Venetian Senate regarding the grant of privileges, but only on the condition that the patent satisfied a subsequent test which, if not passed, would result in the voiding of the patent, 'as though it had never been granted'.[15]

The patent was moreover subject to challenge by way of an 'opposition'. It was during this stage that novelty was generally a matter of examination. Mandich noted that the petition was carefully worded to avoid any accusation of fraud, emphasizing that although the invention was novel this assertion as fact was made 'without prejudice to other patents previously granted'.[16]

The Venetian patent system was not however inflexible. The patent monopoly for instance varied in length depending on the nature of the technology or the recommendation of the examining magistrates. From 1500 to 1550 the typical patent monopoly was 25 years, although this could vary anywhere between five and 50 years. This variability was the result of negotiation between the petitioning author and the examining magistrates and was a reflection of the need to achieve the right balance between the inventor and the State, taking into account both the degree of innovation and the economic importance of the invention to the State's economy.

Unfortunately the Venetian Republic's patent system could not halt the movement of people across its borders and inevitably, whatever competitive advantage was provided by its leading edge technologies, this advantage dissipated. Venetian glassmaking skills were in great demand, and by 1551 this know-how was exported to France by Theseus Mutio, a glassmaker from Bologna, who was granted letters patent over the manufacture of glass in France.[17]

Once know-how had been transferred it was only a matter of time before there were improvements and innovations. These improvements not only produced new and more efficient manufacturing techniques and apparatus but also resulted in new products that met consumer demand. Consumerism is not simply a modern phenomenon; it was as much a driver of innovative products and design in the eighteenth century as it is today and the demand for new, fashionable goods was just as insatiable then among the aristocratic and bourgeois classes. For instance once the basic technology for silk manufacture had spread throughout Europe, competition between the manufacturing cities within Europe drove innovation towards the production of merchandise which denoted its place of origin or manufacture, increasing demand for such merchandise.

BOX 4.1   REPORT FROM THE VENETIAN AMBASSADOR TO PARIS TO THE VENETIAN GOVERNMENT, 14 NOVEMBER 1725

'The very ingenious manufacture of these French materials, which are greatly admired for their low cost, for their lightness and for their colours and appearance, has almost driven out Dutch cloth, which is heavier, much less fine in colour and at least twice as expensive. Nor has English cloth escaped without some losses. But since English products still enjoy their former reputation with the people of note they still retain some of the wealthy trade and draw much profit from this.'[18]

What this illustrates is that Europe's patent systems, common by the eighteenth century, were not key to encouraging innovations in technology or in matters scientific or aesthetic, or indeed key to guaranteeing continuing economic prosperity. They played a part in protecting economies through rewards and punishments designed to control the movement of labour, but their failure to halt the transfer of technical knowledge did not cause what Cipolla calls the 'seven black decades' in northern Italy.[19] The industrial revolution, which commenced in England at the turn of the eighteenth century, would finally take the premiership of wool and silk production away from northern Italy; and while the cause of this region's industrial collapse during the seventeenth century has been the subject of academic study, it is the case that, just as no system of *privilegi* prevented it, no system of *privilegi* caused it.

Similarly other factors are more likely to have led to the *Rinascimento* (the Renaissance), such as political stability, the wealth and power of the Roman Catholic Church, the availability of capital through banking systems, an established legal system, established trade links and networks, and the talent and genius of people like Filippo Brunelleschi (1377–1446), Donato di Niccolo (1386–1466), Donato Bramante (1444–1514), Leonardo da Vinci (1452–1519), Michelangelo Buonarroti (1475–1564), Raffaello Sanzio (1483–1520), Galileo Galilei (1565–1642), Evangelista Torricelli (1608–1647) and Marcello Malpighi (1628–1694). These ultimately proved much more decisive than any system of *privilegi*.

EIGHTEENTH AND NINETEENTH CENTURY DEVELOPMENTS IN CONTINENTAL EUROPEAN PATENT LAW

At the time of France's first patent statute becoming law in 1762 during the reign of Louis XV,[20] France and Austria (eventually joined by the Russian Empire, Sweden, Saxony and Spain) were, and had been since 1756, at war with Great Britain, Prussia, the Electorate of Hanover and Portugal over parts of modern Canada (known as New France). With Prussia signing a treaty of neutrality with Great Britain in 1756 France found itself being squeezed militarily and economically, a situation made considerably worse by the cost of maintaining 3000 troops in North America and the crippling of its Navy. The waging of a losing war coupled with an inefficient taxation system meant that inevitably life in France became extremely difficult. With France eventually losing its North American colonies, a fate sealed on 10 February 1763 by the Treaty of Paris, by the time that Louis XVI[21] came to the throne in 1774 its economy was in recession. The disparity in living standards between the aristocratic, bourgeois and peasant classes was so great that it fuelled a revolution leading to the formation of the National Assembly in 1789 (known as the Legislative Assembly from 1791) – an Assembly which promptly abolished feudalism, cancelled the privileges given to the Roman Catholic Church and its clergy and confiscated its lands. It also set about negotiating a new system of government with Louis XVI.

The result was the French Constitution of 1791. It provided for a constitutional monarchy, abolishing 'irrevocably the institutions which were injurious to liberty and equality of rights' of the French people. It also abolished all crown privileges and gave the French citizenry certain 'guarantees as natural and civil rights', which included the 'inviolability of property' (Title I); codified what the English Parliament had tried to pursue in the seventeenth century, namely that the monarch 'reigns only . . . in the name of the law', and confirmed that 'there is no authority in France superior to that of the law'.[22] Although the French retained the King as Head of State his legislative and taxation powers were irrevocable transferred to the Legislative Assembly. With the individual's right to own property guaranteed by the Constitution, John Locke's[23] idea of the individual's rights to life, liberty and property, as melded into pre-revolutionary France by François-Marie Arouet de Voltaire,[24] was no longer a philosophical theory. It was a reality protected by constitutional law.

Perhaps inspired by the example of the United States of America, in France patents became a priority and, like the US Patents Act 1790 which was passed by Congress on 10 April 1790, the law which Stanislas de

Boufflers[25] introduced into the Legislative Assembly later that year ensured that the grant of a patent in France was a property right. The preamble to the *Décrêt du 30 Decembre 1790* confirmed: 'any new idea of which the demonstration or the development can become useful to the society . . . [belonged] to the one who conceived the idea' and that for the State 'not to look at an industrial discovery as the property of the author [was] . . . an attack on their human rights'. Accordingly Article 1 provided: 'every discovery or new invention, in any industry, is the property of its author; consequently the law therefore guarantees him full and entire enjoyment in the manner and for the time as hereafter provided'.

Like section 1 of the US Patents Act 1790 it used the word discovery – qualified by the words 'in any industry' and 'industrial discovery' in the preamble to the French patent law. Therefore it is unlikely that 'discovery' extended notions of property to the discovery of products of nature. Like the English term 'manner of new manufacture' the word 'discovery', as in the US Patents Act, was directed towards the application of a discovery in an invention.

The term of the patent monopoly was for five, 10 or 15 years and patent fees, ranging from 300 *livres* to 1500 *livres*, were paid by the patent applicant depending on the length of patent protection. As with England and the United States there was no specific patent office, but patent applications were filed with the Bureau of Consultation of Arts and the Trades established in October 1791. The Bureau consisted of 30 academics who were required to examine and report on patent applications, and any subsequent patent grant came with a disclaimer warning that it did not establish the 'merit or success of an invention'.

Within months of the passing of de Boufflers's patent law the Legislative Assembly became deadlocked as differing political factions wrestled for control. With France already in a state of war with Austria and Prussia and the political situation quickly deteriorating, by September 1792, with a new revolutionary movement called the Paris Commune forming a de facto government, the French Constitution of 1791 was suspended. This new revolutionary government, determined to end the constitutional monarchy in France, then set about arresting the aristocracy and those whom it considered to be enemies of the people of France, leading to the trial and guillotining of Louis XVI, Marie Antoinette and thousands of aristocrats, clergy and bourgeois.[26]

1795 saw a new French Constitution ushering in the First French Republic, and within a year France had invaded Italy and, under the command of Napoleon Bonaparte,[27] successfully extended French territory into northern and central Italy. His armies subsequently marched into Austria and his victories extended French territory to include the Low

Countries and the Rhineland. The impact which Napoleon Bonaparte had in Europe at that time was significant, leading the British and French yet again into war and further destabilizing the internal politics of France. However by 1800 he had effective control of France, and by 1802 had negotiated peace with the British (Treaty of Amiens), under the terms of which France was recognized as a republic. In the meantime the Napoleonic Code was drafted and entered into force on 21 March 1804. This Code brought together the existing French laws with Roman law and established a new legal system of civil law which subsequently influenced the development of civil law systems in much of Europe. On the same day the Duc d'Enghien[28] was executed for plotting the assassination of Napoleon Bonaparte, and this event led to Bonaparte's ultimate demand for the restoration of a hereditary monarchy in France. In December 1804 Napoleon Bonaparte and his wife, Josephine, were crowned Emperor and Empress of the French and, although his reign lasted for only 11 years, his abdication in 1814 ironically led in 1815 to the restoration of the House of Bourbon, with King Louis XVIII being installed as King of France. Unfortunately this did not halt the royal power struggle between the various branches of the Bourbons and eventually France, once again, became a republic in 1848, only to see Charles Louis-Napoleon Bonaparte[29] declare the Second French Empire in 1852. Despite this political seesaw Napoleon Bonaparte's lasting legacy to France and to Europe was the Napoleonic Code, and it was through this that the patent law of France was to have a most significant influence on the development of patent law throughout Europe during the 1800s.

PATENT LAW IN CONTINENTAL EUROPE PRIOR TO 1860

By the 1860s Belgium, The Netherlands, the German Confederation (Saxony, Prussia, Bavaria, Hanover, Würtemberg, Grand Duchy of Baden and Petty States of Germany), Russia, Poland, Austria, the Kingdom of Piedmont Savoy and Sardinia, the Roman States, the Kingdoms of Naples and Sicily, Spain and Portugal had all passed patent statutes or had issued decrees establishing their own patent system, very much based upon the French patent law of 1791. Within 70 years the French Patents Law 1791 had left its mark on Continental Europe.

The elements in common with the French model were the application, registration, collection of patent fees and publication of granted patents and the limitation of the maximum patent term to 15 years (with the exception of Belgium, which permitted a patent term of 20 years). Patentable subject matter was not defined by a prescribed term, as it was in the UK, but clearly the objective was to grant patents for innovations which were new and industrially applicable. Only in the Roman States was 'the discovery of a natural product' included as patentable subject matter, and even then it was subject to the condition that the 'invention' not 'endanger the public health or interests of others', a qualification suggesting that farmers, being the most likely users of natural products, would not be prevented from using seeds and growing crops.

Notable similarities were the express exclusions of patentability directed to 'pharmaceutical compositions or remedies of any kind and plans and combinations on credit and finance' (France); 'medicines, cosmetics, food, including articles of luxury intended for consumption, patterns, designs, and general scientific principles' (Saxony); 'the preparations of food, drinks, or medicines' (Austria) and 'medicines' (Piedmont, Savoy and Sardinia). Also excluded were inventions which by their nature endangered 'public safety' (The Netherlands); were 'dangerous to the public safety or health, or contrary to the existing laws' (Austria); or involved 'improvements that cannot be worked for reasons of public health, morals or safety' (Austria). Beyond these specific exclusions was the general exclusion that the invention was 'contrary to the general interests of the state' (Austria) or 'contrary to law' (Piedmont, Savoy and Sardinia). Although these exclusions of patentability were more focused than the general proviso contained in the Statute of Monopolies, namely, 'they be not contrary to the law nor mischievous to the state by raising prices of commodities at home, or hurt of trade, or generally inconvenient', they were designed to tackle monopolies with respect to things which were either vital to the health of the people or damaging to the economic interests of the country. Finally there were exclusions for 'purely scientific theorems' (Austria) or 'purely theoretical inventions' (Piedmont, Savoy and Sardinia). These exclusions reinforced the point that an invention had to have a manifestation in some physical form or result and that pure discoveries which were unable to be worked or which did not produce a useful result in some form of industry were beyond the bounds of patentability.[30]

THE FREE TRADE DEBATE IN EUROPE

The English Prime Minister Peel continued to reduce tariffs between 1842 and 1846 and pursued a free trade policy which commenced in 1825. By 1860 the free trade debate in the UK and Europe was at its peak, with the UK having negotiated bilateral trade agreements with France, the German Confederation, Austria, Sweden, the Hanse towns, Denmark, the United

States and most South American republics with the specific intent of lowering tariffs. Although the UK was ultimately persuaded by the example set by the United States and other European countries to enact specific patent legislation in 1852, this decision was not made without strong opposition from free traders. The patent system was poison for free traders because it created and fostered monopolies; embracing patents was a foolish move, in their opinion, which would smother economic growth in a country the factories of which needed easier access to overseas markets. A free and open market was, in the opinion of free traders, the optimal model for world economic growth.

The debate continued throughout Europe, and despite protectionist opposition the free traders had been making slow but steady progress. In March 1863 the *Verein Deutscher Volkswirte* (The Association of German Economists) passed a resolution at its annual conference calling for the repeal of patent law throughout the German Confederation. Prussia, the largest member of the Confederation, through its government even took up the suggestion, but soon encountered serious opposition from the *Berliner Kaufmannsaeltestenschaft* (The Senate of Berlin's Merchants), the *Technischer Verein für das Eisenhüttenwesen* (The Technical Association for Metallurgical Engineering) and Ernst Werner Siemens.[31]

Siemens, an inventor and industrialist, founded Telegraphen-Bauanstalt von Siemens & Halske in 1847 (becoming Siemens & Halske AG in 1902 and Siemens AG in 1966) and was a very influential businessman. He strenuously opposed any move that would reduce protection for German industry. Rather than the repealing of the patent system Siemens wanted a single German patent system. By the time Bismarck had completed the drafting of a Constitution for the proposed unified Germany in 1867, provision for a national German patent law was included.

The Netherlands on the other hand repealed its patent statute in 1869 and Switzerland, a federation since 1848, continued to refuse to enact a national patent law. Neither country suffered, as was shown by Eric Schiff's famous study.[32] Indeed both countries prospered. For instance Ciba (the Swiss firm today known as Novartis AG, one of the world's largest pharma-bio-agri business conglomerates) did well in this environment. Incorporated in 1884 it was started in 1859 in Basel by Alexander Clavel,[33] a chemist, who simply copied the dye production process that had been patented in France by Renard Frères & Franc. The process produced a synthetic dye called aniline red (fuchsine) used in the production of dyed silk cloth. Similarly in the 1870s in The Netherlands Antonius Jurgens[34] and Samuel van den Bergh,[35] both dairy producers from Oss, adopted an American process for the production of margarine and became two of Europe's largest producers of margarine. They were followed in 1891 by the Philips family who made light bulbs and sold them throughout Europe in competition with Edison.

THE GREAT INTERNATIONAL TRADE FAIRS

In an endeavour to kick-start the French economy after the economic upheaval of the Revolution, in 1798 Paris held the first French national industrial exhibition. It was an opportunity for the new republic to display its agricultural and industrial technologies, and it was designed to encourage trade and commerce within France.

This kind of event, although not attempted again for some time, marked the beginning of what was to become a series of international trade fairs, the first of which was held in Paris in 1844, followed by Berne and Madrid in 1845; Brussels and Bordeaux in 1847; St Petersburg in 1848 and Lisbon and Paris, yet again, in 1849.

These international trade fairs attracted tremendous attention and the British Empire was eager to participate. Prince Albert[36] was the principle architect of the British trade fair, but alongside him were Henry Cole,[37] George Leveson-Cower,[38] Samuel Jones-Loyd[39] and others. Together they served on the Royal Commission for the Exhibition of 1851 which was established in 1850 to oversee its administration. The resulting trade fair, known as the Great Exhibition of the Works of Industry of all Nations, was held in Hyde Park, London, between May and October 1851. Its success was staggering. In generating a net profit of £186 000, a small fortune, the Royal Commissioners decided to use this money for the specific purpose of 'increasing the means of industrial education and extending the influence of science and art upon productive industry'. Indeed some of the profits were used to acquire 87 acres of land in South Kensington in London upon which Imperial College, the Natural History Museum, the Royal Albert Hall, the Royal College of Art, the Royal College of Music, the Science Museum and the Victoria and Albert Museum were built.

Not to be outdone, between May 1855 and November 1855 Paris hosted the *Exposition Universelle des produits de l'Agriculture, de l'Industrie et des Beaux-Arts de Paris* on the Champ de Mars. About 5 000 000 visitors attended the exhibition, 1 000 000 fewer than in London, but unfortunately it was a financial disaster. Its only permanent legacy which remains in use today was the Bordeaux Wine Official Classification System – a system that ranked Bordeaux wines produced by the regions' châteaux from their first to fifth growths, with the *premier crux* wines under this system being produced by Château Lafite-Rothschild, Château Latour, Château Margaux, Château Haut-Brion and Château Mouton-Rothschild.

With the British competitive spirit aroused, between May 1862 and November 1862 London hosted another exhibition, but this time the International Exhibition, as it was known, was nowhere near as grand or as profitable as the Great Exhibition and, although it was not a financial disaster like the *Exposition Universelle,* its profit was insignificant. Among the machines exhibited was the 'analytical engine', a mechanical computer invented by Charles Babbage,[40] as well as new industrial processes for rubber and steel production.

Predictably Paris responded yet again, and between April 1867 and October 1867 hosted another *Exposition Universelle.* On this occasion it was a very grand exhibition, rivalling the Great Exhibition, with some 9 000 000 visitors and 50 000 exhibitors. The funds needed to host the exhibition were provided by the French Government, the city of Paris and public subscription, and although it was not as dramatic a financial disaster as the previous exhibition, the attendance revenue covered only half the costs.

Even the Franco-Prussian War in 1870–1871 was not able to dent the enthusiasm of the Austro-Hungarian Empire. Determined to proceed with its plans, between May and September 1873 Vienna hosted the next world exhibition. The *Weltausstellung* (International Exhibition) was a matter of pride as this was to be the first German-language international fair. Wilhelm von Schwarz-Sendborn, a veteran organizer of Austrian exhibitions at previous world fairs, was appointed its general manager. The site was the Prater, a large city park which was built by redirecting the Danube, and the plans were as grand as those for the Great Exhibition and the *Exposition Universelle* – but its planners had not foreseen the collapse of the Vienna Stock Market on 9 May 1873, an early symptom of the long recession (1873–1896) which started in Europe and spread to the United States and the rest of the world, and which some economic historians believe was the result of the Franco-Prussian War.

Finally it was the turn of the United States, and Philadelphia was the host city. Known officially as the International Exhibition of Arts, Manufactures and Products of the Soil and Mine, it was held, despite the economic situation, between May and November 1876 also as a matter of national pride. The exhibition was held on around 450 acres of Fairmont Park and some 200 buildings were constructed. At its opening on 10 May 1876 President Ulysses Grant[41] was present and in September 1876 it was used to commemorate the centenary of the signing of the Pennsylvania Constitution, one of the milestones towards American independence.

In 1878 Paris again hosted the third *Exposition Universelle* (1 May to 10 November 1878). As with the previous two, the Champ de Mars was its site and most countries (including the colonies and dominions of the British

Empire such as Canada, Victoria, New South Wales, Queensland, South Australia and India) participated by sending delegations, although there was one notable exception – Germany. Some 13 000 000 people came and saw the many inventions that were exhibited, including Bell's telephone and Edison's light bulb, megaphone and phonograph. In addition electrical street lighting was demonstrated throughout the month of June on the Avenue de l'Opéra and the Place de l'Opéra.

There were subsequent international fairs before the turn of the century, and the next were held in Sydney, Australia in 1879; Melbourne, Australia in 1880; Amsterdam in 1883; Antwerp in 1885; Paris in 1889 (for which the *Tour Eiffel* was erected); Chicago in 1893 and finally Paris again in 1900. This was not to be the last and they continued into the twentieth century, with the last great international fair being held in Paris in 1937, but these early fairs played a significant role in the development of patent law (as well as trade mark and copyright law) because they fostered its internationalization.

THE GERMAN PATENT LAW, 1877

For Bismarck nationalism and protectionism were kindred spirits. A devotee of List and a fiercely ambitious man, Bismarck looked to the British Empire with both suspicion and admiration. Unlike the British, who were seeking to expand their Empire's economy by what List saw as 'bringing down' the economic defences of its trading partners through the guise of free trade, Bismarck was determined to build up the economic defences of the fledgling German Empire and was attentive to the ambitions and concerns of Germany's industrialists.

In 1947 Heinrich Kronstein and Irene Till, economic historians, denounced Bismarck as 'the leader of the anti-patent movement';[42] but their criticism was misplaced. Simply that he had delayed establishing a national patent law until 1877 was no proof that he disapproved of patents rather it reflected his wish to have the right patent system for Germany. They ignored two points: first patents were continuing to be granted by the provinces of the former German Confederation and so there was no immediate imperative for a national system, and secondly it was clear to Bismarck that German industrialists, like Siemens and Bayer, were concerned to ensure that the national patent system did not inadvertently suppress Germany industrialization, a concern which he shared and a result that he wished to avoid.

In 1874 the *Deutche Chemische Gesellschaft* (the German Chemical Organization), representing the German chemical industry, collaborated with the representative organizations of other technologies such as the electrical industry to form the *Deutsche Patentschutz-Verein* (the German Patent Protection Association), the sole purpose of which was to guide Bismarck on how to draft the proposed national German patent law.[43] Like Bismarck its president, Siemens, was in favour of a national patent system, but he was not in favour of one that could be used by the British Empire and the United States to suppress German industrialization. To an expert committee, established in 1876 by Bismarck to enquire into the establishment of a national patent system, Siemens made his case:

> Today [German] industry is developing rapidly; and as a result monopolization of inventions and abuse of rights will inevitably expose large segments of industry to serious injury. The government must protect industry against these dangers. From abroad another danger may arise. Inventive work is far more developed in England, United States and France than in Germany. Up to the present the number of patents taken out in Germany by foreigners has been small because of the scope of protection given to the inventor has been insufficient. New legislation will lead to a substantial increase of foreign patentees. We shall experience a wave of foreign – particularly American – patent applications. These patents will not be taken out in order to protect industrial plants established or to be established in Germany; they will be taken out to monopolize production abroad. These articles will be imported into this country. Such a danger must be met. It is not enough to provide that foreign patentees be required to submit evidence that they have established a plant in Germany. Such evidence may be mere shadow; they can merely keep a small domestic production going to maintain their patents.[44]

Equally the chemical industry was concerned to ensure that any new patent law did not protect chemical products per se, just the *processes* of their manufacture. Their strategy was to encourage R&D, so that new and more efficient chemical processes were developed in a field in which Germany had a comparative advantage over its international competitors. Accordingly a patent system like the US and English, which allowed product patents on chemical substances, would act only as a disincentive to that advantage because, if the product was subject to patent protection, then no matter how innovative the processes for their manufacture would be subject to that monopoly.

Bismarck subsequently satisfied each of these concerns. Under the German Patents Act 1877 or *Reichspatentgesetz*, enacted on 25 May 1877, the Act stated:[45]

> Patents are granted for new inventions which permit of an industrial realisation. The exceptions are . . . inventions of articles of food, drinks and medicines as well as of substances manufactured by a chemical process in so far as the inventions do not relate to a certain process for manufacturing such articles [section 1].

Furthermore a German patent would be unenforceable if after three years the patentee neglected 'to work his invention in the Country to an adequate extent or to do all that was requisite for securing the said working'. Moreover, as Siemens was on the patent law drafting committee, the economic protections which he desired included a compulsory licensing power which applied 'when it appear[ed] conducive to the public interest that permission to use the invention be granted to others and the patentee refuse[d] to grant such permission for a suitable compensation and on good security' (section 11).

Siemens believed in the importance and power of collaborative science and engineering, and his approach to innovation involved a combination of both academic and industrial institutions; thus for him it was difficult, if not impossible, to apportion the inventive contribution of one person over another. The German patent law therefore deliberately excluded any reference to 'the inventor' as such, only to the patent applicant – an organization – reinforcing the team approach to technical innovation.

This idiosyncratic approach did not mean however that the framers of the German patent law were determined entirely to ignore the international community. Siemens was rather impressed by the US example, and so the new patent law established the *Kaiserliches Patentamt* (the Imperial Patent Office) in Berlin. The law effected the transition of all existing German provincial patents by giving them national status, but only the German Patent Office would be empowered to grant new patents. Patent examiners were employed by the patent office to examine patent applications for novelty (again adopting the US practice); this examination was to be conducted over an eight-week period and the results were published in an official patent journal. Patent applications were also published. There were two reasons for this: first it enabled members of the public to challenge the assertion of novelty during the examination phase, thereby 'opposing' the grant of the patent, and secondly it ensured that technical information contained in the patent application could be rapidly disseminated. This was different from the US and most European patent systems, which allowed public inspection of the patent application only after grant, and perhaps contributed to Germany's domination of chemicals and electrical products prior to World War I.

Nonetheless a distinctly German solution was devised to resolve priority of invention disputes. The framers adopted the first-to-file threshold which gave priority to the first to file a patent application, not the first to invent, as was then required by the US and British patent laws.[46]

The maximum term of a German patent was left unchanged at 15 years, but patent fees were quite high, being 30 Marks for the first year, 50 Marks for the second, 100 Marks for the third and 50 Marks for every subsequent year. For a 15-year patent this brought the total cost to 780 Marks – a very substantial sum – but a reflection of one of the principal objectives of the framers to encourage collaboration with large German firms and to discourage the over-use of the patent system by small firms and individuals, an over-use which would increase the number of patent applications for trivial inventions and cause an overall slowing down of the examination process.

Unfortunately the prohibition on the patenting of chemical substances was successfully exploited by chemical companies which were established close to Germany, in Basel, Switzerland. Consequently Basel became a source of competition for the German chemical industry because Swiss firms were able to copy the German chemical processes and sell the chemical products in Germany without infringing Germany's chemical process patents. What separated these companies from Germany was merely the River Rhine, providing them with easy access to their German markets.

Calls for patent law reform soon started being heard in the *Reichstag* (German Parliament). Badische Anilin- und Soda-Fabrik (BASF) was particularly keen to neutralize Swiss competition. A Basel firm which was started by Johann Geigy-Merian and Johann Muller-Pack (eventually to become Geigy in 1901, Ciba-Geigy Ltd in 1971 and Novartis International AG after Ciba-Geigy's merger with Sandoz AG in 1996) was sued for patent infringement in the German Federal Court. BASF alleged that in exporting methylene blue (a synthetic dye) to Germany Geigy had infringed its German patent. This was, as the law then stood, impossible. For a start, if the process was copied it was copied outside German territory and therefore was not an infringement in Germany. As there was no patent over chemical substances in Germany, importing and selling such substances in Germany was not an infringement. Neither could the copying of the process in Switzerland, a country which did not have national patent laws, amount to an infringement in Switzerland itself. Nonetheless in its decision of 14 March 1888 the German court held that BASF's patent was infringed because the German patent's monopoly extended to *any* products made by the use of that process. Thus necessity created the 'product-by-process' patent monopoly as a way of attaching liability for the production of the end product of a patented process.

This was a clear victory for German protectionism, but it was not enough to satisfy the demands of the German Chemical Association. Consequently, after the German Government consulted with industry in 1883 and 1886, it amended the patent law on 14 April 1891. The effect of this amendment was not only to codify the court's decision in *BASF* but to shift the burden of proof to the alleged infringer to prove that the chemical product, if it was the same as the product produced by the patented process, was manufactured by a different process. Otherwise infringement of the process would be presumed and infringement proven.

Another reform concerned the German Patent Office. One of the features of the German patent system was that the decisions of patent examiners could be appealed only to the Patent Office. While this seemed appropriate to the framers, it soon became apparent that a lack of independence between examiners at the Patent Office and the Patent Office itself was creating conflicts of interests. Under the original patent law full-time examiners were lawyers, but part-time examiners were not, and were generally chemists or engineers who came from industry. One part-time examiner was Carl Martius,[47] who founded Aktiengesellschaft für Anilinfabrikation in 1867 (re-established in 1952 as AGFA AG and in 2007 divided into three companies: AGFA Graphics, AGFA HCES and AGFA Materials). As a patent examiner Martius had access to patent applications for new chemical processes filed by his firm's competitors, and eventually suspicions were raised over his role in the examination of a patent application for a process filed by Bayer. Bayer's process produced a red synthetic dye (Ponceau 4 RB). Soon AGFA was producing the same red dye as that produced by the Bayer process. Naturally Martius was accused of industrial espionage and was criminally prosecuted, and AGFA, his firm, was sued for patent infringement. Despite the circumstances Martius was acquitted and AGFA was found not to have infringed Bayer's patent because Martius, an excellent chemist, had sufficient skill to design around the Bayer process, and accordingly he was able to prove that the AGFA process was different. Nonetheless the message had been heard, and from 1891 all patent examiners would be employed full-time.

Apart from these amendments the German Federal Court retained sole jurisdiction for infringement actions, while the validity of patents remained with the Patent Office until 1959, when the validity of German patents was transferred to a specific patents court consisting of both lawyers and engineers or scientists. Consequently Germany now has one court for deciding validity and another infringement. This is different from the UK and the US, where infringement and validity are usually decided before the same court in the same proceedings.

There were further calls for reform after 1891, particularly from employee engineers and scientists who believed that the failure of the German patent system to recognize the actual inventor was discriminatory. Calls for reform came from the *Bund der technisch-industriellen Beamten* (Employed Technical and Industrial Engineers' Union), the *Deutscher Juristentag* (German Lawyers' Association) and the *Allgemeiner Deutscher Erfinder-Verband* (German Inventors' Association), and eventually these calls resulted in a proposed amendment in 1913 which would, but for the interruption of World War I, have seen the end of the first-to-file system in Germany. This issue was not revisited until 1936 when the Nazi government finally recognized the role of the inventor.[48]

In 1911 there was one further amendment to the German patent law brought about in a tit-for-tat response to the requirement that British patents must be worked within the UK or be subject to either the grant of a compulsory licence or revocation (section 27, UK Patents & Designs Act 1907). According to this amendment, if the owner of a German patent refused to grant a licence on reasonable terms, 'and the grant of the licence appears desirable in the public interest', the German Patent Office was authorized to 'grant the license unconditionally or subject to conditions as it may think fit', and furthermore, if the patent was 'worked exclusively or principally outside of the German Empire and the German Protectorates . . . [the] patent may be revoked'.[49]

THE SWISS PATENT LAW, 1888, 1907 AND CARTELS

By 1883 the Paris Convention was complete, and by 1887 the accepted view in Europe was that patents were here to stay. Understandably, with The Netherlands being the only other exception to the rule, Swiss resistance to patents had dissipated. Even so when the Swiss patent statute passed into law on 15 November 1888 it was, according to Schiff, 'probably . . . the most incomplete and selective patent law ever enacted in modern times'.[50] It defined patentable subject matter so narrowly that only inventions that could be represented by mathematical models were permitted. Obstinately refusing to allow chemical patents, the Swiss clung onto their competitive advantage.

Naturally the United States, which had joined the Paris Convention Union in 1887, had Switzerland in her sights. She was determined to see reciprocity enforced throughout the world, and so in Brussels in December 1900 proposed that the Paris Convention be amended so that 'any invention that [was] not patentable in the country of origin, may be excluded from protection in any other Member country that [found] it expedient to include it'. By this time even Swiss firms were beginning to file patents in other countries, and this amendment to the Paris Convention placed Switzerland in a difficult situation. Germany followed suit and joined the Paris Convention Union in 1901. It too had grown impatient with the Swiss attitude, delivering an ultimatum that either Switzerland amended its patent law and permitted the patenting of chemical processes by 31 December 1907 or Germany would retaliate by imposing penalty customs duties on Swiss-made chemical products. Consequently on 21 June 1907 Switzerland amended its patent law to comply with US and German demands – but while chemical processes became patentable chemicals and other substances were not, neither were they permitted with respect to food and pharmaceutical products, and unless the patents were worked in Switzerland they were subject to compulsory licensing or revocation.

Although the Swiss had capitulated, by this time Ciba, Giegy and other Swiss chemical firms had become increasingly globalized. They had realized that German and US companies were becoming involved in sharing patents over specific technologies and using these technologies to create industry-wide global cartels. In the electrical industry one such cartel was formed in 1903 between Allgemeine Elecktricitäts-Gesellschaft (AEG) and General Electric (GE), under which they agreed to share patents and home markets, thereby increasing barriers to entry in both home markets for their respective competitors. The same cartelization process was occurring within the chemical industry, as BASF, Bayer and Hoechst used their overseas sales subsidiaries, factories and foreign patents to control competition in their foreign markets, especially with respect to dyestuffs. It was therefore becoming a matter of necessity for the Swiss either to join the German/US cartelization club or not only to risk losing their traditional markets but also face the prospect of increasingly competitive markets at home. According to Kronstein and Till:

> The very fact that the German government and the German chemical industry were demanding that Switzerland grant chemical patents was taken as an indication that the real purpose was to compel Swiss industry to join the German dyestuffs cartel. History proved that this change was correct, for in the end the Swiss industry was compelled to become a junior partner in the German dyestuffs group.[51]

PHILIPS, THE LIGHT BULB, THE NETHERLANDS PATENT LAW AND MORE CARTELS

Gerard Philips,[52] an engineer, and his father, Frederik, a tobacco merchant and banker, opened a small factory in Eindhoven in The Netherlands on 15 May 1891. Four years later they were joined by Gerard's brother, Anton,[53] a stockbroker. Together they manufactured electric light bulbs. So successful were they that by 1912, when the new Dutch patent law came into effect, they were able to list NV Philips Gloeilampenfabrieken on the Amsterdam Stock Exchange and made a small fortune.[54] This achievement was made even more remarkable by the fact that in 1891 the manufacture of light bulbs around the world was controlled by the General Electric Company (GE) through its network of patents and licensees, and that of the three men who established Philips only one was an engineer.

The first electric light bulb, using an incandescent carbon filament encased in a partial vacuum glass bulb, was invented in 1878 by Joseph Swan,[55] an Englishman, and while his invention was a breakthrough it had a life-span of only 13 hours. A year later Thomas Edison,[56] an American, improved upon Swan's invention by using a carbon filament encased in a total vacuum glass bulb. Edison's light bulb had a life-span of about 40 hours. Remarkable as these inventions were, given that they used a new form of energy, electricity, to create light without a flame, in comparison to the existing well-established gas lighting invented by William Murdoch in 1792, neither electricity nor electric light bulbs were readily available or affordable. Moreover electric light bulbs at that time did not burn anywhere near as brightly. Even 13 years after Swan first demonstrated his invention the life-span of electric light bulbs and the brightness of the light they produced were inferior to those produced by gas light.

Apart from these technical hurdles, as the intense rivalry between the Swan Electric Light Company (established in London in 1881) and the Edison Electric Light Company (established in New York in 1878) demonstrated, there were others. Despite the fact that Swan's light bulb was invented before Edison's, Edison claimed to be the first inventor, and while his light bulb was certainly more efficient than Swan's (and different, in that it used a complete vacuum while Swan's did not), it was a claim that was disputed by Swan. Both Swan and Edison were granted patents in the UK and, naturally, both became adversaries in patent litigation fought in the UK. In 1881 the decision of the British courts in *Swan Electric Light Co Ltd v Edison Electric Light Co Ltd* resulted in Edison losing to Swan because, even though Edison was also granted a UK patent for his invention, Swan's patent not only predated Edison's by two years but it claimed a patent monopoly which was broad enough to capture the improvements made by Edison to Swan's invention. In one of the classic examples of how the patent system has been used to undermine technological improvements, Swan's broad patent monopoly meant that Edison either sued to challenge the validity of the Swan patent and win, or faced extinction in the UK.

Shrewdly Edison proposed to Swan that it would be in their mutual interest to merge their companies rather than fight it out through the courts and, just as shrewdly, Swan agreed – leading in 1883 to the formation of Edison & Swan United Electric Light Co Ltd. As a result Edison's improved light bulb remained available for sale in the UK; but, fortunately for Edison, had Swan been more ambitious and tenacious the patent system would have prevented the better bulb from being manufactured and sold in the UK until 1892, only two years before Edison's British patent was due to expire.

BOX 4.2   UK PATENT 4576 TO THOMAS ALVA EDISON

Improvements in electric lamps, and in the method of manufacturing the same

Final Specification Filed 10 May 1880

'First, an electric lamp for giving light by incandescence, consisting of a filament of carbon of high resistance made as described, and secured to metallic wires as set forth; second, the combination of a carbon filament within a receiver made entirely of glass, through which the leading wires pass and from which receiver the air is exhausted for the purposes set forth. Third, a coiled carbon filament or strip, arranged in such a manner that only a portion of the surface of such carbon conductor shall radiate light, as set forth; and fourth, a mode of securing the carbon filament to the leading wires.'

Edison & Swan Electric Light Company v Woodhouse 1886 32 Ch D 520.

Of course in 1891, without a national patent system, the Philips family was spared not only the need to invent around the Swan and Edison patents but also the expense and disruptions caused by patent litigation. Furthermore it avoided the need to secure patent sub-licences from Compagnie Continentale Edison, the French subsidiary of the Edison Electric Light Company and the principal European licensee. Quite apart from the issue of the patent royalties that would otherwise have been payable to Edison, the obligations that these patent licences imposed on licensees were often onerous. For example, in a typical Edison licence granted to Deutsche Edison-Gesellschaft für angewandte Elektrizität (later to become AEG) over Edison's German patents, Schiff wrote:

the [licensee] undertook to uphold the integrity of the German Edison patents even beyond what its own interest might have suggested. It undertook, for example, in case of litigation, not to compromise without the consent of the Paris company. The activities of the German company were further restricted by the provision that they should use only the Edison system in their work, and that they should not acquire any patents, licenses, or other rights pertaining to the exploitation of technical innovations, without the consent of the French company.[57]

As a result Edison's patent licensees were carefully controlled in their ability to develop alternative technologies or even to improve upon Edison's invention, giving Edison a competitive advantage not only for the duration of the patent but even for a significant time afterwards by preventing licensees from springboarding into the market until the patent had expired. Clearly it would take some months or even years for any Edison licensee to establish itself in any market which had been dominated by Edison, both by patent and by trade mark, for at least 15 years.

Furthermore Edison's domination of the light bulb markets in Europe and the UK enhanced its ability to acquire, control and manipulate technologies that would improve light bulb performance and otherwise compete with Edison's core technology. For instance Edison acquired the invention of two Hungarians, Alexander Just and Franz Hanaman, in 1905. They were the first to develop a process which used the metal tungsten in the production of filaments, which significantly improved light bulb performance. Edison, which by 1892 had merged with Thomson-Houston Electric Company to form the General Electric Company (GE), now possessed the patent rights to this breakthrough, and in 1912 was granted US patent 1,018,502.

In the meantime GE had established the GE Research Laboratory in Schenectady, New York and, as can be expected, provided the Just and Hanaman technology to William Coolidge, one of its research scientists. As Edison had done with Swan's invention, Coolidge was able to improve upon the Just and Hanaman process which, although an improvement on Edison's light bulb, produced a tungsten filament which was brittle. Coolidge's process turned a powder metallurgy ingot into wire by using elevated temperatures to deform the tungsten, thus producing small diameter tungsten ductile wires. Thus his process overcame the inherent brittleness of tungsten and substantially improved light bulb performance. The Coolidge invention was also significant in another respect because, in US patent 1,082,933 granted to GE in 1913, it claimed not only the Coolidge process (claim 1) and the tungsten filament (claim 24) but also 'an incandescent electric lamp having a filament of drawn tungsten wires' (claim 25). As such claim 25 effectively gave GE a renewed monopoly over the light bulb itself and, even more importantly, over radio valves – essential components in radios. Almost simultaneously another of GE's research scientists, Irving Langmuir,[58] discovered that if Coolidge's tungsten filament was used in a bulb 'filled with nitrogen carefully purified and free from water-vapor', the light bulb was, in Langmuir's words, 'capable of operating at extraordinarily high efficiency and giving a light of marked intrinsic brightness and whiteness'. As a result in 1916 GE was granted US patent 1,180,159. Finally the modern incandescent light bulb was born.

Coolidge's invention had effectively renewed GE's patent monopoly in light bulbs (as the original Edison patent had expired by 1896) and, in combination with the Langmuir patent, enabled GE and its exclusive licensee in the US, Westinghouse Electric and Manufacturing Company (Westinghouse), further to control the US market domination which GE still enjoyed through the GE trade marks.

Meanwhile in 1910 the decision was made in The Netherlands to reinstate its patent system. The proposed Dutch patent law, following the German patent system, limited the maximum length to 15 years and provided for compulsory licensing after a period of five years if the patent was not worked in The Netherlands. It came into effect on 1 June 1912. Its introduction was deliberately delayed to give Philips and other Dutch firms time to file patent applications ahead of any foreign competition. Indeed Gerard Philips was surprisingly quick to use his own engineering skills 'simultaneously' to invent a process which produced a tungsten filament that protected Philips from GE in its home market until 1927.

In order to survive in this new environment Philips had seriously to develop its own R&D capacity, and by 1914 Gilles Holst, a physicist, was employed to head the new Philips R&D team. Fortunately for Philips his appointment coincided with the beginning of World War I and, with the wartime embargo on the export of German coal, gas production fell dramatically, giving electricity an opportunity to break into a much larger market. By 1915 Holst's team had developed a light bulb which was filled with argon gas, rather than Langmuir's purified and dry nitrogen gas, and by the 1920s his team had gone on to develop X-ray tubes and radio valves. From there Philips went on to become a manufacturer of radios, not just of electrical components, and without doubt the success of Philips in a patent environment is an example of how patents can aid innovation. What cannot be overlooked is that Dutch industrialization was not inspired by any patent system in the first place, and that the ability of the Dutch to copy patented technology ultimately benefited the Dutch economy by enabling Philips and others to establish themselves independently of patent owners and their European licensees. As it turned out this mattered little within a matter of years GE and Philips had come to an agreement that effectively carved up the world light bulb market and was designed to suppress both competition and innovation in the manufacture of electric light bulbs and their components, such as glass.

The only problem for them was that in 1890 the US Congress had passed the Sherman Antitrust Act. The Sherman Act was inspired by John Sherman,[59] and it provided in section 1:

> Every contract, combination in the form of trust or otherwise, or conspiracy, in restraint of trade or commerce among the several States, or with foreign nations, is declared to be illegal.

Section 2 provided:

> Every person who monopolize, or attempt to monopolize, or combine or conspire with any other person or persons, to monopolize any part of the trade or commerce among the several States, or with foreign nations, shall be deemed guilty of a felony.

For GE and Westinghouse the successful prosecution of Standard Oil in 1911[60] meant they too were in the spotlight over alleged anti-competitive practices in the distribution and sale of light bulbs in the United States. Within two months of the Supreme Court decision in *The Standard Oil Company v The United States* (1911) 221 US 1, handed down on 15 May 1911, the Department of Justice sued both GE and Westinghouse under the Sherman Act; but, keen to avoid litigation, both GE and Westinghouse submitted to a Consent Decree which effectively prohibited them from setting prices for their light bulbs beyond their wholesale buyers. Otherwise GE was free to continue with business as usual, and that included using patent licences to set the sale price of light bulbs manufactured by GE and Westinghouse, dividing up the US into discrete wholesale territories with specific market quota, and dictating the kinds and sizes of light bulbs which wholesalers could supply to their distributors. The Consent Decree was hardly an issue for GE and Westinghouse, who then set about circumventing it by restructuring their relationships with retailers by supplying them with light bulbs as consignment inventory in which the light bulbs remained the property of GE and Westinghouse, rather than selling them light bulbs through wholesalers and distributors. Ultimately this new arrangement was the subject of a new complaint in 1924, but the Supreme Court upheld it as legal in *United States v General Electric & Westinghouse* (1926) 272 US 476 and confirmed that the Just and Hanaman, Coolidge and Langmuir patents completely covered 'the making of the modern electric lights with the tungsten filaments', and gave GE 'the monopoly of their making, using and vending'.

This broad approach towards the patentees' rights of exploitation, which the US Supreme Court first adopted in *Bement v National Harrow Co* (1902) 186 US 70, ensured that so long as the patent was operational

GE and Westinghouse were able effectively to ignore the *Sherman Act*. For GE this was ideal: that was until the Third District Court of Appeal decision in *General Electric v DeForest Radio* (1928) 28 F 2d 641 held that all the product claims in the Coolidge patent were invalid, and even though this ruling came down towards the end of the life of the patent on 29 January 1929, after the US Supreme Court refused leave to appeal GE was forced to disclaim the invention defined in claims 14, 16 and 24–31. This included the all-important claim 25, which claimed any bulb that used a tungsten filament.

In any event by 1931 what remained of the Coolidge patent had expired. That of course had not stopped GE and Westinghouse from colluding, and by 1927 their collusion had implicated a number of other American companies, namely Corning Glass Works, American Blank Company, Empire Machine Company, Consolidated Electric Lamp Company, Hygrade Sylvania Corporation, Ken-Rad Tube and Lamp Corporation, Tung-Sol Lamp Works Inc., and one foreign company, namely Philips. According to the Department of Justice indictment of 333 paragraphs,[61] since 1927 these companies had:

> unlawfully conspired to monopolize, attempted to monopolize, and unlawfully contracted, combined and conspired to restrain trade or commerce among the several states, or with foreign nations, in the incandescent electric light lamp industry and more particularly by unlawfully and in violation of Sec. 1 and Sec. 2 of the Sherman Anti-Trust Act.

Furthermore GE, Corning and Philips were separately accused of:

> violating Sec. 73 of the *Wilson Tariff Act* by unlawfully combining and conspiring with and entering into and maintaining unlawful contracts or agreements relating to the importation from foreign countries into the United States of glass bulbs, tubing and cane and machinery for the production of such articles, whereby Philips has been and [was] prevented from importing such articles into the United States, all with the purpose and effect of restraining lawful trade and competition in the United States.

By 19 January 1949, when Judge Foreman of the US District Court handed down his decision in *US v General Electric Co* (1949) 82 F Supp 753 holding each of these companies guilty, nearly 70 years had passed since Edison's light bulb was patented, and around 33 years had passed since Coolidge and Langmuir had patented key improvements to it. This meant that for over 50 years in the case of the former and for over 15 years in the case of the latter GE and Westinghouse had used the market dominance which they had obtained by virtue of various US patent monopolies to maintain and extend that market dominance through various agreements and commercial devices designed illegally to suppress competition. Besides these agreements GE used various devices (such as owning or controlling the manufacture and distribution of all lamp-making machinery; ownership and control with Corning of all types of glass bulb, tubing and cane manufacturing; and ownership and control of all lamp-base manufacturing) to ensure that the equipment needed to manufacture light bulbs was unavailable to competitors which were not parties to the GE and Westinghouse collusion. Moreover they enlisted the support of Philips, the only other company in the world that could pose a significant threat to their de facto monopoly, by effectively bribing Philips to stay out of the US market. This was achieved by a number of agreements, but one known as the Phoebus Agreement, signed in Zurich on 20 December 1924 and renewed in 1941, established a worldwide cartel known as Phoebus SA Compagnie Industrielle pour le Dévelopment de L'Eclairage. Philips, naturally, was a party to that cartel. There were other agreements of course, and one of these was signed by Anton Philips on 15 March 1931. This agreement superseded an earlier agreement signed in 1919 which provided for an exchange of patent rights and market information between GE and Philips, and under this new agreement Philips was granted Holland as its exclusive territory and GE was granted the United States as its exclusive territory. Under the new agreement glass products and machinery were excluded, but otherwise it was business as usual until the agreement expired on 1 July 1955. In 1937 a separate agreement was made between Philips, GE and Corning concerning glass products. Under the terms of this agreement Philips agreed not to sell glass products to the United States or aid anyone in that regard, and gave up its US patent rights to the glass-making technology for ten years to GE, in return for which GE would pay Philips 'a monetary consideration'.

In its concluding remarks the District Court acknowledged that GE's 'industrial achievement has been impressive', but it also found that it 'paced its industrial achievements with efforts to insulate itself from competition', and that it 'sought to stretch the monopoly acquired by patents far beyond the intendment of those grants' by constructing 'a great network of agreements and licenses, national and international in scope, which had the effect of locking the door of the United States to any challenge to its supremacy in the incandescent electric lamp industry'. In this regard the court noted: 'admiration for the business acumen of GE . . . cannot avoid adherence to the philosophy of political economics enunciated in the antitrust laws . . . for as the US Supreme Court stated ". . . our economy is built largely upon competition in quality and prices" . . . and monopoly is a protean threat to fair prices'.

Although this case specifically concerned US law and the US market for electric light bulbs, what it demonstrates is that patent owners in general are never satisfied with the term of any patent monopoly, whether it be for five, ten, 15 or more years. It also shows that The Netherlands, without having a patent law, was able to foster the development of an extremely successful business in a leading edge technology; and it also shows that within a handful of years of a patent law coming into effect in The Netherlands at least one of its key businesses had commenced participating in conduct which was designed to extend whatever patent monopoly to which it was lawfully entitled well beyond that entitlement. That was the purpose of the 1919 agreement with GE and it led Philips deeper into a relationship in 1924 and 1937 with GE and other companies which was equally designed to suppress competition around the world, giving it and members of the worldwide cartel the ability to charge prices and control technological advances in such a way as to maximize the time for which those prices could be charged. It shows that the patent system can be used to control technological development to suit the profit motives of those who dominate a field of technology.[62]

THE NEW EUROPE, THE EUROPEAN PATENT AND THE UK'S MEMBERSHIP OF THE EEC

For the six inaugural members of the European Economic Community (EEC), formed under the Treaty Establishing the European Community signed in Rome on 25 March 1957 (Treaty of Rome), the need to establish and maintain a competitive trading and technological edge in world trade was essential to their plan to protect both themselves and their industries from competition from the United States. By drawing inspiration from the United States, the EEC's mandate was the free movement of goods, services and labour across its international borders. What was missing however was the centralized bureaucratic and administrative agencies and departments that facilitated this process in the United States. Therefore it was obvious that a centralized European patent system, like the US Trade Mark and Patent Office (USPTO), would be necessary if this new paradigm was to function successfully.

In terms of European patent law harmonization by October 1962 the first complete draft of a convention to unify European patent law had been completed under the supervision of Kurt Haertel,[63] President of the German Patent Office between 1963 and 1975. Haertel and his colleagues had been working on the draft proposal since 1959, and it envisaged the establishment of a European Patent Office and a European Patent Court through which a single supranational European patent would apply in all EEC countries. It did not propose the repeal of the national patent systems of member countries, but only that the European-wide patent would operate alongside the national patent systems as an alternative. Thus Haertel avoided the kinds of nationalist rivalries that could easily derail the negotiations. Indeed Haertel was supremely confident that the cost advantages alone would be incentive enough for inventors to prefer the single European-wide patent system over the existing fractured and expensive national patent systems which required translations of patent applications into many languages.

Haertel also avoided arguments over patentability criteria by deliberately following the early drafts of the Convention on the Unification of Certain Points of Substantive Law on Patents for Invention (the Strasbourg Convention), signed in Strasbourg in November 1963.[64]

The Haertel draft was circulated widely throughout Europe[65] and came under consideration not only within the EEC but, in May 1965, by the European Free Trade Association (EFTA), a body in competition with the EEC, of which the UK was a member. Meeting in Vienna the EFTA Ministerial Council established an expert patent working party, chaired by Edward Armitage,[66] and by January 1967 this working party had prepared a further draft patent convention based upon, but different from, the Haertel draft.

This development then led to the formation of another EEC expert working party in 1969, but this time it was chaired by Haertel, not Armitage. A proposal was then made to broaden membership to include non-EEC countries, and in March 1969 the Council of the European Communities established an Inter-Governmental Conference in Brussels which included both EEC and non-EEC participants. This conference took place in May 1969 and was chaired again by Haertel, but on this occasion the United International Bureau for the Protection of Intellectual Property (BIRPI) – now known as the World Intellectual Property Organization (WIPO) – the Council of Europe, the Commission of the European Communities and the International Patent Institute were invited to participate.

What followed was the establishment of an inter-governmental working party made up of delegates from Germany, France, the UK, The Netherlands, Sweden and Switzerland which met in July, October and November 1969 producing a Memorandum on the Establishment of a European System for the Grant of Patents. However rather than rubber stamp the original 1962 Haertel draft, which envisaged a single European-wide patent, the working party instead proposed a bundle of national patents. Even though the European Patent Office (EPO) would remain the central granting authority, this compromise was seen as a backward step as far as Haertel was concerned. This was because the critical issues of the enforcement and validity would then come within the jurisdiction of the respective national courts, removing many of the cost and efficiency advantages that were central to his proposal.

This must have been foreseeable, given the differences in Europe's legal systems; but as if this was not enough to sound warning bells the EPO and its 'independent' appellate bodies, the Technical Board of Appeal and the Enlarged Board of Appeal, would be retained. These bodies would adjudicate on the validity of a granted European patent through the pre-grant examination and post-grant opposition processes. This introduced a further source of confusion because it contemplated that a bundle of national patents could be invalidated by a single agency (assuming that it was challenged in opposition proceedings), but the corresponding national patents could be revoked only by the respective national courts. This would lead to a multiplicity of patent litigation.

Another significant difference from the original Haertel draft was that a European patent application would not be deemed to apply automatically across all members of the proposed EPC (which in 1962 consisted of only EEC members), but would apply only with respect to those countries nominated by the patent applicant at the time of the filing of the application with the EPO (which in 1970 included all EPC countries, not just the EEC). This amendment was unavoidable, given that that the resulting granted European patent would not now be a single pan-European patent but would instead be a bundle of national patents. As such the geographical footprint of a European patent was determined by the patent application much like a patchwork, cut into a shape that corresponded to the national borders of the nominated countries and with respect to which national patents would ultimately be granted.

Despite the foreseeable difficulties the inter-governmental committee considered the proposed EPC worthwhile. Of course the only other alternative was a continuation of the hodgepodge of inefficient and even more expensive national patent laws.

In what was the probably the only opportunity to 'harmonize' European patent laws, the advantages over the *status quo* were several: there would be a single European patent application; the official languages of the EPO would be limited to three (French, German and English); the EPO would be responsible for examination, opposition and appeal and the grant and revocation of a European patent; and there would be one application and patent grant and one set of patent renewal fees. Even though it was not a true European patent as Haertel had first proposed, the Committee decided that it was worth trying.

However by 1978, when the European Patent Convention came into effect, this history and the reasoning behind it had been erased and replaced by the pharmaceutical-patent paradigm which was now entrenched into the very fabric of the European patent system. No longer concerned about the petty squabbles over European trade, European politicians accepted that national patent laws which excluded pharmaceutical products as inventions were unnecessary. The Italians, unfortunately, seemed not to have understood the impact that the EPC would have on their country's vibrant and competitive generic pharmaceutical industry. In 1977 American pharmaceutical companies challenged the validity of the Italian patent law which continued to prohibit the patenting of chemical substances for use in medicines, and these proceedings reached the Italian Court of Cassation, Italy's constitutional court. It ruled in 1978 that the prohibition on the patenting of pharmaceutical products and their processes of manufacture was unconstitutional, and ordered Italy to comply with the EPC. According to FM Scherer,[67] there were a number of immediate consequences:

> (1) no significant increase in Italian drug R&D expenditures relative to world trends; (2) no significant increase in the number of new drug entities introduced by Italian firms; and (3) a sharp deterioration of the Italian trade balance in drugs into the negative realm as export sales faltered and multinational firms imported many of their products into Italy from elsewhere in Europe.[68]

One of the central objectives of the EEC was to guarantee the free movement of goods, workers and services within the EEC area, as provided respectively by Articles 9, 48–51 and 59–66 of the Treaty of Rome.[69] Accordingly this free trade and labour movement objective placed the parochial and protectionist economic agendas inherent in the national patent legislations on a collision course. The price that the EEC membership demanded was the removal of any provision in any national law which tended to undermine these collective objectives. Naturally, restricting compulsory licensing was the next item on the pharmaceutical industry's agenda.

GLOBAL PHARMACEUTICAL CONSOLIDATION

Sensing victory the pharmaceutical industry began consolidating within the EEC where, since the Treaty of Rome, national borders became almost irrelevant in terms of trade and commerce. Consequently in 1972 Beecham (UK) made a takeover bid for Glaxo (UK) and, although the bid failed on that occasion due to the intervention of the UK Monopolies and Mergers Commission, by the late 1980s Beecham had merged with Smith Kline Beecham to become Smithkline Beecham plc (UK). ICI (UK) hived off its biosciences division into a new company called Zeneca Group plc (UK), and by the early 1990s this had merged with Astra AB (Swedish) to become AstraZeneca (UK/Swedish) in 1999. ICI similarly hived off its agrochemical business to Ciba-Geigy (Swiss), itself the result of a merger between Ciba and Geigy in 1973, which in 1994 merged with Sandoz (Swiss) to become Novartis (Swiss). Novartis and AstraZeneca then merged their respective agribusinesses into one mega-agrichemical business corporation called Sygenta AG (Swiss). The Wellcome Foundation (UK) was itself floated in 1986 to become Wellcome plc and in 1995 Glaxo made a successful, though hostile, bid for Wellcome to become Glaxo Wellcome, only finally to merge in 2000 with Smithkline Beecham into the mega-pharmaceutical company, GlaxoSmithKline (UK).

Consolidation also came at a price, as some British companies were fully taken over by, or sold to, foreign pharmaceutical companies. In this regard the pharmaceutical giant Rhône-Poulenc (French) acquired Fisons (UK) and BASF (German) acquired Boots (UK).

Throughout Europe not only did pharmaceutical companies merge but, as they became mega-pharmaceutical companies, they also diversified their businesses into separate companies which themselves then merged into further specialized industrial sectors, such as agribusiness. The Novartis and AstraZeneca move to establish Sygenta (Swiss) is one example, but there are others. Another important merger in 1999 was between Rhône-Poulenc SA (French) and Hoechst Marion Roussel, itself the result of a merger between Hoechst AG (German), Roussel Uclaf (French) and Marion Merrell Dow (US), to form Aventis (French). Then in 2004, after a successful hostile takeover, Aventis merged with Sanofi-Synthélabo to become Sanofi-Aventis (French).

Over in America mergers were also busily happening. Bristol-Myers Squibb (US) for instance was the result of a merger in 1989 between Bristol-Myers and Squibb, and Pfizer (US) swallowed up Warner-Lambert (US) in 2000, itself having acquired Parke-Davis (US) in 1970. In 2002 Pfizer then acquired Pharmacia (US), itself formed by various mergers or acquisitions including Upjohn (US), Searle (US) and Agouron Pharmaceuticals (US).

The world's five largest mega-pharmaceutical-chemical conglomerates in 2008 are Pfizer (US), Bristol-Myers Squibb (US), Novartis (Swiss), GlaxoSmithKline (British) and Sanofi-Aventis (French). These companies have not only significant pharmaceutical interests, but also interests in agribusiness, agrichemicals and biotechnology. Along with Sygenta (Swiss) and Monsanto (US), which is itself a child of Pharmacia and UpJohn, these seven companies effectively control the world's production of medicines, fertilizers, GM seeds and other commodities used in the production of food and medicines. As a consequence there has been a convergence, through biotechnology, of pharmaceuticals, agriculture, organic chemicals, diagnostics and health care in general and, unfortunately, a corresponding explosion in the patenting of biological materials.

NOTES

1. Belfanti, CM (2004), 'Guilds, Patents, and the Circulation of Technical Knowledge', *Technology and Culture*, **45**, 569–89.
2. 1693–1722.
3. Cipolla, CM (1972), 'The Diffusions of Innovations in Early Modern Europe', *Comparative Studies in Society and History*, **14** (1), 46–52, 47–8.
4. Ibid, 50.
5. See Scoville, WC (1952), 'The Huguenots and the Diffusion of Technology II', *The Journal of Political Economy*, **60** (5), 392–411.
6. '[T]hree sorts of engines never before made or used within this our Kingdom of Great Britain, one to wind finest raw silk, another to spin and the other to twist the finest Italian raw silk into organzine in great perfection which was never before done in this our Kingdom, by which means many thousand families of our subjects may be constantly employed in Great Britain, be furnished with silks of all sorts of the manufacture of our subjects, and great quantities exported into foreign parts by being made as good and cheap as any foreign silk can be.' A year before the patent expired in 1732 Lombe's brother, Thomas, petitioned Parliament for an extension and, although a six-year extension was recommended by the Committee established to investigate his claim, George II rejected it, preferring instead that Parliament 'recompense' him in some other way. By Act of Parliament in 1732 Lombe was granted £14 000 as 'a reward for his eminent services done to the nation, in discovering with the greatest hazard and difficulty the capital Italian engines, and introducing and bringing the same to full perfection in this kingdom, at his own great expense'.
7. 1683–1760; King of Great Britain & Ireland, 1727–60.
8. As early as 1290 the Florentine Republic had passed a statute similar to the Statute of Monopolies. See Prager, FD (1946), 'Brunelleschi's Patent', *Journal of the Patent Office Society*, **28** (2), 109–35, 131.
9. Ibid, 131.
10. 1377–1446.
11. Ibid, 131.
12. 1389–1464. See Saalman, H and Mattox, P (1985), 'The First Medici Palace', *The Journal of the Society of Architectural Historians*, **44** (4), 329–45.
13. Mandich, G (1948), 'Venetian Patents (1450–1550)', *Journal of the Patent Office Society*, **30** (3), 166–224 and Mandich, G (1960), 'Venetian Origins of Inventors' Rights', *Journal of the Patent Office Society*, **42**, 378–82.
14. Mandich (1948), above n 13, 189.
15. Ibid.
16. Ibid, 187.
17. Price, WH (2006), *The English Patents of Monopoly* (Clark: New Jersey: The Lawbook Exchange, Ltd.), 4 n 1.
18. Cipolla, CM (1952), 'The Decline of Italy: The Case of a Fully Matured Economy', *The Economic History Review*, **5** (2), 178–87, 181 n 3.
19. Ibid.
20. 1710–74; King of France and Navarre, 1715–74.
21. 1754–93; King of France and Navarre, 1774–91; King of the French, 1791–92.
22. Title III, Chapter II, Art 3.
23. 1632–1704.
24. 1694–1778.
25. 1738–1815.

26. While this political unrest threw the French economy deeper into recession, it failed to benefit one Nicholas Leblanc who had in 1791 invented a process for making soda ash. Leblanc, a doctor, was unfortunately employed by the Duke of Orleans. Leblanc's process, developed to meet France's wartime need for an alternative to potash (an ingredient used in the production of a range of essential goods, such as glass, soap, textiles and paper), along with the factory that the Duke had built and which Leblanc managed, was then confiscated and used without compensation by the new revolutionary government and, although Leblanc survived the guillotine, his misfortunes led him to commit suicide in 1806.

27. 1769–1821; Emperor of the French, 1804–14.

28. 1772–1804.

29. 1808–73; President of the Second French Republic 1848–52; Emperor of the French, 1852–70.

30. Fraser, J (1860), *A Handy-Book of Patent and Copyright Law* (London: Sampson Low, Son, and Co.).

31. 1816–92; von Siemens, 1888.

32. Schiff, E (1971), *Industrialization without National Patents: The Netherlands, 1869–1912, Switzerland, 1850–1907* (Princeton, NJ: Princeton University Press).

33. 1805–73.

34. 1867–1945.

35. 1864–1941.

36. 1819–61; the Prince Consort to Queen Victoria.

37. 1808–82; knighted, 1875.

38. 1815–91; 2nd Earl Granville.

39. 1796–1883; 1st Baron Overstone.

40. 1791–1871.

41. 1822–85; President of the United States, 1869–77.

42. Kronstein, H and I Till (1947), 'A Reevaluation of the International Patent Convention', *Law and Contemporary Problems*, **12** (4), 765–81.

43. Seckelmann, M (2001), 'The Quest for Legal Stability: Patent Protection within the German Empire, 1871–1903', *EBHA Conference 2001*: Business and Knowledge: E2: Patents and Knowledge. Available at http://web.bi.no/forskning/ebha2001.nsf/dd5cab801f172358525647c8/a6cb7066ea59edabc12567f3005bef4d/$FILE/E2%20-%20Seckelmann%20ii.PDF.

44. Kronstein and Till, above n 42, 773.

45. Dutfield, G (2003), *Intellectual Property Rights and the Life Sciences* (Hampstead: Ashgate Publishing Limited; Burlington: Ashgate Publishing Company), 78.

46. Today only the US maintains the first-to-invent requirement. All other countries subsequently adopted the German approach of first-to-file. For an interesting account of the development of the history of the US first-to-invent system see Frost, GE (1967), 'The 1967 Patent Law Debate: First-to-Invent vs. First-to-File', *Duke Law Journal*, **5**, 923–42.

47. 1838–1920.

48. Gispen, K (2002), *Poems in Steel: National Socialism and the Politics of Inventing from Weimer to Bonn* (Oxford and New York: Berghahn Books).

49. Schuster, EJ (1913), 'Germany', *Journal of the Society of Comparative Legislation,* New Series, **13** (2), 302–3.

50. Schiff, above n 32, 93.

51. Kronstein and Till, above n 42, 779.

52. 1858–1942.

53. 1874–1951.

54. As Koninklijke Philips NV it is currently the world's largest electronics company employing over 120 000 people. Sales revenue from its electronic equipment in 2006 was €27 billion and, according to WIPO, it was the world's leading patent filing company, followed by Matsushita, Siemens, Nokia, Bosch, 3M, BASF, Toyota, Intel and Motorola.

55. 1828–1914; knighted, 1904.
56. 1847–1931.
57. Schiff, above n 32, 60–61.
58. 1881–1957; Nobel Prize, 1932.
59. 1823–1900; US Secretary of the Treasury, 1877–81; US Secretary of State, 1897–8.
60. Although it took some time, by 1911 the Sherman Act had been used successfully against Standard Oil, a company controlled by John D Rockefeller (1839–1937), breaking it up into 34 separate entities to be operated by separate company boards.
61. The Department of Justice also alleged that they had, by effect of their collusion: '(a) obtained and now hold a monopoly of patents relating to glass bulbs, tubing and cane and the manufacture thereof in the United States; (b) obtained and now hold a monopoly of patents relating to incandescent electric lamps and the manufacture thereof in the United States; (c) established and now hold a monopoly in the manufacture, distribution, and sale of such lamps in the United States; (d) unreasonably restricted and now restrict the production of such lamps in the United States; (e) unreasonably restricted and now restrict the distribution and sale of such lamps in the United States; (f) fixed and now maintain non-competitive prices on approximately 80% of such lamps manufactured and sold in the United States; (g) obtained and now maintain monopolies on glass bulbs, tubing and cane on lamp bases; (h) restrained and now restrain trade in other essential parts and materials for incandescent lamps; (i) eliminated the importation into the United States of glass bulbs, tubing and cane, machinery relating to the manufacture of such glass parts; lamps, lamp parts and lamp-making machinery; (j) discouraged and impeded the progress of science and the useful arts, and have used the patent laws of the United States for purposes inconsistent with the constitutional basis of these laws; and (k) monopolized interstate and foreign trade and commerce and have unreasonably restrained such trade and commerce in violation of the laws of the United States': US Complaint, *US v General Electric Co et al* (1949) 82 F Supp 753, 766.
62. Finally on 2 October 1953 Forman J made the following order: '[t]he defendants are each, jointly and severally, ordered and directed, forthwith upon entry of this Judgment, to dedicate to the public any and all existing patents on lamps and lamp parts': *US v General Electric Co et al* 115 F Supp. 835.
63. 1910–2000.
64. The Strasbourg Convention was ratified or acceded to by 13 European countries, including the UK, and it sought, as its title suggests, to harmonize certain aspects of European patent law. Consistently with the Strasbourg Convention it provided for a patent system which prohibited the kind of compulsory licensing allowed by section 41 UK Patents Act 1949 (Art.136); treated pharmaceutical substances as patentable subject matter (Arts 9–10); and provided for a 20-year patent term (Art. 23).
65. Oudemans, G (1963), *The Draft European Patent Convention* (London: Stevens & Sons Ltd; New York: Mathew Bender & Co. Inc.).
66. UK Comptroller-General of Patents, 1969–77.
67. Scherer, FM (2000), 'The Pharmaceutical Industry and World Intellectual Property Standards', *Vanderbilt Law Review*, **53** (6), 2245–54.
68. Ibid, 2250.
69. See http://www.hri.org/docs/Rome57/.

5. The internationalization and harmonization of the patent systems

[S]ix billion people, most of whom are poor and battling a crippling disease burden with little or no help from their governments . . . with the amendment in the Indian Patent Act (in effect from January 1, 2005) in compliance with WTO patent laws and TRIPs . . . will no longer be able to [access] cheap generic copies of patented medicines.

Dr Yusuf K Hamied, Chairman, Cipla Limited, India, 2005

Despite the Industrial Revolution and the technological innovations which it inspired; the public display of inventions in grand international industry fairs held throughout Europe during the 1840s, 1850s and 1860s; the significant reduction in the cost of patenting inventions in the US and the UK; and the growing economic and political power of corporations in both the US and Europe, by 1873 the patent systems in Europe and the UK were in danger. While the British Empire, then the world's military and economic superpower, had not yet done away with its patent system, by this time enough questions had been raised about the role of the patent system that free traders were close to getting their way. It was the same in Europe, and it would have taken only a British decision, following the Dutch example in 1869, for a domino effect to have been triggered. In 1873 patents were not considered to be the harbingers of technological innovation that they are today. Rather they were understood to be a policy tool which sought to protect the domestic economy by encouraging domestic production, manufacturing independence and employment through industrialization. Invention may have been the threshold of that policy, but its true objective was to foster economic growth. Indeed free traders believed that there were better ways to achieve that objective – ways that did not involve the creation of private monopolies.

In their study of invention in Victorian England, Christine MacLeod and Alessandro Nuvolari[1] observed that those who made significant technological, scientific and medical contributions, such as William Thomson[2] and Joseph Lister,[3] were rewarded through 'unprecedented elevations to the peerage'[4] and 'the erection of statues in city centres'.[5] Whether their ingenuity was motivated by the grant of patents or by their personal ambitions is a matter of speculation, but according to MacLeod and Nuvolari about 40 per cent of such people never obtained a patent, and of these 'the majority . . . had elected not to'.[6] Was this an act of public philanthropy or was it simply that patents were not, in Victorian England, the motivators of technological innovation?

Despite their common ancestry, by 1873 the US and the UK were diverse countries; economically, politically and socially. The United States had its own Constitution – the UK had not; the US was a republic – the UK was a constitutional monarchy; the US was a country – the UK was the seat of the greatest Empire the world had ever known. More importantly, Americans perceived themselves as living in a country that gave any man the ability to transcend class – something impossible in Victorian England. Any male citizen could, theoretically, become its President and anyone could become wealthy through their own ingenuity, perseverance and good luck. In a country whose people believed in the individualism engendered by a pioneering spirit, it is unsurprising then to find here the first dedicated patent office in the world. In 1836 the US Patent Office (USPTO) was created by statute and empowered, separately from the executive government, to create a personal property right in the form of a patent to the 'first and true inventor'. While the earlier patent statutes of 1790 and 1793 were biased in favour of US citizens and permanent residents, by 1870 foreign inventors were treated more or less equally with American inventors. Although there still remained aspects of the American patent system which

---

BOX 5.1   A BRIEF INQUIRY INTO THE PRINCIPLES, EFFECT, AND PRESENT STATE OF THE AMERICAN PATENT SYSTEM

H & C Howson, Philadelphia, 1872

'Our Patent Laws are, undoubtedly, the most truly liberal of any. They more clearly than any other recognize the truths that productive industry is the basis of natural wealth and power; that such industry will flourish in proportion as it is made a secure course of individual profit; that true invention is intellectual production of the most beneficial kind, and that, therefore true policy, which is always just, demands that it shall be made, as far as possible, a secure source of individual profit.'[7]

gave its citizens advantages over foreigners, the American attitude towards patents was markedly different from that in Europe and the UK. That the patent was seen as a *public reward* available to anyone who produced an invention, something that would contribute to the progress of the economy and its people was quintessentially an American perspective.

MacLeod and Nuvolari found, in a country which lacked the class structure of England, only 6 per cent of 'America's "great inventors" active between 1790 and 1846 held no patent'. This, they believed, may have been explained by 'the relative cheapness and accessibility of the American patent system, which increased the general propensity to patent inventions'. On the other hand, they said, 'it may owe something to the high esteem in which the British held public-spirited inventors who foreswore intellectual property rights, thereby enhancing their reputation as disinterested benefactors'. Whatever the real reasons, by 1873 a patentless world was not an acceptable option to Americans.

INTERNATIONALISM, VIENNA, 1873 – THE ROAD TO THE PARIS CONVENTION

By 1870 travel times across the Atlantic had shrunk as coal powered passenger ships like the *SS Great Britain* became increasingly common. With the invention of the telephone in the 1860s, communication, likewise, had become more rapid and, although it would not be until 1896 that Guglielmo Marconi[8] would invent the radio, undersea telegraph cables had been operating since 1858. Inevitably with both the end of the disruption caused to its economy by the American Civil War (1861–1865) and the relative ease of new forms of travel and communication, foreign trade and commerce had become increasingly important to the American economy. Isaac Merritt Singer (1811–1875), the American inventor of the Singer sewing machine, had already collaborated with other American inventors to form a sewing machine patent pool in 1856. So successful was his idea that within four years IM Singer & Co was producing 13 000 sewing machines. Eventually reorganizing itself into The Singer Sewing Machine Company, Singer built a factory in Glasgow, Scotland, 'deliberately [to] . . . produce for a foreign market on a regular basis . . . not [as] a safety valve to handle an occasional domestic surplus', according to American historian Robert Davies.[9] Singer, an early American success story, intrigued Europeans, and while his use of their patent systems to establish 'a permanent market as part of a desire to saturate the world market'[10] was a great business strategy, it also raised eyebrows.

Before long US manufacturers had become sensitive to how foreign patent laws, or their lack thereof, could actually work to their disadvantage, and their growing sensitivity to this issue explains why by 1872 Americans were developing a somewhat guarded approach to participating in international trade fairs. In contrast to their participation in the grand London and Paris exhibitions of the 1850s and 1860s, as the *Weltausstellung* of 1873 drew nearer Americans began to vocalize their concerns. On 19 December 1872, during a debate in the US House of Representatives over a Bill for the appropriation of US$100 000 'to enable the people of the United States to participate in the advantages of the international exposition to be held at Vienna in 1873', Samuel Shellabarger,[11] a congressman from Ohio, objected. According to him, 'an exhibition of patented and patentable articles would be exceedingly disadvantageous to our inventive and industrial people'. What had prompted this American politician to rise to his feet in Congress was an article that had been published in *Scientific American*, the 'substance and effect' of which, he said showed 'that both the law of Austria and the practice of that Government [were] such as that the exhibition of any of the inventions of our country there will result practically in a surrender of those inventions'.[12] He had been alarmed to learn that without patent laws which provided reciprocal protections, publication of an invention by an American inventor before filing a patent application in Vienna could destroy its patentability in countries of the Austro-Hungarian Empire.

This however was only one of many concerns that Americans had about foreign patent systems. Other concerns included the lack of any thorough pre-grant examination; a concept of novelty that permitted the import of inventions from abroad; compulsory licensing; and obligations for foreign patentees to work inventions within a certain period of time or have them revoked. This last concern was especially worrisome to Americans after the US Patents Act 1836 was amended in 1870. Until then it had been a defence to patent infringement if an American could prove that the foreign inventor 'had failed and neglected for the space of eighteen months from the date of the [US] patent, to put and continue on sale to the public, on reasonable terms, the invention or discovery for which the patent issued'. While this was not the same as a requirement to work the US invention or risk its revocation, this defence nonetheless provided foreign inventors with an incentive to work a US patent in the United States. Clearly with the success of men like Singer and others like Thomas Edison[13] and Alexander Graham Bell,[14] both of whom were to become industrial celebrities by the end of that decade, American policy-makers foresaw that they needed to lead by example. Appreciating that they were exposing their economy to foreigners, American policy-makers believed that they had more to gain from their foreign markets than to lose from foreigners in their local market; that was so long as American inventions could be adequately protected in those foreign markets.

While Shellabarger's attempt to stop American participation at the *Weltausstellung* failed, he succeeded in highlighting an issue which had become a thorn in the side of American industry. In fact, unnerved by the prospect of an American boycott, the Austro-Hungarian Empire had already sought to placate America's inventors by amending its patent law so that all exhibitors would enjoy a grace period of two months after the close of the exhibition during which time they could file a patent application for an Austrian patent and not risk the invention's patentability. Also in a further attempt to stave off further criticism and to demonstrate its magnanimity, the Austro-Hungarian government, at the suggestion of the US government, issued an invitation to all other world governments to come to the *Weltausstellung* and participate in the world's first international patent meeting.[15]

In accepting the invitation on behalf of the United States, Columbus Delano[16] optimistically wrote on 29 May 1873 to the Austro-Hungarian government that, while he believed the meeting would be 'of the very greatest importance . . . if the American [patent] system can be properly presented before that Congress, discreetly and cautiously sustained with facts and figures, I feel confident that the best results can be expected'. On 7 June 1873 President Ulysses Grant[17] appointed the Assistant Commissioner of Patents, John Marshall Thacher (who was to serve as the US Commissioner of Patents in 1874–1875), to head the US delegation. Thacher's objective was, according to a report of the events published by *Scientific American* on 6 September 1873, 'to discuss the propriety of establishing a uniform patent law in Europe . . . and also to suggest, to the several governments, the general principles and features which such a law ought to embrace'.

Thacher's mission was made easier by the presence of Ernst Siemens, the German industrialist who was a keen supporter of a national German patent system and who was appointed to chair the Vienna meeting, and Thomas Webster, a London patent barrister who had not only argued for the retention of the British patent system during the 1864 Royal Commission but had championed a US-style pre-grant examination system during the patent inquiry held in 1851. The other delegates who were appointed by their respective governments, no doubt also because of their experience with their own patent systems, were also naturally sympathetic to patents and so at the end of the meeting a predictable resolution was passed that called upon their governments to accept that 'the protection of inventions should be guaranteed by the laws of all civilized nations under the condition of a complete publication of the same'. The delegates also resolved that the world's patent systems should provide a 'right . . .

[for the] legal protection of intellectual work'; be 'the only practical and effective means of introducing new technical ideas, without loss of time and in a reliable manner, to the general knowledge of the public'; 'the protection of invention renders the labor of the inventor remunerative, and induces thereby introduction and practical application of new and useful technical methods and improvements, and attracts capital from abroad, which, in the absence of patent protection, will find means of secure investment elsewhere'; with 'the obligatory complete publication of the patented invention the great sacrifice of time and of money, which the technical application would otherwise impose upon the industry of all countries, will be considerable lessened'; 'by the protection of invention the secrecy of manufacture, which is one of the greatest enemies of industrial progress, will lose its chief support'; 'great injury will be inflicted upon countries which have no national patent laws by the native talent emigrating to more congenial countries, where their labor is legally protected'; and 'experience shows that the holder of a patent will make the most effectual exertions for a speedy introduction of his invention'.

Accordingly, through these resolutions, the delegates provided their governments with a set of principles that would constitute 'an effective and useful patent system': prescribing 'only the inventor himself, or his legal representatives, should be entitled to a patent'; 'a patent should not be refused to a foreigner'; a 'system of preliminary examination' be introduced; 'a patent be granted for a term of fifteen years, or be permitted to be extended to such a term'; 'the expense of obtaining a patent should be moderate'; 'facilities should be given by a well-organized patent-office to obtain in any easy manner the specification of a patent, as well as to ascertain what patents are still in force'; 'legal rules' be established 'to which the patentee may be induced, in cases in which the public interest should require it, to allow the use of his invention to all suitable applicants, for an adequate compensation'; and 'non-application of an invention in one country shall not involve forfeiture of the patent'. Finally it was agreed that preparations be made for the establishment of an international patent organization through which dialogue to continue patent harmonization would take place.

PATENT LAW REFORM A CENTURY LATER

More than 100 years later however the American vision of a single uniform patent system based upon the US template was not a reality. Despite the resolutions passed at the Vienna meeting the American patent system was not universally adopted in Europe; although many of its features, including the establishment of dedicated patent offices and pre-grant examination, found their way into the German patent law of 1877 and the UK patent law of 1883, it was not until the European Patent Convention (EPC) in 1978 that Europe, which now included the UK, relinquished the economic protections that had been provided by its previous national patent systems. Nonetheless the Vienna meeting in 1873 was a watershed in the history of patents. Not only did it stop the free trade movement against the retention of a patent system in the UK but it also provided the stimulus for the drafting of the world's first international patent, trade mark and copyright treaty, the Paris Convention for the Protection of Industrial Property of 1883 (the Paris Convention), which by 1893 had led to the formation of *Bureaux Internationaux Réunis pour la Protection de la Propriété Intellectuelle* (United International Bureau for the Protection of Intellectual Property, BIRPI). For members of the Paris Union, signatories to the Paris Convention, the BIRPI, headquartered in Berne, remained the principal route through which intellectual property, as it had become known, would be discussed and administered internationally. Eventually the Convention Establishing the World Intellectual Property Organization was signed in Stockholm on 14 July 1967, and in 1974, in accordance with that Convention, the BIRPI became the World Intellectual Property Organization (WIPO), headquartered in Geneva.

WIPO is a specialized agency of the United Nations which currently administers 24 international treaties, has 184 countries as members and employs nearly 1000 people from 95 countries. In terms of patent law treaties it administers: the Paris Convention; the Patent Cooperation Treaty, 1970; the Strasbourg Agreement Concerning the International Patent Classification, 1971; and the Budapest Treaty on the International Recognition of the Deposit of Microorganisms for the Purposes of Patent Procedure, 1977.

THE PARIS CONVENTION, 1883

The Paris Convention was first signed by Belgium, Brazil, El Salvador, France, Guatemala, Italy, The Netherlands, Portugal, Serbia, Spain and Switzerland and, by the time it came into effect on 7 July 1884, by Great Britain, Tunisia and Ecuador. It came into force in the United States in May 1887. Although without patent systems at the time, The Netherlands and Switzerland were inaugural members of the Paris Convention Union because the Convention also dealt with trade marks and copyrights and both countries had laws with respect to these forms of intellectual property.

THE PATENT COOPERATION TREATY, 1970

The Patent Cooperation Treaty (PCT) was signed in Washington, DC, in June 1970 and became operational in January 1978. One hundred and thirty six countries are currently signatories to the PCT and members of the International Patent Cooperation Union (IPCU). According to the PCT a single patent application filed in any IPCU national patent office (that is, within 12 months of the provisional or first patent application) can nominate other IPCU member countries to patent the same invention. This then becomes an *international application* (which is a misnomer as there is no single international patent available, but the term simply recognizes that it is the patent applicant's intention to seek a patent under the national patent laws of the designated countries through the PCT). An international patent search is then conducted to assess novelty and an international search report is prepared, usually by the originating patent office. Copies of the international application and the international search report are sent to WIPO.

WIPO publishes the international application and the search report 18 months after the filing date in one of eight international languages. After 30 months the international application enters the *national phase*, where the national patent offices of each of the designated ICPU member countries will examine the patent application under the applicable national patent law as if it was filed as a national patent application. Herein lies the advantage of the PCT. Through one administrative action and filing fee (1400 Swiss Francs as at May 2008) patent applicants are able to file patent applications simultaneously as if they were filing individual patent applications in the national patent offices of each designated country. This is advantageous because it saves foreign patent applicants the expense of filing separate patent applications in every patent office from which the applicant seeks patent protection. Nevertheless if and when patents are granted they are all national patents, not a single international patent, and they are each subject to scrutiny and revocation under the national laws applicable in the country of grant.

THE STRASBOURG AGREEMENT CONCERNING THE INTERNATIONAL PATENT CLASSIFICATION, 1971

The Strasbourg Agreement was designed to overcome the difficulties caused by the diverse national patent classification systems. The US established the first patent classification system to assist in the US pre-grant examination system created in 1836. As other countries eventually adopted pre-grant examination they developed their own patent classification systems. The common idea was to provide a library system for searching that would assist patent examiners in retrieving patent documents that would contain information relevant to the assessment of novelty and inventive step. The classification systems were an integral part of an effective pre-grant examination system, but with the internationalization of patent systems by the 1970s it was clear that a uniform system was required.

Accordingly the Strasbourg Agreement established a common classification system to ease patent searching throughout the world, and it is reviewed every five years to ensure that the classification groupings remain up to date. The sixth edition of the classification system is presently in use and it is divided into eight main sections,[18] 20 subsections, 118 classes, 624 subclasses and over 67 000 groups (of which approximately 10 per cent are main groups and the rest subgroups).

THE BUDAPEST TREATY ON THE INTERNATIONAL RECOGNITION OF THE DEPOSIT OF MICROORGANISMS FOR THE PURPOSES OF PATENT PROCEDURE, 1977

The Budapest Treaty was signed on 28 April 1977 and came into force on 9 August 1980. It allows for 'deposits of microorganisms at an international depository authority to be recognized for patent procedure', and this eliminates the need for patent applicants who are claiming microorganisms as 'inventions' (a) to describe in words the nature of the microorganism to meet the written description (or sufficiency of disclosure) requirements common to patent law around the world or (b) to deposit a microorganism in more than one recognized depository anywhere in the world.

THE PATENTING OF CHEMICALS IN EUROPE – A STEP TOWARDS HARMONIZATION?

Like the patent systems of most other European countries of the day Germany's national patent system of 1877 prohibited patents over chemical and pharmaceutical substances. That prohibition, although relaxed in 1891 with respect to products-of-processes, was completely repealed by the Bundestag only in September 1967. Under the influence of Kurt Haertel, while serving as President of the German Patent Office, the West German government of Kurt Kiesinger,[19] which was also sympathetically inclined towards the EEC and a unified European patent system, was persuaded to fall into line with the new pharmaceutical patent paradigm. Haertel was convinced that it was no longer possible to justify the century-old European practice of excluding chemical and pharmaceutical substances from patentability, especially given that neither Anglo-American patent model contained such an exclusion and the European pharmaceutical industry needed to be able to compete with Japanese and American counterparts. Accordingly Article 52(1) of the European Patent Convention of 1973 (EPC) stipulated: 'European patents shall be granted for any inventions, in all fields of technology, provided that they are new, involve an inventive step and are susceptible of industrial application'. The words 'in all fields of technology' enshrined the pharmaceutical patent paradigm into European patent law, making it clear that any technological discrimination was prohibited so long as the patent pertained to something that was an 'invention'.

In terms of what was and what was not capable of 'invention', however, the EPC did not adopt the Anglo-American approach which expressly defined the word in terms of either a 'manner of new manufacture' (as in section 6 of the Statute of Monopolies) or 'patentable subject matter' (as in section 101 of the US Patents Act 1952). Rather, Haertel and his colleagues preferred not to define an invention, and instead provided only a list of exclusions. Accordingly Article 52(2) expressly excluded: (a) discoveries, scientific theories and mathematical methods; (b) aesthetic creations; (c) schemes, rules and methods and programs for computers; (d) presentation of information; and Article 52(4) expressly excluded methods for the treatment of the human or animal body by surgery or therapy and diagnostic methods practised on the human or animal body.

The list of excluded subject matter nevertheless appeared to coincide with the effect of the Anglo-American approach which also provided, through patent jurisprudence, that these types of things were neither a 'manner of new manufacture' nor 'patentable subject matter'. It would seem that the EPC, even though it did not provide an express definition of the word invention, for all intents and purposes was trying to achieve the same result; and with respect to what was an invention there would be no technological discrimination.

Moreover the absence of an express definition of 'invention' did not mean that literally anything that was new, involved an inventive step and was susceptible to industrial application and not specifically excluded was, by default, an invention. This was made clear by the inclusion of the word 'invention' in Article 52(1) as a *prerequisite* and *separate condition* of patentability to the subordinate conditions of patentability of novelty, inventive step and industrial application. (Excluding the word 'invention' from Article 52(1) would otherwise provide that European patents should be granted for *any* product, process or method.) This was consistent with the Anglo-American approach which distinguished between an 'invention' on the one hand and a 'patentable invention' on the other, and was furthermore reinforced by the EPO patent examiner's manual which advised that 'the basic test of whether there is an invention within the meaning of Article 52(1) is separate and distinct from the questions whether the subject-matter is susceptible of industrial application, is new and involves an inventive step'.

So what the examiner's manual required was for examiners to consider the invention in a patent as a separate and distinct issue from whether that invention was patentable. Therefore in determining whether there was a patentable invention there were two thresholds. The first: was the technology defined in the patent claims and described generally in the patent specification an invention? If the answer was in the affirmative, the questions would then be asked: (a) was that invention novel?; (b) did that invention involve an inventive step?; and, (c) was that invention industrially applicable? Only if the answers to all questions were in the affirmative would the requirements of Article 52(1) be satisfied.

With respect to the first question, the issue that has subsequently caused the most disquiet is the relationship between Article 52(1) and 52(2) and (4): in defining an 'invention' under Article 52(1) were the exclusions in Article 52(2) and (4) exhaustive? In other words was this list of things that could never qualify as inventions definitive, or could it be that other things might not qualify as inventions either, but were not specifically mentioned? In this respect the House of Lords in *Biogen, Inc v Medeva plc* [1997] RPC 1 took the view that this list was not definitive. Lord Hoffmann, who wrote the unanimous decision, explained: 'in the absence of a definition one cannot say with certainty that one might not come across something which satisfied all the conditions but could not be described as an invention'.

This reasoning accords with the Anglo-American approach which applies a combination of statutory language and judge-made jurisprudence to provide a purposive construction in terms of defining 'patentable subject matter'. Accordingly, although the US Patents Act 1952 expressly defines an 'invention' in section 101 to be 'any new and useful process, machine, manufacture, or composition of matter, or any new and useful improvement thereof', as the US Supreme Court confirmed in *Laboratory Corporation of America v Metabolite Laboratories* (2006) 126 S Ct 2921, this definition '[e]xclude[s] from . . . patent protection . . . laws of nature, natural phenomena, and abstract ideas'. The rationale for this subject matter exclusion was necessary, as Justice Breyer explained, 'to avoid the dangers of overprotection'. According to him the optimal balance between the competing interests of the public at large and inventors, under the US patent system, was to be achieved by allowing 'certain types of invention and discovery within the scope of patentability while excluding others'. As to whether a specific technology defined in a patent claim to *be* an invention was truly an invention within the meaning of section 101, both the patent examiner and any subsequent court must not only ensure that it comes within one of the things expressly defined to be something capable of being an invention, but that it must not be something that was inherently excluded by the common law.

Irrespective of whether or not the legislative scheme upon which a patent system is based provides an express definition of the word 'invention', what is important is that the technology that is defined to be the invention in the patent claims is indeed an 'invention'; discoveries about the natural world, such as isolated biological materials, are clearly always going to pose a problem in this regard.

Indeed by 1980 it had become apparent that advances in biotechnology were seriously challenging the ability of the EPC to provide patent protection for the types of biological products and processes that were being developed. Global pharmaceutical corporations were also beginning to invest in biotechnology; and being familiar with the pharmaceutical patent paradigm they naturally expected patent law to provide patent protection for isolated biological materials and the processes of their manufacture. However the idea that naturally occurring organisms could be genetically manipulated so that they could produce other biological substances caught everyone's attention, and this led to an unprecedented level of publicity, controversy and scrutiny, especially over whether such things were truly inventions. Amid conflicting decisions between differing national European courts as well as between national European courts and the appellate tribunals of the EPO, judicial tensions began building. The EPO was determined to resolve the issue of the legitimacy of patenting isolated biological materials, especially given that the USPTO had been granting patents to US corporations and universities for such processes and products since about 1974, and began granting European patents for these materials. The UK courts were not so sure – their jurisprudence, developed over the past 400 years, was consistent with a statutory requirement that allowed patents only with respect to things that were a 'manner of new manufacture'. Moreover while the EPC may have systematized the grant of European patents through the EPO, the fact remained that patent enforcement was a matter of national jurisdiction. For example in 1988 the

UK Patents Court invalidated a European patent which claimed an isolated form of the protein human tissue plasminogen activator (t-PA) as an invention, for the reason that it was not an 'invention' within the meaning of that word in section 1(1) of the UK Patents Act 1977. Unimpressed by the uncertainty in the law created by disparate decisions over the patenting of isolated biological materials, the pharmaceutical and biotechnology industry mobilized internationally and the result was a joint statement issued in 1988 by the EPO, the USPTO and the Japanese Patent Office (JPO) which said:

> Purified natural products are not regarded under any of the three laws as products of nature or discoveries because they do not in fact exist in nature in an isolated form. Rather, they are regarded for patent purposes as biologically active substances or chemical compounds and eligible for patenting on the same basis as other chemical compounds.[20]

Clearly this was an attempt by the world's principal patent offices to deliver certainty to the world's main patent systems; but it failed.

Within a year the UK's Court of Appeal had upheld the decision of the UK Patents Court on Genentech's European patent for isolated t-PA. The decision not only ignored the joint statement, but made it look ridiculous as not just one, but two, courts had held that, as a matter of law, isolated proteins that were identical to naturally produced proteins, such as t-PA, were not 'inventions' under Article 52(1). Furthermore the Court of Appeal had not just invalidated the patent claims to the isolated proteins, but they had invalidated the entire patent, including the claims to the processes that manufactured these isolated proteins. In what was without doubt an unexpected blow to the framers of the EPC, the EPO went into damage control. The law had to be changed!

THE EUROPEAN BIOTECHNOLOGY DIRECTIVE, 1998

If isolated biological materials were truly 'inventions' within Article 52(1) EPC, why was the Biotech Directive even necessary? According to British patent barrister, Andrew Waugh QC, the Directive was 'clarificatory of the law',[21] while, according to Mustill LJ, one of the two judges who invalidated Genentech's t-PA patent, it was one of the 'necessary repairs . . . [to the] deep flaws . . . in the current [patent] regime'. Whether it was 'clarificatory' or simply a 'necessary repair' the purpose and intent of the Directive was to overturn the Court of Appeal in its Genentech t-PA decision.

Accordingly Article 5(2) of the Directive, which came into force throughout the EPC in July 2000, provided:

> An element isolated from the human body or otherwise produced by means of a technical process, including the sequence or partial sequence of a gene, may constitute a patentable invention, *even if the structure of that element is identical to that of a natural element.*[22]

What Article 5(2) meant to do was to define a human gene that had been isolated from the human body as an 'invention' under the EPC, and while this apparently removed any obstacle for its patenting under the EPC the problem was that there was no legislative or jurisprudential precedent to support such an approach anywhere else in the world. It seemed the European Parliament had passed the Directive oblivious to the Agreement on Trade Related Aspects of Intellectual Property (TRIPS) signed by the European Union in 1994, which provided in Article 27.1 that 'patents shall be available for any inventions'. What the European Parliamentarians had failed to appreciate was that, in light of the binding effect of TRIPS upon the European Community, they were not free to pass a law that sought to make something that was inherently unpatentable patentable. Not only was the word 'invention' included in Article 27.1 TRIPS, but the word was used in the context of defining what was patentable subject matter. Even though TRIPS did not provide any express definition of the word 'invention' per se, it did not mean that anything could be made to be an invention by way of legislative discretion. This is precisely what the UK Court of Appeal had decided was not an 'invention' under Article 52(1) EPC and its reasoning also applied to Article 27.1 TRIPS, given that it had effectively adopted the exact same wording. Clearly it had not occurred to these parliamentarians that the inclusion of the word 'invention' in Article 27.1 TRIPS was the result of collective drafting effort which involved delegates from the US as well as Europe. It could never be said that the TRIPS Agreement was drafted with the parties completely ignorant of the impact that a word such as 'invention' in Article 27.1 TRIPS would have on their respective patent laws. It would be extremely unlikely that, during the TRIPS negotiations which took place during the Uruguay round of the GATT between 1986 and 1994, the US delegates would agree to the inclusion of this word in the text of a document that would be binding on the United States if that word was to have a meaning that was inconsistent with US patent law. That being so, if an isolated biological substance was not an 'invention' under US patent law, then it could not be made to be an invention in contravention of Article 27.1 TRIPS. Arguably Article 27.1 TRIPS and Article 5(2) of the Directive are inconsistent.

In passing the Directive the European Parliament opened a Pandora's box and, as the Danish Council of Bioethics put it:

> [I]t cannot be said with any reasonableness that a sequence or partial sequence of a gene ceases to be part of the human body merely because an identical copy of the sequence is isolated from or produced outside of the human body. . . . [T]he principal objection to the wording of the directive was precisely that in reality it rubber-stamps the practice that has gradually evolved in the USA, Japan and Europe whereby, under certain conditions – which it turns out to be very hard to get a grasp on in practice – parts of the human body can nevertheless be patented.[23]

Nonetheless in the absence of an express definition of 'invention' some legal scholars have argued that anything – including a human gene (whether isolated or not) – is, or can be deemed to be, an invention. For example Li Westerlund argues, 'in principle it does not prevent the exclusion of naturally occurring substances, such as genes and cells, from patent protection'.[24] Others, such as Nuno Pires de Carvalho, argue that 'inventions' are 'artificial creations that stem from the need to solve technical problems', whereas 'discoveries' are 'not the result of creation – even if creativity has been needed to reveal information concealed in nature'.[25] De Carvalho therefore suggests that a human gene, even one that has been isolated, is not and cannot be an invention because it is a natural phenomenon, and information about its role in the human body is a discovery, something that is expressly excluded from being an invention by Article 52(2)(a) EPC.

The complete lack of any judicial and scholarly consensus on this issue has created dysfunctional patent systems, not only in Europe but elsewhere. While attempts further to harmonize patent law have progressed at diplomatic levels, at a deeper level, where the law is subject to interpretation and reconciliation with its historical development, judicial review and scholarly analysis, this process of harmonization has been significantly retarded. Even within the EU the requirement under the EPC that national courts retain jurisdiction over the enforcement and validity of European patents suggests that individual countries are not comfortable with the idea of relinquishing national sovereignty over these ancient privileges – privileges that have more to do with national economic protection than the specific advancement of industry and science. The judicial tension between UK patent judges and their European colleagues in the EPO is far from being resolved. In 2004 the House of Lords held invalid claims to isolated erythropoietin – claims that the EPO had granted in 1984. In trying to explain away the disparate results their Lordships had to admit to being 'a little puzzled'[26] by the EPO's reasoning.

BOX 5.2   JUDGE CALLS FOR EUROPEAN PATENT LITIGATION SYSTEM

Managing Intellectual Property, 20 March 2008

A leading UK judge has called for a 'one-stop patent shop' to cater to companies that do business across Europe, after finding a patent invalid just days after it was upheld by a court in the Netherlands. Lord Justice Jacob made his comments in a Court of Appeal ruling in a dispute between the European Central Bank and Document Security Systems (DSS), a US company that has accused the Bank of infringing its technology in the production of euro bank notes. The Court yesterday backed the UK High Court, which ruled in March 2007 that DSS's European patent EPUK 0 455 750 was invalid. Since then, the patent has been upheld in first instance courts in the Netherlands and Germany but invalidated in France. Jacob described the different rulings as 'deeply regrettable'. 'It illustrates yet again the need for a one-stop patent shop (with a ground floor department for first instance and a first floor department for second instance) for those who have Europe-wide businesses'. . . . In his judgment yesterday, which was supported by Lord Justice Lloyd and Sir John Chadwick, Jacob highlighted comments made by Mr Justice Kitchin, the High Court judge who heard the case at first instance, in which he said that the positions adopted by DSS in the UK court and the CFI were 'radically different'. Kitchin had gone on to say that the case illustrates why it is desirable to try infringement and validity issues together, where at all possible: 'If they are tried separately it is all too easy for the patentee to argue for a narrow interpretation of his claim when defending it but an expansive interpretation when asserting infringement.'

THE GATT AND INTELLECTUAL PROPERTY ISSUES

By 1980 multinational corporations wanted intellectual property protection and an effective international mechanism to enforce those laws. While the GATT was not the right place, it was the only place in which to raise this issue outside WIPO, an organization which, according to Peter

Drahos, 'was no longer a forum that could be trusted to deliver the standards'[27] being demanded by the US, Europe and Japan. By 1985 the GATT had failed to halt the international trade in counterfeit trade-marked goods, serving to reinvigorate a more general debate about effective intellectual property enforcement – a debate that now had the support of both the Office of the US Trade Representative (established under Presidential Executive Order 12188, (1980)) and the European Commission of the European Economic Communities. The developing world was beginning to pose a significant competitive threat to Japanese, European and US multinational corporations and, alarmed by what they considered to be 'unfair competition', they began to agitate for intellectual property enforcement as part of the GATT. These corporations, used to the monopolies provided to them by intellectual property, now not only wanted mechanisms through which to control competition in their mature final markets, but, increasingly, wanted effective enforcement in economies that provided them with cheap labour and significantly lower manufacturing costs but had poor intellectual property laws and enforcement. The significant profit potential provided by these low cost economies was enticing, but the potential losses through uncontrollable counterfeit production was a significant risk. Of even greater risk however was the potential damage that counterfeit products could inflict on their home markets.

In this regard American policy-makers had been alert to the potential ever since World War I, when Germany's domination of the world's chemical and dye production had caused massive shortages of chemicals needed for American textile manufacture and hospitals. The consequent retaliatory action (which involved the confiscation of hundreds of millions of dollars worth of enemy assets, such as German-owned US patents over pharmaceuticals, and led to the establishment of America's chemical and pharmaceutical companies) gave American policy-makers an incentive to create mechanisms to protect themselves from the effects of 'unfair competition'.

In 1930 Congress had passed the US Tariff Act 1930 which provided in section 337 the outlawing of 'unfair methods of competition and unfair acts in the importation of articles into the United States . . . the effect or tendency . . . of which is to destroy or substantially injure an industry . . . in the United States'. Clearly designed to deal with the effects of dumping, it was only a matter of time before this provision began to be used to halt the importation of products which infringed US patents. Goods that were produced in countries which had no patent protection or which did not permit patents over chemical substances, such as was the case in Germany until 1968, exposed US manufacturers to what they called 'unfair competition'. The Europeans saw the situation differently; they preferred instead to characterize section 337 as a trade barrier that was contrary to the GATT.

In 1953 Linde Air Products, a subsidiary of Union Carbide, used section 337 to halt the importation of synthetic star rubies and sapphires into the US on the ground that these goods infringed its US patent. The importer Van Clemm, a European national, then sued in the US Federal Court to obtain a declaration of non-infringement (a process that would take some time to be determined), alleging that the US patent was invalid; but as the US International Trade Commission (ITC), the administrative body established under the Tariff Act 1930, was unable to test the validity of a US patent due to constitutional law restraints (and was not prepared to wait for the Federal Court's determination), it *prima facie* accepted the validity of the US patent and held that Van Clemm's conduct amounted to 'unfair competition'. Van Clem appealed this decision to the Court of Customs and Patent Appeals but failed (*In re Van Clemm*, (1955) 229 F 2d 441).

The significance of this case here is that it showed how an administrative trade mechanism (as opposed to the courts adjudicating on patent validity) enabled US patent owners to close off the US market to European manufacturers using the allegation of patent infringement, which (even unproved) translated to being 'unfair competition'. The mere allegation of patent infringement coupled with a presumption under US law that a granted patent is valid (a presumption that does not exist in other countries) meant that US Customs could seize these goods at the port of entry into the United States.

By the 1980s the continued use of section 337 by US corporations became the subject of international argument, not just between two companies, but between the world's two principal trading blocs: the EEC and the US. A review of section 337 by the GATT was prompted after the ITC made an exclusion order in 1985 against the importation of aramid fibres produced by Akzo NV, a Netherlands company, using a process which allegedly infringed a patent owned by Du Pont, a US company. This material was an essential ingredient in a product sold by Du Pont as 'Kevlar' and was used in goods such as bullet-proof vests, tyres and cables. Between them Akzo and Du Pont owned 95 per cent of the world market for aramid fibres. The ITC found the Du Pont patent valid and infringed by Akzo, and its decision was upheld by the Federal Court (*Akzo NV v ITC* (1986) 808 F 2d 1471). Akzo then sought leave to appeal to the US Supreme Court, but leave was denied ((1987) 107 S Ct 2490).

What started as a commercial dispute between two very large and sophisticated multinational companies had by January 1988 turned into a full scale trade dispute between the EEC and the US. At issue was not just whether section 337 was inconsistent with the GATT Agreement, but the effectiveness of the GATT itself in mediating the dispute – and with a commercial settlement being reached between Akzo and Du Pont in May 1988, the EEC continued with its argument that section 337 violated the GATT. According to the EEC section 337 created an administrative regime, separate from the Federal Courts which enforced US patents, that focused on controlling imported goods, and this, when coupled with a dispute over the validity of US patents, amounted to a denial of national treatment under the GATT.

The case brought into sharp focus the effectiveness of the GATT because, in the absence of a world trade administrative body (given that the proposed International Trade Organization never eventuated), there was no intergovernmental mechanism beyond the GATT. Despite the fact that the US had consented to the establishment of the GATT review panel, when the panel's report in November 1988 went against the US it simply refused to accept it. Then when other countries moved that the Council of the GATT adopt the panel report, the US not only criticized the report's rationale but blocked its adoption. The GATT lacked teeth and, absent an international trade enforcement body, there was little that the EEC could do, other than impose retaliatory penalties against the United States.

Of course the source of this dispute was as multi-faceted as solutions to it. For the US the GATT panel report was one-sided because the panel focused on assessing national treatment in the absence of intellectual property. The United States was determined to protect its manufacturers and its domestic market from what it saw as 'unfair competition' from Europe, and its withdrawal of opposition to the panel's report would happen only if the GATT accepted a universal enforceable regime for intellectual property. In the absence of a global commitment to recognizing and reciprocating intellectual property rights, the price of free trade would be too high for the United States; and in the absence of the ITO, the last institution envisaged at Bretton Woods in July 1944, there was no other international mechanism which satisfactorily dealt with these issues.

INDIA: ACCESS TO MEDICINES AND THE ROAD TO TRIPS

Indian policy-makers had well understood that India needed to continue to industrialize. Moreover it was a matter of national security that India provide medicines at prices which Indians could afford and which provided treatment for diseases and illnesses that were specific to the Indian subcontinent. Under these circumstances, the Indian Government rejected the pharmaceutical-patent paradigm; and, given the precedent provided by nineteenth century English politicians such as Lloyd George and patent law commentators such as Fulton, they used patent law to do for India what it had done for Britain and Germany. But according to Kalpana Chaturvedi and Joanna Chataway, the Indian Patents Act 1970 'propelled Indian firms on [a] reverse engineering path';[28] however, this description ignores the fact that process patents were still permitted. For all intents and purposes the policy behind the law was no different from the policy which applied in West Germany until 1968.

Facilitating access to medicines in India was not just a matter of a new patent law. A regime of price control on drugs was already in place, and this policy continued. Under the Drugs (Display of Prices) Order of 1970, not only were prices of 18 key medicines regulated but a profit ceiling was also imposed by the Ministry of Chemicals and Fertilizers on all pharmaceutical production. By 1978 the Indian Government had also implemented a policy which was biased in favour of Indian pharmaceutical producers and which encouraged them to produce 'bulk drugs'.[29] Under this policy, apart from not being given this allowance, non-Indian pharmaceutical producers and their Indian subsidiaries had to manufacture medicines in India within two years of commencing foreign sales, and those producers with turnovers above 50 million rupees were required to maintain a research and development capacity in India having budgets equal to at least 4 per cent of sales. In 1979 a new Drugs (Display of Prices) Order was issued. This was much more complex than the previous order, and it now applied to 347 drugs – about 90 per cent of Indian production. Medicines were classified as either: lifesaving; essential; less essential; or non essential; all of which, with the exception of those classified as 'non-essential', were subjected to both price and profit controls. Also exempted from these regulations were Indian producers.

This mix of policies successfully made India self-sufficient in pharmaceutical production[30] and a net exporter of reliable, safe and cheap generic medicines. This achievement, clearly, was not simply the result of 'reverse engineering', but involved a considerable innovative capacity which developed over time, with the support of policies designed to encourage pharmaceutical R&D within India. The result saw key Indian producers such as Cipla, Ranbaxy, Dr Reddy's, Lupin, Sun, Torrent, Cadila, Dabur and Zydus expanding their repertoire of drugs, and some, like Dr Reddy's and Ranbaxy, even establishing offices in the United States to supply generic off-patent medicines to the North American market.[31] Consequently, once the Italian generic pharmaceutical industry was put out of business as a result of the EPC, the Indian pharmaceutical industry replaced it.

The experience of India demonstrates the inherent flaw in the pharmaceutical-patent paradigm. Even with the leg-up that local Indian producers undoubtedly received as a result of the new patent law, what history shows is that within 20 years India's pharmaceutical industry had matured from copier into innovator. What was initially needed was a capacity for production, but once that capacity was reached Indian pharmaceutical companies inevitably progressed to develop innovative drugs at prices that were affordable to Indians as well as peoples in developing countries. An example of this kind of innovation was Cipla's release in 2001 of the HIV drug Triomune, the world's first fixed-dose anti-retroviral drug that combined the antiretroviral drugs Stavudine, Lamivudine and Nevirapine (all patented drugs except in India). Cipla sold Triomune at US$600 per year, reduced to US$1 per day to *Médecins Sans Fronitières* – a price much less than US$10 000 per year that it cost to acquire a combination of three drugs separately in the United States and Europe (and not produced as a single drug). In addition, Cipla also developed Duovir-N, Duovir, Viraday and Efavir, each of them drugs useful in the treatment of AIDS; and while it is true that these used otherwise patented ingredients, Cipla's innovation came in developing a drug which combined two or more of these ingredients into one, simplifying the dosage regime and improving AIDS treatment. Indeed, Viraday not only contains ingredients that treat HIV, but because of the way it has been formulated (which is less toxic than if the ingredients are taken separately) it can be taken together with tuberculosis medicine, something that was not possible before then.

Apart from the innovation that Cipla demonstrated with its combined HIV anti-retroviral drugs, its aggressive pricing encouraged Merck, a US pharmaceutical company, to reduce the price of Crixivan, a protease inhibitor, to about the same price, which in turn caused Bristol Myers Squibb and GlaxoSmithKline to follow suit. Moreover Abbott Laboratories, the holder of patents over Kaletra, another HIV drug, came to an agreement with the Brazilian Government reducing the price by 30 per cent – a saving to Brazil of US$10 million per year. Cipla also took the initiative of making its drugs available to miners in South Africa, a country where about 11 per cent of the entire population is HIV positive, by using Anglo-American, a major mining company, to distribute its drugs free-of-charge to its workers.

Unfortunately, during the time that Cipla was making these new drugs available it was also facing the prospect that India would soon become compliant with the Agreement on Trade Related Aspects of Intellectual Property (TRIPS), as required under the World Trade Agreement which came into effect in January 1995. The end of the 10-year TRIPS moratorium required countries like India to allow for patents over chemical substances from 2005.

THE TRIPS NEGOTIATIONS

According to Peter Drahos,[32] Pfizer, the largest US pharmaceutical company, played a major behind-the-scenes role leading up to and during the TRIPS negotiations. The story that was being told to US policy-makers by Pfizer during the 1970s was that the profitability of US corporations was being eroded by 'copycat' products made in low cost manufacturing countries and that this was undermining the price advantage that patents provided. Pfizer's call to arms had been answered – TRIPS was on the GATT agenda.

When the TRIPS negotiations opened in March 1987, the chief US negotiator, applying the Pfizer rationale, blamed the 'deficiencies in protection of intellectual property rights'[33] as the cause of a distortion of the 'trade in goods', transforming the pharmaceutical-patent paradigm into a multilateral trade issue. It was the firm view of the US TRIPS negotiator that 'the entire trading system as a whole will benefit from eliminating trade distortions resulting from lack of adequate and effective protection of intellectual property rights'.[34] Indicating that there was a need to act 'quickly on a multilateral basis', the negotiator emphasized that 'the problem' was 'growing'.[35]

Naturally the resolution of the Akzo and Du Pont trade dispute between the US and the EEC, which at the time was unresolved, was key to securing the multilateral support that the US required from the EEC. In the meantime, while the EEC was alleging that the US was using patents as a disguised trade barrier, the US was alleging that inadequate enforcement of US-owned patents in Europe amounted to unfair competition.

The developing countries, many of which were worried that bringing intellectual property law enforcement within the GATT would inhibit their right to economic self-determination, were guarded. They believed that the Paris Convention provided flexibility in this respect and that WIPO, which administered this and other intellectual property treaties, was accordingly the appropriate body to facilitate all discussion. In their view the GATT talks which were mandated by the Uruguay Ministerial Council were narrowly confined to trade-related aspects of intellectual property law, not to their wholesale harmonization and enforcement.[36] Indeed the Brazilian negotiator attempted to refocus the talks by emphasizing the historical purpose of these kinds of monopolies, which was always about protecting the domestic production capacity and employment of individual economies over the promotion of free trade. The Brazilians were at pains to explain that countries 'which are not able to take advantage of the incentives' provided by technological development 'are obliged to use such protection in a way that ensures the safeguard of domestic technological development'.[37]

Nonetheless once the EEC/US trade dispute was resolved in November 1989 the EEC and US began openly to collaborate on TRIPS. Indeed without any direction by the chairman, Ambassador Anell, or a resolution of the TRIPS Group, on 29 March 1990 the EEC produced the first draft of the TRIPS agreement.[38] The Group next met between 2 and 5 April 1990 and, according to Anell's meeting notes,[39] the proposal reflected the EEC's 'determination to obtain a comprehensive, dynamic agreement', which should be 'open to periodic review' as technology developed. It also reflected the EEC's 'continued determination' to respect and safeguard the role of other international agreements or organizations.

While Anell noted that 'many participants welcomed the Community's proposal',[40] he also noted that 'some other participants . . . stated their disquiet that the proposal appeared to go beyond what they considered to be trade-related aspects of intellectual property rights',[41] and 'the proposal failed to take on board the concerns of developing countries'.[42]

Indeed in an attempt to address these concerns the EEC and the US used diplomatic channels to encourage Australia, New Zealand, Hong Kong, Finland, Iceland, Norway and Sweden to intervene and apply group pressure to overcome the stalemate between the developed and developing countries. So on 30 March 1990 trade negotiators from these countries produced a paper[43] 'as an aid to discussion' which was, apparently, 'deliberately neutral'.[44] The paper raised the subject of transitional arrangements – particularly that these be incorporated into a TRIPS agreement so that developing and lesser developing countries would be exempted for a period of time from full compliance. The rationale for this proposal was 'to take account of [the different] stages of development', of developing countries that were 'interested in participating in the TRIPS agreement', but which might 'find such an arrangement less "marketable" domestically' because of the fact that their economies were not yet at the same level as those of the EEC, the US, Japan and other developed countries.[45] After some discussion a transition date was set for 1 January 2005 – merely ten years later.

Satisfied that the discussions were now on track, on 11 May 1990 the US TRIPS negotiator submitted a draft in very similar language to the EEC draft. According to Daniel Gervais this was a direct result of 'transatlantic consultations',[46] and although there were slight differences in language from Article 27.1 (the patent provision), ultimately the EEC version was adopted in the final TRIPS document – predictable, given that the language of Article 27.1 was virtually identical to that of Article 52(1) of the European Patent Convention. Thus Article 27.1[47] provided that 'patents shall be available for any inventions' and used the word 'provided' to emphasize that the remaining conditions of patentability were subsidiary.

It is the 'invention' per se that must be 'new, involve an inventive step and capable of industrial application'. Clearly the Article requires that the subject matter of the patent be an 'invention' first and foremost. Thereafter it is the 'invention' per se which must satisfy the three residual parameters of patentability if it is to be a 'patentable invention'.

TRIPS, therefore, became the multilateral mechanism through which the pharmaceutical-patent paradigm became a universal requirement of patent law in all WTO member countries. There were, of course, other developments that had converged to facilitate its transformation from a pharmaceutical-patent paradigm into a technology-patent paradigm. By the mid-1970s biotechnology provided pharmaceutical companies with the promise of patents over a whole range of biological materials, many of which would obviously have pharmacological application by replacing existing drugs with recombinant versions. Human insulin and erythropoietin were two of these, but there were countless others. The potential once again to create patented versions of these materials in low cost fermentation processes made it even more imperative that patents over chemical substances be universally granted and enforced, particularly as the patenting of chemical substances established a precedent for arguing that 'isolated' versions of these natural materials were patentable, just as 'new' chemicals were.[48]

Indian economists, such as Surendra Pattel,[49] were critical, and he noted that 'seeds, plants and biogenetic substances and innovations will have to be patented or given patent-like protection'[50] as a result of TRIPS, and that for countries like India this had ramifications for 'agricultural development'.[51] Biotechnology brought pharmaceuticals and food together and made the patenting of these products, either as recombinant versions or as genetically modified versions, enticing enough for pharmaceutical companies to diversify into seed and plant production.[52]

DEVELOPMENTS AFTER TRIPS

Unfortunately, even with the uniform patent protection and enforcement provided by TRIPS and the WTO, there is now a growing body of evidence that both the rate of drug innovation and pharmaceutical company profits are falling.[53] According to one industry analyst, although Pfizer had 'spent $7.6 billion on R&D [in 2004] . . . [it had not] launched a blockbuster from its own labs since 1998'.[54] More to the point, the kinds of drugs that are in the development pipeline are not necessarily those that will save lives or alleviate human suffering or illness, especially in the developing world. Rather, many of these drugs are cosmetic, such as the penile erection drug Viagra,[55] and anti-obesity drugs, such as Orlistat, Sibutramine, Metformin, Byetta, Symlin and Rimonabant – not the kinds of drugs that Chain had in mind in 1963 when he spoke of the life saving miracles that modern drugs could provide. At the same time the classic pharmaceutical business model that traditionally associated patent protection with huge profits and blockbuster drugs, such as Lipitor (for reducing cholesterol), Nexium (for alleviating stomach ulcers) and Zoloft (for alleviating anxiety and depression), seems to have changed. The reasons for this change have less to do with the patent system and more to do with the need for pharmaceutical companies to 'protect themselves from [product] recalls'[56] and class actions[57] in wealthy and developed countries. Consequently the R&D focus now appears to be on drugs which are much more specific and have much smaller (but wealthier) markets, and not on the kind of drugs or vaccines that are needed by people who are malnourished, suffer from tuberculosis or live in parts of the world in which malaria[58] and other diseases (such as leprosy[59] or trachoma[60]) are endemic. Arguably, if the patent system truly encourages innovation in medicines, one would think that the prospect of eradicating 515 million cases of malaria a year alone would provide sufficient incentive for the necessary R&D into diseases which afflict the developing world. Yet there is still no anti-malarial vaccine.

The example of Cipla and India aside, history shows that patents are not the promoters of innovation that the pharmaceutical industry would like us to believe. Not until November 1888 did Switzerland enact a national patent law, and even then, according to Eric Schiff,[61] it was 'probably . . . the most incomplete and selective patent law ever enacted in modern times'.[62] In fact, it was not until 1907 that Switzerland finally repealed the requirement to lodge a 'model' of the invention, and then it was only in response to pressure from Germany (which had threatened to impose draconian import duties on its manufactured goods) and the United States (which had suggested that the Paris Convention be amended so that patent protection be extended only to members which provided mutual recognition of patented inventions). The Swiss firm Ciba (now Novartis) actually prospered, because it could manufacture and supply chemicals and dyes to Germany while using manufacturing processes that were not patentable in Switzerland as a result of the 'model' requirement. Moreover The Netherlands, which repealed its patent law in 1869 only to reintroduce it in 1912, provided Philips, today the world's largest patent filing company,[63] with a patent-free environment within which to commence operations and prosper with its own innovations to the electric light bulb.[64]

Instead, the overwhelming evidence appears to confirm that, rather than improving access to medicines, the patent system actually encourages research and investment into medicines that produces the greatest profit for the least cost – not necessarily medicines that will alleviate human suffering, especially in developing countries. While some argue that by increasing the costs of medicines in developing countries (by paying for patented medicines at higher prices) research into treatments for common diseases that are endemic will be encouraged, others point out that this will be of little consolation to the poor who will be unable to afford them in the first place. The continuing strengthening of patent laws has not improved access to affordable medicines. Rather, as Mattias Ganslandt, Keith Maskus and Eina Wong[65] explain, 'these problems [of poor access] point squarely to the need for further public involvement in encouraging new drugs and in procuring and distributing medicines'.[66] By this they mean some publicly funded scheme that is subsidized by developed countries to provide pharmaceutical companies with 'a long-term guarantee for new innovations'[67] in medicines at affordable prices, 'but [with] tight controls to prevent the low-cost drugs from escaping those areas'.[68] Whether their proposal is viable is one thing, but the fact that it has been mooted suggests that the implementation of stronger and uniform patent laws has not resulted in new medicines that alleviate human suffering in the developing world. They conclude that 'the prevailing system' of intellectual property rights has failed to provide 'sufficient incentives to develop new treatments and distribute them at low cost'.[69]

What seems to have been either forgotten or ignored by western policy-makers is that until 1970 most industrially developed countries had been extremely careful to ensure that patents were not allowed to be used to undermine the local production and supply of medicines. Even the UK, if only between 1919 and 1949, followed Germany's example by refusing to permit the patenting of chemical substances. Most other European countries, including France and Italy, expressly prohibited the patenting of pharmaceuticals and did so until 1978.

Chain was probably right in 1963 to ask his British audience to accept his argument that collaborative science between academic research laboratories and commercial laboratories was good for innovative drug development, and, perhaps, the success that Stanford University achieved with the licensing of Stanley Cohen and Herbert Boyer's bacterial factory invention[70] in 1976 to Genentech[71] is a good example of this; but, unfortunately, this particular success which encouraged US Senator Birch Bayh to co-sponsor the Bayh-Dole Act in 1980 in the US Congress was not easily replicated by other American universities. Twenty-five years later, as Clifton Leaf in his retrospective piece[72] on the effects of the Bayh-Dole Act explained, only a handful of American universities had actually made any substantial money from their collaborations with the commercial world;

and, worst still, some of these, such as Columbia,[73] had attempted to extend their patent royalty income streams well beyond the original patent term by exploiting a loop-hole in US patent law. Despite the fact that the loop-hole was subsequently closed in 1995, it demonstrated how universities could behave unethically. Consequently, American universities have paid the ultimate price – the loss of their academic independence and the research privileges that once enabled the common law easily to provide universities with an exemption from patent infringement. The decision of the Court of Appeals for the Federal Circuit (CAFC) in *Madey v Duke University* (2002) 307 F 3d 1351 confirmed that any activity, including research, that is engaged in for 'commercial gain' and in 'furtherance of the alleged infringer's legitimate business and is not solely for amusement, to satisfy idle curiosity, or for strictly philosophical inquiry' is not capable of coming within the 'very narrow and strictly limited experimental use defense'. Thus, the CAFC held that, as part of Duke's legitimate business involved recruiting students and that excellence in research was an element of its promotion as an attractive university, Duke fell outside the exemption.

This has had an impact on the way scientists collaborate across universities and disciplines. The secrecy demanded by the patent system, prior to the filing of a patent application, has meant that the type of collaboration that was once open between science and medicine is not possible. Commonplace these days are contractual conditions which impose upon research scientists duties to protect the patentability of their research. Confidentiality agreements and technology transfer agreements are now part of the everyday administrative paper shuffle that research scientists labour over, regardless of the 'profit or non-profit status' of their organization or their research. Universities now demand that their scientists sign over any and all intellectual property, resulting in litigation as some scientists, understandably, leave their universities to commercialize their inventions.[74]

As honourable as Chain's intentions were, and despite his claim of not being 'naïve enough to claim that everything is of a pure white within the pharmaceutical industry',[75] the truth is that he was naïve. The pharmaceutical industry is in the business of making money. That it makes money by producing drugs that may be life-saving does not absolve regulators or politicians or policy-makers from failing to be more circumspect with respect to their commercial activities. Admittedly the anti-trust lawsuits against pharmaceutical cartels over antibiotics in the 1970s and vitamins in the 1990s indicate that they are sometimes scrutinized and occasionally punished for price fixing. Regrettable as this kind of activity is, it is the kind of activity which is easy for politicians to deplore on the one

hand while accepting political donations with the other. Beyond price
fixing there are other kinds of activity that are just as criminal. John
Braithwaite, in his study on the pharmaceutical industry in the 1970s,
exposes the collective mentality that makes this kind of criminality
possible.[76] He explains:

> In hastening to point out that not all pharmaceutical executives are nice guys,
> I am reminded of one gentleman who had a sign, 'Go for the jugular', on the
> wall behind his desk. Another respondent, arguably one of the most powerful
> half-dozen men in the Australian pharmaceutical industry, excused his own
> ruthlessness with: 'In business you can come up against a dirty stinking bunch
> of crooks. Then you have to behave like a crook yourself, otherwise you get
> done like a dinner'.[77]

Braithwaite's 1970s study should be a reminder that corporate collectivism hides a multitude of sins. In late 2006 and early 2007, when
the Thai Government made the legitimate decision to issue compulsory
licences over a number of HIV drugs, the reaction of the pharmaceutical
industry was ferocious. In spite of acting in accordance with Thai law
and within the parameters of TRIPS, the Thai Government's decision
was described by *Managing Intellectual Property*, a leading intellectual property publication read by patent lawyers around the world, as
having '*broken three drug patents* within the past four months'.[78] Rather
than understanding the humanitarianism behind its decision, the patent
attorney profession and the pharmaceutical industry portrayed the Thai
Government as acting duplicitously by 'playing an elaborate game of
bluff, using compulsory licensing as a negotiating tactic to lower the cost
of its highly successful, but increasingly expensive, health programme'.[79]
Even Peter Mandelson, the EU's trade commissioner, wrote to the Thai
Health Minister expressing his concerns 'that the Thai government may
be taking a new approach to access to medicines', taking the opportunity to remind him that his ministry's policy of compulsory licensing
'would be detrimental to the patent system and *so to innovation and the
development of new medicines*'.[80] Ignoring the fact that under the Thai
licence these companies would be paid a royalty of 5 per cent on all
sales, what Mandelson seemed to have rejected is that the Thais were
facing an enormous health catastrophe that required them to have access
to HIV medicines at prices that were *affordable*. Unrelenting, Abbott
Laboratories retaliated by withdrawing seven pending drugs[81] from the
Thai drug regulatory approval process.[82] The reason given by Abbott's
Director of Public Affairs was, unsurprisingly, 'the Thai government's
decision *not to support innovation* by breaking the patents of numerous
medicines'.[83]

BOX 5.3 'EU BROADENS INQUIRY INTO DRUG MARKET'

International Herald Tribune, 14 May 2008

'BRUSSELS: European antitrust investigators are expanding the scope of a major inquiry into the 484 billion pharmaceutical market in a bid to determine whether companies are blocking generics makers from getting less-expensive medicines to market quickly. Lawyers and European Union officials said Neelie Kroes, the European Union competition commissioner, was also casting her net widely in a bid to determine whether drug companies' efforts to block competitors by extending patents were also distracting them from developing new medicines, which have been slow in coming to market in recent years. . . .

Commissioners are proposed by their home government and approved by the European Parliament. Some health and consumer groups also argued that more competition would pressure pharmaceutical companies to develop more new medicines and rely less on extending patent protection and marketing of existing molecules – a practice known as evergreening. 'These companies should be spending money on discovering drugs for diseases that still go uncured,' said David Ortega, in charge of competition issues at the Spanish consumers' organization OCU. . . .'

Since World War II the pharmaceutical industry has pushed the line – if you want more drugs then we need patents! The truth is that it is an elaborate lie devised by the pharmaceutical industry and implemented by policy-makers and politicians who felt so comfortable that world war (or any disaster) would never recur in Europe that they no longer needed to guarantee access to medicines. Despite compulsory licensing being the last safety valve, today even this is in danger of being eradicated. However, the evidence overwhelmingly shows that despite having the strongest and most uniform patent laws in history, the level of innovation in medicines is actually falling. Moreover, if one accepts that the patent system was never designed to encourage innovation, but was actually an economic tool which protected domestic economies from foreign competition, the continued emphasis on patents to encourage the development of new and needed medicines is misplaced. Not only does the patent system not encourage the development of new and better medicines but, if it does, it encourages the development of medicines which maximize the profits of companies that demand the benefit of powerful economic protections which are otherwise unavailable in an international environment – technological monopolies that enable them to control access to, price and the quality of pharmaceuticals. Furthermore patents distort research priorities by encouraging scientists to focus their applied research towards meeting the profit objectives of an industry that is inefficient (because of the economic protections provided by the patent system), unethical (because its primary motivation is money) and predatory (because it focuses on treating diseases prevalent in the developed world), rather than encouraging those whose pure research is meeting an ethical and humanitarian duty aimed at truly alleviating the human suffering of those who are poor, hungry and ill.

True it may be that Louis Pasteur patented a process which improved the quality of beer in 1873,[84] but he never patented the vaccine for rabies. Indeed Pasteur courageously developed this vaccine while powerful men of medicine in Paris scoffed at his theories of infection and immunity. Pasteur laboured on with his research, even risking prosecution,[85] because ultimately he believed that his research would help to end human suffering; and, although Lord Florey modestly repudiated any suggestion that he was motivated to develop penicillin as an antibiotic medicine in order to alleviate human suffering,[86] the fact remains that his work was unmotivated by the promise of a patent.

THE WORLD TRADE ORGANIZATION

Since its formation membership of the WTO has increased from the original 79, which included India, to 150. This does not mean that there is accord between the developed countries of the North and developing countries of the South; there remain many contentious issues between them, and the civil unrest that surrounded the WTO meetings in Seattle in 1999 and Hong Kong in 2005 suggests that harmony remains but a distant ambition. Within the WTO moves have been initiated by the South over access to medicines. The Declaration on TRIPS and Public Health was negotiated in 2001 during the Doha round specifically to clarify that TRIPS does not interfere with the ability of WTO members to promote 'access to medicines for all'. The South's euphoria was short-lived; in 2003 the General Council of TRIPS created a number of pre-conditions that effectively restricted the ability of developing countries to use the mechanisms designed to make that happen.

TRIPS is now one of the three pillars of the World Trade Organization (WTO) which was formed on 1 January 1995. The WTO absorbed the

GATT to become the sole multilateral forum for international trade and tariff negotiations. The inclusion of TRIPS in the WTO was not only a very significant step towards the statutory harmonization and enforcement of all intellectual property law, but it represented a fundamental realignment of trade negotiations. TRIPS was the most controversial of the three pillars because, until the GATT Uruguay round, intellectual property had not been part of GATT; although the counterfeiting of trade-marked goods had been first raised during the GATT Tokyo round (1973–9), the scope of this referral was narrowly confined to the effect of 'unfair competition' upon trade, not on the *enforcement* of trade marks against the manufacturers of counterfeit goods.

The most significant harmonizing requirement of TRIPS was the regularizing of the patent term to 20 years from the date of the patent. All of the other requirements were already part of the patent law of developed countries. So why the controversy?

Essentially TRIPS imposed a one-size-fits-all policy on economic development. While this may have been appropriate for the developed economies of North America, Europe, Japan, the UK and former members of the British Empire such as Australia, Canada and New Zealand, for developing countries some commentators and scholars argued that it was not. The problem for these countries was that since the establishment of the GATT many had become members at a time when intellectual property was not a trade issue and, having done so, rather than become isolated from this international forum once the discussion turned towards the formation of the WTO, they chose to remain a part of it. While India for example had in 1970 passed a patent law that did not comply with TRIPS, resolution for the under-developed and developing countries was by way of the grant of an allowance that gave them until 2005 to get their house in order. Consequently the developing world had a 10-year moratorium – which was fine, until that time arrived.

> One wonders how developing countries can see other than hypocrisy and deceit in a solution that pushes developing country public health officials onto a battleground of legal rules, a battleground that favours those with large litigation budgets and armies of lawyers.

Peter Drahos

NOTES

1. MacLeod, C and A Nuvolari (2006), 'The Pitfalls of Prosopography: Inventors in the Dictionary of National Biography', *Technology and Culture*, **47** (4), 757–76.

2. 1824–1907; knighted 1866.
3. 1827–1912.
4. William Thomson became 1st Baron Kelvin in 1892 and was awarded the Knight Grand Cross of the Victorian Order in 1896 and one of the first 12 to receive the Order of Merit in 1902, the same year that he was made a Privy Councillor. Joseph Lister became 1st Baron Lister in 1883 and was also one of the inaugural recipients of the Order of Merit in 1902.
5. There is a statue to William Thomson in Belfast Botanical Gardens and he is buried in Westminster Abbey alongside Isaac Newton. There is a monument erected to Joseph Lister in Portland Place, London, and a statue of him in Kelvingrove Park, Glasgow.
6. MacLeod and Nuvolari, above n 1, 766.
7. Howson, H and C (1872), *A Brief Inquiry into the Principles, Effect, and Present State of the American Patent System* (Philadelphia: Sherman & Co.).
8. 1874–1937.
9. Davies, RB (1969), '"Peacefully Working to Conquer the World": The Singer Manufacturing Company in Foreign Markets, 1854–1889', *The Business History Review*, **43** (3), 299–325.
10. Ibid, 300.
11. 1817–96.
12. *The Congressional Globe*, 19 December 1872, 252–3.
13. 1847–1931.
14. 1847–1922.
15. Invitation to the First International Congress Concerning the Protection of Patents Vienna, 5–10 August 1873: '[w]e live no longer in the day of Industrial action, which is strictly confined and removed from foreign competition, and where slow communications prevents or delays the utilization of inventions. We live at a time of liberal Customs policy; Steam and Electricity have newly united once isolated seats of industry in a way undreamt of; and the mutual exchange of goods shows today a magnitude which a generation ago one could not have imagined. Under such altered relations the Patent granted for an invention in one country without limitation or increase in price, becomes in an adjoining country common property. The artisan who in one country must work with the auxiliary material there patented and therefore dearer in price, will suffer an essential injury as soon as the same material is produced in the other country, not only without restriction, but with a damaging competition. Moreover a continuance of the hitherto antagonistic views and measures would scarcely conduce to the preservation of general harmony; and if, for example, Patent protection were maintained in one country, so as to attract thereby skilled operatives from another, then the danger of disturbance of the International industrial balance might readily be apprehended. Such and similar inconveniences can only be met by the common action of all civilized States, disposed to the maintenance of Patent protection. Following a suggestion of the Government of the United States of America, the General Direction of the Universal Exposition intends to unite with the Exposition an International Congress, which shall discuss the question of patent rights; should this discussion, as may be foreseen, induce a vote in favour of Patent protection, it will then be the task of this Congress, on the basis of the experience of various countries and the materials collected, to proceed to a declaration of fundamental principles for an International reform of Patent Legislation.'
16. 1809–96; US Secretary of the Interior, 1870–75.
17. 1822–85; President of the United States, 1869–77.
18. The eight main sections are: A. Human necessities; B. Performing operations, Transporting; C. Chemistry, Metallurgy; D. Textiles, Paper; E. Fixed construction; F. Mechanical engineering, Lighting, Heating, Weapons, Blasting; G. Physics and H. Electricity.
19. 1904–88; Chancellor of West Germany, 1966–9.
20. Nuffield Council on Bioethics (2002), *The Ethics of Patenting DNA: A Discussion Paper*, 26, para 3.14, n 9.

21. Transcript, *Kirin-Amgen v Hoechst Marion Roussel* [2005] 1 All ER 667, 13 July 2004, 677.
22. My italics.
23. Danish Council of Ethics (2004), *Report on Patenting Human Genes and Stem Cells*, 98.
24. Westerlund, L (2002), *Equivalence and Exclusions under European and U.S. Patent Law* (New York: Kluwer Law International).
25. De Carvalho, NP (2002), *The TRIPS Regime of Patent Rights* (New York: Kluwer Law International), 145, para. 27.6.
26. *Kirin-Amgen v Hoechst Marion Roussel Ltd and others* [2004] All ER 286, para. 95.
27. Drahos, P with J Braithwaite (2002), *Information Feudalism* (London: Earthscan Publications Ltd), 111.
28. Chaturvedi, K and J Chataway (2003), 'Policy and Technology Co-evolution in the Indian Pharmaceutical Industry', available at http://www.sussex.ac.uk/Units/spru/events/ocs/viewpaper.php?id=288.
29. Ibid.
30. Today it meets 95% of domestic demand (ibid).
31. In 2004 the US was India's biggest export market.
32. Drahos with Braithwaite, above n 27, particularly Chapter 4, 'Stealing from the Mind'.
33. Statement by the United States at Meeting of the TRIPS Negotiating Committee on 25 March 1987. (MTN.GNG/NG11/W/2 3 April 1987).
34. Ibid.
35. Ibid.
36. The Brazilian negotiator argued: '[f]or more than 500 years, the main objective of the protection of IPRs has been the promotion of industrial creativity *to the benefit of a country's social and economic development*. Each State, therefore, recognises IPRs according to well-defined public interests. This basic orientation guides, for instance, the system established by the Paris Convention. It also explains and justifies the differences which naturally exist between various national laws dealing with the subject': MTN. GNG/NG11/W/30, 31 October 1988, para. 13 (my italics).
37. Ibid.
38. MTN.GNG/NG11/W/68 – 92100042.
39. MTN.GNG/NG 11/20 – 92100090, para. 3.
40. Ibid, para. 6.
41. Ibid, para. 7.
42. Ibid, para. 8.
43. MTN.GNG/NG 11/W/69 – 92100047.
44. Ibid, para. 1.
45. Ibid, para. 4.
46. Gervais, D (2003), *The TRIPS Agreement: Drafting History and Analysis* (2nd edn., London: Sweet & Maxwell), 16, para. 1.18.
47. 'Subject to the provisions of paragraphs 2 and 3, patents shall be available for any inventions, whether products or processes, in all fields of technology, provided that they are new, involve an inventive step and are capable of industrial application. Subject to paragraph 4 of Article 65, paragraph 8 of Article 70 and paragraph 3 of this Article, patents shall be available and patent rights enjoyable without discrimination as to the place of invention, the field of technology and whether products are imported or locally produced.'
48. Palombi, L (2004), *The Patenting of Biological Materials in the Context of TRIPS*, PhD thesis, University of New South Wales, Sydney, Australia.
49. A Director of UNCTAD (1969–84) and a former member of the Institute of Economic and Social Research, Ahmedabad, India.
50. Pattel, S (1992), 'Statement to the Group of Ministers on Arthur Dunkel's Draft of the Final Act on Uruguay round of GATT Negotiations', *Social Scientist*, 20 (1–2), 99–107.
51. Ibid.

52. Sygenta, a Swiss agribusiness company, was spun off by Novartis and AstraZeneca; and Monsanto, a US agribusiness, is a product of Pharmacia and UpJohn.
53. See 'Pfizer profits fall' (19 January 2006), MedicalSales.co.uk, available at http://allaboutmedicalsales.com/news/0106/Pfizer_20.html; 'Pfizer to cut 10,000 jobs, shut 5 plants', (22 January 2007) CNNMoney.com, available at http://money.cnn.com/2007/01/22/news/companies/pfizer/index.htm?postversion=2007012216; 'Schering-Plough sees quarterly profits falling 48% on merger costs' (23 April 2008), BloggingStocks, available at http://www.bloggingstocks.com/2008/04/23/schering-plough-sgp-sees-quarterly-profit-falling-48-on-merge/.
54. See 'The Waning Of The Blockbuster Drug', (18 October 2004) *BusinessWeek.com*, available at http://www.businessweek.com/magazine/content/04_42/b3904034_mz011.htm.
55. ABC TV Four Corners (2 November 1998), 'Viva Viagra': Reporter Liz Jackson. It posed the question: is Viagra a medical or marketing miracle?; available at http://www.abc.net.au/4corners/stories/s22482.htm.
56. Above n 54.
57. The Australian law firm Slater & Gordon has brought a class action in the Australian Federal Court for Australians who have been affected by Vioxx, manufactured by Merck. See http://www.slatergordon.com.au/pages/class_actions_vioxx.aspx.
58. For the WHO summary see http://www.who.int/topics/malaria/en/.
59. For the WHO summary see http://www.who.int/lep/en/.
60. 'Chronic eye infection, resembling severe conjunctivitis. The conjunctiva becomes inflamed, with scarring and the formation of pus, and there may be damage to the cornea. It is caused by a bacterium (chlamydia), and is a disease of dry tropical regions. Although it responds well to antibiotics, numerically it remains the biggest single cause of blindness worldwide. In 2001 alone, 6 000 000 people worldwide went blind through trachoma and a further 540 000 000 were at risk. A 2004 study estimated that 18–24% of global blindness (7-9 million people) is caused by trachoma': *The Free Dictionary*, available at http://encyclopedia.farlex.com/Tracoma.
61. Schiff, E (1971), *Industrialization without National Patents: The Netherlands, 1869–1912, Switzerland, 1850–1907* (Princeton, NJ: Princeton University Press).
62. Ibid, 93.
63. WIPO 2007 Patent Statistics. WIPO/PR/2007/476: Record Year for International Patent Filings with Significant Growth from Northeast Asia. Available at http://www.wipo.int/pressroom/en/articles/2007/article_0008.html.
64. Schiff, above n 61, 121; Verspagen, B (1999), 'Large Firms and Knowledge Flows in the Dutch R&D System: A Case Study of Philips Electronics', *Technology Analysis & Strategic Management*, **11** (2), 211–33.
65. Ganslandt, M, K Maskus and E Wong (2001), 'Developing and Distributing Essential Medicines to Poor Countries: The *Defend* Proposal', *The Research Institute of Industrial Economics*, Working Paper No. 552, 2001, available at http://www.naringslivsforskning.se/Wfiles/wp/WP552.pdf.
66. Ibid, 5.
67. Ibid, 17.
68. Ibid, 18.
69. Ibid, 21.
70. US 4,237,224 (2 December 1980), 'Process for producing biologically functional molecular chimeras'.
71. Hughes, SS (2001), 'Making Dollars out of DNA: The First Major Patent in Biotechnology and the Commercialization of Molecular Biology, 1974–1980', *Isis*, **92** (3), 541–75.
72. Leaf, C (2005), 'The Law of Unintended Consequences', *Fortune*, 19 September 2005, available at http://money.cnn.com/magazines/fortune/fortune_archive/2005/09/19/8272884/index.htm.
73. Leaf provides the example of the Axel patents which Columbia had licensed to 11 biotechnology and pharmaceutical companies, permitting them to manufacture 19 different

drugs including Genentech's Herceptin. Leaf writes, '[b]ut when the patent life ran out, Columbia announced that – surprise – it had secured a new patent, issued in 2002, that won't expire until 2019'.

74. A recent example of this type of litigation is *University of Western Australia v Gray* [2008] FCA 498.
75. Chain, EB (1963), 'Academic and Industrial Contributions to Drug Research', *Nature*, **200** (4905), 441–2.
76. Braithwaite, J (1984), *Corporate Crime in the Pharmaceutical Industry* (London: Routledge & Kegan Paul).
77. Ibid, 2.
78. 'Why Thailand is at the centre of a patent storm', *Managing Intellectual Property*, March 2007 (my italics).
79. Ibid.
80. 'More drugs under threat in Thailand', *Managing Intellectual Property*, 24 September 2007 (my italics).
81. These are Kaletra (HIV); Brufen (pain killer); Abbotic (antibiotic); Clivarine (blood clotting); Humira (arthritis); Tarka (blood pressure); Zemplar (kidney disease).
82. 'Drug maker hits back in Thai patent row', *Managing Intellectual Property*, 1 March 2007.
83. Ibid (my italics).
84. US 135,245 (28 January 1973), 'Improvement in Brewing Beer and Ale'.
85. Geison, GL (1978), 'Pasteur's Work on Rabies: Reexamining the Ethical Issues', *The Hastings Center Report*, **8** (2), 26–33.
86. De Berg, H (1967), 'Transcript of Taped Interview with Lord Howard Florey', 5 April 1967, National Library of Australia, Canberra, 9.

PART II

The patenting of biological materials: the monopolization of nature

[The] concern about rights of ownership under the patent system is rooted in a deeper belief that genes are naturally-occurring entities that are there to be discovered, like new species or new planets. They are not invented.

Nuffield Council of Bioethics, 2002

6. The isolation contrivance

[W]hen I isolate the DNA sequence from its natural environment, and when I separate the exons from the introns . . . I have made an invention, since I have isolated via a reproducible technical process the DNA sequence from the human body, and I have made a selection in the sequence, i.e., I have selected those parts of the sequence I am interested in. I will basically also copy that sequence, and then I have made cDNA, which does not occur as such in nature. All these elements make the DNA sequence I have isolated not a mere discovery but an invention, which provides a teaching to methodical action. The isolated sequence is not a product of nature, but a product derived from nature.

Sven Bostyn, European Patent Agent, 2002[1]

In the members' view, it cannot be said with any reasonableness that a sequence or partial sequence of a gene ceases to be part of the human body merely because an identical copy of the sequence is isolated from or produced outside of the human body.

The Danish Council of Bioethics, 2004

1873 was a significant year for patent law. Not only was the first international patent meeting held but Louis Pasteur,[2] the most famous microbiologist of the day, was granted two US patents over the production of beer. The first, US 135,245, was granted on 28 January 1873. Entitled 'Improvement in Brewing Beer and Ale', in one and a half pages it provided details of a process which improved 'the capacity of unchangeableness' of beer and enabled it to be 'transported without detriment or deterioration'. The second, US 141,092, was granted on 22 July 1873. Entitled 'Improvement in the Manufacture of Beer and Yeast', in a little over two pages it provided details of a process and drawings of an 'apparatus' which, when used together, would 'eliminate and prevent the multiplication [of] . . . microscopic organisms . . . in "brewers" yeast, worts, and beer'. According to Pasteur these 'pernicious germs' were capable of 'changing the condition of the product'. In other words they caused beer brewed using traditional methods to spoil. His process involved the heating and cooling of the 'wort' and the use of 'pure alcohol yeast', thereby eliminating 'germs' and producing a beer that could be 'preserved without the aid of ice' and 'made in hot as well as cold climates, as summer as in winter'.

The function of yeast in the brewing process, as Pasteur had discovered while studying the fermentation process in wine in the 1850s, was to convert sugars into alcohol using what he called 'ferments'.[3] Applying this discovery Pasteur went on to develop a process that improved the quality of beer but, inexplicably, in patenting his invention he never claimed his improved beer as an 'invention'. True, beer was not a new product and could not be patented as such; but, given that the beer brewed using his patented processes had a longer shelf life, could be transported without loss of quality and could be made all year round, attributes which traditionally brewed beers lacked, it is curious that there was no product claim to the 'new' beer itself.

This was a surprising omission, especially when it is understood that by 1873 America was home to some 4000 breweries; yet even more surprising was that Pasteur claimed 'pure yeast', defined as '[y]east, free from organic germs of disease', as an invention. Why he claimed an intermediate product used in the brewing process but not the final product – the beer itself – is difficult to comprehend, especially when the final product was not only completely artificial, but was also far more valuable. By contrast pure yeast not only was a derivative of a natural substance but it performed the very same function as natural yeast, with its only distinguishing feature being its purity. While purity was important in terms of the role it played in Pasteur's brewing process, its purity neither changed nor enhanced its ability to perform its natural function. Indeed it was identical to natural yeast.

When the distinguished American patent scholar, PJ Federico, wrote about these two patents in *Science* in 1937[4] he concluded, 'in all likelihood no attempts to commercialize the inventions were ever made' – a surprising outcome, given that in 1876 Pasteur published details of his beer inventions in a book, *Etudes Sur La Bière, Ses Maladies, Causes Qui Les Provoquent, Procédé Pour La Rendre Inaltérable; Avec Une Théorie Nouvelle De La Fermentation.*[5] The book was so popular with brewers that Frank Faulkner, a noted British brewer of the day,[6] translated it into English and published it in 1879 as *Studies on Fermentation: The Diseases of Beer, Their Causes and the Means of Preventing Them.*[7] Impressed with Pasteur's ideas Faulkner wrote, '[t]he more I studied the work, the more I was convinced of its immense value to the brewer as affording him an intelligent knowledge of the processes and materials with which he deals'. Pasteur was also granted patents over the same inventions in France,[8] Italy[9] and the UK.[10] Yet despite the readiness with which his ideas found favour with brewers and the grant of these patents, it would seem that his beer inventions were commercial failures.

One explanation may be that Pasteur was not a particularly astute businessman. Another may be that he was not particularly litigious. Yet another, as Federico hinted, was that the second of his US patents was of questionable validity. Citing *American Fruit Growers v Brogdex* (1931) 283 US 1 he speculated that Pasteur's second patent 'would now probably be refused by an examiner, since it may be doubted that the subject-matter is capable of being patented'. Of course it may have been the case that even in 1873 the patent was considered to be invalid; although *Brogdex* was decided some 50 years later, had its reasoning been applied to the Pasteur patent over 'pure yeast' perhaps it too would have been held invalid.

The question which the US Supreme Court considered in *Brogdex* was: '[i]s an orange, the rind of which has become impregnated with borax, through immersion in a solution, and thereby rendered resistant to blue mold decay, a "manufacture," or manufactured article, within the meaning of ß 31, Title 35, U.S. Code?' In a unanimous decision Justice McReynolds, who wrote the judgment for the Court, held that the answer was no. In describing the Federal Circuit Court of Appeals' ruling as 'not tenable', McReynolds made it clear that it was wrong to construe the invention as 'a combination of the natural fruit and a boric compound carried by the rind or skin in an amount sufficient to render the fruit resistant to decay'. While it was correct to say that 'the complete article [in this form] is not found in nature', this fact alone did not make it an 'article of manufacture'. Rather an indication of invention was whether the orange itself was, as a result of the process described in the patent, given a 'new or distinctive form, quality, or property'. In this respect while the application of borax on the surface of the orange resulted in the orange having a longer shelf life, in truth there was 'no change in the name, appearance, or general character of the fruit'. So while the evidence established that the application of borax on the surface of the orange achieved a useful result, it did not give the patent owner the right to claim a patent monopoly over the fruit itself. That, after all, was not anyone's invention.

Applying this same reasoning to Pasteur's patent for purified yeast, while the natural alcoholic yeast was purified and, like the borax-coated orange in *Brogdex,* not something that existed in nature in that form, it was certainly the case that the purified yeast performed the exact same function. Therefore Pasteur's purified yeast was not something which had a 'new or distinctive form, quality, or property'. It was simply a pure version of natural yeast. While the process that he had invented produced an 'improved beer' and was undoubtedly an 'invention', purified yeast was not.

PRODUCT-BY-PROCESS CLAIMS: CLARIFICATION OR CONFUSION?

Between 1873, when Pasteur's US patents were granted, and 1931, when *Brogdex* was decided, patent law in the United States had undergone something of a transformation. Before 1877 an invention for a product as defined in a patent claim captured that invention regardless of the process used in its manufacture. In terms of Pasteur's yeast patent, the claim to 'pure yeast' was such a claim. On the other hand an invention for a process captured only the use of the process. However in 1877 the US Supreme Court allowed a new type of claim – a *product-by-process* claim. This was a hybrid product and process claim which captured the product, but only if it was made with the use of the process. So if a different process was used, even though the resulting product was identical, there would be no patent infringement. A product-by-process claim was therefore much narrower in scope than a product claim, but broader in scope than a process claim. Concomitantly, with the passing of the German national patent law in 1877 that specifically prohibited patent claims to chemicals as products and permitted only the patenting of the processes of their manufacture, *Smith v Goodyear Dental Vulcanite Company* (1877) 93 US 486 was the first US Supreme Court decision which concerned this new type of claim.

The patent in question was granted in 1865, and it concerned a process which produced 'improvements in artificial gums and palates'.[11] There was nothing actually revolutionary about dentures per se, but this patent concerned a new denture which used 'hard rubber' in what the inventor, a Dr Cummings, claimed to be 'a superior product, having capabilities and performing functions which differ from any thing preceding it'. What distinguished this particular denture from other dentures was the use of '[an] elastic substance, so compounded with sulphur, lead, and other similar substances as to form a hard gum, or whalebone gum, rigid enough for the purposes of mastication, and pliable enough to yield a little to the mouth', in a new process to make a single plate denture. The advantage of this denture over existing dentures was that the teeth could be moulded to fit precisely inside the mouth of the patient, but it was the *process* that Cummings invented which made this particular denture possible.

However on three occasions the USPTO had rejected Cummings' patent application on grounds of obviousness; namely, that vulcanized rubber (or 'hard rubber') was well known and the use of it in a denture an obvious application. Over nine years of wrangling, during which time Cummings nearly went bankrupt, he eventually filed a new patent application with the help of other dentists who had purchased a quarter share of the invention. Finally, these objections were overcome but, as might be expected, this displeased some, like one Mr Smith, who had begun using hard rubber to manufacture single plate dentures. Inevitably Smith sought to have the patent revoked, and eventually the dispute came before the US Supreme Court. Relying on the previous rejections Smith's counsel argued that the use of hard rubber in dentures was obvious; but his argument was rejected because, according to Justice Strong, '[t]he invention . . . is a product or manufacture made in a defined manner'. In other words, Strong used the process of the denture's manufacture to distinguish this particular denture from other single plated dentures. In Strong's opinion, '[i]t is not a product alone separated from the process by which it is created'. As such it mattered not that hard rubber was a well known substance, nor that its use as a component in an article such as a denture was seen as desirable and, to that extent, obvious. While '[t]he properties of vulcanite were well known', the point was, said Strong, 'until Cummings revealed the mode', the use of hard rubber in dentures had 'remained undiscovered'. Consequently, as Smith had made single plate dentures using hard rubber and a similar process to that used by the inventor, Smith had infringed the product-by-process claim – a type of product claim which, as explained, was inextricably linked to the process from which it was made.

The question that soon demanded an answer, however, was whether such a claim could be drafted in such a way that it captured a product made not only by a specific process, but 'by any other method which will produce a like result'. In *Cochrane & Others v Badische Anilin & Soda Fabrik* (1884) 111 US 293 the US Supreme Court was called upon to consider an appeal in respect of proceedings which commenced when the German corporation, BASF, sued an American importer of a dye which was called artificial alizarine. This was one of the new artificial dyes which at the time were state-of-the-art products made with the aid of synthetic chemistry. In what was considered to be amazing science, artificial alizarine was made from anthracene, a chemical by-product of coal-tar distillation, but it looked and behaved like natural alizarine, a dark reddish coloured natural dye which had been available for over 2500 years.[12] In its natural form alizarine was extracted from the madder plant root, and in the early nineteenth century, just prior to the breakthrough by two BASF chemists, Carl Graebe[13] and Carl Liebermann,[14] most of the world's alizarine was sourced from Dutch madder plant plantations.

In the United States BASF was initially granted US patent 95,465 on 5 October 1869 for an 'improved process of preparing alizarine' which used bromide or chlorine (the original Graebe and Libermann process) but, as a result of the development of a new process which used sulphuric acid, BASF applied to have the '465 patent reissued. On 4 April 1871 it was re-issued as US 4,321 for 'improvement in dyes or coloring matter from anthracene'. In fact the development of the new process was not exclusive to BASF; William Perkin,[15] an English chemist, had simultaneously invented it. Indeed it was so close a contest between Perkin and Graebe, Libermann and Heinrich Caro (also a BASF scientist who had joined the team),[16] that BASF managed to file a British patent application only one day before Perkin on 25 June 1869. About seven months later, on 26 January 1870, BASF filed a US patent application over the sulphuric acid process, and on 28 July 1874 US patent 153,536[17] was granted.

In the meantime, before the '536 patent was granted, BASF had no patent specifically over the sulphuric acid process and, knowing that Perkin's sulphuric acid process was available and being legitimately used in Germany to manufacture artificial alizarine, it decided to use the '465 patent reissued as '321 in an attempt to extend the scope of the existing patent monopoly (over the bromide/chlorine process) by using the words 'by any other method'.[18] The reissued patent was therefore significantly broader in scope because it claimed artificial alizarine produced 'by any other method which will produce a like result' and not simply artificial alizarine manufactured using the bromide/chlorine process. Thus BASF was seeking to extend its patent monopoly to capture artificial alizarine no matter how it was made – a classic product patent monopoly. Having secured the reissued '321 patent, BASF then sued the American importers of artificial alizarine who, purportedly, had 'legally purchased artificial alizarine in Germany' from a manufacturer which used Perkin's patented process. The idea, clearly, was to eradicate any competition that BASF might have in the US market.

Unfortunately, BASF had underestimated the tenacity of the American importers. Not only did they challenge the validity of the '321 patent on the ground that artificial alizarine (as originally disclosed in the '465 patent) was 'not a composition of matter' and therefore was not an 'invention', but they took their challenge all the way to the US Supreme Court.

Their attack on the validity of '321 was based upon the fact that natural alizarine (as extracted from the madder plant) was indistinguishable from the artificial alizarine produced with the bromide/chlorine process originally disclosed in the '465 patent. In fact they used as evidence statements made by Graebe and Liebermann in 1869 that there was 'no difference between the natural and artificial alizarine' and that their 'characteristic colors' were 'perfectly identical', in support of their case. They were able to additionally show that the chemical formula for natural alizarine, first deduced by Adolph Strecker[19] in 1866, $C_{14}H_8O_4$, was identical to the chemical formula of the artificial alizarine produced using the bromide/chlorine method.

BASF countered the defendant's argument by claiming that the words 'by any other method which will produce a like result' captured artificial alizarine made using a sulphuric acid process, and this was different from natural alizarine and artificial alizarine made using the bromide/chlorine process as, first, the chemical formula was $C_{14}H_8O_5$, and, secondly, it contained 'anthrapurpurine, isopurpurine and other bodies, not known to have existed before they were produced by Graebe and Liebermann'. Accordingly, the artificial alizarine made using the sulphuric acid process was different from natural alizarine.

The issue, therefore, was whether BASF's claim in the reissued patent '321 was permissible as a product-by-process claim.

At the trial in the District Court and on appeal to the Federal Court of Appeal BASF's argument prevailed. Both courts held that although alizarine was a natural product the artificial alizarine produced using synthetic chemistry was not, because it was not 'chemically pure'. In what was the reverse of the Pasteur 'pure yeast' distinction, which sought to turn a natural product into an artificial product on the basis that the artificial was free of bacteria and 'pure', these judges reasoned that it was not natural because the artificial alizarine was impure. On this basis they held that artificial alizarine was a 'new' composition of matter that was patentable as an invention.

At a practical level, however, if BASF was able to extend patent protection to capture artificial alizarine made by *any process* then the availability, production and price of this dye would be controlled by BASF, a German company. As a result the American textile industry would have to pay a much higher price for this dye, which in turn would have meant that American textiles would have been less competitive.

Before the US Supreme Court, a court which was more attuned to the economic impact of patents, as in this case – on America's textile industry, a different approach was taken. According to Justice Blatchford the words 'by any other method' in the '321 patent could not be interpreted to mean literally any method because 'we then have a patent for a product or composition of matter, which gives no information as to how it is to be identified': the point being that if the scope of the product monopoly was not confined to the process defined in the patent then a product-by-process claim would be incapable of definition and, accordingly, would bring a product, however produced, within the scope of the patent monopoly, thereby rendering the distinction between a product claim and a product-by-process claim otiose. It followed then, as Blatchford explained, '[e]very patent for a product or composition of matter must identify it so that it can be recognized aside from the description of the process for making it, or else nothing can be held to infringe the patent which is not made by that process'. Therefore the words 'any other method' could not be interpreted to include artificial alizarine made using the Perkin sulphuric acid process.

Furthermore, in Blatchford's view, the product or composition of matter of that process had to be identifiable, 'aside from the description of the process for making it'. In this respect the sulphuric acid process produced artificial alizarine having the chemical formula $C_{14}H_8O_5$, whereas natural alizarine and the alizarine produced using the bromide/chlorine process both had the chemical formula $C_{14}H_8O_4$. This meant that, while the artificial alizarine made with the bromide process was chemically identical to natural alizarine, the artificial alizarine made with the use of the sulphuric acid process was not; and although this difference between the two artificial alizarines was a single oxygen atom the evidence showed that this was not trifling because of the presence of anthrapurpurine, a substance not found in natural alizarine or alizarine made using the bromide/chlorine process. Therefore Blatchford concluded the product-by-process claim of the '321 patent was not infringed as, first, the words 'by any other method' could not include the sulphuric acid process nor extend to the product of that process and, secondly, the artificial alizarine produced by the bromide/chlorine process described and claimed in the original '465 patent was different from the artificial alizarine produced by the sulphuric acid process. Thus the attempt by BASF to broaden the scope of its patent monopoly through the reissued patent to include artificial alizarine made 'by any other method', which the USPTO and the lower courts allowed, was disallowed by the US Supreme Court.

Blatchford then turned to the issue of validity. Focusing on the chemical formula $C_{14}H_8O_4$, Blatchford agreed with Graebe and Liebermann that there was 'no difference between the natural and artificial alizarine' made using the bromide process. In fact, '[i]t was an old article'. He held that by being chemically indistinguishable from natural alizarine, the product-by-process claim was directed to something which was excluded from patentability, a product of nature. Moreover, as he stated, '[c]alling it artificial alizarine did not make it a new composition of matter, and patentable as such, by reason of its having been prepared artificially for the first time from anthracene, if it was set forth as alizarine, a well known substance'. Applying this reasoning it followed that the product-by-process claim in the reissued '321 patent was invalid.[20]

Without doubt Blatchford's reasoning was correct, but the BASF cases illustrate that when an invalid patent is granted by the USPTO and the lower courts fail in their duty as gatekeepers to rid the US economy of an illegal monopoly, it is only the tenacity, perseverance and deep pockets of such American defendants which help the US Supreme Court to do so. In this situation, not only was the distinction between a product and a product-by-process claim maintained as being relevant, but an illegal patent monopoly that would have significantly and adversely impacted upon the American textile manufacturers was removed. It also reinforces the importance of understanding the true role of patents as an economic protection and how to balance this protection against a number of other important factors, such as encouraging innovation on the one hand and the restrictions these monopolies impose on the use of the 'invention' on the other, to create competition in price and also in innovation. It is precisely because of the latter factor that the German patent system, which at the time this case was heard in 1884 was only seven years old, expressly prohibited product patents over chemical substances and would continue to do so until 1968. BASF, being a German company, well knew the reasoning behind such a ban; but how curious it is that this company persisted with an argument through every level of the US court system knowing that it was completely contrary to that reasoning. Clearly it was prepared to exploit the apparent readiness of American patent attorneys to seek patents for their German clients and a patent office which was so enamoured with itself and the 'perfect' US patent system, wherein the attorneys, the USPTO and the US lower courts all failed to recognize how their actions could undermine the capacity of the American textile manufacturers to access artificial alizarine at competitive prices.

BLURRING THE JUDICIAL DISTINCTION BETWEEN PRODUCT CLAIMS PER SE AND PRODUCT-BY-PROCESS CLAIMS

The US patent in issue in *Scripps Clinic & Research Foundation & Others v Genentech, Inc., & Another and Scripps Clinic & Research Foundation and Another v Chiron Corporation* (1991) 927 F 2d 1565 was reissued patent US 32,011 entitled 'Ultrapurification of Factor VIII Using Monoclonal Antibodies'. The patent, US 4,361,509, was owned by Scripps and was originally granted on 30 November 1982. In its reissued form the '011 patent consisted of three types of claims. The first was the process claims and the first of these was claim 1, which defined the invention as a process involving five steps with the end result being a 'highly purified and concentrated [Factor] VIII:C' product. The second was product-by-process claims and the first of these was claim 13, which defined the invention as a '[h]ighly purified and concentrated human or porcine VIII:C [product] prepared in accordance with the method of claim 1'. The third was product claims and the first of these was claim 24, which defined the invention as 'a highly purified Factor VIII:C preparation' (meaning that it was a product essentially free of fibronectin or fibrinogen, two glycoproteins made in the liver and normally present in blood). In this purified form Factor VIII:C was not found in normally healthy humans; in fact without these two glyc-oproteins blood would not congeal. In every other respect, however, the purified Factor VIII:C was identical to that found in the human body.

Scripps sued both Genentech and Chiron for patent infringement, relying on the '011 patent. Understandably, given that their own patent portfolios contained a myriad of patents and patent applications over isolated biological materials and the processes of their production, neither Genentech nor Chiron challenged the validity of the '011 patent on the ground that the purified Factor VIII:C product was not an invention within the meaning of section 101. Instead they preferred to rely on the argument that the product claims could not include, within the scope of their patent monopolies, purified Factor VIII:C produced using *a different process* from that of claim 1. Indeed if the product claims could be inter-preted to capture purified Factor VIII:C howsoever made, then product-by-process claims would be redundant.

In what was *BASF* revisited, the product claims in *Scripps* were directed to achieving the same broad patent monopoly for the product, except that in *BASF* the patent owner attempted to do this by inserting the words 'by any other method' in the product-by-process claim, whereas here the reissued '011 patent simply contained claims to the product per se. Just as BASF had tried to patent artificial alizarine howsoever made, Scripps was now trying to hold on to its patent over purified Factor VIII:C howsoever made. Once again the USPTO and American patent attorneys were pre-pared to stretch the envelope, apparently ignorant of or indifferent to how such a patent monopoly would impact on other American companies and industry.

The analogy to *BASF* was made even stronger when the Federal District Court and the CAFC upheld the validity of the reissued patent. That the CAFC did this was indicative of its ambivalence towards the authority of the US Supreme Court on patent issues. Contradicting *BASF*, Judge Pauline Newman held that the 'correct reading of product-by-process claims is that they are not limited to product prepared by the process set forth in the claims', and in so doing she literally gave patent attorneys the green light to use their drafting skills to turn product-by-process claims into product claims. Her decision was not only wrong as a matter of princi-ple but understandably proved to be controversial. On this occasion unfor-tunately it went no higher, and so the US Supreme Court was deprived of the opportunity to set the record straight.

Within a year, however, the CAFC revisited the topic with respect to another product-by-process claim in *Atlantic Thermoplastics Co. v Faytex Corp.* (1992) 970 F 2d 834. This time the CAFC not only ruled against the patent owner but, surprisingly, actually applied *BASF*, and in so doing tried to reverse the effect of Newman's decision; clearly someone had had a word with the CAFC that her decision was having an adverse impact on the American economy and industry.

The patent in this case was US 4,674,204, entitled 'Shock Absorbing Innersole and Method of Preparing Same'. The invention was a process for the manufacture of shock absorbing innersoles. The claim under scrutiny was a product-by-process which defined the invention as '[t]he molded innersole produced by the method of claim 1'. The issue was whether the supply by Faytex of shock absorbing innersoles manufactured by a third party using a different process from that of claim 1 was an infringement. Atlantic argued that the claim's patent monopoly captured the Faytex innersoles because the process employed to manufacture them performed *substantially the same function* to produce *substantially the same result*. In reply Faytex answered that even if this was the case there were two limitations in the claim language of claim 1 which restricted the scope of the patent's monopoly over the process. Indeed without these limitations the USPTO would not have granted the process claims in the first place.

Judge Rader, who authored the CAFC's decision, agreed with Faytex. He reviewed the US Supreme Court authorities, including *Goodyear* and *BASF,* concluding: 'the Supreme Court enunciated a rule for products claimed within process limitations', namely: 'nothing can be held to infringe the patent which is not made by that process'. The supply of innersoles by Faytex could not infringe Atlantic's patent, he concluded, '[as] product-by-process claims are limited by and defined by the process'. More to the point he was critical of Newman who, he said, had 'ruled without reference to the Supreme Court's previous cases involving product claims with process limitations'.

There the issue remained unresolved until, six years later, a Federal District Court was placed in the difficult situation of trying to make sense of the judicial schism created by the CAFC. In *Trustees of Columbia University v Roche Diagnostics GmbH* (2000) 126 F Supp 2d 16 Judge Gertner expressed her frustration by reprimanding 'the Federal Circuit' which, she said, had been 'less than helpful in providing guidance'.

Before her were US 4,399,216, 4,634,665 and 5,179,017. Each of these biotechnology patents concerned a processes over what was called 'cotransformation'. According to the inventors of this process, cotransformation 'involved insertion of "more than one different gene" into the host (or recipient) cell'. The end result was a genetically modified organism which had two functions. The first was the expression of a protein coded for by the foreign DNA which was inserted into the host cell. The second was the expression of a protein which assisted in the identification and isolation of cells which had achieved the first function successfully. This second function was particularly useful as a research tool because it helped to eliminate cells which did not process the required characteristics.

The relevant product-by-process claimed a eukaryotic cell or a mammalian cell 'into which foreign DNA I has been inserted in accordance with process of claim 54'. The issue that faced Gertner was: 'whether . . . the transformed cell with multiple copies of both DNA I and DNA II, can be claimed in the patent without regard to the process used to create it?' Again the issue was whether a product-by-process claim limited the scope of the patent monopoly to the specific process defined in the process claim.

Unfortunately Gertner was unable to reconcile the differing opinions of the CAFC other than by following *Scripps,* simply because it predated *Atlantic*. Hardly a satisfactory outcome in view of the US Supreme Court in *BASF*.

MUDDYING THE WATERS . . .

Six years later the issue again returned to the CAFC. The case concerned paroxetine (PHC), a compound which had originally been discovered by scientists at the Danish company Ferrosan AS and found to be useful as an anti-depressant and an anti-Parkinson's agent. Ferrosan was granted US 4,007,196 over PHC as a product in 1977 and it maintained its monopoly over PHC until the patent expired in 1998. In the meantime scientists at SmithKline Beecham (SKB) in England had developed a hemihydrate form of PHC (PHCh), which was apparently more stable than PHC, and in 1988 SKB was granted US 4,721,723 over PHCh (but expressly excluding PHC) as a product. Then in 1994 SKB scientists reformulated PHCh into a tablet form (PHCht) and applied for a product-by-process patent over PHCht. In 1996 SKB commenced selling PHCht under the trade mark Paxil, and in 2000 PHCht was made the subject of US 6,113,944. By 2006, when the '723 patent expired, SKB's worldwide sales of Paxil had a value of US$3.2 billion per year. SKB could well appreciate that the expiration of Ferrosan's '196 patent would permit generic manufacturers to enter the US market with PHC and, with about eight years to run on its '723 patent and about 18 years to run on its '944 patent, SKB was keen to keep generic medicines out of the market for obvious commercial reasons.

As was to be expected, in 1998 the Canadian generic pharmaceuticals manufacturer Apotex applied to the FDA to enter the US the market with a tablet form of PHC. Of course Apotex had every right, subject to FDA approval, to do so, since the '196 patent had expired or was about to expire and the '723 patent expressly excluded PHC; but, having been alerted to Apotex's application (which is a requirement of the FDA approval process), SKB instructed its patent lawyers to find ways to stop it. They dutifully came up with a clever plan, the foundation for which was scientific evidence which showed that Apotex would necessarily make trace amounts of PHCh in the process of making PHC, thereby infringing (a) the product claim in '723 to PHCh and (b) the product-by-process claim in '944 to PHCht. Another strategic element of their plan involved suing Apotex separately using the different patents, thereby ensuring that Apotex's legal costs would be maximized.[21]

In *SmithKline Beecham Corp v Apotex Inc* (2006) 439 F 3d 1312, the first of these proceedings, SKB argued that PHC infringed the product-by-process claims to PHCht in its '944 patent, but Apotex responded by pointing out that if that were so then the '944 patent was invalid because PHCht, in light of the '723 patent, was not new. Indeed this simple argument, which seemed to have eluded SKB's patent lawyers, made perfect sense, given that PHCht was nothing more than PHCh in tablet form. On this occasion the Federal District Court (the trial court) agreed with Apotex and held the '944 patent invalid.

On appeal to the CAFC SKB attempted to have this ruling reversed by arguing that the product-by-process claims to PHCht contained limitations which narrowed the scope sufficiently so that the '723 patent did not anticipate (in other words was novel). However Judges Schall and Dyk, the majority, simply avoided the 'controversy' between *Scripps* and *Atlantic* because in their view 'the ultimate issue' was 'simply' whether 'the prior art disclosure of a product precluded a future claim to that same product when it was made by a novel process'. The resolution of that issue did not turn on how broadly or narrowly they construed the '944 patent's claims, for they held, 'it is undisputed that the product that is the subject of the patent's claims is PHCh'. In other words no matter how narrowly one defined the scope of the product-by-process claim, the fact remained that the '723 product claim to PHCh anticipated it. More importantly, however, Schall and Dyk held, 'once a product is fully disclosed in the art, future claims to that same product are precluded, even if that product is claimed as made by a new process'.

This was a significant concession, particularly by Schall, who 13 years earlier (as one of the three CAFC judges) decided in *In re Bell* (1993) 991 F 2d 781 that a patent application[22] which defined the invention to be the purified genetic material of a human gene which coded for the protein called insulin-like growth factor was a patentable invention. Thus in *Bell* Schall held as valid a patent which claimed a purified version of a human gene which coded for a protein which was itself well known and in the public domain[23] on the basis of the *process* which was used to isolate and purify the genetic material; thus the process distinguished it from the natural human gene. The fact that the genetic material was already in existence in nature was able to be ignored by Schall by using this reasoning. In this instance it illustrated how the CAFC's agenda of providing patent protection for biotechnology took priority over the consistent development of patent law. Indeed by narrowly reading 'disclosed in the art' to exclude anything other than information which was published about the genetic sequence of the human gene, the CAFC in *Bell* went further and held that even knowledge of the amino acid sequence to the coded protein, despite the known relationship between the nucleic acid sequence to the amino acid sequence, was insufficient to render the 'invention' obvious.[24]

Newman, the author of *Scripps* and a member of the appeal panel, was annoyed by Schall and Dyk. In addition to describing their reasoning as 'seriously flawed', she accused them of perpetuating 'a confusing misunderstanding of precedent governing product-by-process claims'. Using the opportunity, she attempted to answer the criticism that had been directed against her ruling in *Scripps* by Rader in *Atlantic* by suggesting that, '[w]hen correctly viewed', *Scripps* and *Atlantic* were 'not in conflict' but simply dealt with 'different situations'. Taking the position that it was for SKB to define what was within the scope of the patent monopoly and what was not, if SKB chose to confine the scope of PHCht to the process used to make it, then that limitation was relevant in differentiating PHCht from PHCh. 'The term "anticipation" in patent usage', she argued, meant 'the invention was previously known to the public; that is, that it previously existed in the precise form in which it is claimed, including all of the limitations in the claim.' Thus consistently with the approach she followed in *Scripps*, regardless of the evidence to the effect that PHCht was the same as PHCh, if a patent attorney was able to draft a patent claim that said otherwise then the court, according to her, should have ignored the evidence and upheld the validity of the patent.

This was quite a ridiculous result, given that by 1994 PHCh was well known and that its production in tablet form was not a significant advance in medicine, nor in the treatment of depression or Parkinson's. Still the market for Paxil was worth US$3 billion a year to SKB and, with another 15 years to run before the '944 patent expired SKB (an English company) sought an *en banc* review, that is it asked the CAFC to rehear the appeal with a full complement of CAFC judges.

Unlike the first appeal which was as of right and which was presided over by three judges, an appeal *en banc* was available only with leave. In June 2006 a panel of ten judges heard SKB's petition for leave. Predictably it was Newman, the author of *Scripps,* and Rader, the author of *Atlantic,* who were in favour of granting leave. They wanted the *en banc* panel effectively to resolve the argument between them. While Newman believed that there was 'no conflict' between *Scripps* and *Atlantic,* preferring to lay the blame for the 'apparent uncertainty [on] the patent community', Rader believed that there was 'an apparent conflict' which needed resolution. The majority of seven judges, however, did not agree, and so leave was refused and these particular proceedings went no further.

The US Supreme Court was eventually brought into the other case in *SmithKline Beecham Corp v Apotex Inc* (2006) 547 US 1218 but, unlike the other proceedings which involved the '944 patent, this appeal concerned the validity of the product claim 1 to PHCh in the '723 patent.

In this case, the Federal District Court had tried to balance the rights of Apotex (Canadian), SKB (British) and the American public's need for cheaper drugs by holding the claim to PHCh in the '723 patent valid but not infringed. According to the District Court PHC was different from PHCh because the process which Apotex used to make PHC was different from the process claimed in the '723 patent. On appeal the CAFC disagreed with the Federal District Court, ruling instead that claim 1 was invalid due to the public use of PHCh (because trace amounts of PHCh were necessarily made during the manufacture of PHC) for more than one year prior to the filing of the patent application. Ironically it was SKB's own evidence which it tried to use against Apotex in the '944 patent case which undermined it in the '723 case.

An *en banc* hearing of the CAFC subsequently vacated this first decision and, having directed the CAFC on the law, remanded the appeal back to the CAFC. The CAFC duly delivered a second decision ((2005) 403 F 3d 1331), this time ruling against the validity of claim 1, but for different reasons. In its second attempt to invalidate the patent the CAFC held that claim 1 was invalid because the ''723 patent was inherently anticipated by the prior art covered by the '196 patent'. This, they said, was an example of 'a prior art reference' because, even though PHCh was *undisclosed* in the '196 patent, it was nonetheless a 'feature of the claimed invention'. In their opinion, as it was 'necessarily present, or inherent' in the production of PHC, it could anticipate. It was irrelevant that in 1977 the inventors of PHC were unaware that PHCh was produced (even in minute amounts) and had therefore failed to disclose it in the '196 patent. Citing *Schering Corp v Geneva Pharmaceuticals* (2003) 339 F 3d 1373 with approval, the CAFC reinforced that *'inherent anticipation* does not require a person of ordinary skill in the art to recognize the inherent disclosure in the art at the time the prior art is created'.

In what had become a marathon of litigation when it reached the US Supreme Court even the US Solicitor-General (SG) filed a brief as *amicus curiae,* that is as a friend of the Court. This then provided the US Government with an opportunity to make its views publicly known. While the ultimate legal issue in these proceedings was whether the original patent for PHC granted to Ferrosan AS, which had expired in 1998, anticipated the '723 patent claim to PHCh, the ultimate political issue was the price of medicines for US citizens. In his *amicus curiae* brief, in which the SG agreed with the CAFC, he argued that the US Constitution's grant of power to Congress to promote the progress of science meant that 'patent protection applies only to novel inventions'. He confirmed, ' "[a] claimed invention may be inherently anticipated by a prior art disclosure if the claimed invention *necessarily or inevitably flows from the prior art*", see e.g., *Cruciferous Sprout,* 301 F.3d at 1349'.[25] Thus the SG accepted that the production of trace amounts of PHCh was an 'inherent anticipation' because, on the evidence, it was an inevitable by-product of PHC. Describing it as a 'bedrock principle of patent law', he argued: 'if granting patent protection on the disputed claim would allow the patentee to exclude the public from practicing the prior art, then that claim is anticipated, regardless of whether it also covers subject matter *not in the prior art*'.

For SKB, having lost the '944 patent before the CAFC, this application for leave to appeal to the US Supreme Court was extremely important, given that the market for Paxil was worth billions of dollars. Naturally SKB tried to neutralize the SG's line of reasoning by arguing that such an interpretation of the law posed a general threat to 'the innovation that the patent laws are designed to protect'. The SG countered by pointing out that the more specific and narrower claim to its use as a pharmaceutical to treat anti-depression (claim 5) still provided SKB with patent protection for PHCh as a medicine. 'In this fashion', the SG argued, 'they may retain protection for the actual, practical applications of their new discoveries even if their broader claims to the bare compound are ultimately rejected.' Unfortunately for SKB the US Supreme Court refused leave. That PHC was in the public domain meant that Apotex had every right to manufacture and sell, subject to FDA approval, PHC as a generic medicine. This was good not only for Apotex but also for the American people who needed PHC and would now be able to purchase it at much lower prices.

What is revealing about the history of this litigation is that in 1993 the CAFC had overlooked the SG's reference to the 'bedrock principle' of inherent anticipation in *Bell,* and so upheld as valid a patent over isolated and purified nucleic acid materials which coded for a known protein, whereas in the case of PHCh it applied that very principle to strike down a clearly invalid patent claim which should never have been granted in the first place. Some would argue that the history of the *SKB v Apotex* litigation is a reflection of how *well* the patent system works, as the invalid patent claim was revoked.

What this case demonstrates instead is just how easy it is for unmerito-rious patent claims to be granted, even with extensive pre-grant examina-tion, and how complex, expensive and time-consuming patent litigation is. The irony is that, had it not been for SKB suing Apotex for patent infringe-ment, the validity of these patent claims would not have been scrutinized and probably would have remained on the patents register until their expiry. SKB had enjoyed a lengthy period of patent monopoly protection with PHC and then PHCh, but it sought to use the US patent system to maximize its profits to the detriment of the American people. SKB was not concerned to help those who for many years had been forced to pay a higher than normal price for PHC, and had it not been for the determina-tion of Apotex and its deep pockets it is likely that nothing would have changed. Rather than being an example of how well the US patent system works, this litigation marathon is an example of how inefficient the US patent system is and how the enormous costs of patent litigation (of great benefit only to the patent lawyers involved) is damaging the US economy and is inequitable to the American people.

That, in addition, patents are still being granted for things that are merely isolated versions of naturally existing biological materials is an outcome that must be questioned. Patent law requires more than the mere identification or isolation of a product of nature to qualify as an invention. Given that even the SG accepts that the public domain is the repository of common property that should not be controlled unjustifiably by patents, and that anything inevitably flowing 'from the prior art' is part of the public domain, then it follows that products of nature, even those that are unknown or unappreciated at the time, must be part of the public domain. If patent laws are to be permitted to remove something from the public domain, then there must be some proper basis to justify that removal, even if it be for only a limited period of time and eventually to return to the public domain. That the patent system, despite the law, continues to condone such removal through the administrative actions of patent offices, merely on the basis that isolating a product of nature is an 'invention', means that the patent system is not working as it should and that patent offices are acting *ultra vires*, that is beyond their powers. Even with the pre-grant examination of patents, the patent system remains open to abuse.

The British pharmaceutical company SKB was not in the end deprived entirely of patent protection. Even if the product-by-process claim was invalid, it retained patent protection over the specific process for PHCh production and PHCh as a drug until the '723 patent expired in 2006. In this regard, much like the German patent system which operated between 1877 and 1968, the US patent system seeks to encourage the development of better processes – an incentive that would been removed if a claim over a product per se were allowed to stand. According to the SG, 'a patent on a new process does not prevent others from using prior art processes, whereas under the petitioners theory their patent on a "new" product would block others from manufacturing the prior art product that inevitably produces the new one'.

But if knowledge need not be actual, and can be inferred even with the benefit of hindsight, what is the difference between the situation in this case and one where the process is natural and the products of that natural process are products of nature? Surely if it is known that the human body makes, for example, the hormone erythropoietin through a natural human process which takes place inside the human body, does not its human production anticipate its production through an artificial process? Surely the process may be novel and inventive, but the product of that process is not. More to the point, even if the nucleotide or genetic sequence of a human gene is unknown, is the human gene nonetheless a product that anticipates it?

PATENTABLE SUBJECT MATTER AND ANTICIPATION

The US Supreme Court in *Diamond v Chakrabarty* (1980) 447 US 303 explained that an assessment of patentable subject matter is a separate assessment from the other 'conditions and requirements' of novelty (section 102) and nonobviousness (section 103). Thus the word 'new' in section 101[26] is not the same as 'novelty' in section 102,[27] although the association can be difficult to separate; the difference is that, under section 101, unless the subject matter of the patent is *new* then it is not something capable of being an 'invention'. However once that hurdle is overcome, if the 'invention' is not 'novel' as statutorily defined in section 102 it is incapable of being a patentable invention. For instance section 102(a) excludes from patentability 'an invention' which 'was known or used by others'. This is a narrower enquiry although, clearly, if an invention is used in public or is known about then it also cannot be said to be 'new'. This distinction between invention and patentable invention has been repeatedly reinforced and is well recognized to be a fundamental principle of patent law throughout the world.[28] The US Supreme Court in *Diamond v Diehr* (1980) 450 US 175 held: '[t]he question therefore of whether a particular invention is novel is "wholly apart from whether the invention falls into a category of statutory subject matter" '. Moreover in *In Re Nuijten* (2007) 500 F 3d 1346 Judge Linn of the CAFC explained that the word 'new' in section 101 means 'patentable subject matter . . . must not be pre-existing in nature; it must be, literally, an invention'.

With this principle in mind in *Smithkline Beecham Corp v Apotex Inc* (2005) 403 F 3d 1331 Judge Gajarsa had raised the issue of patentable subject matter *sua sponte* (that is, of his own volition) because in his words there was a 'significant public policy interest in removing invalid patents from the public arena'. Thus, even though the parties in this litigation had not raised section 101 as an issue, according to Gajarsa, by effect of US Supreme Court authority 'established long ago', whether something 'is patentable or not is always open to the consideration of the court, whether the point is raised by the answer or not'.

Unfortunately, having then raised the issue of patentable subject matter, he proceeded to make a classic error, namely to find that the distinction between 'products and process of nature' that were not patentable subject matter and those that were was dependant upon whether they were 'human-made or synthetic'. That something is human-made or synthetic or isolated or purified is not, by itself, enough to distinguish it as a product of man over a product of nature. This is what the US Supreme Court held in *BASF* in 1884, in *Brogdex* in 1931 and in *Chakrabarty* in 1980. Indeed Rebecca Eisenberg, an American law professor, noted in 1987 that 'the Supreme Court did not reach the issue of whether naturally-occurring microorganisms that have been newly isolated or purified also fall within the ambit of "manufactures" or "compositions of matter" ' and although, in *Nuijten*, Gajarsa seemed to have modified his position by stating, 'artificiality is insufficient by itself to render something a "manufacture" ', the fact remains that even if an isolated biological material is tangible and artificial enough to be an 'invention' under section 101 how can it be so if, as Linn said in the same case, it is something that is 'pre-existing in nature'?

NOTES

1. He is not an inventor and is merely describing the process from the point of view of a patent agent.
2. 1822–95.
3. Which led Eduard Buchner to discover in 1897 that yeast contained an enzyme, which he called 'zymase', and it was this enzyme which caused sugars to ferment and for which he was awarded the Nobel Prize in Chemistry in 1907.
4. Federico, PJ (1937), 'Louis Pasteur's Patents', *Science*, New Series, **86** (2232), 327.
5. (Paris: Gauthier-Villars, 1876).
6. Author of *The Art of Brewing* (London: FW Lyon, 1878).
7. (London: MacMillan & Co, 1879).
8. No 91,941, 28 June 1871; No 98,476, 8 April 1872.
9. 8 April 1872 and 10 July 1873.
10. No 2225, 24 August 1871 and No 1106, 25 March 1873.
11. Originally granted as US 43,009 on 7 June 1864 to John A Cummings, the inventor, it was re-issued as 1,904 on 21 March 1865 to Dental Vulcanite Company as the assignee of the patent.

12. As a result the price per kilo of alizarine fell from about 200Marks in the early 1870s to 9Marks by 1886. See also Chandler, AD (1992), 'Organizational Capabilities and the Economic History of the Industrial Enterprise', *The Journal of Economic Perspectives*, **6** (3), 79–100.
13. 1841–1927.
14. 1842–1914.
15. 1838–1907; knighted, 1906.
16. 1834–1910.
17. The judgment refers to US 154,536, however, the correct patent number is US 153,536.
18. US 4,321 claimed '[a]rtificial alizarine produced from anthracene or its derivatives by either of the methods herein described, or by any other method which will produce a like result'.
19. 1822–71.
20. Blatchford did not go so far as to rule the patent invalid, because '[i]t is so clear that the defendants are not shown to have infringed, that we have not deemed it necessary to consider other questions any further'. Nonetheless, it is clear that, had this option not been available, he would have ruled the patent invalid.
21. The '944 patent trial was before US District Court for the Eastern District of Pennsylvania (Judge R Barclay Surrick), whereas the '723 patent trial was before US District Court for the Northern District of Illinois (Judge Richard A Posner). It is also the case that SKB's lawyers would have been aware that separating the trials enabled them to make arguments that they knew would have been more difficult to make before the same judge. Thus the argument that the '944 patent was infringed because of the trace amounts of PHCh made during the production of PHC, which by implication threatened the validity of the '723 patent on the ground of obviousness, remained quarantined from the trial judge.
22. Once granted it became US 5,405,942, (11 April 1995) 'Prepro insulin-like growth factors I and II'.
23. The patent specification confirmed that the protein had been in the prior art since 1983: '[t]he chemical synthesis of biologically active IGF-I has been reported. Li et al. (1983) Proc. Natl. Acad. Sci. USA 80:2216–2220. See also copending application Ser. No. 487,950, filed Apr. 25, 1983, which discloses the expression of synthetic genes for IGF-I and IGF-II in yeast.'
24. Indeed the patent did not make a claim to the process used (because it was not new), nor even to the product of that process; it made a claim to the actual purified gene as a product per se. Of course the protein and the gene are not the same thing, but they are inextricably linked because the gene contains the biological instructions that enable the human body's processes to produce the protein; but so determined was the CAFC to ensure that the biotechnology industry was able to patent isolated genes that the three judges, Rich, Lourie and Schall, decided that a protein and its DNA were not linked via the genetic code because the *degeneracy* of the genetic code made it impossible for a skilled person to extrapolate the gene sequence from the protein sequence. This was a fantastic conclusion, especially given that both the USPTO examiner and the US Board of Patent Appeals and Interferences found otherwise.
25. My italics.
26. 'Whoever invents or discovers any new and useful process, machine, manufacture, or composition of matter, or any new and useful improvement thereof, may obtain a patent thereof'.
27. 'A person shall be entitled to a patent unless–
   (a) the invention was known or used by others in this country, or patented or described in a printed publication in this or a foreign country, before the invention thereof by the applicant for patent, or
   (b) the invention was patented or described in a printed publication in this or a foreign country or in public use or on sale in this country, more than one year prior to the date of the application for patent in the United States, or . . .'.

28. See for instance the High Court of Australia in *NV Philips Gloeilampenfabrieken v Mirabella International Pty Limited* (1995) 183 CLR 655. There the Court explained: 'In the light of what has been said above about what is involved in an alleged manner of new manufacture, that threshold requirement of "an alleged invention" will, notwith-standing an assertion of "newness", remain unsatisfied if it is apparent on the face of the relevant specification that the subject matter of the claim is, by reason of absence of the necessary quality of inventiveness, not a manner of new manufacture for the purposes of the Statute of Monopolies. *That does not mean* that the threshold requirement of "an alleged invention" *corresponds with or renders otiose* the *more specific requirements of novelty and inventive step* (when compared with the prior art base) contained in section 18(1)(b). It simply means that, if it is apparent on the face of the specification that *the quality of inventiveness* necessary for there to be a proper subject of letters patent under the Statute of Monopolies is absent, one need go no further': 663–4. (my italics). Also see Mustill LJ in *Genentech Inc's Patent* [1989] RPC 147 where he explains (at 262 lines 6–15) in the context of the European Patent Convention (which applies in 32 countries) that there is a distinction between an invention and a patentable invention.

7. Anything under the sun made by man

> Because that fragment is identical in primary structure in the DNA sequence to the original one that was put into the plasmid or virus it is said to be cloned and it really gives you then the ability to isolate in almost unlimited quantities and in relatively pure form a single DNA sequence or a single gene out of the originally very complex genome of an individual or of another species.
>
> John Shine, testimony to the Federal Court of Australia, 2 July 1996

Before a Congressional hearing on the proposed new patents legislation in 1951 PJ Federico, the principal draftsman of the Bill, testified: 'under section 101 a person may have invented a machine or a manufacture, which may include anything under the sun that is made by man'. About 30 years later, in *Diamond v Chakrabarty,* the US Supreme Court referred to this testimony in a footnote, and almost immediately his words became famous in patent law circles around the globe. Indeed as the Advocate General explained to the European Court of Justice in *The Netherlands v European Parliament* (2000) ECR 1-6229, only after *Chakrabarty* did 'the biotechnological industry develop seriously'.

DIAMOND, THE COMMISSIONER OF PATENTS v CHAKRABARTY (1980) 447 US 303

The phrase 'anything under the sun made by man' is synonymous with the word 'new' in section 101, and while what is new and what is not seems an easy distinction to make, deciding whether something is 'made by man', God or nature is not. Fortunately Chief Justice Burger was quite specific about what kind of human intervention would transform a product of nature into a product of man, but in the resulting stampede which marked the beginning of the biotechnology gold rush this qualification was simply ignored.

The invention described in US 3,813,316 entitled 'Microorganism having multiple compatible degradative energy-generating plasmids and preparations thereof' granted on 28 May 1974 was a genetically modified bacterium. Six years later, amid enormous controversy, the US Supreme Court confirmed it to be a 'new' composition of matter and, therefore, patentable subject matter. Although it was derived from nature the Court found that, unlike the natural bacterium, it contained 'two stable energy-generating plasmids, each of which provided a separate hydrocarbon degradative pathway', which the natural bacterium did not. Dr Chakrabarty's insertion of these two plasmids through the use of what was then a leading edge molecular biological technique was held by the Chief Justice to have transformed a natural bacterium into something that was 'made by man' because 'the patentee has produced a *new* bacterium with *markedly different characteristics from any found in nature* and one having the potential for significant utility'.[1] By a narrow majority of five to four the Court ruled that Chakrabarty's discovery was 'not nature's handiwork, but his own; accordingly it [was] patentable subject matter under ß 101'.

Undoubtedly it was artificial in some degree. Undoubtedly it was derived from nature. Undoubtedly it had a commercial and industrial application and undoubtedly it was valuable. However what actually convinced the Court that it was a new 'composition of matter' was that it displayed 'markedly different characteristics from any found in nature'. Indeed the biological function it performed had no natural precedence. For the first time ever an organism was capable of degrading crude oil. The Chief Justice emphasized that this was a significant degree of artificiality – one that so changed the organism that it could no longer be said to be a product of nature. The Chief Justice considered three characteristics about Chakrabarty's bacterium to be crucial: the level of human intervention, the end result (its function) which was unprecedented in nature and the significant utility that this function had.

In the first instance the artificial bacterium in *Chakrabarty* was *significantly modified* when compared to any natural microorganism, not just the bacterium in issue. The human intervention involved the genetic modification of a natural bacterium through the insertion of two plasmids which were not found in any naturally occurring microorganism.

In the second instance the microorganism displayed *markedly different characteristics from any found in nature;* namely it degraded crude oil. There was no naturally occurring microorganism or anything close to it that performed this function. The Court's emphasis here was not on the artificial bacterium performing a new function in comparison to the natural bacterium, but on the artificial bacterium performing a function different from *any* found in nature. It did more than simply *replicate or reproduce* an identical substance or thing already produced in nature, such as insulin, human growth factor, hepatitis C virus, erythropoietin, human tissue plasminogen activator or Factor VIII: C.

Finally the microorganism's ability to degrade crude oil had the *potential for significant utility* that was directly attributable to its new characteristics – characteristics that were alien to nature.

Only in satisfying all three criteria did the US Supreme Court rule that Chakrabarty's bacterium was something that was an 'invention', or patentable *subject matter*. Of course to be a patentable invention Chakrabarty's invention had also to satisfy the secondary conditions of patentability: namely novelty, obviousness and written description. Thus the US Supreme Court emphasized that it was the *new* characteristics per se which possessed the potential for *significant* utility, not simply the artificiality of the bacterium per se that proved decisive. What was crucial in this process of transformation was the degree of human intervention, which was significant, and how that directly contributed to its *new* function of degrading crude oil. The microorganism was not merely 'isolated' from its natural environment nor purified through a process of manufacture.

THE IMPACT OF REVISIONIST PATENT LAWYERS

Twenty years later the Chief Justice's decision was the subject of some discussion before the US House of Representatives Judiciary Subcommittee on Courts and Intellectual Property,[2] which was undertaking an enquiry into the impact of biotechnology patents on medical and scientific research. There had been growing disquiet among scientists for some time over the impact that biotechnology patents were having on scientific research. For instance Harold Varmus[3] a former Director of the National Institutes of Health, explained to the House Subcommittee that he had 'significant concerns about whether [the patent] system [was] being used optimally to realize the opportunities offered by modern molecular genetics to improve the health of the public'.[4] The ensuing biotechnology gold rush saw thousands of patents being granted over human genes, viruses, proteins and the processes of their biological manufacture, and it had become evident that perhaps things had gone too far. Varmus testified that he was particularly 'troubled by widespread tendencies to seek protection of intellectual property increasingly early in the process', because, he said, 'such practices can have detrimental effects on science and its delivery of health benefits'.[5]

His concerns had also been raised by other eminent researchers such as David Baltimore,[6] John Sulston[7] and Francis Collins,[8] yet, despite these concerns, Andrea Ryan, the then President-Elect of the American Intellectual Property Law Association, an association of US patent attorneys, downplayed their importance by testifying that the US patent system was 'providing unprecedented hope for the nation's sick and infirm while serving the biotechnology community'.[9] She also explained that the patent system was not encroaching upon scientific research because patents 'do not extent [*sic*] to . . . a naturally occurring biological material, such as a gene, a hormone, an enzyme'. Indeed the impression that she wished to convey to her political audience (which was understandably ignorant of the technicalities of patent law) was that the patent system did not restrict the ability of researchers to work with naturally occurring biological materials to develop new medicines and treatments for illness and disease, and allowed for the patenting of these materials only 'in the isolated or purified form *that does not exist in nature*'.[10] In fact, 'the Supreme Court ruling in Chakrabarty', she said, confirmed 'any product of nature is patentable if it is transformed *in some way* by man and it is also new, useful, and non-obvious'.[11]

The unmistakable message from her testimony was that researchers like Varmus and Baltimore were misinformed and their apprehensions were misplaced. She expressly used the phrase 'in some way' deliberately to suggest that the US Supreme Court in *Chakrabarty* had ruled that any human intervention would be sufficient to distinguish a product of nature from a patentable biological material; yet the US Supreme Court in *Chakrabarty* had said no such thing. The Chief Justice had made it clear in his decision that what was required for a biological material to meet the threshold of invention was the display by the modified biological material of markedly different characteristics from any found in nature (that is it performed a function that was unprecedented in nature and had significant utility), and Ryan well knew that the mere isolation or purification of a biological material came nowhere near satisfying that criterion. Unfortunately her misdescription of the Chief Justice's reasoning could not be dismissed as a mere oversight, but was a deliberate attempt to misinform, because she then persisted by suggesting that the real issue in patent law in the light of Chakrabarty was no longer 'whether an isolated or purified product obtained from nature, such as a gene-based invention, [was] eligible for patenting', but what was 'the proper form and scope of the application and claims for the patent to be granted?'[12] In other words the Subcommittee was invited to accept that the US Supreme Court permitted the patenting of isolated or purified biological materials, and if there were problems that needed to be addressed in terms of the impact which the US patent system was having on medical and scientific research, then the solutions were to be found in the way the patent system was being administered. Indeed, in her opinion, the problem was the USPTO's 'ballooning workload',[13] and the solution was for Congress to provide it with 'adequate . . . funding'.[14] Of course what she failed to explain was how the USPTO's failure properly to apply the patentable subject matter standard in section 101 of the Patents

Act 1952 and how the CAFC's decisions in *In re Bell* and *In re Deuel* had directly contributed to that ballooning workload.

What had in fact happened in the intervening 20 years was that the issue of patentable subject matter had been to all intents and purposes ignored by the USPTO, those who challenged US patents and the US judiciary, particularly the CAFC, which had decided that the US biotechnology industry was deserving of patent protection – a view generally subscribed to by US policy-makers and the US Government. In two landmark cases involving claims to biological materials the CAFC held that it was not obvious for a person of ordinary skill in the art to deduce the amino acid sequence (proteins) from the nucleotide sequence (DNA) and visa versa because of the degeneracy of the genetic code, that is the ability of one amino acid to be substituted for another in the replication process. In these two cases, *In re Bell* (1993) 991 F 2d 781 and *In re Deuel* (1995) 51 F 3d 1552, the CAFC completely ignored the issue of patentable subject matter. As a result the CAFC gave the green light to patents over isolated and purified biological materials, and it was Arti Rai, a US professor of patent law, who pointed the finger at the CAFC in a paper[15] suggesting that the CAFC's treatment of DNA-based inventions 'as just another species of chemical compound had substantially diminished the balance between property rights and the public domain achieved by various patentability requirements'.[16]

The attempt to extend patentable subject matter into fields previously excluded is continuing, except that the subject matter that is now being considered is not isolated biological materials but financial service products, such as 'a method practiced by a commodity provider for managing (i.e., hedging) the consumption risks associated with a commodity sold at a fixed price'.[17] The patent application in *In re Bilski*[18] was rejected by the USPTO and the Board of Patent Appeals and Interferences on the ground that the alleged invention was merely an 'abstract idea' which used a 'mathematical algorithm'. Accordingly they both found that the technology did not pertain to an 'invention' within section 101. Specifically the Board observed that the claims which defined the alleged invention did not stipulate how to 'implement' the invention, and that the language used was 'broad enough' to capture within the scope of the proposed patent monopoly the performance of the invention 'without any machine or apparatus'. Indeed, there was nothing 'expressly or impliedly' stated in the claims which required 'any physical transformation of physical subject matter, tangible or intangible, from one state into another', or which produced, 'any electrical, chemical or mechanical act or result', or which transformed data 'by a mathematical or non-mathematical algorithm'. In fact the invention: 'could be performed entirely by human beings'.[19]

On 12 May 2008 the CAFC heard an *en banc* appeal in which 12 judges participated. That by 1pm, an hour before the appeal was to be heard, there was a queue of 200 people waiting to enter the courtroom in Washington, DC,[20] was an indication of its importance, not just to the inventors but to the 'eager members' of the patent community. In fact the decision will be important also to the financial services industry in America and the rest of the world, for, as Charles Macedo, a patent attorney, was reported to have said on the steps of the courtroom, 'Financial service patents are an important part of the economy. . . . Financial services is one of our biggest industries – it's not good for the economy if we don't protect innovation'.[21]

So are patents about 'inventions' or are they about creating private monopolies that help specific industries, whether they be pharmaceutical, biotechnological or financial, to operate without competition?

THE EUROPEAN COMMUNITY AND THE UNITED KINGDOM

A report by the European Commission to the European Parliament and the European Council about the European Biotechnology Directive (EBD),[22] entitled *Development and Implications of Patent Law in the Field of Biotechnology and Genetic Engineering*,[23] explains that recital 21 of the EBD[24] stipulates that 'an element from the human body, including a sequence or partial sequence of a gene' qualifies for patentability under the EPC only if it is 'the result of technical processes which have identified, purified, characterised and multiplied it outside of the human body. Apparently, so the report stated, '[s]uch techniques cannot be found in nature.'[25]

Therefore a human gene is not patentable until it has been isolated. Somehow the act of isolation (which is performed using well known methods and techniques) is an act performed in a laboratory which transforms a naturally occurring human gene into an invention. In fact even if 'such techniques' cannot be found in nature, what the report is incapable of explaining is how an 'element from the human body, including a sequence or partial sequence of a gene' which is substantially identical to that element's natural counterpart is any different from what it was before its isolation: namely, the sequence of a human gene or a protein.

It should be obvious that a human gene which codes for a particular protein remains *substantially the same* even if it is isolated using techniques which are not found in nature, and even if the protein it codes for is produced by 'such techniques'. In truth the only way of distinguishing the resulting 'artificial' protein to its natural counterpart is by the method used to produce it; but, while the process may be patentable (if it satisfies the patentability conditions), what the report failed to explain is how the protein itself was patentable when it was not *new*. Indeed this is precisely the point that was made by the UK House of Lords in *Kirin-Amgen, Inc v Hoechst Marion Roussel Ltd* [2005] 1 All ER 667[26] when it held Amgen Inc's European patent claims to purified erythropoietin invalid.

Even though the EBD, which took effect in July 2000, did not apply at the time when the patent to Kirin-Amgen Inc was granted in 1984, the fact remains that the central rationale of the EBD presupposes that it is the process which is applied to the isolation of the human element, or the process used to produce the human element, which distinguishes the human element from its natural counterpart and which therefore makes the human element somehow artificial, thus becoming man-made technology. This rationale is difficult to accept, especially when the patent monopoly is directed not only to the process itself but also to the *product* of that process. As already discussed, in 1884 the US Supreme Court held in *BASF* that a product-by-process claim to a product which had the same atomic structure as one existing in nature 'could not be patented', and even though this decision was strictly about US patent law clearly Lord Hoffmann in *Kirin-Amgen* was making a similar point in the context of the European Patent Convention. So too was the Chief Justice in *Chakrabarty* when he emphasized the need for 'markedly different characteristics' to be displayed between the natural and the artificial – namely that natural phenomena and anything like them are not patentable subject matter even if they are made artificially.

Despite the European Commission conceding that, '[t]aken out of their natural context, elements isolated from the human body cannot be exploited on an industrial basis', its report ignored these judicial authorities and tried to justify the EBD's rationale by focusing only on the artificiality of the processes used to separate those elements from the human body or to produce them outside the human body. Notwithstanding these artificial methods or techniques, if the 'invention' is an 'isolated' human element or the production of an 'isolated' human element which is identical to the natural human element, then the artificiality of the 'isolated' human element is negated by its identity with the natural human element. As the Danish Council of Bioethics concluded, 'it cannot be said with any reasonableness that a sequence or partial sequence of a gene ceases to be part of the human body merely because an identical copy of the sequence is isolated from or produced outside of the human body'.[27]

It follows then that if the 'isolated' human element is indistinguishable from its natural counterpart the grant of a patent right over the 'isolated' human element per se is tantamount to the grant of a patent right over the natural human element per se. This is the dilemma which confronted the

European biotechnology industry in 1989 when Mustill LJ of the English Court of Appeal in *Genentech Inc's Patent* [1989] RPC 147 zeroed in on how '[this] explosively new technology . . . has exposed some deep flaws even in the current regime'.

This problem, which the decision in *Genentech* highlighted, had to be overcome by any means for the reason which the European Commission gave to the European Parliament, namely: 'life sciences and biotechnology are widely recognised to be, after information technology, the next wave of the knowledge-based economy, creating new opportunities for our societies and economies'.[28] European business was demanding patent protection for biotechnology and the European Commission obliged, especially since 'Europe is faced with a major policy choice: either accept a passive and reactive role, and bear the implications of the development of these technologies elsewhere, or develop proactive policies to exploit them in a responsible manner, consistent with European values and standards. The longer Europe hesitates, the less realistic this second option will be'.[29] If those standards required patent law to apply to things that were not 'inventions' within the meaning of Article 52(1) EPC, then according to the European Commission the law naturally had to be changed. The result, the EBD, therefore transformed patent law because it was no longer about 'inventions' – it was about creating private monopolies over biological materials which had a commercial application in medicines, diagnostics, therapeutics or other life science industries.

GENENTECH INC's PATENT

In *Genentech* the UK Court of Appeal decided that a purified version of human tissue plasminogen activator (t-PA) produced by recombinant technology – an 'isolated protein'–was not an invention within the meaning of the word in section 1(1)[30] of the UK Patents Act 1977. This decision was relevant not only in terms of the UK's patent legislation but also to European patent law under the EPC because section 130 of the UK Patents Act 1977 requires its provisions to be as 'nearly as practicable' to the EPC. Accordingly section 1(1) mirrors Article 52(1) of the EPC.

The subject of the patent was purified t-PA, a protein normally produced and used by the human body in the process of dissolving blood clots. Purified t-PA became available as a therapeutic agent in large industrially produced quantities, and its availability in this form and quantity was a very useful development in human health. However before purified t-PA could be produced by recombinant technology it was first necessary to identify the human gene that coded for t-PA. It was generally known that all proteins consisted of amino acids, but the complete amino acid sequence of t-PA was not known. The patent disclosed then for the first time the DNA sequence of the t-PA gene and the complete amino acid sequence of t-PA.

Claim 1, the product claim of the patent, defined the scope of the patent monopoly as 'recombinant human tissue plasminogen activator essentially free of other protein of human origin'. Claim 3, the product-by-process claim, defined the scope of the patent monopoly as 'human tissue plasminogen activator as produced by recombinant DNA technology'. Both of these claims were product claims to an isolated or purified form of t-PA, meaning that the product claims were not directed to the form in which t-PA was produced in the human body but to t-PA produced outside the human body.

Both at first instance and on appeal these and other claims were held to be invalid. Purchas LJ held that the genetic sequence of t-PA in 'figure 5' of the patent was the 'underlying discovery'.[31] However from this underlying discovery came two possible classes of products, neither of which had been available before. One class was genetic sequence probes, with respect to which no claim was made by the patentee because '[they] would be of little or no commercial value now that the full molecular structures are known'.[32] The other class was components or intermediate products used in the recombinant process, that is 'expression vectors, including the DNA gene coding for t-PA'.[33]

In terms of the production of the latter class of products, he held that '[the] method embracing [the] discovery of the full molecular structure of DNA coding for t-PA and the full amino acid sequences of the latter'[34] was a 'discovery' within section 1(2)(a) and thereby expressly excluded from being an 'invention' within section 1(1). Purchas accepted that section 1(1) contained a legal prerequisite that required the patent to disclose an 'invention'. However as to what constituted an 'invention' he deferred to section 1(2). In his opinion the list of prohibited subject matter was an exhaustive definition of the subject matter of what was not an 'invention' in section 1(1). Therefore unless the subject matter of the claim was expressly prohibited by section 1(2), it was an invention for the purposes of section 1(1).

In his opinion claims 1 to 6, the primary product claims to purified t-PA, were 'discoveries' within section 1(2)(a)[35] because they were claims to t-PA per se, 'in one form or another and prepared by one method or another'.[36] Also the plasmids or vectors described in the patent and 'the plasmids or vectors readily available within the state of the art or their immediate derivations or variations and incorporating genes resulting from minor adjustments to the molecular structure of the t-PA gene'[37] were not 'inventions' because they were not 'clearly identified and defined' in such a way as to 'exclude any speculative element'.[38] He held that the plasmid and vector claims (claims 16 and 17) were not 'inventions' within section 1(1) because such claims 'protected against any use of this information, howsoever this may be achieved in the future',[39] and therefore they were 'for protection of the discovery as such',[40] within section 1(2)(a).

Discoveries about the natural world had never been considered patentable subject matter; and certainly, when the framers of the EPC had deliberately excluded 'discoveries', it was with the understanding that, while the application of a discovery in something that was an invention which was patentable could be the subject of a patent, it was never the case that the discovery itself would be patentable. Accordingly what Purchas found unacceptable was that the claims to purified or isolated t-PA were nothing more than claims to something which was identical to natural t-PA; therefore the amino acid sequence (the protein sequence) disclosed and claimed in the patent was the disclosure of information about the natural world. In the same way, the plasmids and vectors which contained the genetic information (the nucleic acid sequence) of the gene that was encoded t-PA could be nothing more than a discovery. His concern in this respect was that he understood that the claims to the vectors and plasmids extended patent protection over the genetic sequence contained within them, and this he said was tantamount to patenting 'the discovery as such'.

Elaborating further he postured that it was theoretically possible for plasmids or vectors which incorporated the 'discovery' of a DNA sequence to be inventions, conceding that he 'would have probably taken a different view if claims 16 and 17 had been more specifically drafted',[41] but he did not elaborate and explain how this would be possible. Presumably if it were possible to define a claim so that the scope of the monopoly was 'clearly identified and defined' so as to 'exclude any speculative element' then such a claim might be defensible on the basis that the plasmid or vector would make use of the genetic sequence for a particular purpose. But the problem that Genentech would have encountered, had it done so, is that the scope of the patent monopoly would have been rendered worthless, as competitors would have been able to create plasmids and vectors which avoided infringing the patent. Indeed it is difficult to imagine a drafting scenario that would have satisfied Purchas's requirements and at the same time have provided Genentech with what it perceived to be a fair monopoly, that is to purified t-PA howsoever produced.

Nonetheless the fact remains that the protein t-PA and its function were known *prior* to the elucidation of the complete amino acid sequence of t-PA (only the partial amino acid sequence was known before the patent was published). Accordingly t-PA, as a substance, was not *new*. So in an attempt to overcome this patenting obstacle Genentech fashioned its case by relying upon the fact that the *complete* amino acid sequence of t-PA was unknown, to argue that without this additional information t-PA was not characterized and therefore, to that extent, was not new. Purchas remained unimpressed because, if the argument was true, then Genentech would be able to monopolize 'any use of this information, howsoever this [could] be achieved in the future'. Accordingly he made it clear that while this new information was important to science, it did not change the fact that t-PA, even in a purified form, was not new.

Mustill LJ held that patentability could not be decided by reference only to the three patentability conditions contained in sections 1(1)(a)–(c). In his opinion such an argument tended 'to mask a more fundamental require-ment that must be satisfied before a patent can properly be granted, namely that the applicant has made an "invention" '. Indeed he was 'fortified'[42] by the *Guidelines for Examination in the EPO* which provided that the four parameters of patentability are:

1.   There must be an invention.
2.   The invention must be susceptible of industrial application.
3.   The invention must be new.
4.   The invention must involve an inventive step.[43]

In his opinion it was possible for the subject matter of a patent not to be a 'discovery' within section 1(2)(a) and also not be an 'invention' within section 1(1). In this regard his approach diverged from that of Purchas because he was not prepared to define invention by reference *only* to the excluded subject matter in section 1(2). Mustill believed that the list of excluded subject matter was not exhaustive, while Purchas believed that it was.

Furthermore the word 'recombinant', explained Mustill, did not describe 'the product itself, but its history'.[44] Thus, he believed, to describe t-PA produced by *recombinant* means was misleading because it suggested that '[the] protein molecules with the amino acid sequences shown in figure 5 and the functional characteristics set out in the specification' were new, when in fact they, 'have existed since far into the distant past'.[45] In his opinion the technical process used to mass produce purified t-PA did not result in a product that was any different from the t-PA produced by the human body, concluding: '[t]he t-PA which Genentech made [was] neither more nor less than t-PA'.[46]

He compared the purified t-PA that was defined in the primary claim by reference to naturally produced t-PA. The fact that it was recombinantly produced did not alter his opinion that it was identical to its natural counterpart. Genentech's ability to control the production of purified t-PA by recombinant technology suggested to him that it was of 'more than academic interest'[47] to understand precisely what the claimed invention was, as well as whether 'the applicant has made an "invention" ' because section 1(1) contained, in his opinion, a 'fundamental requirement' of invention which had to be satisfied prior to, and independently of, 'the three conditions precedent to the grant of a patent set out in paragraphs (a) to (c) of section 1(1)'.[48]

He concluded that the products defined by claims 2 and 4 were not inventions and 'should fall at the very first hurdle'.[49] Similarly he concluded that the products defined in claims 1 and 3 were equally incapable of being patented because 'there is no difference between recombinant t-PA and any other kind of t-PA. If so, claim 3 must, like claims 2 and 4, be unsound. Genentech did not invent t-PA. At most, they invented a new way of making it. The same objection is, in my view, fatal to claim 1'.[50]

The component and process claims were also unacceptable to Mustill, but not because they were incapable of being inventions in theory. Like Purchas' his reasoning permitted claims to components or processes in recombinant production, but not in this case. In this respect even though claims 9 and 19 were to a specific plasmid and to a process that could use that plasmid and were theoretically inventions, he nevertheless held these claims to be invalid because they lacked an inventive step. In the end he held all claims to be invalid because they were 'so wide as to embrace products which Genentech have not invented, and which others may invent in the future'.[51] He concluded: 'Genentech [was] not entitled to any reward through the medium of a patent monopoly'.[52]

Despite the distinction that he made between the product claims to t-PA, which he held not to be inventions, and the component and process claims to t-PA, which he held to be inventions but not patentable inventions, he was undoubtedly of the opinion that Genentech was not entitled to a patent monopoly over t-PA howsoever produced. Moreover for Genentech to have narrowed the component and process claims so that they were valid would have meant reducing the scope of protection to the point of being practically worthless because it would have left the door open for others to produce purified t-PA by other recombinant means.

Both Purchas and Mustill had come to the same conclusion. They both held that purified t-PA was not an invention within section 1(1) or under Article 52(1) of the EPC. Where they diverged is with respect to this question: does section 1(1) require an examination of the word 'invention' separately from the excluded subject matter in section 1(2)? In this regard Purchas was of the view that the word 'invention' was inextricably linked to section 1(2), and therefore the categorization of subject matter as an 'invention' in section 1(1) depended upon whether it was or was not included in the list of excluded subject matter contained in section 1(2). This implied that the list was exhaustive. Whereas for Mustill, although sections 1(1) and (2) were related, the word 'invention' in section 1(1) required an enquiry in an appropriate case, distinct from section 1(2). In his opinion it was possible for something not to come within section 1(2) and also not be an 'invention' within section 1(1). Therefore the list of excluded subject matter was not exhaustive, and it was possible for something not to be a 'discovery' within section 1(2)(a) and also not be an 'invention' within section 1(1).

THE ROLE OF THE EUROPEAN PATENT OFFICE IN EUROPEAN PATENT LAW JURISPRUDENCE: THE EPO v THE JUDICIARY

It is necessary to look at two decisions of the EPO which have considered Article 52 of the EPC in order better to appreciate the EPO's position on the patentability of this type of subject matter. While the decisions of the EPO are strictly the decisions of a patent office and are not judicial (therefore they are not truly independent), the House of Lords still held in *Biogen* that the '[d]ecisions of the EPO on questions of law are . . . of considerable persuasive authority', and therefore cannot be ignored. Moreover section 91(1)(c) of the UK Patents Act 1977 mandates the UK courts to take judicial notice of 'any decision of, or expression of opinion by, [the EPO] on any question [concerning the EPC]'. No doubt the reason for this policy is based on the need for the harmonization of patent law between the EPO and EC national courts, but, as Nicholls J properly noted in *Re Gale's Application* [1990] RPC 305, 'this should be a two-way flow . . . [so that] in appropriate cases, the European Patent Office has regard to, and takes into account, decisions of the courts of this country as well as decisions of the courts of other contracting states'.[53]

Even so it must be recognized and acknowledged that the EPO appellate process is not independent of the organization which is charged under the EPC with the specific task of 'granting' patents – the EPO itself; therefore it is appropriate that the national courts treat EPO decisions with some degree of scepticism, if for no other reason than to provide a check on how the EPO may influence the development of European patent law. After all, propriety dictates that judge and jury should be independent of each other.

BOX 7.1 ARTICLE 52(1) EUROPEAN PATENT CONVENTION, 1973

'European patents shall be granted for *any inventions*, in all fields of technology, provided that they are new, involve an inventive step and are susceptible of industrial application. . . .'

Article 52(2)
'The following in particular shall not be regarded as inventions within the meaning of paragraph 1:

(a) discoveries, scientific theories and mathematical methods;
(b) aesthetic creations;
(c) schemes, rules and methods . . . and programs for computers;
(d) presentation of information.'

Unfortunately the flow of judicial influence as not been two-way. Instead, as Peter Drahos correctly observed, the EPO has been 'singularly successful in giving a narrow reading to the limits on invention and patentability contained in Articles 52 and 53 of the EPC'.[54] The result has been to so weaken the patentability restrictions that they barely function. Drahos's conclusion has been corroborated by the Nuffield Council on Bioethics which, in its 2002 report entitled *The Ethics of Patenting DNA: A Discussion Paper*, concluded: 'patent offices maintain that the DNA sequences claimed in patents are not natural phenomena . . . [and] have concluded, genetic information [in a cloned artificial molecule] is essentially part of an "invention", a molecule which is human handiwork, and can be patented as such.'[55] In fact the source of this misinformed policy was traced by the Nuffield Council to a communiqué which was issued in 1988 by three of the world's largest patent offices – the EPO, the USPTO and the Japanese Patent Office (JPO). In this communiqué they ignored the contemporary judicial rulings of the day, such as *Chakrabarty* and *Genentech*, and gave their support to a policy of patenting whereby:

Purified natural products are not regarded under any of the three laws as products of nature or discoveries because they do not in fact exist in nature in an isolated form. Rather, they are regarded for patent purposes as biologically active substances or chemical compounds and eligible for patenting on the same basis as other chemical compounds.[56]

1984: VICOM AND THE TECHNICAL CONTRIBUTION APPROACH

Vicom's bundle of European patents granted by the EPO as a 'European patent' was one of the first patents to be reviewed by the EPO's Technical Board of Appeal (TBA) on the ground that it was not about an invention within Article 52(1) of the EPC. The technology involved here was not biotechnology but computer technology. It was about the operation of a mathematical algorithm as an electrical signal, and how the algorithm enhanced the performance of a computer's processing speed. Accordingly the subject of the patent was artificial in every respect, as was the technology within which it operated – a computer. Both the algorithm and the computer existed only because of human intervention.

In reviewing the decision of the Opposition Division of the EPO the TBA was invited to find that an algorithm per se was not an 'invention' because it was 'an abstract concept' which produced no 'direct technical result'. On the other hand, it was argued that, while an algorithm per se may have been an abstract concept, it was also part of a computer which in its totality was capable of being an invention. Once again the kind of reasoning that the US Supreme Court held to be 'untenable' in *Brogdex* (because there the alleged invention – a borax-coated orange – was still 'an orange') was replayed, but in a different technological context. In fact just as the application of borax to the surface of the orange was an incremental improvement over untreated oranges and did not make the orange in its totality an 'invention', neither could a new algorithm make a computer in its totality an 'invention'.

Unfortunately the *Brogdex* scenario did not square with the EPO's policy of expanding the boundaries of patentability, and so the TBA determined that as the 'technical contribution' – the algorithm – made a measurable improvement to the overall performance of a computer, that in being part of the computer it was capable of being an 'invention'. According to the TBA, because the algorithm was (a) used in 'a technical process' that was (b) carried out on 'a physical entity by some technical means' and (c) produced 'a certain change in that entity', regardless of the fact that it was only the 'algorithm' that distinguished the computer as a whole from anything in the prior art, the entity as whole was deemed to be the invention. Thus, the mere application of the algorithm in a computer was enough to sidestep the express exclusion from patentability under Article 52(2)(c); namely 'programs for computers'.

Five years later when the English Court of Appeal in *Genentech* examined the reasoning in *Vicom* it expressly disapproved of it. Understandably Purchas found the literal application of *Vicom* to the facts of *Genentech* unsatisfactory because it would have enabled Genentech to be 'protected against any use of this [genetic sequence] information, howsoever this may be achieved in the future'. This was not, in his opinion, consistent with either the EPC or the UK Patents Act 1977. Mustill, also critical, found the TBA's decision to be 'so compressed' as to be 'almost incomprehensible'. Moreover he believed that the 'controversy raise[d] a puzzling question' in respect of the contention that the discovery of the genetic sequence of t-PA was a 'step towards or even preceded by the creation of the expression vectors' which, in his opinion, was not unequivocally supported by the evidence. Indeed, according to Mustill, 'the factual assumptions of the argument on section 1(2)(a) . . . [and] the close attention focussed on the discovery may have been misplaced'. Although, in the end, nothing in *Genentech* turned on the latter point, it was clearly a necessary comment because so much of the *Vicom* decision relied upon the nexus between the 'technical contribution' and the enhanced performance of the computer to overcome the prohibition.

1994: HOWARD FLOREY INSTITUTE

In this Opposition Article 52 of the EPC was considered in the context of a patent which claimed as the invention: 'DNA fragment encoding human H2-preprorelaxin, said H2-preprorelaxin having the amino acid sequence set out in Figure 2'. The patent for Relaxin EP 0,112,149 claimed priority from Australian provisional patent application AU 7247/82 filed with the Australian Patent Office in December 1982, and was one of a number of international patent applications filed in December 1983 under the PCT.

The Opponents challenged the patent on the ground that Relaxin was a discovery within Article 52(2)(a) and therefore expressly excluded from being an invention within Article 52(1); however both the Examining and Opposition Divisions of the EPO rejected this argument. In their view the 'long standing' practice of the EPO was to allow such claims because the *EPO Examiners Guidelines* stated: 'if a substance found in nature has first [been] isolated from its surroundings and . . . can be properly characterised by its structure and it is new in the absolute sense of having no previously recognised existence, then the substance per se may be patentable'. Following on from this they believed that Relaxin had no previously recognized existence since the inventors had 'developed a process for obtaining Relaxin and the DNA encoding it'. That is, they had 'characterised [Relaxin by its] chemical structure and . . . found a use for [it]'. The fact that Relaxin was a known substance produced naturally in humans was ignored by the Opposition Division. Instead the disclosure of its genetic structure meant that Relaxin had 'been made available to the public for the first time'. While conceding 'the mere finding of something freely occurring in nature [was] not an invention', they believed that Relaxin 'had a technical character, i.e. it constituted an industrially applicable technical solution to a technical problem [that could be] reproducibly obtainable without undue burden'.

The problem with their reasoning was that nowhere did the Opposition Division refer to any European national court decision, nor was there any discussion about what constituted an 'invention' within the meaning of Article 52(1) beyond the *EPO Examination Guidelines*. In this respect, even though *Chakrabarty* was not binding on the EPO, it was a decision of a superior appellate court that would have provided the EPO with some guidance with respect to the issue of patentable subject matter. Particularly relevant in this context were the facts: the DNA fragment encoding human Relaxin did not involve any significant modification; the Relaxin produced by means of the use of the DNA fragment was identical to human Relaxin produced by the human body and did not display any characteristics different from human Relaxin; and finally the human Relaxin produced by use of the DNA fragment did not possess any utility above and beyond human Relaxin produced by the human body. Furthermore, although *Genentech* was not binding on the EPO either, it was nevertheless a decision of a superior European appellate court that was directly on point. The decisions of both Purchas and Mustill LJJ were clearly relevant to Article 52(1) and (2) despite the fact that their reasoning contradicted EPO policy. While it may have been true that the 'H-2' human gene was first identified and its genetic sequence elucidated by the 'inventors', the purpose and functional properties of human Relaxin had been known to the skilled person and part of the scientific literature since 1926. Moreover, Relaxin had been synthesized in the late 1970s using recombinant means. Indeed the case was analogous to *Genentech*, the only material difference being the protein in issue. In *Genentech* the protein was isolated t-PA, whereas in this case it was isolated Relaxin. Applying the reasoning of Purchas in *Genentech* the patent claim to Relaxin was nothing more than a claim for the protection of the discovery as such, and not patentable. However, while the Court of Appeal invalidated the t-PA patent, the Opposition Division of the EPO upheld the Relaxin patent.

A MATTER OF COMMERCIAL SUPERIORITY AND THE IMPLICATIONS ON MEDICAL AND SCIENTIFIC RESEARCH AND ULTIMATELY PUBLIC HEALTH

The introductory words of the European Biotechnology Directive[57] (EBD) state: 'biotechnology and genetic engineering are playing an increasingly important role in a broad range of industries and the protection of biotechnological inventions will certainly be of fundamental importance for the Community's industrial development'. They make it clear that the patenting of isolated biological materials and the processes of their production is about promoting business within the European Community.[58] That is the central objective. It is not about rewarding ingenuity – although that is supposedly the trigger through which the process of meeting the central objective is initiated. Much like the patent systems which existed before and after the Statute of Monopolies 1624, the modern patent system which operates throughout Europe (and which today incorporates the UK) is about giving businesses within the European Community a competitive edge. In terms of the policy behind the EBD, if that means extending patent protection to include isolated biological materials and their processes of manufacture then so be it.

The litigation between Amgen and TKT epitomizes the transatlantic battle for commercial superiority and global market dominance; through the patents Amgen was granted it was able to control the market for purified erythropoietin throughout the world, and by 2006 had grown to be the world's largest biotechnology company on the back of its first and only major breakthrough –the discovery of the human erythropoietin gene.

Ironically it was the success of American biotechnology companies like Amgen, Inc and Genentech, Inc that encouraged the European Commission to support the EBD in the 1990s – and the significant beneficiaries of the EBD have not been European biotechnology companies but American. It is worth noting that, 10 years after the EBD was passed by the European Parliament, the EBD has yet to deliver the anticipated and hoped for industrial growth in the EC region. According to a study commissioned by the European Commission and published in November 2006,[59] of the thousands of patents that had been granted over human DNA, 94 per cent were granted by the USPTO, whereas only 13 per cent were granted by the EPO. Indeed the report confirmed the European Commission's worst fear that the 'majority of granted DNA patents at the USPTO and EPO were held by US-based assignees' and, even worse, that 'Japanese and [EU] assignees had very small shares of the patent awarded at the USPTO'.[60] The data made it clear that, 25 years later and despite the EPC, the EPO's policy of expanding patentability to isolated biological materials and the EBD, the United States was winning the world biotechnology trade war.

The authors conducted surveys and interviews and found that 'granted patents are primarily on research tools, diagnostics and therapeutics, with the majority suggesting research tools made up the largest proportion of their [patent] portfolios'.[61] This is significant, given that research tools are intermediate products used in the research and development of final products such as new diagnostics, therapeutics and pharmaceuticals; unlike the control of final products, the control of tools for medical and scientific research gives patent owners the legal right to restrict and manipulate this medical and scientific research. Indeed, 'a minority of biotech firms and five of the nine pharmaceutical firms'[62] were so worried that DNA patents would restrict their ability to undertake research that they employed a deliberate patenting strategy designed to 'spoil competitors chances of excluding others from commercialisation opportunities'.[63] The report concluded that while this tended to 'ensure "freedom to operate"'[64] in the field, there was no guarantee that this strategy would be successful in the long run.

The most disturbing aspect of this DNA patenting trend is that for the most part the patent system has been used inappropriately in order to give the first to discover these materials the kind of monopoly protection that in the past has been reserved for inventors of new machines, devices and medicines. The distinction between invention and discovery has now become so blurred that policy-makers and, tragically, many academics and patent lawyers have ignored the impact that patent law has in creating private monopolies, which in turn discourages competition in every respect (and that includes innovation) and lower prices. The result is that the general public is paying a higher than normal price for basic diagnostics, therapeutics and pharmaceuticals when they need not be. A perfect example of this is the experience of the patenting of the BRCA 1 and 2 human gene and gene mutations that are associated with breast and ovarian cancer, which resulted in charges of over US$2500 being paid to Myriad for every diagnostic test on a patient in Europe. Gert Matthijs from the Centre for Human Genetics at the University of Leuven believes that 'as a result of the granting of the patents, the BRCA1 testing would either become impossible in the European laboratories, or become significantly more expensive'.[65]

It is the absolute level of unaccountable legal control given to a patent owner that is one of the most significant issues. Professor Jon Merz from the Department of Molecular and Cellular Engineering at the University of Pennsylvania testified before the US House Subcommittee[66] which was investigating gene patents about the results of a study that he and his colleagues, Drs Anna Schissel and Mildred Cho, had conducted. They found that 27 gene patents used in the diagnosis of various human diseases, such as Charcot-Marie-Tooth disease, Spinocerebellar Ataxia, Apolipoprotein-E in Alzheimer's Disease and BRCA 1 for breast and ovarian cancer, raised a variety of concerns over 'the pattern of exclusive licensing'. Primary among these was that some licensees exercised their patent rights to 'prevent physicians – in particular, molecular patholo- gists – from performing genetic testing of their patients'. Furthermore, having conducted a pilot survey of 74 laboratory physicians Merz found that, of these, '25% reported abandoning a clinical test that they had developed, and 48% reported that they had not developed a clinical test because of patents'. Yet defenders of patents over biological materials, such as Stephen Crespi, pointed out a decade ago that there was little empirical evidence to support the kinds of complaints that were being made at the time. His retort was: '[a]n embargo on gene patents . . . is not the answer'.[67] He claimed that the excesses of the patent system could be ameliorated through 'an open policy of licensing the patent rights on terms which are reasonable and defensible in relation to the budgets of public health care authorities'.[68] While this sounded like a reasonable option to US and European policy-makers, commercial reality has meant that such a policy has never been implemented. The simple truth is that for all the talk about patent pools and patent sharing, including non-exclusive licens- ing, the desire of patent owners to exercise exclusive control is absolute. The experience with Chiron should be evidence enough that the patent system is incapable of dealing with issues of public health in an equitable and appropriate manner. Indeed the patent system aided and abetted a company which in the early to mid-1990s ruthlessly ignored the need to develop anti-HCV immunoassays that were capable of detecting HCV antibodies in human blood and blood products elicited from persons who had donated or sold their blood and who were infected with a strain of HCV other than strain 1a. Scientific evidence confirmed that a secondary immunoassay was required to deal with borderline positive or negative diagnostic results (about 10 per cent in Australia), yet in spite of the call Chiron ignored them.[69] Doggedly pursuing its own commercial agenda, Chiron prohibited (which it could do because of its patents over HCV polypeptides and nucleotides) its licensees and any other third party labo- ratory from developing such immunoassays that could have satisfied that need.[70] Indeed it was only when Murex looked as if it would prevail over Chiron in patent litigation in Australia that Chiron relented and settled its dispute.[71] This then allowed Murex to manufacture and sell an anti-HCV immunoassay in Australia and supply the rest of the world with an HCV serotyping assay.[72]

NOTES

1. My italics.
2. US House of Representatives, Judiciary Subcommittee on Courts and Intellectual Property, *Gene Patents and Other Genomic Inventions*, 13 July 2000.
3. 1939–; Nobel Prize, 1989; Director, National Institutes of Health, 1993–99; National Science Medal, 2001.
4. Above n 2, Statement of Harold Varmus, 13 July 2000.
5. Ibid.
6. 1935–; Nobel Prize, 1975; President Caltech, 1997–2006; President of the American Association for the Advancement of Science, 2007.
7. 1942–; Nobel Prize, 2002.
8. 1950–; Team leader of Human Genome Project.
9. Above n 2, Statement of M Andrea Ryan, 13 July 2000.
10. Ibid, my italics.
11. Ibid, my italics.
12. Ibid.
13. Ibid.
14. Ibid.
15. Rai, A (2000), 'Addressing the Patent Gold Rush: The Role of Deference to PTO Patent Denials', USD School of Law, Public Working Paper No 5 and Law and Economics Research Paper 2, *SSRN*, 223758.
16. Ibid, 202.
17. *Ex parte Bernard L Bilski and Rand A Warsaw*, Appeal No 2002–2257, Application 08/833,892, Board of Patent Appeals and Interferences, 8 March 2006, 2.
18. Ibid.
19. Ibid, 6.
20. Managing Intellectual Property (12 May 2008) *Federal Circuit Seeks New Patentability Test in Bilski.*
21. Ibid.
22. Directive 98/44/EC of the European Parliament and of the Council of 6 July 1998 on the Legal Protection of Biotechnological Inventions: '[w]hereas biotechnology and genetic engineering are playing an increasingly important role in a broad range of industries and the protection of biotechnological inventions will certainly be of fundamental importance for the Community's industrial development' . . . Recital 20: '[w]hereas, therefore, it should be made clear that an invention based on an element isolated from the human body or otherwise produced by means of a technical process, which is susceptible of industrial application, is not excluded from patentability, even where the structure of that element is identical to that of a natural element, given that the rights conferred by the patent do not extend to the human body and its elements in their natural environment;' . . . 'Article 3(2): Biological material which is isolated from its natural environment or produced by means of a technical process may be the subject of an invention even if it previously occurred in nature'.
23. European Commission report of 7 October 2002, COM(2002)545, available at http://europa.eu/scadplus/leg/en/lvb/l26026a.htm.
24. Above n 22, Recital 21: '[w]hereas such an element isolated from the human body or otherwise produced is not excluded from patentability since it is, for example, the result of technical processes used to identify, purify and classify it and to reproduce it outside the human body, techniques which human beings alone are capable of putting into practice and which nature is incapable of accomplishing by itself'.
25. See also the report of the European Commission to the European Parliament, The Council, The Economic and Social Committee and the Committee of the Regions (2002), *Life Sciences and biotechnology – A Strategy for Europe.*
26. *Kirin-Amgen Inc v Hoechst Marion Roussel Ltd and others* [2005] 1 All ER 667 per

Lord Hoffmann, para. 132. 'were determined to try to patent the protein itself, notwithstanding that, *even when isolated*, it was not *new*' (my italics).

27. Danish Council of Ethics (2004), *Report on Patenting Human Genes and Stem Cells*, 98.

28. Report of the European Commission, above n 25.

29. Ibid.

30. 'A patent may be granted *only for an invention* in respect of which the following conditions are satisfied, that is to say (a) the invention is new; (b) it involves an inventive step; (c) it is capable of industrial application;' (my italics).

31. Purchas LJ considered whether 'the other claims can be brought under the umbrella of a claim to an invention which incorporates the figure 5 data as its underlying discovery, in contrast to a claim to the figure 5 data as such': *Genentech Inc's Patent* [1989] RPC 147, 226 lines 47–8.

32. Ibid.

33. Ibid.

34. Ibid, 228 lines 47–9.

35. 'It is hereby declared that the following (among other things) are not inventions for the purposes of this Act, that is to say, anything which consists of (a) a discovery . . .'.

36. Ibid, 229 lines 1–2.

37. Ibid, 228 lines 5–10.

38. Ibid, 228 line 52.

39. Ibid, 228 lines 14–15.

40. Ibid, 228 lines 15–16.

41. Ibid, 234 lines 34–5.

42. Mustill LJ, ibid, 262 line 5.

43. Ibid, 262 lines 6–15.

44. Ibid, 262 line 10.

45. Ibid, 262 lines 13–16.

46. Ibid, 262 lines 1–6.

47. Ibid, 262 line 21.

48. Ibid, 262 lines 33–6.

49. Ibid, 264 line 33.

50. Ibid, 270 lines 25–8.

51. Ibid, 271 lines 20–21.

52. Ibid, 287 lines 11–12.

53. *Re Gales's Application* [1991] RPC 305, 323.

54. Peter Drahos argues: '[p]atent offices are hybrid creatures, business bureaucracies which make their living from granting more rather than less patent registrations, from ensuring the repeat custom of their transnational clientele and from going on proselytising missions in those developing states or new market economies which are in the middle of acquiring patent systems. Patent offices can, through their decisions, include more things in the scope of patentability or narrow the operation of restrictions on patentability. Moreover, if they are supranational entities, as in the case of the EPO, they can exercise a profound harmonising influence on national systems. English courts, for example, have pointed out that it is of the "utmost importance" that the exclusions in section 1 of the U.K. Patents Act 1977 should have the same interpretation as the EPO gives to the exclusions contained in Article 52 of the EPC': Drahos, P (1999), 'Biotechnology Patents, Markets And Morality', *European Intellectual Property Review*, **21**(9), 441–9.

55. Nuffield Council on Bioethics, *The Ethics of Patenting DNA: A Discussion Paper*, July 2002, 3.11, 3.21.

56. Ibid, 3.14.

57. Passed into law in 1998 and effective from 2000.

58. 'The top ten public sector organisations in DNA patenting were exclusively US-based, with the exception of the Ludwig Institute of Cancer Research. The top ten firms were mainly US-based, with GSK and Roche being the only non-US representatives (the latter being in the top ten due to its large equity stake in the US biotechnology firm

Genentech). In general US assignees failed to replicate the same degree of success in obtaining US patents at the EPO and JPO, although assignees long established in the field of biotechnology patenting such as Amgen, Genentech, and the NIH enjoyed some success': *The Patenting of Human DNA: Global Trends in Public and Private Sector Activity* (The PATGEN Project) November 2006, viii. Available at http://www.sussex. ac.uk/spru/1-4-3-1-2html.

59.   Ibid.
60.   Ibid, p viii.
61.   Ibid, p vii.
62.   Ibid, 28.
63.   Ibid, 28.
64.   Ibid, 28.
65.   Matthijs, G (2006), 'The European Opposition Against the BRCA 1 Gene Patent', *Familial Cancer*, **5**, 95–102, 97.
66.   Above n 2, Statement of Jon F Merz, 13 July 2000.
67.   Crespi, S (2000), 'Patents on Genes: Can the Issues be Clarified?', *Bio-Science Law Review*, **3** (5), 199–204.
68.   Ibid.
69.   The first affidavit of Stephen Alister Locarnini filed in *Murex Diagnostic Australia Pty Ltd v Chiron Corp* in the Federal Court of Australia, New South Wales District Registry, Action No NG 106 of 1994.

At para. 6.7 he testified: 'The problem I have as a medical virologist in setting up hepatitis C testing in Victoria is that only approximately 45% of persons infected with hepatitis C are genotype 1a; 5–10% are genotype 1b; and 45% are genotype 3a. There are two sources which support these statistics. One source is the data being generated at the moment from my own laboratory at Fairfield. This is not yet available in a published format. The other source has been published in a report prepared by the Hepatitis C Task Force of which I am the chairman, entitled *"Report On The Epidemiology, Natural History And Control Of Hepatitis C"* and tabled with the NH & MRC in November 1993.'

At para. 6.9 he testified, "The concern of the Hepatitis C Task Force is the strong and unequivocal evidence indicating that, despite the use of second generation anti-HCV screening assays as supplied in Australia, there were antibody negative HCV infectious blood donors in Australia. So in the opinion of the Hepatitis C Task Force there is sufficient evidence to indicate that there are genotypes of hepatitis C in Australia which may not be detected by the current anti-HCV screening assays."

At para. 6.10 he testified: 'In my view which is supported by the published literature, the anti-HCV screening assay that is produced by Ortho or licensed by Chiron to Abbott Laboratories in Australia, is only 90% sensitive in relation to genotype 1a and probably much less so with respect to genotypes 3 or 5. I have written a paper with Dr. A. Breshkin entitled *"Comparison of Three Second Generation Immunoassays for Detection of Hepatitis C Virus Antibody"* published in *Australian Journal of Medical Science, Vol. 14, February 1993.*'

At para. 6.11 he testified: "I am aware, from my position as chairman of the Hepatitis C Task Force, that the level of sensitivity referred to in paragraph 6.10 is not acceptable to blood banks in Australia. What is acceptable is the benchmark set for HIV which is 99.4% sensitive and specific. The current Chiron anti-HCV screening assay which is no more than 90% sensitive, is clearly unacceptable and must be improved upon. Sensitivity is defined as the ability of a diagnostic test to actually find those who are truly infected to be positive, whereas specificity is to find those that are truly not infected to be negative, so when the test is evaluated for sensitivity one finds a high risk group that are likely to be infected. For specificity, one finds a low prevalence group.".

At para. 6.17 he testified: "With hepatitis C it is now suspected, due to the fact that anti-HCV screening assays/diagnostic kits have not achieved sensitivity above 90% and the numbers of indeterminants that have been recorded, that many of the immune responses are conformation dependent. In other words there are nuances of the three-dimensional folding which are critical to antibody detection. It is extremely difficult to reproduce the natural three dimensional folding of a protein containing an epitope in *E.coli* or yeast fusion protein systems. With such systems all that is produced is a linear epitope of one small fragment of the genome of a strain of HCV inserted in the *E.coli* or yeast expression protein. The difficulty with hepatitis C is that a person is not infected with *E.coli* containing clone 5.1.1 proteins, or c-100-3 proteins; that person is infected with the whole native hepatitis C virus of a particular genotype."

At para. 6.18 he testified: "There is also evidence emerging that some third generation kits such as the Abbott Laboratories anti-HCV diagnostic kits have no greater sensitivity than the second generation kits, even though the manufacturer has included longer fusion protein inserts (i.e., more genetic material) into the kits."

70. For more information about Chiron's patent licensing strategy see Cohen, J (1999), 'The Scientific Challenge of Hepatitis C', *Science*, New Series, **285** (5424), 26–30 which was critical and Chiron's reply: Blackburn, RP (1999), 'Chiron's Licensing Policy', *Science*, New Series, **285** (5430), 1015.

71. Indeed the settlement between Murex and Chiron occurred within one week of Burchett J, the trial judge, making an order that Chiron produce all documents relating to communications between it, William Rutter and other officers and employees and Lynx Therapeutics and Prof Sydney Brenner. On 21 August 1996 Burchett explained in his judgment, 'the role of Dr Brenner as scientific adviser to Aldous J, and later as scientific adviser to the Court of Appeal, in the English proceedings concerning the United Kingdom equivalent of the patent with which I am concerned' was relevant, given that Chiron was seeking to rely on the English court decisions in support of its case in Australia. Burchett explained:
'the evidence [which] has been tendered on the motion to show prima facie that Dr Brenner, while adviser to one or both of Aldous J and the Court of Appeal, was sitting, as a director, on the board of a company, together with the President and founder of Chiron, which owned a significant part of the shareholding of the company in question; that this company, to which Dr Brenner was also a scientific consultant, had a collaboration agreement with Chiron; and that Dr Brenner stood to gain financially, to some degree, from that collaboration, and from his association with the company.'

72. The dispute was settled on a worldwide basis on 28 August 1996 in Sydney, Australia while Robert Blackburn, Chiron's chief patent counsel, was being cross-examined by David Catterns QC, counsel for Murex. Murex was subsequently fully acquired by Abbott Laboratories in March 1998 and was delisted from NASDAQ (Code MURXF). Blackburn, coincidentally, was co-counsel with Donald Chisum, a noted US patent law academic and lawyer, who appeared for the patent owner and argued the case before the CAFC in *Bell*.

8. The invention of nature?

And God created great whales, and every living creature that moveth, which the waters brought forth abundantly, after their kind, and every winged fowl after his kind: and God saw that it was good.

King James Bible: Genesis 1:21

In 1624 when James I signed Lord Coke's Statute of Monopoly into law the idea that a natural phenomenon could be a 'manner of new manufacture' would have been as repugnant to him as the idea that God did not exist, for he believed that his entitlement to reign was a sacred contract between God and himself. Indeed so fundamental was his belief that ultimately his son, Charles I, would rather die than relinquish it. Indeed it was deeply ingrained into every Protestant and Catholic that God created the world and everything on it, and no man or woman could claim something God-made as his or her own. So it was that when Burger CJ in *Chakrabarty* held once again that 'laws of nature, physical phenomena and abstract ideas'[1] were not patentable subject matter, he was applying a legal precedent which acknowledged that from the very beginning of Anglo-American patent law these things were to be 'free to all men and reserved exclusively to none'.[2]

Yet when Kyle Jensen and Fiona Murray published the results of their study in their *Science* paper, 'The Intellectual Property Landscape of the Human Genome'[3] they showed 'nearly 20% of human genes are explicitly claimed as US IP'.[4] Of the 23 688 human genes that made up the human genome database of the National Center for Biotechnology Information, their study revealed that 4382 were the subject of 4270 patents within 3050 patent families[5] and controlled by 1156 patent owners, of which 63 per cent were private firms.[6] The largest single patent owner of some 2000 human genes was Incyte Genomics, a US corporation.

As Jordan Paradise, Lori Andrews and Timothy Holbrook, professors of intellectual property law, pointed out in their *Science* paper,[7] when it comes to human gene sequences 'the "invention" is the information',[8] that is the 'invention' is information about the natural world. As a result they argue, '[g]ene patents, especially, limit what can be done in the realm of scientific research and medical care because there are no alternatives to a patented gene in diagnosis, treatment, and research'.[9] Naturally if a gene

250

patent is to have any commercial value, it is the information about the natural world contained within the scope of the patent monopoly which underpins that value. It is this information that holds the key to the diagnosis and treatment of human genetic disease and illness because, in the final analysis, it is this which will make the 'invention' useful as a diagnostic, therapeutic or pharmaceutical. So when Amgen, Inc patented erythropoietin in 1984 it claimed as its invention a substance made artificially by the use of a recombinant gene even though, as the Federal District Court in *Amgen, Inc v Chugai Pharmaceutical Co and Genetics Institute, Inc* (1989) 13 USPQ2D 1737 found, it was 'the same product' as erythropoietin made by the human body. Not only that, according to 'overwhelming evidence' the Court found 'the [erythropoietin] gene used to produce [recombinant erythropoietin was] the same [erythropoietin] gene as the human body uses to produce [erythropoietin] . . . [and] by all criteria examined, [recombinant erythropoietin was] the "equivalent to the natural hormone" '.

Quite apart from the fact that the *quid pro quo* that an inventor supposedly pays society in return for the grant of a 20-year patent monopoly is a thorough and complete description of how the invention was made so that others can make it, as Paradise, Andrews and Holbrook have found that 'many patents [claim] far more than what the inventor actually discovered', while others claim 'discoveries' which the patent holder has not 'specifically' described.[10] This raises a question mark over the adequacy of the USPTO patent examination and suggests that lax scrutiny of patent applications has contributed to the explosion of gene patents.

Nonetheless the real problem, as David Olson, a Resident Fellow at Stanford Law School, suggests in his article, 'Patentable Subject Matter: The Problem of the Absent Gatekeeper'[11] is 'the federal courts' abandonment of any subject matter gatekeeping role'.[12] This, he believes, is 'bad for society, because it results in patents being granted in areas in which inventors do not need the incentive of monopoly grants'.[13] Even if such an incentive is considered to be appropriate his criticism raises this question: is the patent system the only option or are there other alternatives? Olson is justified in blaming the US Court of Appeals of the Federal Circuit (CAFC) for, as Judge Gajarsa held in *SmithKline Beecham v Apotex* (2006) 453 F 3d 1346, there is a 'significant public policy interest in removing invalid patents from the public arena' and the fact is that, particularly during in the 1990s, the CAFC failed to be that gatekeeper. Only since 2007 has the CAFC started to show signs of contrition, and then only at the direction of the US Supreme Court.

During the 2006 and 2007 terms the US Supreme Court granted *certiorari* in an unprecedented number of appeals concerning patents. *Laboratory Corporation of America Holdings v Metabolite Laboratories, Inc* (2006) 126

S Ct 2921 was one of these. Although it subsequently withdrew *certiorari* (leave to appeal) Breyer, Stevens and Souter JJ, in their powerful dissent, made it clear that patentable subject matter was an important threshold which should not be transgressed. They were critical of a patent that sought to control the diagnosis of a vitamin deficiency based upon the measure of a naturally occurring amino acid, homocysteine, in the human body. Unfortunately LabCorp had failed to raise the issue of patentable subject matter before the lower federal courts, and raised the issue only before the US Supreme Court in its application for *certiorari*. This meant that there was an absence of evidence upon which the appeal court could properly assess the issue; at least this was the view of the US Attorney-General and the majority of the Supreme Court. In referring to the principle of US patent law which 'excludes from patent protection . . . laws of nature, natural phenomena and abstract ideas', Breyer confirmed that 'this principle finds its roots in both English and American law' and he explained that its existence 'does not lie in any claim that "laws of nature" are obvious, or that their discovery is easy, or that they are not useful'. '[T]o the contrary', he held, 'research into such matters may be costly and time consuming; monetary incentives may matter; and the fruits of those incentives and that research may prove of great benefit to the human race'; but even so, 'the reason for the exclusion is that sometimes too much patent protection can impede rather than "promote the Progress of Science and useful Arts."' This in turn led to the problem:

> that arises from the fact that patents do not only encourage research by pro-
> viding monetary incentives . . . [but] sometimes their presence can discourage
> research by impeding the free exchange of information, for example by forcing
> researchers to avoid the use of potentially patented ideas, by leading them to
> conduct costly and time-consuming searches of existing or pending patents, by
> requiring complex licensing arrangements, and by raising the costs of using the
> patented information, sometime prohibitively so.

INSULIN

Insulin is a peptide hormone (a protein of 51 amino acids) that is made naturally and exists in a pure form in humans and animals. It is made in the pancreas and it has several important functions in a normal healthy person and animal, one of which is to cause liver and muscle cells to absorb glucose as glycogen, which in this form is stored in those cells for later use. Essentially it enables the body to extract and use energy provided by the digestion of carbohydrates which enter the blood stream through the intestines, and so it regulates the blood sugar level. Without insulin liver and muscle cells are unable to absorb glucose from the blood stream, glucose is then excreted in urine. Consequently a diabetic has higher than normal blood sugar levels (hypoglycaemia) and suffers from symptoms which include excessive urination (polyuria), excessively sweet urine (glycosuria), increased level of fluid consumption (polydipsia) and increased food consumption (polyphagia).

The association of hypoglycaemia, polyuria and glycosuria with the lack of a pancreas was first made in 1889 by Oscar Minowski[14] and Joseph von Mering[15] after they conducted an experiment on a dog which involved the surgical removal of its pancreas (pancreatectomy). This association enabled them and other scientists to conclude that a malfunctioning pancreas was the cause of diabetes. Naturally that discovery directed the medical and scientific research to the identification and isolation of a pancreatic substance and to the development of that substance so that it could be used in the treatment of diabetes in humans.

It is mostly accepted that Frederick Banting[16] and Charles Best,[17] working at the laboratory of JJR Macleod[18] at the University of Toronto, did the crucial experimental work that led to the isolation of the pancreatic substance which they called insulin. However in 1971 Ian Murray, at the time a professor of physiology at the Anderson College of Medicine in Glasgow and a founding member of the International Diabetic Federation, convincingly argued in a paper entitled 'Paulesco and the Isolation of Insulin'[19] that credit for the discovery of insulin should have been shared with Nicholae Paulesco,[20] a Romanian-born professor of physiology, who published a scientific paper in August 1921 and 'proved convincingly', according to Murray, 'that he had succeeded in isolating the antidiabetic hormone of the pancreas and demonstrating its actions in lowering the blood sugar in both diabetic and normal dogs'.[21] Even more puzzling was why Best, who actually worked with Banting on the crucial experiments, was not awarded the Nobel Prize while Macleod, who was holidaying in Scotland at the time, was. No one will ever know the real reason this occurred, but the Committee's decision sufficiently disturbed the conscience of Arne Tiselius[22] that in December 1969, while he was the Director of the Nobel Institute, he tried to right the wrong. According to a letter he wrote, 'Paulescu was equally worthy of the award'.[23] Also unhappy was Roif Luft, the chairman of the Nobel Committee for Physiology and Medicine in 1971, who wrote in a paper entitled 'Who Discovered Insulin?' that the Nobel Prize for the isolation of insulin, 'without any doubt, [should] have been shared between Paulescu, Banting and Best'.[24]

The controversy over attribution aside, few would doubt that the research that led to the isolation of this pancreatic substance was risky, difficult, time-consuming and expensive; but while they all merited the highest praise for their breakthrough the fact is that none of them invented what Banting and Best ultimately called insulin. The isolation of this substance from the animal pancreas, though a very important step in the treatment of diabetes, did not make insulin their invention. True, they were able to show that it reduced hypoglycaemia in animals, but it needed further development before it could be used to treat diabetes in humans; and it was the work of James Collip,[25] a biochemist at the University of Alberta who joined Macleod's Department of Physiology, that enabled Banting and Best to extract toxin-free insulin from animal pancreases for use in human clinical studies. These clinical experiments were crucial to proving its efficacy in humans, but its mass production as a pharmaceutical posed other problems which required the input of others.

In this regard George Clowes[26] of Eli Lilly & Company (formed in 1876), a US pharmaceutical company in Indianapolis, Indiana, played a major role. Clowes, a biochemist, had in 1919 become Eli Lilly's director of biomedical research; immediately recognizing the obvious business potential of insulin as a pharmaceutical, he was determined to guide Banting and Best towards the conclusion that patenting insulin would be the only way in which they could ensure that insulin would be readily produced and supplied as a pharmaceutical throughout the world. This was a most controversial idea in 1922. Walter Cannon,[27] a noted American physiologist and a Harvard professor, expressed the view that '[t]he evils of patenting substances which may be essential for further advance in biology or which may be of therapeutic value . . . are clear enough'.[28] Yet under Clowes's influence Banting and Best felt that they had no choice, and in May 1922 they sought the permission of the University of Toronto to apply for patents. Eventually on 9 October 1923 Banting, Best and Collip were named inventors on US 1,469,994. The patent however was not owned by them. They had assigned their rights to the University of Toronto for one Canadian dollar in an attempt to overcome the stigma associated with their decision.

The practical reality was all too clear. The inventors needed to partner Eli Lilly, a company that could manufacture, distribute and sell insulin in large quantities. With the ethical question resolved, an advisory board was established by the University of Toronto during 1922 to administer the patent rights. Known informally as the Toronto Committee it included a patent attorney. Under the terms of an agreement that was negotiated and signed on 30 May 1922 Eli Lilly was given the exclusive right to manufacture and sell insulin for only one year, after which time the Committee could license to whomever it wanted. In return for this period of exclusivity Eli Lilly agreed, among other things, to provide insulin for human clinical assessment free of charge for one year and transfer all patent rights on any future improvements to insulin to the Committee. The title of US 1,469,994 was 'Extract Obtainable from the Mammalian Pancreas or from the Related Glands in Fishes, Useful in the Treatment of Diabetes Mellitus, and a Method of Preparing It'. It was three pages in length and the product claim to insulin, claim 1, read as follows:

> A substance prepared from fresh pancreatic or related glands containing in concentrated form the extractive from the ducts less portions of the glands sufficiently free from injurious substances for repeated administration and having the physiological characteristics of causing a reduction of blood sugar useful for the treatment of diabetes mellitus.

The main process claim, claim 5, provided for:

> A method of obtaining a potent substance from the ductless portion of pancreatic or related glands in concentrated form and practically free from impurities having the hereindescribed physiological characteristics, which consists of extracting said substance, precipitating said substance from the solution practically free from injurious substances, and making a sterile aqueous solution of said substance.

Claim 1 was broad enough to cover any insulin, including human insulin, 'prepared from fresh pancreatic or related glands' that was 'concentrated' and 'sufficiently free from injurious substances'. The inventors, taking their lead from Pasteur's purified yeast patent, claimed the invention was the 'purified insulin' since the only distinction between natural insulin and insulin as a pharmaceutical was its purity. This however was no trifling distinction because only in this purified form was insulin extracted from animal pancreatic tissue able to be safely administered to humans. Therefore the purification of insulin derived from animal tissue was vital. Even so the purification distinction mattered little in terms of the natural function of insulin. It was true that pure insulin as made in an animal or human pancreas was not available without a purification step, but this had nothing whatsoever to do with the insulin per se and had everything to do with its source, namely the surrounding pancreatic tissue from which it was extracted. The purification step therefore did not improve or enhance the normal function of insulin. Rather it enhanced the performance of the raw biological material that came from pancreatic tissue which contained insulin that was mixed with other biological substances. This was no different from the situation with Pasteur's patent for pure yeast; while the purification process certainly purified insulin derived from animal pancreatic tissue, it did not justify a claim to purified insulin per se.

Nonetheless, as granted, claim 1 gave the Toronto Committee legal control over any insulin derived from pancreatic or related tissue; but the question remained whether claim 1 was a valid claim in light of what the US Supreme Court had held in *BASF* in 1884 and what that Court was soon to hold in *Brogdex* in 1931? In terms of patentability the problem was that purified insulin, in the words of *Brogdex*, 'had not been manufactured into a new and different article, having a distinctive name, character or use' from that of natural insulin. Furthermore there was a problem regarding the patentability of the process, because the process claim did not define a specific method, but covered *any* method or process 'which consists of extracting' purified insulin from pancreatic tissue, and this was a claim which *BASF* held to be contrary to law. Probably what saved the patent from being attacked was that, first, Eli Lilly had partnered the Toronto Committee and accordingly was not an adversary and, secondly, beyond the first year the Committee was free to grant non-exclusive licences around the world, meaning that there was little incentive for anyone to challenge the patent.

Despite the breadth of the process and product claims in US 1,469,994, on 23 December 1924 the USPTO granted US 1,520,673, entitled 'Purified Antidiabetic Product and Process of Making It', to George Walden of Indiana. This intriguing patent was a product of Eli Lilly's research laboratory, and Walden sought to distinguish his invention from US 1,469,994 by claiming that his invention provided 'a suitable method of extraction and an efficient method of purification' that produced an 'anti-diabetic substance' which had a 'residual-nitrogen content' no greater than '0.1 milligrams per unit of anti-diabetic activity'. Walden's patent thus claimed a purer form of insulin and one which displayed 'a stability many times as great and a purity ranging from ten to one hundred times as great as the best product obtainable prior to [his] invention'. Moreover Walden claimed that his invention showed 'no diminution in potency after a lapse of three months from the time of its preparation' and, to his knowledge: 'not a single instance of sensitization or induration or any deleterious effect [had] been reported'. Rather boldly, especially in the light of the significance of the scientific breakthrough made by Banting, Best and Collip, Walden conceded that while his process 'used the principle of isoelectric precipitation', as did 'Banting, Best and Collip in their work in Toronto', his process used it 'for different purposes and with different effects'. Specifically he claimed that, while Banting, Best and Collop's process used 'the idea of precipitating undesirables, and of leaving the anti-diabetic hormone in the solution and throwing away the precipitate obtained . . . [his process] use[d] it to precipitate and conserve the anti-diabetic product, and leave the undesirables in the solution'. Therefore his process was more efficient because 'the solution' in which the insulin was contained was discarded only after 'all of the anti-diabetic hormone has been separated from it'.

In contrast to US 1,469,994, which consisted of three pages and eight patent claims, Walden's patent consisted of seven pages and 30 patent claims. The claims were to the method (claims 1–5); the processes employing the method (claims 6–20); '[a]n anti-diabetic product derived from the pancreas' (claims 21–27) and '[a]n anti-diabetic product containing the active anti-diabetic principle or hormone derived from the pancreas' (claims 28–30).

The fact that Walden was granted US 1,520,673 shows how the pre-grant examination system was simply incapable of filtering out invalid patents. Ignoring for the moment that insulin was a natural 'anti-diabetic' substance produced in its most pure form *in vivo* and in this form was not a new composition of matter, the USPTO failed to recognize that even if Walden's insulin was purer than 'the best product obtainable prior to [his] invention', the scope of claim 1 of US 1,469,994 was so broad that any insulin, no matter how pure, came within the scope of its patent monopoly. According to claim 1 of '994 it did not matter whether pure insulin was derived from the pig, cow, fish or human pancreas, so long as the insulin was 'sufficiently free from injurious substances for repeated administration ... for the treatment of diabetes mellitus'. Indeed there were no limitations regarding the source of the insulin, its purity, its biological activity or its efficacy as a pharmaceutical. Therefore not only was Walden's product claim not patentable subject matter because it was not new, but it lacked novelty because it had been anticipated.

Precisely because this was an outstanding scientific achievement the USPTO was most likely persuaded, even if it acted contrary to law, to grant US 1,469,994; but subsequently to grant US 1,520,673 for a substance that fell squarely within its scope for simply taking the next and frankly obvious step of purifying insulin even more was plainly mischievous.

In fact across the Atlantic the British Medical and Research Council (MRC) was very unhappy about the patenting of insulin; but the UK Government wanted insulin manufactured in the UK and made available to Britons. While the MRC initially rejected the Toronto Committee's offer of a patent licence it eventually changed its position, principally because it wanted to be able to regulate the production of insulin in the UK for the purpose of promoting its standardization and ensuring its safety. Unfortunately it also became the regulator of all research relating to insulin and this, according to Alison Li in her biography of James Collip, brought criticism because 'its involvement in patenting was ... leading to the commercialization of science'.[29]

In the absence of a pharmaceutical regulator (like the FDA in the United States) it was nonetheless felt that the MRC was in the best position to ensure its safety. It was not until after the UK Therapeutic

Substance Act 1925 had been passed and a new government regulator installed that the MRC, according to Li, 'deemed the patents no longer necessary for ensuring the quality of the product'[30] and relinquished its regulatory role. Not only that, but in 1931, some six years before the expiry of the UK patent, the MRC stopped the payment of all royalties to the Toronto Committee. Consequently in the UK the MRC opened up insulin production with its most pressing concern being, according to Li, 'to ensure that patents would not become an obstacle to further research by other scientists'.[31]

Dovetailing with the expiry of the original insulin patents, a new anti-diabetic substance was developed by Hans Hagedorn[32] and B Norman Jensen in 1936.[33] Its main advantage over previous insulin products was that it was longer-acting; in order to achieve this effect its developers did a most interesting thing – they mixed insulin and protamine together. This was not an intuitive step, and in the 1930s, given how little was known about biochemistry, it was probably a very risky thing to do, particularly as protamine was derived from fish sperm. Nevertheless they made this insulin product using protamine and made a significant breakthrough in the process.

According to Elliot Joslin,[34] reputedly the first American doctor to specialize in the treatment of diabetes and who went on to found the Joslin Diabetes Center in Boston, this new substance was 'the most important advance made in the treatment of diabetes since the discovery of insulin in 1921',[35] because in practical terms it meant that the frequency of injections which diabetic patients required to undergo on a daily basis was reduced to a few. Naturally Nordisk,[36] the Danish organization which developed it patented the new diabetic treatment – to which it was perfectly entitled because this was a new substance that displayed characteristics not found in nature.

The next significant development in the treatment of diabetes came in 1946 when Nordisk scientists, C Krayenbühl and T Rosenberg,[37] developed a method of crystallizing protamine insulin. This then enabled Nordisk to produce a rapid-acting and long-lasting insulin medicine, which it called Neutral Protamine Hagedorn (NPH), by combining protamine insulin with rapid-acting insulin without the loss of efficacy of either component. This was also patented. Then in 1953 Kund Hallas-Moller at Novo developed a new long-lasting insulin which chemically combined insulin and zinc, and this was sold under the trade mark Lente. Again this was patented.

There was however a difference between the purified insulin derived from the animal pancreas and human insulin made *in vivo*, the significance of which was not fully appreciated until *after* the breakthrough made by Frederick Sanger,[38] who was Head of the Division of Protein Chemistry at the MRC when he elicited the complete amino acid of bovine insulin for which he received his first Nobel Prize in 1958. Sanger confirmed that the difference between the chemical structure of insulin in pigs, sheep, horses, whales and cows was only three amino acids, leading him to conclude: 'the exact structure of the residues in this portion is not important for biological activity'.[39] This molecular similarity explained why insulin derived from animal pancreatic tissue was efficacious in humans.

Despite these developments in insulin and Sanger's efficacy conclusion, by the mid-1960s it was becoming evident that bovine- and porcine-sourced insulin was responsible for the growing number of allergic reactions in humans. Coupled with the realization that animal pancreatic tissue was also a finite resource the direction of research moved towards the chemical synthesis of insulin. Sanger's breakthrough in the 1950s was the starting point, but scientific knowledge of the molecular structure of insulin grew rapidly, and by 7 January 1969 the USPTO granted US 3,420,810, entitled 'Process For Joining The A And B Chains of Insulin', to the US Atomic Energy Commission. The patent however contained no claim to the synthesised insulin – only to the processes. The inventors, PK Patchogue and AM Tometsko, confirmed that their invention was 'not limited to any particular source of A or B chain of insulin and it permits combining, for example, . . . the A chain of human insulin, with the B chain of the same or another species'. The advantage of their invention, so they claimed, was that it provided greater yields of insulin than 'the known conventional processes for combining the A chain and B chain to produce insulin'.

It was also becoming evident that some diabetics were developing antibody resistance to insulin, as one inventor explained in US 3,591,574 (granted 6 July 1971), entitled 'Tri-N-Phenylglycyl Derivatives of Insulin', where the patent specification was for 'new acyl-substituted-insulins . . . wherein all of the free amino groups in insulin have been substantially completely substituted by reaction with a reagent forming the acyl group'. According to this invention the primary source of the insulin remained animal-derived insulin, but this would be subjected to molecular modification with the result that its 'antibody-binding capacity' was 'very much lower than standard beef insulin and substantially less than that of pork insulin'. The patent's two claims were to insulin 'wherein substantially all of the free amino groups . . . are substituted by acyl groups'. In this way the product claims were not to natural insulin but to a modified insulin that was materially *different* because of its antibody resistance. However with the advent of recombinant DNA technology that was all about to change, as patents would soon claim isolated genetic materials and proteins as 'inventions'.

RECOMBINANT DNA BIOTECHNOLOGY

Although Chakrabarty's famous patent had not yet been the subject of legal argument before the US Supreme Court, it was only a matter of weeks away when the USPTO granted US 4,190,495 entitled 'Modified microorganisms and method of preparing and using same' to Roy Curtiss of Research Corporation on 26 February 1980. Bearing a priority date of 27 September 1976 this patent contained only two prior art references. One of these was to a letter entitled *Potential Biohazards of Recombinant DNA Molecules* which was signed by Paul Berg,[40] David Baltimore,[41] Herbert Boyer,[42] Stanley Cohen,[43] Ronald Davis, David Hogness, Daniel Nathans,[44] Richard Roblin, James Watson,[45] Sherman Weissman and Norton Zinder. Apart from being among America's most accomplished molecular biologists they were members of the Committee on Recombinant DNA of the National Research Council. Their letter was published in *Science*[46] on 26 July 1974 and it commenced rather modestly by describing as 'recent advances' the breakthrough that had been made by Cohen and Boyer and others 'in techniques for the isolation and rejoining of segments of DNA [which] now permit construction of biologically active recombinant DNA molecules in vitro'.

Details of the these breakthrough experiments had been published by Cohen and Annie Chang in *Proceedings of the National Academy of Sciences*[47] (*PNAC*) and by Morrow, Cohen, Chang, Boyer, Howard Goodman and Robert Helling in *PNAC*,[48] and confirmed in separate experiments conducted by Hogness, Davis and Boyer that had been written up and submitted but were yet to be published. The letter explained that the Cohen *et al.* and Morrow *et al.* papers demonstrated how to break up DNA into fragments and recombine it in a plasmid (for example a bacterium) which contained both its own and inserted foreign DNA and express the protein that was coded for by the foreign DNA. The potential of this technology was not only significant but obvious.

By way of introduction the Committee's letter confirmed the importance of this research, but it also addressed another more sinister issue: the potential danger posed to humanity should any new and experimental bacteria escape the laboratory. Its purpose therefore was to advise scientists of the Committee's recommendation to the National Institutes of Health (NIH) that there be a moratorium 'until attempts have been made to evaluate the hazards and some resolutions of the outstanding questions has been achieved'.

Curtiss cited this letter because it referred to Cohen and Boyer's ideas and, undoubtedly, he had applied their ideas in making the invention, which he described as a 'recombinant DNA-containing vector . . . capable of having recombinant DNA or foreign genetic information introduced thereinto and recovered therefrom along with its expression or production of useful gene products'. His patent also contained claims to various microorganisms which he declared were suitable for use in his invention. His patent was essentially for a biological toolbox.

Apart from its being one of the first patents that was granted by the USPTO in the biotechnology gold rush, what was particularly noteworthy about it was an acknowledgement that the US Government had rights to the invention which was 'made in the course of work under . . . [a] grant from the National Science Foundation and . . . from the Department of Health, Education and Welfare'. The US Government now had an interest in biotechnology.

Perhaps the conflict of interest that this gave rise to was not immediately apparent to the USPTO or to the US Government, or indeed to scientists, but it seems obvious that once the US Government had a legal interest in an invention then the USPTO, being an agency of the US Government, could no longer act impartially. Consequently whether Curtiss's patent was valid or not, the fact that it was granted sent the message to the US business community and universities that the fledgling biotechnology industry would be supported by the USPTO. In the space of 50 years scientists who believed it to be unethical to commercialize the science that had been developed with public money were by 1980 the entrepreneurs of the biotechnology industry, and the US government was prepared to facilitate their transformation. That the US taxpayer was funding this kind of research was no longer a reason for universities to ignore the patent system.

Indeed it was a timely meeting between Robert Swanson,[49] a Silicon Valley venture capitalist, and Herbert Boyer that resulted in the incorporation of Genentech, Inc on 7 April 1976. On 14 October 1980, when Genentech's shares became open to the public, the share price soared to US$89 and Boyer, who then owned nearly 1 000 000 shares, become an instant multi-millionaire. In what was a classic rags-to-riches story Boyer became America's science poster boy, and there is no doubt that Genentech's rapid success was partly behind the change in government policy at that time. Not only did Genentech's success make Boyer rich, but it changed the status and career path of many scientists who were now attracted to industry. Higher levels of pay and better working conditions meant that the scientific research landscape had changed. By 1981 Genentech employed 40 PhDs and 65 researchers, with Boyer in charge of its research. He also went from earning US$10 500 per year as a university researcher to US$50 000 per year at Genentech, and in an article published by *Time Magazine* in March 1981 Boyer was quoted as saying, 'You'll never get rich in a university'. What had attracted Swanson to Boyer was not only the invention which Cohen and Boyer had assigned to Stanford University so that it could be patented, but the obvious commercial application of their invention in the production of such things as insulin.

By patenting the results of their research – research which they had conducted with the benefit of public research funds – Stanford University went on to earn about US$40 million in patent royalties over the life of the patent. Thus Cohen and Boyer's decision to patent their invention, which at the time was made reluctantly and with only a week to spare before a patent deadline would render it unpatentable, proved to be decisive, as Sally Smith Hughes, an economic historian, explained in her paper, 'Making Dollars Out of DNA: The First Major Patent in Biotechnology and the Commercialization of Molecular Biology, 1974–1980'.[50] It also provided US policy-makers and politicians with the kind of hard evidence that they needed to make legislative changes governing the relationship between American universities and commerce. In a speech he made to the NIH on 25 May 2004 Birch Bayh, a US Senator and one of the co-sponsors of the Bayh-Dole Act 1980, explained that this legislation was designed to restore America's 'technological advantage'.[51] By the late 1970s, he said, the United States 'had lost [its] number one competitive position in steel and auto production . . . [t]he number of patents issued each year had declined steadily since 1971 [and the] . . . number of patentable inventions made under federally supported research had been in a steady decline [so that] . . . [i]nvestment in research and development . . . was static'.[52]

Twenty-two years later the *Economist* described the Bayh-Dole Act as '[p]ossibly the most inspired piece of legislation to be enacted in America over the past half-century'.[53] Not everyone agreed; and in an article entitled 'The Law of Unintended Consequence' its author, Clifton Leaf,[54] was scathing. Rather than encouraging innovation in science Leaf believed that it had encouraged litigation, noting: '[f]rom 1992 to September 2003, pharmaceutical companies tied up the federal courts with 494 patent suits'. He emphasized his point by saying: '[t]hat's more than the number filed in the computer hardware, aerospace, defense, and chemical industries combined'. Furthermore he argued that it transformed universities from being 'public trusts into something closer to venture capital firms', with the result that '[w]hat used to be a scientific community of free and open debate now often seems like a litigious scrum of data-hoarding and suspicion'. Unfortunately this change in policy also put enormous pressure on the USPTO to support the restoration of America's technological advantage; inevitably patents began to be seen as the way forward for the new biotechnology industry.

Cohen and Boyer were granted US 4,237,224 on 2 December 1980, having filed their patent application on 4 November 1974. Entitled 'Process for producing biologically functional molecular chimeras' it was granted to the Board of Trustees of the Leland Stanford Jr University and it was directed to a process that was useful as a molecular biological tool. The patent specification described the process thus:

> The process of this invention employs novel plasmids, which are formed by inserting DNA having one or more intact genes into a plasmid in such a location as to permit retention of an intact replicator locus and system (replicon) to provide a recombinant plasmid molecule. The recombinant plasmid molecule will be referred to as a 'hybrid' plasmid or plasmid 'chimera.' The plasmid chimera contains genes that are capable of expressing at least one phenotypical property. The plasmid chimera is used to transform a susceptible and competent microorganism under conditions where transformation occurs. The microorganism is then grown under conditions which allow for separation and harvesting of transformants that contain the plasmid chimera.

While it is clear that plasmid chimeras produced in accordance with this process were artificial, it is also clear that the 'foreign DNA' (which was cut and spliced, and then inserted into a foreign host cell to create a plasmid chimera) was identical or substantially identical to the DNA from which it was sourced. The source of that foreign DNA could be 'derived from: 'eukaryotic or prokaryotic cells, viruses, and bacteriophage'. They also anticipated the use of 'synthetic genes' – genes that were synthetic in the sense that they were recombined fragments of DNA, but beyond that they were not truly synthetic in the artificial sense. Indeed it was obvious that the patent taught that the proteins which would be expressed by these vectors would be identical or substantially identical to natural proteins. After all it was its capacity for natural mimicry that made the invention so useful and brought Cohen and Boyer instant fame.

That Swanson recognized the commercial potential of this new tool is a credit to him, but that he went directly to Boyer was a masterstroke. Under Boyer's guidance Genentech immediately set its sights on producing human insulin. In order to do that, however, it first had to find the human gene that coded for human insulin, and to do that it would need the help of Arthur Riggs and Keiichi Itakura, who were at the time at the City of Hope National Medical Center (CHNMC).

GENENTECH AND RECOMBINANT HUMAN INSULIN

On 18 May 1976, as the CEO of Genentech, Swanson sent a letter to CHNMC proposing that in return for providing US$300 000 over a two-year period, Riggs and Itakura undertake research to 'complete the synthesis of genes coding for somatostatin and insulin'. That offer was accepted and an agreement between the parties was concluded in August 1976. Under the terms of the Agreement Genentech would retain the patent rights but would pay the CHNMC 'a royalty of two percent of the net sales of all polypeptides sold by [Genentech] or its affiliates, provided only that manufacture of the polypeptide employs DNA synthesized by CITY OF HOPE under this agreement and provided to GENENTECH by CITY OF HOPE'. One of the polypeptides in question was human insulin and, according to the Agreement, production by Genentech of these polypeptides required 'synthetic DNA which codes for the production of a particular polypeptide when incorporated in a bacterial or other plasmid'. Essentially Genentech proposed using the Cohen and Boyer process to manufacture human insulin. In what was an obvious step too for Walter Gilbert[55] and his start-up biotech company, Biogen, the race was on; and the prize of recombinant insulin would go to the first to isolate the human insulin gene.

As the amino acid sequence for insulin was already known, Riggs and Itakura were able to complete their work within a year and by November 1977 Genentech had filed its first patent application. A year later, in December 1977, in a *Science* paper[56] Itakura and his team confirmed that Genentech had been successful. Genentech's patent application was not however directed only to the production of human insulin, but included other proteins such as somatostatin. What was key to this technology, as Itakura explained, was the employment of 'heterologous DNA coding for virtually any known amino acid sequence'. He predicted that this would enable the production of 'mammalian hormones . . . [such as] somatostatin, human insulin, human and bovine growth hormone, leutinizing hormone, ACTH, pancreatic polypeptide, human preproinsulin, human proinsulin, the A and B chains of human insulin and so on'.

On 26 October 1982 Genentech was granted US 4,356,270 (its third US patent) entitled, 'Recombinant DNA cloning vehicle'. The principal invention was:

> A recombinant microbial cloning vehicle comprising a first restriction endonuclease recognition site, a structural gene coding for the expression of the amino acid sequence of a mammalian polypeptide, and a second restriction endonuclease site, at least a majority of the codons of said structural gene being codons preferred for the expression of microbial genomes.

Effectively the patent claimed, as an invention, genetically modified microorganisms which were capable of producing pure human insulin and other mammalian proteins. Subsequently Genentech was granted US 4,571,421 (18 February 1986); US 4,704,362 (3 November 1987); US 5,221,619 (22

June 1993) and US 5,583,013 (10 December 1996), all of which were related to the original patent application filed in November 1977.

What these patents did not claim was pure insulin as an invention. What they did do however was to claim the DNA to the gene that coded for insulin in the context of a genetically modified organism; and this they were not entitled to do as DNA was not something that they had invented. The breakthrough was what Boyer and Cohen had achieved in 1973. After that it was merely a case of finding the gene, and Itakura's paper confirmed that. Genentech just happened to have been the first to isolate the insulin gene.

AMGEN AND RECOMBINANT ERYTHROPOIETIN

On 25 July 1990 the European Patent Office (EPO) had granted Amgen EP 0,148,605. It was an exceptionally broad patent which included product claims to purified erythropoietin itself. During the early to mid-1990s the patent was subjected to rigorous scrutiny by the EPO as various opponents challenged the patent's validity; but ultimately Amgen prevailed on each occasion. However, some six weeks before the patent was due to expire, the UK House of Lords delivered the decision in *Kirin-Amgen v Hoechst Marion Roussel and TKT* which held the product claims to isolated erythropoietin invalid and the process claim not infringed. It was the culmination of another marathon episode of patent litigation that had started in the UK Patents Court and progressed to the Court of Appeal and ultimately to the House of Lords. Indeed so complex was the appeal that it was heard over a two-week period in July 2004. For over 20 years[57] Amgen had fought hard to retain its exclusive patent monopoly over purified erythropoietin in Europe and it had mostly succeeded; but this decision of the House of Lords brought its winning streak to an end. Perhaps this loss was not important to Amgen, given that the patent had provided it with a monopoly for almost 20 years, but the decision was important for other reasons. Finally the highest appeal court in the UK had ruled that erythropoietin, a naturally occurring human protein, was not new when it was made using recombinant DNA technology.

As is typical in biotechnology cases, the process claims in EP 0,148,605 were not challenged; Transkaryotic Therapies Inc (TKT), a US biotechnology company, had developed its own biological process for making erythropoietin that it too had patented.[58] TKT preferred instead to focus its attack on the product claims to isolated erythropoietin. Apart from the fact that these were an easier target, once they were declared to be invalid there would be nothing that Amgen could do to stop TKT using its own patented process to make erythropoietin. The downside to this strategy

---

BOX 8.1   CLAIM 1, EP 0,148,605

'A DNA sequence for use in securing expression in a procaryotic or eucaryotic host cell of a polypeptide product having at least part of the primary structural confirmation [*sic*] of that of erythropoietin to allow possession of the biological property of causing bone marrow cells to increase production of reticulocytes and red blood cells and to increase hemoglobin [*sic*] synthesis or iron uptake, said DNA sequence selected from the group consisting of: (a) the DNA sequences set out in Tables V and VI or their complementary strands; (b) DNA sequences which hybridize under stringent conditions to the protein coding regions of the DNA sequences defined in (a) or fragments thereof; and (c) DNA sequences which, but for the degeneracy of the genetic code, would hybridize to the DNA sequences defined in (a) and (b).'

---

however was that Amgen had alleged that TKT's process was an infringement of its recombinant process. If Amgen's argument was upheld then the invalidity of the product claims would be irrelevant and TKT would be liable for infringing the process claims. TKT's strategy was therefore risky; but in view of its own patent, it had no other choice.

Just as BASF had attempted to do in 1884 with the process for artificial alizarine, Amgen had formulated an argument which attempted to capture within the scope of its patent monopoly any biological process that produced erythropoietin. Key to this argument was the isolation of the human erythropoietin gene which, Amgen argued, justified a broad interpretation of its process claim. Therefore, according to Amgen, because TKT's process used the 'isolated DNA' of the erythropoietin gene to make erythropoietin it infringed its patent. Indeed Neuberger J in the Patents Court was persuaded to the view 'that it was the "discovery" of the gene sequence for EPO which effectively provides the basis for the whole 605 patent'.[59] Thus, Neuberger held: '[c]laim 1 is to a DNA sequence which is "suitable for" the claimed purposes' and agreed with Amgen's submission, 'it [was] "plainly the application of the discovery which is capable of industrial application (whatever the origin of the DNA sequence)"'. The significance of this argument unfortunately was perhaps not fully appreciated by Neuberger, and in agreeing with it he had effectively given Amgen a patent monopoly over purified erythropoietin howsoever produced. In effect the invention was the isolated human erythropoietin gene.

TKT appealed to the Court of Appeal,[60] which was not so easily persuaded. In rejecting Amgen's argument the Court held that it was 'not possible to obtain a patent for the discovery of a gene which by definition is found in the human body', and therefore construed the ambit of the process claim much more narrowly. Accordingly the Court confirmed that under European patent law Amgen 'could not monopolise the gene per se as that existed in nature'. It could however monopolize 'the DNA sequence encoding for DNA when isolated and in that respect was suitable for use to express EPO in a host cell'. In other words Amgen's patent had to be confined to a specific process and could not extend to purified erythropoietin however produced. Obviously the Court had accepted the argument that isolated DNA was different from natural DNA; while this was a conclusion that was completely unjustified on the evidence, where in fact there was no real difference between them, the Court used the distinction to drive the message home to Amgen that its process claim was to a specific biological process that made use of that isolated DNA. In this respect the Court concluded that TKT's process was different from Amgen's process, and so there was no infringement.

Predictably Amgen appealed to the House of Lords and there acquainted the Appellate Committee with its principal argument. Andrew Waugh QC, Amgen's counsel, argued:

> The DNA which is suitable for in whichever way you have made it suitable, is capable of industrial application. *It is no longer a mere discovery.* It has entered into the realms of technical utility. I can take that sequence. I can have that sequence. I can really turn that sequence to my advantage to make erythropoietin. Again, whether I do it by taking the erythropoietin DNA out or whether I do it by taking the shuttle vector to the DNA and then making new copies of the DNA *is beside the point. In each case I have been able, with the knowledge of the erythropoietin, to turn it to technical account.*[61]

The problem with this argument is that it described what the Court of Appeal had held in *Genentech* to be 'a claim for protection of the discovery as such', and therefore was not an 'invention' within Article 52(1) of the EPC. Unperturbed, Amgen's counsel continued:

> The fact of the matter is this inventor has provided new DNA sequences which were not available to the public before and has published them in this patent and claimed them as suitable for the expression of erythropoietin in a host cell. On that basis, as a chemical, TKT have little factories that make new copies of this chemical, albeit 14 on average per little factory. They are making the chemical. They are hooking that chemical up to other chemicals that will activate it and cause it to do something else, but at the end of the day this is precisely the technical application of claim 1 which is not excluded by patentability.[62]

The House of Lords however disagreed. The crucial distinction was the words 'in a . . . host cell' in claim 1. Lord Hoffmann, who wrote the unanimous decision, explained that claim 1 required the DNA sequence to be exogenous to a host cell, whereas the TKT process used DNA sequences upstream of the whole Epo gene sequence to switch on the endogenous encoding sequence of the gene to produce erythropoietin. Accordingly he held that TKT had not infringed Amgen's process claim. Having disposed of this issue, Lord Hoffmann then addressed the validity of the product claims to purified erythropoietin. In this regard he had no difficulty in concluding that they were invalid, simply because: 'even when isolated, . . . [erythropoietin] was not new'.[63]

However in the United States, where Amgen was also suing TKT for patent infringement, a completely different approach was adopted by the CAFC. Predictably, given its readiness to ignore US Supreme Court authority, it did not import the House of Lord's limitation into the US process claim in US 5,618,698 (one of the many US patents that were derived from the discovery of the human erythropoietin gene). Rather it held that TKT had 'improperly' sought to 'import the "exogenous" limitation into the claims'. In dismissing TKT's argument the CAFC concluded that '[t]he plain meaning of the claims controls here, and they plainly are not so limited'.[64] Indeed the process claims to the same 'invention' in the United States made no mention of the words 'in a . . . host cell', even though all of Amgen's patents were born from the same single discovery – the discovery of the human erythropoietin gene. The key to Amgen's process invention was therefore the same all over the world, but the claims that were drafted were not.[65]

Why it took another 13 years for these US patents to be granted made little sense, until it is understood that by doing so Amgen effectively extended the term of its patent monopoly in the United States. Indeed, unlike the situation elsewhere where its patent expired in December 2004, in the United States Amgen maintains patent rights to erythropoietin as a pharmaceutical product until April 2012. Moreover by delaying filing its patent applications Amgen's patent department had time to assess the strengths and weaknesses of its foreign patent claims. This delay therefore not only enabled it to secure a significantly longer patent monopoly in the United States but it provided Amgen with an opportunity to tailor its US patent claims with the benefit of knowing how they could be attacked by its competitors. In learning from this European setback, Amgen used different claim language in the US product process claims. Accordingly claim 4 of US 5,618,698 granted on 8 April 1997 defined the invention thus:

A process for the production of a glycosylated erythropoietin polypeptide having the in vivo biological property of causing bone marrow cells to increase production of reticulocytes and red blood cells comprising the steps: a) growing, under suitable nutrient conditions, vertebrate cells comprising promoter DNA, other than human erythropoietin promoter DNA, operatively linked to DNA encoding the mature erythropoietin amino acid sequence of FIG. 6; and b) isolating said glycosylated erythropoietin polypeptide expressed by said cells.

As a result Amgen achieved in the United States what it was not able to achieve in the UK. In a perfect example of how the fractured national patent systems that individually make up the patchwork of patent systems which cover the globe, Amgen's deliberate and perfectly legal manipulation of the US patent system worked to its advantage. More to the point, in the United States Amgen has a patent monopoly over erythropoietin howsoever made – in view of what the US Supreme Court said in *BASF*, clearly something that is repugnant to US patent law.

Common sense would suggest that one invention means the same patent all over the world covering the same invention, but this is clearly not the case. Amgen has been able to obtain many patents around the world by using differently worded claims creating layers of patent monopolies covering a multitude of inventions arising from one single discovery. Even so, when the validity of EP 0,148,605 was challenged in the UK, the House of Lords never looked across the Atlantic to see what Amgen was claiming as its corresponding invention. Perhaps if this had been done Lord Hoffmann would have better understood why it was that Amgen had consistently made the same argument he had rejected. Unfortunately while reading a limitation into the European patent enabled him to find that there was no infringement of the process claim, it also enabled him to ignore the most disturbing aspect of this patent. How Amgen had put its case showed, without any doubt, that it was seeking to patent the isolated DNA – fundamental to both the process claim and the production of purified erythropoietin. That Amgen had consistently made this argument before the Patents Court, the Court of Appeal, the House of Lords and the CAFC in the United States meant that Amgen, the patentee, was seeking to patent something which was fundamentally unpatentable – the human erythropoietin gene itself.

In this respect Amgen's first US patent, US 4,703,008, granted by the USPTO on 27 October 1987 and entitled 'DNA sequences encoding erythropoietin', is revealing; even though the patent specification was almost identical to that in EP 0,148,605 the claim language was not. In this instance, rather than define the invention in terms of a process, the US equivalent went straight to the point and claimed '[a] purified and isolated DNA sequence encoding erythropoietin'. This then is what Amgen was after all over the world; and if that was so then EP 0,148,605 should never have been granted for the same reason that US 4,703,008 should never have been granted. That this gene was 'purified and isolated' made no difference to what it was; and, just as Lord Hoffmann concluded that erythropoietin, 'even when isolated, was not new', neither was the human gene that coded for this protein.

THE IMPACT ON UNIVERSITY RESEARCH

The Bayh-Dole Act 1980 deliberately encouraged universities to behave more like corporate entities than institutions devoted to independent research and teaching. Over the subsequent 22 years, while America regained its 'technological advantage' and some universities, like Stanford and Columbia, prospered from the millions of dollars in patent royalties, the vast majority of American universities did not. Worse still, and much to their surprise, American universities discovered that they had lost the benefit of a common law exemption from patent infringement.

According to the CAFC in *John MJ Madey v Duke University* (2002) 307 F 3d 1351 (US Supreme Court denied *certiorari* (2003) 539 US 958) even a university researcher and the university itself can be guilty of patent infringement. Summarizing its position with regard to the issue of experimental use as a common law defence, the CAFC held:

> In short, regardless of whether a particular institution or entity is engaged in an endeavor for commercial gain, so long as the act is in furtherance of the alleged infringer's legitimate business and is not solely for amusement, to satisfy idle curiosity, or for strictly philosophical inquiry, the act does not qualify for the very narrow and strictly limited experimental use defense. Moreover, the profit or non-profit status of the user is not determinative.

This reasoning was an inevitable consequence of this entrepreneurial policy; and, as bad as this was, the situation was about to get worse.

On 13 June 2005 the US Supreme Court delivered its opinion in *Merck KGaA v Integra Lifesciences I, Ltd* (2005) 545 US 193. This appeal concerned the operation of the Federal Food, Drug, and Cosmetic Act, which empowers the Food and Drug Agency to regulate, among other things, the provision of pharmaceuticals in the United States. Under the system of regulatory approval provided by the legislation, applicants for FDA approval must file various applications at various stages in the approval process. One of these applications is for an investigational new drug (IND) which is to be the subject of human clinical trials. Another is for a new drug that, having undergone human clinical trials, is to be marketed in the United States.

Here David Cheresh, a medical researcher, and the Scripps Research Institute, his employer, were found guilty of infringing a US patent owned by Integra. The basis of this finding was a series of experiments which were conducted by Cheresh and Scripps on behalf of the drug manufacturer Merck KgaA (a German company, not to be confused with Merck, a US company). Naturally there was an agreement in place between Merck and Scripps which set out the terms under which these experiments would be performed. Thus the agreement provided that Merck would fund Scripps. During the conduct of these paid experiments Scripps made use of certain products that Integra held patents for. Eventually the successful experiments led Merck to make an IND application to the FDA which, under the legislation, was mandated to assess whether 'the drug involved represents an unreasonable risk to the safety of persons who are the subjects of the clinical investigation'.

Before the District Court and the CAFC Cheresh and Scripps argued that their activities were exempted because section 271(e)(1) of the Drug Price Competition and Patent Term Restoration Act of 1984 provided that experiments conducted 'solely for uses reasonably related to the development and submission of information under a Federal law which regulates the manufacture, use, or sale of drugs' were not to be construed as patent infringement. The CAFC disagreed because the experiments were conducted prior to the IND application and were in any event in the 'hunt for drugs that may or may not later undergo clinical testing for FDA approval'. In other words the CAFC held that the link between the experiments and the IND was too tenuous for the exemption to apply.

On appeal to the US Supreme Court the US Acting Solicitor-General (ASG) submitted, in an *amicus curiae* brief in support of *certiorari*, that the CAFC's view of the law was 'likely to restrict significantly the development of new drugs', and that the CAFC's decision posed 'a direct and substantial threat to new drug research by dramatically narrowing the scope' of the patent infringement exemption. The ASG also explained, 'although the patent system provides important incentives for innovation, pre-clinical research into investigational new drugs is of tremendous importance to the public health'. In terms of the effect which the CAFC's decision has had on research generally the ASG submitted, '[the] FDA is aware of anecdotal evidence that the decision is adversely affecting the legal advice given on drug researchers regarding their ability to use patented inventions in new drug research'. Others such as Rochelle Dreyfuss, John Duffy, Arti Rai and Katherine Strandburg, all professors of US patent law, were also critical of the CAFC's reasoning. In their view the narrowing of the patent infringement exemption meant that 'the power of the patent system to promote the progress of science and technology will suffer'.

Given these submissions it was not surprising that the US Supreme Court granted *certiorari*, but what was surprising was those which supported the

CAFC's approach. For instance Wisconsin Alumni Research Foundation, the American Council on Education, Boston University, the Regents of the University of California, Research Corporation Technologies, the Salk Institute for Biological Studies, University of Alberta and University of Oklahoma, all of which held US patents over biological research tools, were concerned that the value of their patent portfolios would be destroyed if the exemption could apply to commercially supported research. The case highlighted how the policy which the Bayh-Dole Act effected to encourage universities to become entrepreneurial was being compromised by an exemption that was, ironically, directed towards the encouragement of innovative pharmaceuticals. Admittedly this was a problem; but Scalia J, who authored the unanimous decision, was unsympathetic to the protestations of the universities and, in rejecting the CAFC's approach, expressed the view that 'the relationship of the use of a patented compound in a particular experiment to the "development and submission of information" to the FDA does not become more attenuated (or less reasonable) simply because the data from that experiment are left out of the submission that is ultimately passed along to the FDA'. Although the result was unpalatable to universities, Scalia's approach reflected the fact that all economic policies, no matter what their objective, may at some point collide and that making sense of the consequences of such a collision must involve the prioritization of those objectives. The consequential balancing act that followed meant, on the facts of this case, that the drug innovation was more important to the American economy than the preservation of patent monopolies over research tools.

As for regaining America's technological advantage, David Mowery[66] and Bhaven Sampat,[67] in their paper 'The Bayh-Dole Act of 1980 and University-Industry Technology Transfer: A Model for Other OECD Governments?',[68] have argued: '[the] characterizations of the positive effects of the Bayh-Dole Act cite little evidence to support their claims beyond simple counts of university patents and licenses'. In point of fact they suggest that 'these "assessments" . . . fail to consider any potentially negative effects of the Act on U.S. university research or innovation in the broader economy'.

NOTES

1. *Diamond v Chakrabarty* (1980) 447 US 303, 309 citing *Parker v Flook* (1978) 437 US 584; *Gottschalk v Benson* (1972) 409 US 63, 67; *Funk Brothers Seed Co v Kalo Inoculant Co* (1948) 333 US 127, 130; *O'Reilly v Morse* (1854) 15 How. 62, 112–21; *Le Roy v Tatham* (1853) 14 How. 156, 175.
2. *Funk Brothers Seed Co v Kalo Inoculant Co* (1948) 333 US 127, 130.

3. Jensen, K and F Murray, (2005), 'Intellectual Property Landscape of the Human Genome', *Science*, **310** (5746), 238–40.
4. Ibid, 239.
5. Ibid.
6. Ibid, 240.
7. Paradise, J, L Andrews and T Holbrook (2005), 'Patents on Human Genes: An Analysis of Scope and Claims, *Science*, **307** (5715), 1566–7.
8. Ibid, 1566.
9. Ibid.
10. Ibid.
11. Olson, DS (2006), 'Patentable Subject Matter: The Problem of the Absent Gatekeeper', *Social Science Research Network*, *(SSRN)*, 933167.
12. Ibid, 3.
13. Ibid, 1.
14. 1858–1931.
15. 1849–1908.
16. 1891–1941; Nobel Prize, 1923; knighted, 1934.
17. 1899–1978; Companion Order of Canada (COC), 1967.
18. 1876–1935; Nobel Prize, 1923.
19. Murray, I (1971), 'Paulesco and the Isolation of Insulin', *Journal of the History of Medicine*, April, 150–57.
20. 1869–1931.
21. Murray, above n 19, 153.
22. 1902–71; Nobel Prize, 1948.
23. Weber, M (1976), Book Review: Pavel, I (1976), *The Priority of N.C. Paulescu in the Discovery of Insulin*, Academy of the Socialist Republic of Romania, *The Journal of Historical Review*, **5** (1), 101–5.
24. Ibid.
25. 1892–1965.
26. 1877–1958.
27. 1871–1945.
28. Li, A (2003), *J.B. Collip and the Development of Medical Research in Canada* (Montreal, Canada: McGill-Queen's University Press), 77.
29. Ibid, 78.
30. Ibid, 80.
31. Ibid, 79.
32. 1888–1971.
33. Hagedorn, HC, BN Jensen, NB Karup and I Wodstrup (1936), 'Protamine Insulinate', *Journal of the American Medical Association*, **106**, 177–80.
34. 1869–1962; Joslin, EP (1919), *A Diabetic Manual for the Mutual use of Doctor and Patient*, 2nd edn (Philadelphia: Lea & Febiger).
35. Novo Nordisk History, 6, available at http://www.novonordisk.com/images/about_us/history/history_uk.pdf.
36. Hans Hagedorn and August Krogh (1874–1949; Nobel Prize, 1920) were licensed by the Toronto Committee in 1923 to manufacture and sell insulin in Denmark and they formed Nordisk Insulinlaboratorium. Today Novo Nordisk A/S, formed in 1989 when Novo and Nordisk merged, is a Danish pharmaceutical company which earned revenues in 2006 of US$6.9 billion.
37. Krayenbühl C and T Rosenberg (1946), 'Crystalline protamine insulin', *Rep Steno Mem Hosp Nord Insulinlab*, **1**, 60–73.
38. 1918–; Nobel Prizes, 1958 and 1980.
39. Sanger, F (1958), 'The Chemistry of Insulin', *Nobel Lecture*, 11 December 1958, 543–66, 556.
40. 1926–; Nobel Prize, 1980.
41. 1938–; Nobel Prize, 1975.
42. 1936–; National Medal of Science, 1990.

43. 1922–; Nobel Prize, 1986.
44. 1928–; Nobel Prize, 1978.
45. 1928–; Nobel Prize, 1962.
46. Berg, P et al, *Science*, **185** (4148), 303.
47. Cohen, SN, ACY Chang, HC Boyer and RB Helling (1973), 'Construction of Biologically Functional Bacterial Plasmids In Vitro', *Proceedings of the National Academy of Sciences of the United States of America*, **70** (11), 3240–4.
48. Morrow, JF, SN Cohen, ACY Chang, HW Boyer, HM Goodman and RB Helling (1974), 'Replication and Transcription of Eukaryotic DNA in Escherichia coli', *Proceedings of the National Academy of Sciences of the United States of America*, **71** (5), 1743–47.
49. 1947–99.
50. Hughes, SS (2001), 'Making Dollars out of DNA: The First Major Patent in Biotechnology and the Commercialization of Molecular Biology, 1974–1980', *Isis*, **92** (3), 541–75.
51. Statement of Senator Birch Bayh to the National Institutes of Health, 25 May 2004, 1.
52. Ibid, 1.
53. 'Innovation's golden goose', *The Economist*, **365** (8303), 3 (14 December 2002).
54. Leaf, C (2005), 'The Law of Unintended Consequences', *Fortune*, 19 September 2005, available at http://money.cnn.com/magazines/fortune/fortune_archive/2005/09/19/8272884/index.htm.
55. 1932–; Nobel prize, 1980.
56. Itakura, K, H Tadaaki, R Crea, AD Riggs, HL Heyneker, F Bolivar and HW Boyer (1973), 'Expression in *Escherichia coli* of a Chemically Synthesized Gene for the Hormone Somatostatin', *Science*, **198** (4321), 1056–63.
57. The patent monopoly period runs from the date of the patent application once the patent is granted. In this case, from 12 December 1984.
58. US 5,968,502 (19 October 1999), 'Protein production and protein delivery' and US 6,048,524 (11 April 2000), 'In vivo production and delivery of erythropoietin for gene therapy'.
59. *Kirin-Amgen Inc v Hoechst Marion Roussel Ltd and others* [2002] RPC 1 at 142, para. 534.
60. *Kirin-Amgen v Hoechst Marion Roussel Ltd and others* [2003] RPC 31.
61. Andrew Waugh QC, Transcript of the House of Lords Appeal in *Kirin-Amgen, Inc v Hoechst Marion Roussel Ltd and others*, 13 July 2004, 674 lines 6–15 (my italics). [2005] 1 All ER 667.
62. Ibid, 673 line 23–674 line 2.
63. *Kirin-Amgen Inc v Hoechst Marion Roussel Ltd and others* [2005] 1 All ER 667 per Lord Hoffmann, para. 132.
64. *Amgen Inc v Hoechst Marion Roussel, Inc and Transkaryotic Therapies, Inc* (2003) 314 F 3d 1313, 1329.
65. As 'disconformity' was removed as ground of revocation in 1949 when the UK Patents Act 1949 replaced the Patents & Designs Act 1907. Under the EPC disconformity was never a ground for revocation and therefore was not available to attack the validity on the Amgen patent.
66. Hass School of Business, UC Berkeley.
67. Georgia Institute of Technology.
68. Mowery, DC and B Sampat (2004), 'The Bayh-Dole Act of 1980 and University–Industry Technology Transfer: A Model for Other OECD Governments?', *The Journal of Technology Transfer*, **30** (1–2), 115–27.

9. Gene wars

We don't think it's right for someone to decode genomes, perform no research and then be able to make outrageous claims.

Spokesman for F Hoffmann-La Roche AG, *Die Zeit*, 36/2001[1]

In November 2006 Michael Hopkins and other researchers at the University of Sussex published a report entitled *The Patenting of Human DNA: Global Trends in Public and Private Sector Activity*.[2] The study that formed the basis of their report found that between 1980 and 2003 15 000 patent families (which suggests that there are tens of thousands of individual DNA patents) claiming human DNA had been granted around the world. The report's authors would have found, had their study extended beyond human DNA, many more claiming non-human DNA, and even thousands more again claiming the cellular components involved in the production of naturally occurring proteins. Without any doubt by 2006 virtually anything that was naturally occurring but 'isolated' was the subject of a patent giving their owners the legal right exclusively to control their 'inventions' for at least 20 years.

Undoubtedly the proliferation of patents over such things and the frustrating need to seek patent licences even to undertake basic research prompted a spokesman from F Hoffmann-La Roche AG to criticize those who 'decode genomes', but, given that Genentech was then a company which Roche controlled and which had been established in 1976 to do precisely that, the criticism was made either in ignorance or as part of a lie that was designed to elicit sympathy from European regulators. In fact Roche was once very critical of Chiron, a Californian company which for many years excluded it from the world hepatitis C virus diagnostics market by effect of its network of hepatitis C virus patents; but once Roche had brokered a settlement with Chiron that criticism became an accident of history.[3]

The truth is that once Cohen et al[4] (November 1973) and Morrow et al[5] (May 1974) had published their papers, information about the genetic manipulation of vectors (such as the insertion of foreign genetic material into bacteria and yeast cells and the subsequent expression by those vectors of proteins that were coded for by the foreign genetic material) became part of the stock of common general knowledge of molecular biologists.

Thereafter, to meet their objective of producing purified proteins, scientists needed either to isolate the natural gene encoding the protein or synthesize it using the knowledge of the protein's amino acid sequence. The next step in meeting the objective involved tweaking the genetic material of both the vector and the gene.

By 1980 molecular biologists had become something like mechanics – the Cohen and Morrow papers had made much of what they were doing with vectors and genes, the equivalent of hotwiring a car. While they needed to do some genetic fiddling in order to marry the genetic material to the vector of choice, they knew that through a process of trial and error eventually they would get the 'car' to 'start'. Furthermore they knew that the amino acid sequence of the expressed protein would be identical, or substantially identical, to the protein encoded by the gene. This explains why, after 1980, the biotechnology industry provided patent offices around the world with a 'ballooning workload' or, as John Sulston described it, a reason for permitting them to stake 'claims in the biotechnology Klondike'.[6]

Yet despite supposedly being the rewards for invention, gene patents kept rolling out of patent factories about as quickly as these biological mechanics ticked off the protein checklist, starting with insulin in 1977. Since the patent system gives all the credit to the first to invent (in the United States) or the first to file (the rest of the world), in this winner-takes-all scenario, inevitably gene wars broke out over who invented what, when and where. These wars continue and involve battalions of patent attorneys, lawyers and expert scientists, many of whom have made careers and fortunes along the way, mostly convinced there is nothing wrong with patenting genes.

ERYTHROPOIETIN

Almost the instant that Amgen's patent over isolated and purified eryth-ropoietin gene sequences was granted on 27 October 1987 it declared war on Chugai Pharmaceuticals and Genetics Institute, Inc. In *Amgen, Inc v Chugai Pharmaceutical Co and Genetics Institute, Inc* (1989) 706 F Supp 94 the US District Court had to resolve 'a battle over turf', as Judge Young described it. The turf was the human erythropoietin gene, and victory depended on whether Lin, from Amgen, or Fritsch, from Genetics Institute, was the first to 'invent' it. Eventually the litigation reached the CAFC,[7] but in the meantime a Federal Magistrate[8] had decided that Amgen's patent, US 4,703,008, was valid and infringed, while Genetic Institute's patent, US 4,677,195, was also valid and infringed. The parties were at a stalemate, and this effectively meant that, while third parties were unable to make use of the invention without the permission of both Amgen and Genetics Institute, the real irony was that neither could make it without the permission of the other. It was a ridiculous situation and the CAFC was determined to resolve the deadlock.

The problem was that both parties had made claims to the DNA sequence of the human erythropoietin gene; so, being the impartial umpire that the CAFC was required to be, Judge Lourie commenced by making it clear that 'neither Fritsch nor Lin invented [erythropoietin] or the [erythropoietin] gene'.[9] This of course created a paradox because, if neither of them invented the gene, then neither could be an inventor, and thus how could he resolve the deadlock? Unfortunately it was beyond his power to rule that neither of them had any right to a patent; after all the USPTO had granted not just one patent, but two, over the same human gene – the 'invention'. To resolve the paradox Lourie needed to display some imagination, and this he did when he concluded that Amgen's patent was about the 'purified and isolated sequence which codes for EPO'. By employing the isolation contrivance, the legal fiction that transforms a product of nature into a product of man, Lourie was then able to resolve the argument because the act of invention was the isolation and purification of the gene, and this was a matter of evidence.

According to Lourie, priority of invention went to the first person who could demonstrate 'the structure or physical characteristics' of the erythropoietin gene and 'had a viable method of obtaining it'. In other words the act of invention was in characterizing the gene. Cloning the gene was one such method, according to Lourie; so after reviewing the evidence presented at the trial in the District Court he made a most astounding finding. He held that the bipartisan nature of the expert evidence indicated that 'success in cloning the [erythropoietin] gene was not assured until the gene was in fact isolated and its sequence known'. In his opinion the gene's identification by its isolation and the sequencing of its DNA were the inventive steps – without these steps being taken the protein erythropoietin, which the gene coded for, could not be synthesized outside the human body. He was reinforced in his conclusion by the 'lack of information concerning the amino acid sequence of the [erythropoietin] protein'. This led him to hold that 'the trial court was correct in concluding that neither party had an adequate conception of the DNA sequence until reduction to practice had been achieved; Lin was first to accomplish that goal'. He discounted Fritsch's approach, even though it was obvious to any skilled worker that its methodology was sound, since '[c]onception of a generalized approach for screening a DNA library that might be used to identify and clone the [erythropoietin] gene of then unknown constitution is not conception of a "purified and isolated DNA sequence" encoding human [erythropoietin]'.

In resolving the inventorship issue in favour of Lin, Lourie confirmed that first prize went to the first person to sequence and characterize a human gene. Unfortunately he completely ignored the US Supreme Court's reasoning in *Chakrabarty,* which held that for something natural to be patentable subject matter it had to display 'markedly different characteristics to anything found in nature'. Lin's invention, being nothing more than the 'purified and isolated sequence which codes for EPO', simply did not meet that criterion. Indeed this was confirmed by the Federal Magistrate earlier in the proceedings, when he had found:

> the overwhelming evidence, including Amgen's own admissions, establishes that [natural erythropoietin] and [recombinant erythropoietin] are the same product. The [erythropoietin] gene used to produce [recombinant erythropoietin] is the same [erythropoietin] gene as the human body uses to produce [natural erythropoietin]. The amino acid sequences of human [natural erythropoietin] and [recombinant erythropoietin] are identical. . . . There are no known differences between the secondary structure of [recombinant erythropoietin] produced in a Chinese hamster cell and [erythropoietin] produced in a human kidney. Amgen's own scientists have concluded that by all criteria examined, [recombinant erythropoietin] is the 'equivalent to the natural hormone.'[10]

Neither party in this case was particularly interested in raising the issue of patentable subject matter, and the CAFC deliberately decided not to raise it, although it could have,[11] because it was determined not to open the Pandora's box of 'invention' and in the process derail America's opportunity to dominate the world in the field of biotechnology and in the production of pharmaceutical substances made with the use of recombinant DNA technology. Indeed the CAFC decisions in *Bell*[12] in 1993 and *Deuel*[13] in 1995 secured that market for Americans by holding that knowledge of the amino acid sequence of a protein or the DNA sequence of a human gene was not capable of rendering 'obvious', respectively, the DNA which coded for the protein or the amino acid sequence of the protein.

HEPATITIS B SURFACE ANTIGEN

In August 1981 both the University of California (UC) and Genentech filed patent applications for DNA expression vectors which comprised a promoter capable of expression in a yeast host cell, a DNA sequence which encoded the hepatitis B virus surface antigen (HBsAg), and the translational start and stop signals. The principal claims in the patents in issue, one to UC[14] and the other to Genentech,[15] were directed only to the HBsAg proteins themselves – proteins that were 'virtually identical to that of authentic 22 nm HBsAg particles' and to the genetic material that encoded them within a yeast cell. UC's patent also claimed the use of HBsAg proteins 'capable of eliciting antibodies reactive with HBsAg' in an HBV vaccine (claim 4), which was quite an amazing claim, given that the patent specification did not disclose how to make such a vaccine. Rather, the *assumption* of its author appeared to be that these isolated HBsAg particles would work in an HBV vaccine without the need for undue experimentation.

The issue in this litigation was, once again, who was the first true inventor? The alleged inventors were William Rutter from UC, a professor from UC Berkeley and founder of Chiron in San Francisco, and Ronald Hitzeman from Genentech. The forum of the dispute resolution was the Board of Patent Appeals and Interferences' judgment in *Hitzeman et al v Rutter et al* (1999) Pat. App LEXIS 26.

Apart from the fact the claim language and the descriptions in the respective patent specifications differed significantly, both patents were directed to the same biological material – the invention was purified HBsAg – and both used yeast cells as vectors to express the purified HBsAg. Where they varied was in the precise genetic manipulations carried out on the respective yeast cells. This suggests therefore that the genetic manipulation of yeast cells themselves, while important to getting them to express the protein, was not the inventive step. Indeed these differences were quite immaterial in distinguishing between the two inventions because it really did not matter how Rutter or Hitzeman had arrived at his invention, what was the key – the inventive step, if you like – was the genetic material that coded for the protein.

Although at the time the use of yeast cells for human protein expression was regarded as being something of a technical achievement, it was obviously not crucial to the resolution of the inventorship dispute. While these two patents described for the first time how to use yeast cells to express HBsAg proteins, the fact is that their use had already been contemplated and it was only a matter of time before someone actually did it. Certainly by 1979 DNA transfer vectors suitable for transfer and replication in yeast had already been developed.

So if one disregarded the yeast cells as having anything to do with the inventive step, the only remaining missing piece of the invention jigsaw puzzle was the gene which encoded HBsAg. The inventive step being thus defined Judge Ellis soon zeroed in on the experimental evidence that linked those 'DNA fragments' with the expression of HBsAg proteins in yeast cells. The question for him was: did Hitzeman's laboratory notebooks show that he had 'a definite and permanent idea of the complete and operative invention'? Hitzeman, being from Genentech, called on his colleague David Goeddel to corroborate his invention story. Given that *mental conception* of the invention was crucial to proving priority, Goeddel recalled, 'having a conversation with Dr. Hitzeman within a few days after the successful expression of interferon, where he and I talked about using the ADH and the yeast 3-phosphoglycerate kinase (PGK) gene to express other heterologous proteins in yeast, including the hepatitis surface antigen'. Goeddel's testimony therefore confirmed that Hitzeman had contemplated the use of yeast cells to express HBsAg, knowing that they had already been successfully used to express interferon. Goeddel was trying to neutralize UC's submissions that Hitzeman had yet to prove, in a laboratory, that this idea would actually work.

Judge Ellis was in fact unimpressed with this evidence; he believed that Hitzeman had, at best, 'a hope that [HBsAg] particles would be produced' using his methodology, and this hope, he said, was 'immaterial' to resolving the dispute. In his opinion, '[k]nowledge of the cellular mechanisms for expressing DNA sequences, in general, does not demonstrate conception of the expression of a DNA sequence in yeast which results in the production of HBsAg particles having a sedimentation rate which is virtually identical to that of authentic 22 nm HBsAg particles'. Therefore it was not possible to predict that Hitzeman's ideas would work.

The only evidence that Ellis believed was consistent with 'the doctrine of simultaneous conception and reduction to practice' (citing *Amgen v Chugai and Genetics Institute* as authority) was actual experimental evidence of the use of recombinant DNA technology to express a DNA sequence encoding HBsAg in a transformed yeast cell. Therefore, 'until reduction to practice had been achieved', that is until he had experimental proof that the yeast cells expressed HBsAg, the invention was not complete. According to Ellis, Hitzeman's invention story did not reach that threshold, whereas Rutter had reached it, so he held that Rutter was the first true inventor.

In truth it should not have mattered that Rutter was the first to make a yeast cell express HBsAg proteins in a laboratory because he did not invent the 'DNA fragments' – the biological blueprints to the crucial protein that Rutter called the 'S-protein'. Ellis however was bound to follow the authority of the CAFC, and accordingly he made the same mistake that was made by Lourie in *Amgen v Genetic Institute*.

BOX 9.1   CLAIM 1, US 4,769,238

'A protein preparation (Y-HBsAg) comprising particulate aggregates of S-protein chains of identical primary structure and molecular weight of the hepatitis B surface antigen, synthesized by yeast transformed with a DNA segment encoding the S-protein of hepatitis B virus, all of said S-protein being in unglycosylated form.'

This mistake was further compounded by the fact that Rutter's invention was actually about the process which he had employed, but was claimed to be the actual gene and the protein in isolated forms – both virtually identical to their naturally occurring equivalents. While Rutter tried to distinguish his protein from natural HBsAg by calling it a 'protein preparation (Y-HBsAg)', it was in practical terms the same as natural HBsAg. He also tried to distinguish Y-HBsAg from HBsAg by limiting the claim to the protein in an 'unglycosylated form'. This was nothing more than biological semantics, and no more convincing than distinguishing natural HBsAg from 'isolated and purified' HBsAg. By being in an unglycosylated form the Y-HBsAg proteins were without the polysaccharide chains which natural HBsAg proteins had, but this did nothing to enhance its function. Finally, while Rutter's invention was a genetically modified protein, it simply did not meet the criteria stipulated in *Chakrabarty* for the simple reason that Y-HBsAg did nothing more than what HBsAg did naturally and the genetic modifications were immaterial to that reaction. Rutter's Y-HBsAg proteins did not display markedly different characteristics from those found in nature; rather they displayed *exactly* the same characteristics as natural HBsAg. While Rutter may have been the first scientist actually to have yeast cells express Y-HBsAg proteins in a laboratory, and this is noteworthy, he did not invent the Y-HBsAg proteins. The natural equivalents already existed in nature and, even though isolated and purified, Y-HBsAg was not 'new' within the meaning of that word in section 101.

Critical to demonstrating a useful application of 'protein preparation Y-HBsAg' was its obvious use in an HBV vaccine – the hypothesis being that the human body's immunological reaction to it would match the reaction to natural HBsAg. Indeed it was obvious, as the paucity of experimental data in the patent specification confirmed, that the skilled ordinary virologist was expected to have made that assumption. Nonetheless, that Rutter also claimed the use of Y-HBsAg in a vaccine as an invention proved two things: first, that the protein Y-HBsAg was coded for by the corresponding natural equivalent and, secondly, that Y-HBsAg and natural HBsAg were identical in every material respect. If they were not, then clearly the human body was not to be expected to mount an immunological reaction to Y-HBsAg, and without an immunological response it would have been useless in an HBV vaccine. Which is why Rutter's main invention, Y-HBsAg, described the invention as comprising 'aggregates of S-protein chains of identical primary structure and molecular weight of the hepatitis B surface antigen'. That the 'S-protein' was encoded by the natural viral 'gene' was confirmed in Rutter's patent: '[t]he translation product of the HBV surface antigen gene is termed the S-protein. S-protein has 226 amino acids whose sequence has been inferred from the nucleotide sequence of its gene and by partial sequence analysis'.

Rutter's real aim was to gain a patent for an HBV vaccine that used Y-HBsAg proteins, but one could be forgiven for not discerning this from the title: 'Synthesis Of Human Virus Antigens By Yeast'. Indeed there is no mention of the word 'vaccine' until one reaches claim 4, which defines the invention as '[a] vaccine for protecting a subject against hepatitis B infection which comprises the Y-HBsAg of claim 3 in admixture with a pharmaceutically acceptable carrier'. Likewise claim 5 claims '[a] method of immunizing a subject against hepatitis B infection which comprises administering to a subject in need of such immunization the vaccine of claim 4'.

The US patent system left the door wide open to this kind of abuse, and the USPTO, if it had been doing its job properly, should never have allowed these vaccine claims given that, first, the Y-HBsAg proteins were not patentable subject matter and, secondly, their natural equivalents were already known to induce an immunological reaction. Indeed HBV surface antigens had been used in an HBV vaccine since 1980. Under those circumstances a vaccine as defined by claims 4 and 5 was not novel; indeed the fact that the existing vaccine used natural HBsAg could not, on the basis of US Supreme Court authority, make Rutter's vaccine new. The first generation HBV vaccine[16] was developed by Baruch Blumberg[17] and Irving Millman[18] within four years of Blumberg's discovery of the causative agent of the disease[19] which became known as hepatitis B in 1965; and by 1981 the FDA approved the use in the United States of the second generation of HBV vaccines that used anti-HBV collected from human plasma as a component. So how could Rutter's vaccine be novel? Plainly it could not be, and the US Supreme Court confirmed this in 1884 in *BASF*.

Even if Rutter had invented a truly revolutionary new HBV vaccine –which he clearly had not – one would have expected to see detailed experimental data in the patent specification that established how and why the Y-HBsAg proteins worked in an HBV vaccine in humans. Unfortunately there were no such data. The only data came from animal experiments that showed promising results; and while it is the case that before human clinical experiments can be conducted animal experimental data are required by the FDA, these data hardly established the efficacy of the experimental vaccine in humans. Surely one would have expected the patent specification to explain how Rutter made an HBV vaccine for use in humans so that others reading the patent would be informed of how to make it. After all, is not one of the premises upon which patents are granted to disseminate knowledge? But the patent specification did not contain any information of this kind. The reason for this was that when UC filed the patent application, that work had not yet been done. Under those circumstances it was unacceptable for the USPTO to grant a patent monopoly to an HBV vaccine for use in humans. Rutter would no doubt argue that human data were unnecessary because it was already known that an HBV vaccine containing natural HBsAg would create a life-long immunity in humans to HBV infection; but if this was predictable, why was the University of California granted a patent to HBV vaccines in the first place? Where was the inventive step?

HEPATITIS C VIRUS

By 1981 Rutter had teamed up with Edward Penhoet and Pablo Valenzuela, two of his colleagues from the University of California, Berkeley, to incorporate a new company. That company, Chiron, was principally established to take advantage of Rutter's hepatitis B vaccine 'invention', but he and his colleagues had their eyes on other biological targets as well. Starting modestly with ten employees Chiron set up its operations in Emeryville, a San Francisco suburb near the Berkeley campus. Rutter was the Chairman of the Board, Penhoet was the CEO and President and Valenzuela was the Vice-President of R&D. Within a year Chiron made what was to be a very important decision. It employed Michael Houghton, a young PhD who had for ten years been a research scientist at Searle Research & Development in Buckinghamshire in England. As the project leader of a team which had for four years been working with recombinant DNA technology on interferons, his decision to leave England and come to San Francisco was to be an equally momentous decision for him.

Eleven years later in a witness statement which Houghton made in legal proceedings brought before the UK Patents Court by Chiron, in which it accused Organon Teknika, Murex Diagnostics and United Biomedical of infringing its UK patent GB 2,212,511 for isolated genetic and biological materials derived from the hepatitis C virus,[20] Houghton recalled this history. He explained how he had wanted to continue his work with interferons, but as 'Chiron's corporate objectives were to concentrate on healthcare . . . it was mutually agreed that [he] work on NANBH'.

In 1981 NANBH was the acronym which virologists and medical doctors used to refer to 'non-A non-B hepatitis', that is to a type of hepatitis that was caused by neither the hepatitis A nor the B virus. In fact the cause of NANBH was a mystery, and solving that mystery was something that Chiron wanted to do before anyone else. In fact within the decade Chiron had achieved its goal, and by 1992 NANBH became known as hepatitis C. After patenting the isolated hepatitis C virus (HCV) polypeptides and nucleotides around the world, Chiron became involved in a major patent battle in the UK, and Houghton and his colleagues at Chiron, Qui Lim Choo and George Kuo, had become famous. Their main claim to this fame was that their 'invention' enabled the use of HCV proteins that were antigenic (that is contained epitopes or antibody binding sites to HCV) in immunodiagnostics designed to detect the presence of antibodies to HCV. A positive result from such a test was an indicator that the patient had been infected with HCV and the availability of such a test provided blood banks with a way to screen donated blood and body organs for HCV infection, thereby dramatically reducing the spread of what had previously been called 'post-transfusion NANBH'.

BOX 9.2　CLAIM 1, GB 2,212,511/EP 0,318,216

'A polypeptide in substantially isolated form comprising a contiguous sequence of at least 10 amino acids encoded by the genome of hepatitis C virus (HCV) and comprising an antigenic determinant, wherein HCV is characterized by:

  (i)　a positive stranded RNA genome;
 (ii)　said genome comprising an open reading frame (ORF) encoding a polyprotein; and
(iii)　said polyprotein comprising an amino acid sequence having at least 40% homology to the 859 amino acid sequence in Figure 14.'

The grant of GB 2,212,511 (which subsequently became EP 0,318,216) meant that Chiron had patent monopolies in Europe over all isolated HCV polypeptides (proteins) and nucleotides (RNA – as HCV is a single-stranded RNA virus) and their derivatives used in virtually any medical, scientific or industrial application (such as cDNA), including the diagnosis of HCV using standard antibody-antigen diagnostic (ELISA) technology.

The discovery of HCV had been acknowledged as an outstanding scientific achievement, and by 1992 Houghton had been awarded a number of scientific prizes including the Karl Landsteiner Memorial Award. Chiron's stock price was rising, and this was good news for Rutter and his colleagues, as well as for the American biotechnology industry generally. In fact Houghton, Choo and Kuo's discovery made Rutter, Penhoet and Valenzula very rich. Through its broad HCV patents Chiron controlled

HCV diagnostics.[21] Chiron became a major player in the blood screening market throughout the world. Having partnered Ortho, a subsidiary of Johnson & Johnson, and appointed Abbott Laboratories and Institute Pasteur as licensees for specific technologies within specific geographic regions, Chiron was in an enviable position.

Chiron was not content to claim only the use of specific HCV proteins in an immunoassay as an invention. Claim 1, the principal invention, claimed any 'substantially isolated' proteins consisting of at least ten amino acids that were immunogenic to HCV, and was defined as including anything that had an RNA genome and the amino acid sequence of which comprised 'at least 40% homology to the 859 amino acid sequence in Figure 14'.

This was an extremely broad invention. Apart from the fact that the 859 amino acids were only a fraction of the approximately 10 000 amino acids which made up the complete genome, their location in the non-structural region of the HCV genome (the NS-4 region), which was highly sensitive to immunological pressure, meant not only that they were susceptible to mutation but, combined with the threshold of 'at least 40% homology', made it conceivable that other viruses (known and unknown) causative of hepatitis or hepatitis-like symptoms in humans and primates, such as Ross-River Virus, could potentially come within the scope of the patent's monopoly.

Consequently Chiron's patent claims were quite controversial; but in the background lurked another issue – inventorship. Being protective of its patent position, especially as the USPTO had yet to grant Chiron any HCV patents, Robert Blackburn, Chiron's Chief Patent Counsel, was particularly sensitive to any suggestion that the Chiron scientists were not the exclusive 'inventors'. In fact so sensitive was Chiron that until May 1988, when Chiron publicly announced the discovery of HCV, Daniel Bradley, a virologist at the Centers for Disease Control and Houghton's principal collaborator, was denied access to any information that may have hinted that his name was not included in any of Chiron's HCV patent applications. Indeed it had come as a terrible disappointment for Bradley to learn from Rutter that, while Chiron accepted his contribution to the collaboration to have been important, his work was considered irrelevant to the invention.

Back in 1982, however, it was a different story. Bradley and the CDC had already been searching for the causative agent of NANBH for five years. After acquiring samples of Factor VIII product which had been implicated in infecting haemophiliacs with NANBH in 1977, Bradley had attempted to visualize the causative agent (which he believed to be virus-like) using electron microscopy and immune electron microscopy. Having failed with these experiments he began thinking about how he could improve its identification, theorizing that its presence in low concentrations in biological materials was part of the problem and devising an experiment that applied an algorithm he had calculated. On 16 February 1978 he infected four laboratory research chimpanzees using the infectious Factor VIII materials. One of these four chimps was codenamed 'Don' and another 'Rodney', and together they were to become the main source of biological materials, Bradley's constant objective being to concentrate the infectious agent so that it could be identified. Bradley, a noted virologist around the world, also discussed his ideas, and by 1980 he had published two important papers.[22]

Bradley therefore was someone whom Houghton believed he needed if he was to have any chance of identifying the causative agent of NANBH. Apart from knowing nothing himself about NANBV, having spent the last four years working with interferons, Houghton was a molecular biologist, not a virologist. Furthermore Chiron was a small company which could barely afford to employ 20 people, let alone operate an experimental animal laboratory that housed chimpanzees. The annual costs alone of such a laboratory in 1982 was around US$100 000 per chimp and the CDC, a US government agency, had allocated four chimpanzees to Bradley.

Consequently in early November 1982 Houghton arranged to meet Bradley. Within days of their meeting Rutter wrote to the CDC on 10 November 1982 confirming that Chiron and the CDC had entered into an 'open collaboration', the objective of which 'was to clone HCV', as Houghton subsequently confirmed in evidence he gave to the Australian Federal Court on 9 July 1996.[23]

On the basis of this understanding between Chiron and the CDC, Bradley and Houghton commenced their collaboration. The idea was to combine Houghton's molecular biological skills with Bradley's skills as a virologist. Cloning the causative agent required access to biological materials that were known to contain the candidate agent, and Houghton knew that Bradley had been developing pools of this material based upon his hypothesis as to when to maximize the concentrations of this agent in blood and liver samples extracted from his laboratory's four chimpanzees, but particularly from the chimps Don and Rodney.

Bradley's role in the collaboration, ultimately, went beyond merely being the source of chimpanzee biological materials. During the course of the collaboration he attended joint meetings, was involved in discussions concerning results of the molecular biological experiments, discussed theories and ideas and produced a specifically enriched three-litre plasma pool derived exclusively from the plasma collected from Rodney over a six-year period. According to Bradley he even suggested to Houghton in 1984, after reading a scientific paper[24] by Richard Young and Ronald Davis, both Stanford University researchers from the Department of Biochemistry, that he should consider using the Young and Davis approach which used the expression vector lambda gt11. Bradley told Houghton that they could make 'millions of clones from cDNA libraries created from infected liver or plasma could be screened expeditiously with chronic-phase infected sera either from chimpanzees or humans'. This approach, according to Bradley, had 'the added substantial advantage of providing an immediate immunoassay for the detection of a virus-specific antibody'.[25]

Even George Kuo, another of Houghton's colleagues at Chiron, had by June 1985 made a similar overture, but he went further and sketched out the methodology for an experiment. Kuo's idea was simple: like Bradley he suggested applying the Young and Davis approach and although, as in any experiment, there was no guarantee of success, he believed that it was worth trying. After all, Houghton had tried just about everything else, so what did he have to lose? Kuo suggested that they amplify random segments of genetic material that was contained within the pooled Rodney sera in the hope that one or more of the library of clones which were produced using this vector contained one or more clones which would hybridize to human anti-HCV antibodies. That hybridization, if it were to happen, would give them a genetic handle (that is, a physical link to the virus that caused hepatitis C) on the candidate agent. Once they had that genetic handle they could use it to narrow the field of their search for more parts of the genome by making probes that would hybridize to more and more of the genome. This would take time, but finally they would have enough of the genome then to verify that the candidate agent was truly causative of NANBH.

Kuo's idea, according to Houghton, was a long shot, and he immediately rejected it – just has he had rejected Bradley's suggestion because he was concerned about 'spending a lot of time and precious resources looking for antibodies that might not exist at sufficient levels'.[26] His reaction was understandable, given that at the time he was under 'considerable pressure from management', particularly as, Houghton believed, 'at least one member of management' was 'trying to remove' him as the project leader.[27] Nonetheless by October 1985 he commenced preparing the first clone libraries using the Rodney plasma. At first he encountered difficulties because he found the plasma to be 'a complex substance with many proteins and other components which interfere with the extraction of the genome', but in November 1986 he repeated the experiment, making a number of changes to the methodology 'in an attempt to improve the overall efficiency'.[28] This second library of clones he called the 'C' library. Finally in January 1987 Houghton asked Qui Lim Choo, another Chiron scientist, to screen the 'C' library with serum from a chronically infected NANBH patient, code-named patient 'L', in the expectation that this patient's 'unusually high ALT elevations' which corresponded with 'a severe hepatitis' could, 'through a correspondingly large immune response', produce a positive result.[29] Then on 27 January 1987 Choo identified five positive clones, one of which was dubbed 'clone 5-1-1'.

At that point, Houghton only cautiously acknowledged success. Apart from keeping this news quarantined within Chiron's inner circle (excluding Bradley and the CDC), Houghton's Chiron team then proceeded to verify that the 'putative clone 5-1-1' was, in fact, a true clone of the causative agent of NANBH. This painstaking and vital work continued throughout 1987 and into 1988 and required further biological material from the CDC, which Bradley and the CDC continued to supply, unaware that Houghton had identified five potential NANBH clones.

The verification work was of course necessary, especially given that, until confirmed, '[c]lone 5-1-1 was just another putative positive' which, according to Kuo, 'no-one at that time believed . . . was truly a clone derived from the causative agent of NANBH'.[30] This verification work included the production of a prototype diagnostic assay for NANBH, which again required biological material supplied by Bradley and the CDC. This assay, in turn, was tested against the 'Alter panel' which had been:

> set up by Dr. Harvey Alter of the [National Institutes of Health] in the early 1980s and was widely used as the qualifying panel for putative NANBH assays. The panel consisted of proven infectious sera from chronic NANBH carriers, infectious sera from implicated donors and infectious sera from acute phase NANBH patients in duplicate. Samples were also included from highly pedigreed negative controls and other disease controls.[31]

The assay was subjected to two Alter panels and, having passed both, confirmed that NANBV genomic material was contained in the assay and that clone 5-1-1 was a true clone of NANBV. Final confirmation was given by letter from Dr Alter to Chiron on 10 June 1988.

During this time Houghton and Chiron kept from Bradley and the CDC all information about the success of these experiments. Instead they prepared patent applications, the first of which was filed with the USPTO on 18 November 1987. It was not until May 1988, and after signing a two-page confidentiality agreement, that Bradley was told by Houghton about the events which had transpired between January 1987 and November 1988. Bradley assumed that his name would be included on any patent application, but that was not to be.

Houghton and Chiron then deliberately went about underplaying Bradley's contributions to the collaboration and, crucially, his role in the identification of clone 5-1-1, confining his role as the supplier of biological materials. For example, under cross-examination on 9 July 1996 conducted at the Australian Federal Court, Houghton testified under oath:

'Do you deny that you relied upon any of Dan Bradley's hypotheses to successfully screen or successfully obtain clone 511? – *To a large extent, yes.*

So you did not rely in any way upon that hypothesis in obtaining nucleic acids, from the stage of obtain nucleic acids to the stage of screening 511? – *No.*

Do you deny that you relied upon any views or advice or discussions with Dr Bradley other than the ones you mentioned about expression screening and screening with patient sera in carrying out your work that lead to the successful cloning? – *I essentially deny that, yes.*'[32]

Bradley however considered the enriched Rodney plasma pool to be 'the common factor involved in every step of the . . . cloning process . . . [because it] was used to generate cDNAs, the many individual genetic elements within the source [that] become physically integrated into the cloning process and [remain] there throughout the process'.[33] In fact, as Bradley correctly pointed out, the 'genetic code of clone 5-1-1 was within the Rodney high titre plasma all along' and the 'cloning tool merely captured it as a separate element'. Bradley was, nearly ten years later, annoyed that Chiron had persisted in perpetuating a story which failed to recognize the true role he had played in the work which Houghton, Kuo and Choo had claimed as their own. 'Chiron', he said, 'did not create clone 5-1-1 out of thin air'.[34]

The importance of Bradley's unique biological materials to the cloning experiments for NANBH was, in any event, corroborated by Gregory Reyes, who had also been working during the 1980s on identifying the cause of NANBH. Reyes and Genelabs, his employer, had also approached the CDC, and Bradley had agreed to provide Reyes with biological materials from an enriched plasma pool derived from the chimp Don. Reyes, in his testimony, not only confirmed that he believed that the Young and Davis approach that he adopted would work, but confirmed: 'Dr. Houghton was basically using the same set of assumptions that I and my colleagues at Genelabs were using for our calculations and in our procedures'. Those assumptions were: '(a) that the agent was a virus; (b) that there was a sufficiently high titer of the virus in the CDC chimpanzee plasma to clone the virus; (c) that detectable levels of antibodies would be produced to infection from the virus and (d) these antibodies could be used to identify a virus specific clone using expression cloning protocols'.[35] In other words Houghton, like Reyes, knew that so long as there were high concentrations of NANBV present in the materials Bradley and the CDC were supplying them, these materials were, as Reyes testified, 'critical to our success'.[36]

Even so at the time Reyes had not realized that he too had cloned HCV, and it was not until Chiron had published its results that Reyes went back to his results and was able to confirm that his experiment had indeed been successful.[37]

Unfortunately for Bradley, this version of events did not support the strategic decision which Chiron had made about the role Bradley had played in the work leading to the identification of clone 5-1-1. Consequently, in the first patent application filed with the USPTO on 14 November 1987, Bradley was not even mentioned. Although by the time the fifth patent application was filed on 26 October 1988 Bradley was mentioned, it was only as the supplier of '[s]erum samples from eleven chimpanzees'. Clearly the failure of Chiron to give Bradley proper attribution was threatening the validity of any patent that might issue, but Chiron was supremely confident that it would be able to neutralize this threat.

Eventually a deal was brokered on 12 March 1990 with the aid of Joseph Califano,[38] then a senior partner in the Washington, DC, law firm Dewey Ballantine. Under the terms of this agreement the CDC would receive US$2.25 million and Bradley US$337 500 over five years; but the issue of inventorship was not resolved. These payments were intended to be interim payments pending an independent investigation into the events leading to the invention being conducted at the expense of Chiron.[39] It was only if the investigation concluded that Bradley was not a co-inventor that the payments were to be treated as final. However in the event that a decision favourable to Bradley was reached, then there would be other consequences, which included amending the patent applications to include Bradley as a co-inventor. At least this is what Bradley believed was the effect of the final agreement.

However, as the agreement was being signed someone inserted some handwritten words next to the typed text of the agreement. Bradley, who did not have the benefit of his own legal counsel, was relying upon the CDC in-house legal team, and they had been instructed by the CDC to do the deal. Without the support of the CDC Bradley had little choice but reluctantly to sign the document that now included the handwritten words: 'CDC and Dr. Bradley hereby assign to Chiron any and all right title and interest in or to Chiron Patents and the inventions claimed therein'.[40]

The agreement defined the term 'Chiron Patents' as US patent applications (no US patents had yet been granted); but the agreement failed to mention any of Chiron's patent applications outside the United States. This would have been a significant omission had the true objective of the agreement been to transfer Bradley and the CDC's interest in the invention to Chiron, especially given that patentability is limited to the territory of the granting patent authority. Accordingly that agreement was confined, by effect of the schedule, to the territory of the United States, and that very issue was to become *the* issue in future litigation.

Subsequently Chiron undertook the enquiry as foreshadowed in the agreement. It was conducted by Donald Chisum, a well respected professor of US patent law and then also a member of the patent law firm Morrison & Foerster. His report concluded that Bradley was not a co-inventor. Unfortunately Chisum defined the relevant inventive steps as the construction of the C library, the identification of clone 5-1-1 and the subsequent verification of that clone. Thus the narrow scope of his enquiry avoided his having to deal with the fact that without Bradley the chances of Houghton, Kuo and Choo cloning HCV were extremely small. Moreover he failed to delve into the history of the collaboration between Bradley and Houghton, the joint purpose of which, in Houghton's own words, was 'to clone HCV'.[41]

Although Bradley did sign the agreement, he subsequently brought proceedings in a US Federal District Court against Rutter, Penhoet and Chiron[42] in 1994 alleging that he had done so under pressure and without the benefit of independent legal advice; but Bradley's lawsuit was dismissed by Judge Claudia Wilken, who refused to allow a jury trial that would investigate these events. She ruled that the agreement was conclusive. On appeal the CAFC affirmed; but this was a poor decision and subsequently acknowledged as such by the CAFC in *PAE Government Services, Inc v MPRI, Inc* (2007) US App LEXIS 29221 which confirmed: 'though the Federal Circuit reached a contrary conclusion in *Bradley v Chiron Corp* (1998) 136 F 3d 1317, 1326 no other court of appeals has followed that decision, and we decline to do so'. Unfortunately Bradley did not have the financial resources to appeal to the US Supreme Court.

It must be remembered that Bradley was, after all, a virologist and not a patent lawyer, and accordingly it was very unfair that he be required to sign an agreement that at the very last minute was made materially different by the insertion of some handwritten words. Apart from Joseph Califano's high level involvement, both the CDC and Chiron were keen to put the dispute behind them and Bradley was standing in the way. Bradley was therefore placed under considerable pressure to sign a document that he did not fully understand in circumstances which were highly prejudicial.

Meanwhile F Hoffmann-La Roche AG, a Swiss pharmacetucial company, had been trying for years to negotiate an HCV licence with Chiron but, like most others, it had been rebuffed. While pursing a legal battle before the EPO over the European HCV patent[43] La Roche was desperate enough to seek out Bradley. In November 1997 Bradley reluctantly agreed to help La Roche and assigned, as La Roche wanted, his residual non-US patent rights to the company. It was only a matter of time however before Chiron became aware of what had transpired and sued both La Roche and Bradley.

Indeed when Chiron sued Bradley and La Roche in January 1998 Chiron relied on the handwritten words in the agreement to assert that it exclusively owned the rights to the invention of HCV polypeptides and nucleotides around the world, not just in the United States. Judge Wilken once again came to Chiron's rescue, wasting no time in agreeing with Chiron and throwing La Roche's defence out of court.

Nevertheless whatever Chiron and Houghton thought about Bradley's role in the 'invention', the scientific community believed that Bradley had played a very significant role in the identification of HCV and so, along with Houghton, Choo and Kuo, he also shared the Karl Landsteiner Memorial Award in 1992[44] awarded for 'the molecular cloning and characterization of the genome of the causative agent of hepatitis C'. In 1993 he also shared the Robert Koch Prize with Houghton; in 1994 he, Houghton, Choo and Kuo shared the William Beaumont Prize in Gastroenterology, and in the same year Bradley was awarded the Priscilla Kincaid-Smith Award by the Royal Australasian College of Physicians.

Remarkably Chiron was granted patents for isolated HCV polypeptides and, although the claims varied from patent to patent, in the Australian (AU 624,105) and the UK patents (GB 2,212,511) claims to the use of HCV polypeptides in HCV vaccines and pharmaceuticals were included. Chiron's rationale was that knowledge of the genetic sequence of HCV and the ability synthetically to manufacture HCV proteins was all that scientists needed to know in order to make human vaccines and medicines to treat humans infected with HCV or to prevent HCV infection. Claims of this kind were made by Chiron in 1988 and granted in 1992 in Australia and the UK. Some 16 years later there are still no pharmaceuticals or vaccines which effectively treat or prevent HCV, demonstrating the flaw in this kind of reasoning – a flaw that was recognized fairly promptly by the UK Patents Court in 1993.[45]

As a result the HCV vaccine claims, which the UK Patent Office had allowed, were invalid because the patent specification failed to teach the ordinary skilled worker how to make a vaccine to prevent or treat HCV in humans.[46] Indeed the entire patent specification was written on the basis of an incredible assumption, namely: '[a]nything that is done with the HCV virus is covered by this patent and all research and development on the virus is subservient to it'. Baruch Blumberg, an independent expert in the case, believed that the patent claims were so 'broad' that, 'if I were a research director for anti-virals and had the option of working on several viruses, the existence of this patent would weigh against my deciding to undertake HCV research'. Indeed he described the patent as so 'intimidating' that a 'company, or even an academic laboratory, might well be deterred from conducting research on HCV'.[47]

In June 2000 the Technical Appeal Board of the European Patent Office (TBA) heard La Roche's opposition to EP 0,318,216 and, although it upheld the validity of the patent, it held invalid all claims other than five entirely new claims to HCV nucleotides.[48]

HUMAN INSULIN-LIKE GROWTH FACTOR-I: THE SWISS APPLY GERMANY'S PRE-WORLD WAR I STRATEGY

By 1995 Rutter had become a veteran intellectual property litigator; not only was Chiron embroiled in international patent litigation concerning HCV, but it was also fighting with Genentech over the rights to a 'DNA construct' of human insulin-like growth factor-I (IGF-I),[49] a battle which now not only concerned two American corporations but involved two of the world's pharmaceutical giants. By this time Ciba-Geigy (which merged with Sandoz AG in 1996 to become Novartis) had taken a substantial stake in the ownership of Chiron[50] and F Hoffmann-La Roche had taken control of Genentech. Thus, the fight between Chiron and Genentech, two American biotechnology companies, was actually part of a much bigger international skirmish for market dominance between two Swiss pharmaceutical giants; and ironically it was the American patent system that was providing them with the battleground (the US courts) and the ammunition (US patents) needed to dominate the US market. In an almost repeat performance of Germany's pre-World War I strategy, what the CAFC, US policy-makers and legislators had overlooked in their determination to provide patent protection to the 'inventions' of the American biotechnology industry was how easy it was for the Swiss pharmaceutical industry to use US stock markets to infiltrate and take control of the US market for recombinant pharmaceuticals.

HUMAN PROINSULIN

UC and Eli Lilly however were neither Swiss nor controlled by Swiss interests. Eli Lilly, although now a global pharmaceutical company, something that it owed both to insulin and to the patent system, was still an American company. Indeed it was the deal struck in 1922 between the Toronto Committee and Eli Lilly that helped to transform this small Indiana company into a global entity. Eli Lilly had since retained its interest in insulin products, and the patent litigation with UC was simply a consequence.[51]

Seventy years after its isolation and purification from the animal pancreas, insulin was still worth fighting over and the patent system was the ready facilitator. It was an all-American affair – a fight over the use of recombinant DNA technology in the production of human insulin. Rutter was named as an inventor on both UC patents which were the subject of this litigation, and so he was one of the prime targets for Eli Lilly's attack. Indeed although the focus of this discussion will be on the patent issues in this case it will also consider the conduct of some of the scientists involved, unfortunately demonstrating how the commercialization of American universities and their academics produced consequences that perhaps Senator Bayh did not foresee when he co-sponsored the the Bayh-Dole Act 1980 – conduct that was to have dire consequences for UC in the course of this litigation.

All of the UC patents that were the subject of this litigation had been examined by the USPTO and granted. Judge Dillin explained that in order to succeed Eli Lilly had to prove 'by clear and convincing evidence that the patent in issue is invalid'.

In both these patents Rutter was named as a co-inventor. US 4,431,740, entitled 'DNA transfer vector and transformed microorganism containing human proinsulin and pre-proinsulin genes', was granted on 14 February 1984. US 4,652,525, entitled 'Recombinant bacterial plasmids containing the coding sequences of insulin genes', was granted on 24 March 1987. Another co-inventor on both patents was the Nobel prize-winning laureate Howard Goodman, and although these patents were separated by several years in terms of grant dates, in terms of their application dates they were separated by only about a year. Gene patents were now coming through thick and fast – just about as fast as it took researchers to identify the key genetic materials.

There was no argument that the key to these inventions in each case was the DNA of the relevant proteins, which for the '740 patent was the human insulin gene;[52] and if there was any doubt that the key to the invention was a naturally produced human gene, then the claims in this patent dispelled all such doubts.

BOX 9.3   CLAIM 1, US 4,431,740

'A DNA transfer vector comprising an inserted cDNA consisting essentially of a deoxynucleotide sequence coding for human pre-proinsulin, the plus strand of said cDNA having a defined 5' end, said 5' end being the first deoxynucleotide of the sequence coding for said pre-proinsulin.'

The invention of claim 1 was a genetically modified microorganism – the 'DNA transfer vector'. What actually distinguished this microorganism from its pre-genetically modified state, and what made it industrially useful by producing pre-proinsulin (something which in its pre-genetically manipulated state it would not do) was the biological information that was inserted into it. While this suggests that the 'DNA transfer vector' of claim 1 was an 'invention' within the ambit of the US Supreme Court's ruling in *Chakrabarty*, it was not. Unfortunately what the USPTO examiner overlooked was that the end result of the invention, pre-proinsulin, had a natural precedent. Pre-proinsulin was a naturally existing substance (messenger RNA or mRNA) produced during the production of insulin by the human body. It was an intermediate product of human insulin production. More than that, the pre-proinsulin was already known to science. That was not the case in *Chakrabarty*.

The insertion of a 'DNA transfer vector' which contained sufficient parts of the complementary DNA (cDNA) corresponding to the DNA of the human insulin gene for it to produce pre-proinsulin (an mRNA of insulin) was, by comparison, simply elementary. It merely replicated nature. Indeed there was nothing to distinguish the pre-proinsulin produced by recombinant DNA technology from the pre-proinsulin produced in the human body. What was critical to claim 1 was the cDNA to the protein, and this was nothing more than a derivative of the DNA of the human insulin gene.

That this would work was quite predictable by 1984. Indeed it had been predictable since about 1973. Therefore, minus the DNA vector and the methodology pioneered by Cohen et al., the only thing that was new, as far as this invention was concerned, was the human genetic information contained within the DNA vector, and this was not something that Rutter or any of the co-inventors had actually deduced or invented. Therefore the entire invention either consisted of unpatentable subject matter (the DNA vector containing the human genetic information for pre-proinsulin) or achieved an end result that was obvious to a person of ordinary skill (the methodology of making pre-proinsulin using a DNA vector). Naturally the end product, the pre-proinsulin itself, was also identical to that which was made naturally in the human body.

ANTICIPATION AND US 4,431,740

However this was an argument that Eli Lilly (for obvious commercial reasons) was not interested in making. Rather there was another issue which Lilly preferred to rely upon in its validity attack – *anticipation*.

Lilly asserted that the amino acid sequence for human pre-proinsulin protein was well known before the patent's priority date, and therefore the genetic information (the cDNA) which corresponded to that protein and which was inserted into the 'DNA transfer vector' was not novel in 1984. According to the judge Lilly claimed that the amino acid sequence 'was reported not only in the *Atlas of Protein Sequence and Structure*, a reference book whose name is indicative of its contents, but also was reported in other literature in the discipline'. That literature included a scientific paper which was published in 1971 by Oyer et al.[53] The naturally produced protein, pre-proinsulin, was well known – even its protein sequence had been published prior to 1984. What this meant, if Lilly was right, was that there was absolutely nothing about the invention of claim 1 that was patentable.

UC disagreed. It countered that the Oyer et al publication did not publish the complete amino acid sequence and was, at best, a speculative attempt at arriving at about 90 per cent of the complete protein sequence. The trial judge was unimpressed, saying that he was 'convinced' that the protein sequence was 'known at least as early as 1971'.

This was a significant finding in itself; but with regard to patentable subject matter the evidence that Walter Gilbert,[54] an expert in molecular biology, gave was crucial in explaining the role that the pre-proinsulin protein played in the natural production of insulin and the importance of preserving the pre-proinsulin molecule if it was to fulfil its natural role. In answering why all mammals shared the same 'dibasic residues' and why it was important, Gilbert said:

> Because [that] part of the molecule has an essential function; and therefore, a mutation which changes the amino acid tends to inactivate the molecule. Part of the molecule that doesn't have an essential function, which is sort of waving in the wind over here, when you change that amino acid, it doesn't matter. But if I've got to do something very special with that piece of the molecule and I try to change it, then I'm in trouble.

What Gilbert was clearly saying was that if someone – even a Nobel prize winner – tinkered with the part of the molecule that actually made it work then the likelihood was that the molecule would be rendered useless. So, given that it was critical to the invention of claim 1 to have the recombinant pre-proinsulin mimic natural pre-proinsulin *in vivo*, it can be assumed that the genetic manipulation involved in the making of the 'DNA transfer vector' was of a rudimentary and mechanical kind – the kind performed by biological mechanics.

This evidence was however given in another context: namely with respect to whether the 1971 publication of the incomplete amino acid sequence of pre-proinsulin was sufficient to anticipate the invention of claim 1. In this respect Gilbert's evidence was 'highly persuasive', the trial judge found, because it confirmed that by 1971 'experts in the field had no reason to doubt not only the composition of the dibasic amino acid residues in human proinsulin, but also the order of those residues'. In fact so important was this part of the pre-proinsulin molecule to its biological action *in vivo* that the human insulin gene protected this highly conserved region of the molecule from mutation, with Gilbert testifying that the 'likelihood of a single mutation occurring is approximately a one percent chance in every million years'.

So if this was known to Gilbert then surely it was known to Goodman and his other co-inventors; and, if so, how could the USPTO overlook this information when examining the patent application? Clearly the patent applicant owed the USPTO a duty of candour which required the disclosure of all relevant information – positive as well as negative. The negative, in this instance, was that the amino acid sequence of the human pre-proinsulin protein was known before 1978 and, although this was different in kind from the nucleic acid sequence of the human insulin gene (and supposedly 'new' information), the relationship between a gene and a protein meant that a skilled person could extrapolate one from knowledge of the other.

Unfortunately the patent specification was deliberately written so as to downplay the significance of the amino acid sequence. It was not until an expensive patent trial, when a mountain of evidence was produced and extensive cross-examination conducted, that the truth was revealed. The trial judge concluded on the basis of this evidence 'that even UC believed that the amino acid sequence was in the art as early as 1977'.

So if UC knew this, so must have its inventors and its patent attorneys. In fact so elementary was this knowledge, apparently, that it was surprising that the USPTO examiner, Alvin E Tanenholtz, had not discovered it for himself. He had of course; and as a result he specifically required that the claims be limited in their scope so as to surrender coverage of DNA to pre-proinsulin which encoded a fusion protein. This limitation, the trial judge found, was also known and accepted by UC; so, while he held that the '740 patent was not invalid on this ground because of the limitation, he also held that Lilly did not infringe since its process for making human insulin did not make or use DNA constructs or microorganisms.

Anticipation was not the only ground of invalidity that Lilly relied upon. It also alleged that there had been inequitable conduct in the procurement of US 4,652,525 and US 4,431,740; that is it alleged that UC had failed to disclose material information, or submitted false material information, with an *intent to mislead* the USPTO.

INEQUITABLE CONDUCT AND US 4,652,525

It will be recalled that Paul Berg and some of America's most distinguished molecular biologists of the day[55] had signed and published a letter entitled *Potential Biohazards of Recombinant DNA Molecules*.[56] The letter communicated a recommendation that they had made to the NIH that researchers be compelled to seek ethical clearance before embarking upon experiments involving the genetic manipulation of biological materials 'until attempts have been made to evaluate the hazards and some resolutions of the outstanding questions has been achieved'. Acting upon their recommendation the NIH subsequently established the Recombinant DNA Molecule Program Advisory Committee, and on 23 June 1976 safety guidelines were published by this Committee. Under these guidelines any institution that was funded by the NIH had to appoint a principal investigator who was responsible for supervizing 'the safety performance of the staff to ensure the required safety practices and techniques employed'. The UC's animal experiments regarding pre-proinsulin were NIH-funded and were conducted subject to these guidelines.

The problem, as alluded to in the letter from Cook-Deegan (opposite), was that the plasmid which the UC researchers used in their initial experiments, pBR322 (an E. coli plasmid developed by Boyer), had not yet been authorized for use under the guidelines, and Lilly argued that these experiments had been deliberately concealed from the USPTO in order to avoid inculpating the university and the inventors in this breach. Lilly pleaded that this concealment amounted to a material non-disclosure made with an intent to mislead the USPTO, rendering the patent unenforcable.

The trial judge agreed. He said, 'we find Rutter and Goodman's trial testimony regarding the letters not credible' and, worse, 'Goodman and Rutter did not decide to abandon use of the pBR322 DNA clones after they learned of pBR322's uncertified status'. This led the trial judge to conclude 'by clear and convincing evidence that UC representatives continued to use at least the fruits of the uncertified plasmid in sequencing experiments well beyond the time they learned that such use was inappropriate'.

What a *Science* reporter, Nicholas Wade, had unearthed during his investigations (as a result of a tip-off which probably came from Goodman's own laboratory at UC) was that UC's scientists had given scant regard to these safety guidelines, and that they had then tried to cover their tracks by writing self-serving letters to each other (which they had a reasonable expectation of relying upon) to explain away the impropriety of their actions to internal investigating regulators. Lilly then relied on the *Science*

BOX 9.4 'INSULIN GENE PATENT LITIGATION'

Science, Vol 278, 24 October 1997, pp. 560–561

'I found Eliot Marshall's article (News, 22 Aug., p. 1028) about the 1977 cloning of the rat insulin gene and the subsequent patent litigation engrossing. However, some remaining uncertainties need to be resolved.

1. If the letters Judge Hugh Dillin characterized as "smoking guns" were intended to make a record of what transpired, why were the letters and the events they recorded never mentioned in the 14 October 1977 memo by William Rutter and Howard Goodman? The University of California, San Francisco, biosafety committee and the National Institutes of Heath (NIH) administrators investigating the events surely would have found the letters directly pertinent. The statement by Rutter and Goodman in the NIH files says nothing about retaining DNA.

2. Was the DNA from the original pBR322 experiment retained or not? If so, what was done with it? The chronology is puzzling. It seems that destruction of the original pBR322 clones happened on 19 March and the registered letters saying that not all the DNA was destroyed were dated several days later. But the claim seems to be that DNA was neither retained nor used.

3. What are the accession numbers of the pMB9 deposits at the American Type Culture Collection (ATCC) mentioned in the final paragraph of the article? Sequencing the original pMB9 clones might indeed resolve some of the controversy (although, depending on any subcloning process details, it might not). I asked ATCC staff about these, but to date they have not been able to identify any such deposits.

Robert Mullan Cook-Deegan
Director, National Cancer Policy Board,
Institute of Medicine, and
Commission on Life Sciences,
National Academy of Sciences,
Washington, DC 20418, USA'

article, entitled 'Recombinant DNA: NIH Rules Broken in Insulin Gene Project',[57] as the first step in building its case against UC.

BOX 9.5 'RECOMBINANT DNA: NIH RULES BROKEN IN INSULIN GENE PROJECT'

Science, Vol 197 (30 September 1977) pp. 1342–1345

'UCSF's pre-eminence in the gene-splicer's art has brought it some mixed blessings. Because of the practical implications of what its researchers are doing, a company called Genentech has established a relationship with Herbert Boyer, one of the pioneers of the technique. Members of the insulin team have set up a non-profit corporation, the California Institute for Genetic Research. These commercial developments are a tribute to the department's success, but have also created internal stresses. "Capitalism sticking its nose into the lab has tainted interpersonal relationships – there are a number of people who feel rather strongly that there should be no commercialization of human insulin," says UCSF microbiologist David Martin.'

The relevant experiment using pBR322, which was not approved under the safety guidelines until 7 July 1977, was conducted in early 1977 and the results published in an article by Ullrich et al, entitled 'Rat Insulin Genes: Construction of Plasmids Containing the Coding Sequences'.[58] According to the article the experiment was conducted using plasmid pMB9, a plasmid which had been approved under the safety guidelines on 18 April 1977. The objective of the experiment, as stated in the article, was '[t]o determine the structure of the insulin gene . . . [and] to investigate the possibility of the synthesis of insulin in an alternative biological system such as bacteria'.[59] To do this they used rat insulin mRNA to isolate the cDNA of the rat insulin gene. Practically speaking they were inserting rat genetic material into a bacterium.

Suspicions were aroused in UC when the experiment was successfully completed using pMB9 within a matter of weeks. Normally these kinds of experiments would take much longer. The implication was that the experimental data described in Ullrich et al were derived from an experiment conducted before approval had been given to use pMB9. What subsequently transpired was that it was not the pMB9 experiment data that had been used at all, but the pBR322 experimental data. The impact of this breach, however serious from an ethical perspective, had not resulted in bio-hazard breach. Nonetheless, as Wade pointed out, what really troubled everyone was 'the possibility that the insulin team [at UC] might have gained an unfair advantage over other researchers who had abided by the NIH rules'.[60] This was a significant advantage, especially as evidence from the trial revealed that within days of the experiment's completion Goodman had approached both Genentech and Lilly, companies which had interests in the commercial production of human insulin, with the objective of commercializing the research results obtained using the pBR322 data. According to the trial judge, Goodman had called Robert Swanson, Genentech's CEO, the day after the experiment had been completed and attended a meeting on 12 March 1977 at Genentech during which, according to Goodman's own notes, discussions were had that raised issues of 'money for salaries, supplies, equipment, shares (common) . . . [and] consulting for me'. During another meeting he attended at Lilly on 14 March 1977 Goodman admittedly 'told those present that what he wanted in exchange for what he had to offer included "money for lab" and "consulting"'.

It transpired that Goodman did not act alone. Rutter was also involved, and, according to the trial judge, although he 'was not present at the first' Genentech meeting, 'Rutter was involved in all subsequent meetings'. This finding undermined Rutter's credibility because during the trial evidence was tendered of his testimony given to a US Senate Committee where he denied 'that continued use of the fruits of the pBR322 research was driven by commercial interests'. Clearly that is precisely what drove the experiment forward.

If true, these allegations were very damaging to UC because it was the experimental data in Ullrich et al that were, according to Lilly, 'material to patentability of the '525 patent'. Indeed the trial judge relied on Goodman's own notes that recorded a telephone call to Swanson on 15 March 1977 to come to the same conclusion. Goodman wrote: 'Problem in Boyer plasmid. Lay low. Not approved. Can't apply for patent yet'.

The trial judge thereupon held that there was:

> a substantial likelihood that a reasonable examiner would have considered UC's unauthorized use of pBR322 important in his patentability determination . . . [and] [c]onsidering the admissions contained in the exchange of letters between Rutter and Goodman, we find no room for doubt that UC's failure to reveal its unauthorized use of pBR322 was intentional . . . [and] was meant to deceive or mislead the PTO examiner.[61]

The judge believed that 'UC was aware of its violation of the NIH safety guidelines', and that its motivation for deliberately misleading the patent examiner was its concern 'that the PTO would endorse neither its experimental use of uncertified pBR322 nor its use of the results of that experiment in the '525 patent application'.

In light of this decision UC had no choice but to appeal to the CAFC;[62] although the CAFC reversed the trial judge with respect to his findings on inequitable conduct, it lost the appeal on all other issues. The result left UC with a legal bill of approximately US$12 million and one patent which was not infringed. Apart from losing substantial patent revenues, the CAFC's reversal on inequitable conduct did not ameliorate the damage done to the reputation of UC's scientists, as the reversal was allowed on a technicality. Essentially the evidence about the misuse of pBR322 was not, as a matter of law, of the kind that a reasonable examiner would have considered to be material to patentability simply because 'UC got no advantage in the patent examining process'.[63]

THE HUMAN BREAST AND OVARIAN CANCER GENE MUTATIONS

Like Boyer, Rutter and others, who had started as scientists at American universities and now had their own companies, by 1991 Gilbert, the Nobel prize-winning expert whom Judge Hugh Dillin was to find so credible in 1995 in the UC and Lilly battle over pre-proinsulin, had also amassed a fortune thanks to patents. Biogen, a company which he co-founded in 1978, had made him a multi-millionaire (with a market capitalization in 2008 of about US$19 billion) and he used his newly found wealth, together with his growing business experience, to find new ventures in the field of biotechnology or genomics, a term that by the early 1990s was being bandied about by venture capitalists to describe a field which offered potential. Biotechnology companies were now genomic companies.

In May 1991 Mark Skolnick, a scientist from the University of Utah, and Peter Meldrum, a venture capitalist, formed Myriad Genetics, Inc. Within a year Gilbert had joined Myriad as a 'founding scientist' and became Vice-Chairman of the company's board of directors, as had Kevin Kimberlin, another venture capitalist whom Gilbert already knew.

Myriad was formed for a specific purpose: to identify the gene on human chromosome 17 which was linked to breast and ovarian cancer. The idea was to patent and exploit this genetic information by using 'genomics' to test women's genetic susceptibility to these diseases. The promoters of Myriad, all of them men, realized that there was a fortune to be made if they could control the patent rights to the genetic marker of these human diseases – mainly women's diseases.

It was Mary-Claire King who, in 1990, after 16 years of research and then a professor of genetics and epidemiology at UCSF, discovered that hereditary breast and ovarian cancers were linked to a single gene on human chromosome 17. The head start that King had given everyone by narrowing the search down to one human chromosome was invaluable, but on the basis that the first and only prize goes to those who isolate the gene, her contribution to scientific and medical knowledge was to be regarded as incidental. Skolnick's experience in the 1980s, after he discovered the link between neurofibromatosis, another human genetic disease, and chromosome 17, made him determined to win the race to the gene and patent it. According to Skolnick, 'it was a bit of a disappointment to be left out of really the final prize of discovering what was the gene that caused the disease [neurofibromatosis] that we'd been working on now for ten years'. That prize, 'the real fruit', said Skolnick, was in 'isolating and discovering the underlying gene'.[64]

By 1991 there was no doubt about what was to be done with this genetic information. Whoever it was who isolated the gene to breast and ovarian cancer would use that information to monopolize the market for a genetic test for those diseases. It was hardly surprising therefore that Skolnick was 'able to convince investors that we had a reasonable chance of finding that gene'. Of course they did – King had given them a treasure map.

In his own words he described the 'prize': it was not an invention, it was 'that gene'. So this was no more than a treasure hunt – one that took place after King had given everyone the map to the island on which the treasure was buried. What helped Skolnick find it before anyone else was his team and their tools. Skolnick subsequently said:

> We took an approach that used what are called bacterial artificial chromosomes, or BACs, where some of the competitors used yeast artificial chromosomes, or YACs, and as fate would have it, there was a hole, not well covered by YACs, where the BRCA1 gene was, and it was covered by BACs. So were we lucky that it was covered by the reagent we chose to use, are we, were we smart in choosing a reagent that covered the gene? Is the cup half full, is the cup half empty?[65]

The prize, according to Skolnick, was the whole gene, and once his team at the University of Utah had isolated it they went about patenting it.

PATENTING THE BRCA 1 GENE IN THE UNITED STATES AND EUROPE

Myriad called the breast and ovarian cancer susceptibility gene on chromosome 17 'BRCA 1'. It is a 220-kilodalton nuclear phosphoprotein and in its normal state suppresses the production of tumours. However inherited mutations of this gene impair this natural function, and in this altered state it accounts for about 7 to 10 per cent of all breast and ovarian cancers. Women who have inherited mutations to this gene have a lifetime risk of breast cancer of between 56 and 87 per cent and a lifetime risk of ovarian cancer of between 27 and 44 per cent. One thing is clear: no one invented the gene containing these mutations. They are a natural by-product, albeit deleterious, of human reproduction.

Despite this, on 2 December 1997 the USPTO granted Myriad its first US patent over this gene and its genetic mutations. US 5,693,473, entitled 'Linked breast and ovarian cancer susceptibility gene' defined the principal invention as '[a]n isolated DNA comprising an altered BRCA1 DNA having at least one of the alterations set forth in Tables 12A, 14, 18 or 19 with the proviso that the alteration is not a deletion of four nucleotides corresponding to base numbers 4184-4187 in SEQ. ID. NO:1'.

There was no question about what it claimed as an invention – the human gene with genetic mutations called BRCA 1. The relevant DNA was isolated, but essentially and practically this was a claim to DNA that contained the very same genetic information that exists in the genomes of some people, as a result of which some are predisposed to breast and ovarian cancer. This DNA was not something that the named inventors either conceived of or invented or made. They merely discovered the gene that contained these genetic mutations on human chromosome 17 – the very same chromosome which only a few years earlier King had identified and linked to breast and ovarian cancers.

In Europe it took the European Patent Office (EPO) until 28 November 2001 to grant Myriad EP 0,705,902, entitled '17q-Linked breast and ovarian cancer susceptibility gene'. This patent was about the same invention as US 5,693,473, but it was the second patent to issue, the first being EP 0,699,754 entitled 'Method for diagnosing a predisposition for breast and ovarian cancer' and granted on 10 January 2001.

Claim 1 of the '902 patent defined the invention as '[a]n isolated nucleic acid which comprises a coding sequence for the BRCA1 polypeptide defined by the amino acid sequence set forth in SEQ. ID. NO:2, or an amino acid sequence with at least 95% identity to the amino acid sequence of SEQ. ID. NO:2'. Claim 2 defined it as '[a]n isolated nucleic acid as claimed in claim 1 which is a DNA comprising the nucleotide sequence set forth in SEQ. ID. NO:1 from nucleotide 120 to nucleotide 5708 or a corresponding RNA'.

SEQ. ID. NO:1 is the genetic sequence which corresponds to the human BRCA 1 gene. It is a double-stranded molecule made of cDNA (complementary DNA) consisting of 5914 base pairs (that is the sequence of nucleotides A, T, G, and C in base pairs which Watson and Crick deduced to be in a helical formation). SEQ. ID. NO:2 on the other hand is the amino acid sequence for the protein which is coded for by the nucleotide sequence of SEQ. ID. NO:1. It consists of 1864 amino acids.

Again there was no question about what these two claims were about – the BRCA 1 gene with genetic mutations and the protein that the gene coded for. Again both were naturally made, except that the cDNA was made by humans. Apart from this the genetic information contained in the molecule described as SEQ. ID. NO:1 was identical to the defective human gene.

As an aside, while US 5,693,473 listed Donna Shattuck-Eidens, Jacques Simard, Francine Durocher, Mitsuuru Emi and Yusuke Nakamura as the sole inventors, EP 0,705,902 listed Donna Shattuck-Eidens as an inventor but not any of the other inventors named on the US patent, but it did list Mark Skolnick, David Goldgar, Yoshio Miki, Jeff Swensen, Alexander Kamb, Keith Harshman, Sean Tavtigen, Roger Wiseman and Andrew Futreal. The reason for this discrepancy is that on 20 January 1998 the USPTO granted Myriad its second US patent, US 5,710,001 entitled '17q-Linked breast and ovarian cancer susceptibility gene'. Claim 1 defined the principal invention as:

> A method for screening a tumor sample from a human subject for a somatic alteration in a BRCA1 gene in said tumor which comprises gene comparing a first sequence selected from the group consisting of a BRCA1 gene from said tumor sample, BRCA1 RNA from said tumor sample and BRCA1 cDNA made from mRNA from said tumor sample with a second sequence selected from the group consisting of BRCA1 gene from a nontumor sample of said subject, BRCA1 RNA from said nontumor sample and BRCA1 cDNA made from mRNA from said nontumor sample, wherein a difference in the sequence of the BRCA1 gene, BRCA1 RNA or BRCA1 cDNA from said tumor sample from the sequence of the BRCA1 gene, BRCA1 RNA or BRCA1 cDNA from said nontumor sample indicates a somatic alteration in the BRCA1 gene in said tumor sample.

Indeed all of the claims in US 5,710,001 were to methods. None were to either the BRAC 1 gene or the protein that it coded for. Nonetheless US 5,710,001 corresponded to EP 0,705,902, but in name only. The claims, or the inventions as defined in those claims, were quite different. US 5,693,473 actually corresponded more closely to EP 0,705,902, and even more confusingly EP 0,699,754 corresponded more closely to US 5,710,001. So the relevant US and European patents over the BRCA 1 *gene* were US 5,693,473 and EP 0,705,902 and over the *diagnostic method* for screening breast and ovarian cancer they were US 5,710,001 and EP 0,699,754. (There are legal implications which flow from this, but these will not be discussed in this book: they are mentioned because it is relevant to understand why the titles of the US and EP patents to the same inventions differed.)

Ignoring the patents for the diagnostic methods and focusing only on the patents for the BRCA 1 gene, it is fair to say that what Myriad had patented was a cause of human disease in the form of a defective human gene. Accordingly it has a 20-year patent monopoly on the components of that gene and the protein that it codes for. It may not own the BRCA 1 gene in the sense that one does in terms of physical property; after all those people who carry that gene in their genomes own that gene and the potential consequences. However in the sense that Myriad can control what others can do with the genetic information contained within the genetic components of the gene, to all intents and purposes it has the exclusive rights to the BRCA 1 gene and the corresponding protein for 20 years. That is the consequence of these two patents in the US. In Europe, however the situation is not as certain as powerful opponents have objected to Myriad's European patents, and that fight is continuing.

THE INVENTORSHIP DISPUTE IN THE UNITED STATES

The conception and reduction to practice of an invention are key thresholds to inventorship in the United States. It is only when both of these events have occurred that the invention is complete; and under the first-to-invent patent system, which applies only in the United States, this means that it is the first person or persons to satisfy these thresholds that have the right to a US patent. So when *Science* announced on 14 September 1994 that it was to publish a paper about the cloning of the BRCA 1 gene in the 7 October issue,[66] the race to patent the BRCA 1 gene was over. In fact so news-breaking was the announcement that *Science* released the paper to journalists the day before it made the official announcement. The media frenzy which followed was in the expectation that the cloning of the BRCA 1 gene would lead to a universal genetic test for all breast and ovarian cancer. Unfortunately this was not be. For the 173 000 American women each year who contract a non-hereditary form of breast cancer this news was very disappointing. In the same issue of *Science,* a paper authored by Andrew Futreal, a member, and others wrote a paper entitled 'BRCA 1 Mutations in Primary Breast and Ovarian Carcinomas'[67] confirmed that the gene was linked only to hereditary forms of these diseases. The authors concluded, 'the data from primary tumors . . . raise the possibility that BRCA 1 may have only a minor role in sporadic breast and ovarian tumor formation. . . . Ultimately, it will be important to identify the other genes in the pathway of tumor suppression in which BRCA 1 participates'.

Despite the fact that Skolnick's team was actually unsuccessful in identifying the gene causative of non-hereditary forms of breast and ovarian cancer, representing about 95 per cent of these cancers, they were the first to show a link between the BRCA 1 gene and hereditary forms of these cancers, and on this basis alone made a claim to the gene and all its known and potential uses.

The problem was that some of Skolnick's team were left off the patent application which was filed with the USPTO on 12 August 1994 (US 289,221). What Myriad and the University of Utah had attempted to do to the NIH was what Chiron had successfully done to the CDC, only this time Myriad was not as lucky as Chiron. Roger Wiseman and Andrew Futreal from the National Institute of Environmental Health Sciences, a division of the NIH, had done some of the key sequencing work; so the NIH threw down the gauntlet by filing its own patent application. This posed a significant threat to the validity of any patent that might have been granted to Myriad and the university. Sensing danger Myriad and the University of Utah took a pragmatic approach, and within six months had resolved the inventorship dispute with the NIH without the need for litigation. As a result the patent application was amended to include those previously left off and the US Government became a co-patent applicant with an entitlement to a quarter of all the patent revenues.

That the US Government itself had an ownership interest in the patent may have been fair enough in those circumstances, but only if the patent application was with respect to something that was patentable subject matter. When it came to the BRCA 1 gene however, this was another matter. Indeed one has to question the ability of US government departments to be impartial observers with respect to this issue, given the obvious conflict of interest which ownership of these types of patents create.

THE PATENTING OF THE BRCA 2 GENE IN THE UNITED STATES

Futreal's observations in his 1994 *Science* paper that it would be necessary to 'identify other genes in the pathway of tumor suppression' made sense, especially as the location of the BRCA 2 gene had been pinpointed on human chromosome 13 by Mark Stratton's team at the British Institute of Cancer Research. Stratton's team was at that time still part of Skolnick's team and, according to Skolnick, getting the BRCA 2 gene 'was the local next step', particularly given that Myriad's commercial objective was 'to offer a complete diagnostic . . . for both genes, not just one gene'. In the paper authored by Wooster et al. and entitled 'Localization of a Breast Cancer Susceptibility Gene, BRCA 2, to Chromosome 13q 12-13', published in *Science* on 30 September 1994,[68] Stratton's team had effectively done what King had done with BRCA 1. The race to patent BRCA 2 was now on.

Unfortunately for Skolnick one consequence of the inventorship brawl that followed the patenting of BRCA 1 was a growing disquiet in Europe over Myriad's commercialization plans for the proposed diagnostic test. Politically it was no longer seen as appropriate for European scientists to be aiding American industry to win a race which was clearly going to produce a financial bonanza for Myriad and, now, the US Government. This political tension, together with the implications for European science and European health care budgets, meant that Stratton and Skolnick had to part company. The rivalry between these two groups became intense and for Myriad, the entire commercialization strategy of which would be in tatters if it did not obtain the patent rights to the BRCA 2 gene, winning the patent rights to BRCA 2 was crucial.

It actually took Skolnick's team only another 14 months to clone the BRCA 2 gene. By December 1995 Myriad, Endo Recherche, the University of Pennsylvania and the HSC Research and Development Limited Partnership had applied for a US patent over the BRCA 2 gene, and on 17 November 1998 the USPTO granted Myriad US 5,837,492, entitled 'Chromosome 13-linked breast cancer susceptibility gene'. Claim 1 defined the invention: '[a]n isolated DNA molecule coding for a BRCA 2 polypeptide, said DNA molecule comprising a nucleic acid sequence encoding the amino acid sequence set forth in SEQ ID NO:2'. Claim 2 was defined as '[t]he isolated DNA molecule of claim 1, wherein said DNA molecule comprises the nucleotide sequence set forth in SEQ ID NO:1'.

According to the patent specification, '[t]he coding sequence for a BRCA 2 polypeptide is shown in SEQ ID NO:1 and FIG. 3, with the amino acid sequence shown in SEQ ID NO:2'. In other words both claims were over the same BRCA 2 gene even though claim 1 defined the 'invention' by reference to the protein (amino acid sequence) coded by the BRCA 2 gene and claim 2 defined the same 'invention' by reference to the DNA of the BRCA 2 gene.

The problem for Myriad was that Stratton's team claimed to have done the same. In December 1995 *Nature* published a letter by Stratton's group entitled *Identification of the breast cancer susceptibility gene BRCA 2*.[69] Skolnick's team however had claimed to have beaten Stratton's team to the prize; the day before the *Nature* announcement Skolnick's team announced that it had cloned the BRCA 2 gene and deposited the entire gene in GenBank, a genetic database. So another dispute arose over who was entitled to the patent rights over the BRCA 2 gene.

It took a little longer for Skolnick's team to present the results of its work, given the strict requirement of secrecy required by the patent system, but eventually in a letter published in *Nature Genetics* authored by Tavtigian et al,[70] it claimed, 'Wooster et al reported a partial BRCA 2 sequence and six mutations', but that this represented only 'two thirds of the coding sequence and [only] 8 out of 27 exons were isolated and screened'. Had Stratton's group been defeated? Skolnick's group claimed to have won the race but the jostling over the patent prize was far from over.

In fact Cancer Research Campaign Technology Limited (CRCTL), an English company which represents the commercial interests of Stratton's Institute of Cancer Research, and Duke University, which is where Futreal (and also an original member of Skolnick's BRCA 1 team) was from, had also applied for a patent over the BRCA 2 gene.[71] Effectively Stratton's team claimed patent priority over the BRCA 2 gene, outside the United States and under Europe's first-to-file patent system, because its British patent application was filed on 23 November 1995, whereas Skolnick's team filed its US patent application (US 573,779) on 18 December 1995, some three weeks later. Stratton's team then used its British patent application to apply for a US patent, and on 4 April 2000 the USPTO granted both CRTCL and Duke University US 6,045,997. Claim 1 of this US patent defined the invention: '[a] nucleic acid molecule consisting of the sequence set forth in SEQ ID NO:1 . . . or portion of said sequence of at least 20 consecutive bases'.

Even though the patent specification conceded that the complete BRCA 2 gene sequence was not disclosed, it argued that the inventors were justified in making a claim to the entire BRCA 2 gene because, '[f]ollowing the initial sequencing of the BRCA 2 gene described above, and using the information contained in FIGS. 1 to 3 (SEQ ID NOS: 1-14), the skilled person could readily assemble the full length sequence of the BRCA 2 gene included in the Internet sequence using the techniques described in detail below'. Indeed there was a precedent for this, as Chiron had disclosed only 77 per cent of the RNA sequence of HCV, but nevertheless claimed anything that shared at least a 40 per cent homology with a small section of the NS-4 region of the genome. So the USPTO obliged, and of course this did not make Myriad's commercialization plans any easier. The breadth of the claims that were granted by the USPTO in US 5,837,492 and US 6,047,997 meant that both Myriad and CRCTL had patent rights in the United States over the BRCA 2 gene.

BOX 9.6   '"LEAK" RUMOURS FUEL DEBATE ON GENE PATENT'

Nature, Vol 379, 15 February 1996, 574

'Two research groups potentially engaged in a priority dispute over the discovery of the second hereditary breast cancer gene, BRCA 2, have entered negotiations over the terms under which each may let the other look at data used in preparing patent applications that were filed only days apart. . . . In addition to indicating whether the patent claims are in conflict, the British scientists may be hoping that access to Myriad's patent data will throw some light on the truth or otherwise of rumours that the US team was assisted in its search for the full BRCA 2 sequence by a "leak" of critical information from one of the teams with which they were collaborating.'

In what was a case of *déjà vu*, Myriad was soon potentially facing a repetition of its US litigation. OncorMed, Inc, a company which had also obtained a US patent over the BRCA 1 diagnostic, brought an infringement action against Myriad after the USPTO granted it US 5,654,155 on 5 August 1997, some four months before it granted Myriad US 5,693,473 on 2 December 1997. Then on that very day Myriad retaliated by filing its own patent infringement proceedings against OncorMed, but, fortunately for Myriad and possibly the shareholders of OncorMed, the litigation was soon resolved on 18 May 1998 with Myriad acquiring all of OncorMed's patents.

On this occasion however Myriad did not face an aggressive litigator; and indeed its own aggressive litigation threats in the two years before the CRCTL US patent was granted effectively delivered the US diagnostics market for BRCA 1 and BRCA 2 to Myriad.

THE PATENTING OF THE BRCA 2 GENE IN EUROPE

Mike Stratton and CRCTL had declared war on Skolnick and Myriad and he and other like-minded scientists were determined to ensure that Myriad did not obtain a stranglehold on breast and ovarian cancer diagnostics. They opposed the patenting of the BRCA 1 gene and believed that it would have been better for the genetic information to be freely available. However faced with the realization that the most strategic way to stop

Myriad achieving its goal was themselves to apply for a patent over the BRCA 2 gene, when Stratton's team had made the critical breakthrough in September 1995 that is precisely what they did. This led to the grant, on 11 February 2004, by the EPO of EP 0,858,467 entitled 'Materials and methods relating to the identification and sequencing of the BRCA 2 cancer susceptibility gene and uses thereof'. The named inventors were Phillip Futreal, Richard Wooster, Alan Ashworth and Michael Stratton and the owners were CRCTL and Duke University.

For Myriad, which had also been granted a European patent for the BRCA 2 gene on 8 January 2003, this was not good news. The EPO granted Myriad EP 0,785,216 entitled, 'Chromosome 13-linked breast cancer susceptibility gene BRCA 2'. The named inventors were Sean Tavtigian, Alexander Kamb, Jacques Simard, Fergus Couch, Johanna Rommens and Barbara Weber and the owners were Myriad, Endo Recherhe, the University of Pennsylvania and HSC Research and Development. The patent defined the invention in claim 1 as '[a]n isolated DNA comprising a cDNA coding for a BRCA 2 polypeptide defined by the amino acid sequence set forth in SEQ. ID. NO:2 or a corresponding RNA'.

Myriad also faced other foes across Europe. From Austria came the Austrian Society for Human Genetics. From Belgium came the Belgian Society of Human Genetics, Vlaamse Anti-Cancer League and the Belgian Federation Anti-Cancer League. From the Czech Republic came the Society of Medical Genetics. From Denmark came the Danish Society for Medical Genetics. From France came the Curie Institute, the Public Hospitals of Paris, the Gustave-Roussy Institute and the French Society of Human Genetics. From Germany came the German Association for Human Genetics. From Greece came the Greek National Centre for Scientific Research. From Italy came the Italian Society of Human Genetics, the Angela Serra Cancer Research Association and the Italian Association for the Study of Gastrointestinal Hereditary Tumours. From The Netherlands came the Foundation of Associations of Clinical Genetics. From Switzerland came the Swiss Society of Medical Genetics and from the UK came the British Society for Human Genetics. They all formally opposed the grant of this patent to Myriad and, although the process under the European Patent Convention (EPC) is a post-grant procedure, it is equivalent to an appeal which involves a complete re-examination of the patent by the EPO.

In a tactical response to this opposition, Myriad amended its European patent during oral opposition proceedings at the EPO in January 2005. Claim 1, and now the only claim, defined the invention as follows:

Use of an isolated nucleic acid which comprises the coding sequence set forth in SEQ. ID. NO: 1 from nucleotide position 229 to nucleotide position 10482 and further comprising the mutation associated with a predisposition to breast cancer, wherein T at nucleotide position 6174 is deleted, for diagnosing a predisposition to breast cancer in Ashkenazi-Jewish women in vitro.

By effect of this amendment Myriad was substantially limiting its patent monopoly over the BRCA 2 gene in Europe to women of Ashkenazi-Jewish descent. Apart from representing a significant reduction in scope, it was unprecedented for a patent monopoly to apply only to a specific race of people, and it prompted the European Society of Human Genetics to claim: 'Jewish women in Europe may face genetic discrimination in access to breast cancer diagnosis'.[72] Given that only one in 100 Ashkenazi-Jewish women actually carried the BRCA 2 gene, this was an absurd outcome. Claus Bartram, the Director of the Institute of Human Genetics at the University of Heidelberg, described the Myriad patent as 'nonsense'.

Nonetheless on 29 June 2005 the EPO decided to uphold Myriad's BRCA 2 patent. While this was a technical win for Myriad, the Opposition had inflicted irreparable damage on its commercialization plans in Europe. According to Peter Rigby, the Executive Director of the Institute of Cancer Research, the grant of a European patent to CRCTL meant that the BRCA 2 gene would be 'freely available to our colleagues throughout Europe to research'.

This gene war however continues. Myriad has opposed CRCTL's BRCA 2 patent; and Europe's opposition to Myriad's other BRCA 1 patents continues. It will be some time before the final outcome is known.

NOTES

1. Source: 'The True Cost of Gene Patents', Greenpeace, 2004. Available at http://weblog. greenpeace.org/ge/archives/1study_True_Costs_Gene_Patents.pdf.
2. Hopkins, MM, S Mahdi, SM Thomas and P Patel (2006), *The Patenting of Human DNA: Global Trends in Public and Private Sector Activity* (Project Report, SPRU, Science and Technology Policy Research, University of Sussex). Available at http://www.sussex.ac.uk/spru/1-4-3-1-2.html. For further details of the report's findings see Chapter 7.
3. Chiron SEC Form:10-Q Filing; 7 November 2001: 'Chiron was involved in certain previously reported litigation in the U.S. and several other countries with F. Hoffman-LaRoche AG and related foreign entities (collectively "Roche") concerning infringement and/or validity of certain patents related to HCV and HIV technology. In October 2000, Chiron and Roche resolved all litigation regarding HCV and HIV nucleic acid technology. Among the settlement provisions, Chiron granted Roche licenses to manufacture and sell HCV and HIV nucleic acid clinical diagnostic tests. In May 2001, Chiron further granted Roche licenses to manufacture and sell HCV and HIV nucleic acid tests for blood screening.'
4. Cohen SN, ACY Chang, HC Boyer and RB Helling (1973), 'Construction of Biologically Functional Bacterial Plasmids In Vitro', *Proceedings of the National Academy of Sciences of the United States of America*, **70** (11), 3240–44.

5. Morrow, JF, SN Cohen, ACY Chang, HW Boyer, HM Goodman and RB Helling (1974), 'Replication and Transcription of Eukaryotic DNA in Escherichia coli', *Proceedings of the National Academy of Sciences of the United States of America*, **71** (5), 1743–7.

6. Sulston, J (2006), 'Staking Claims in the biotechnology Klondike', *Bulletin of the World Health Organization*, **84** (5), 412–13.

7. *Amgen Inc v Chugai Pharmaceutical and Genetics Institute* (1991) 927 F 2d 1200.

8. *Amgen Inc v Chugai Pharmaceutical and Genetics Institute* (1989) 13 USPQ 2D 1737.

9. Above n 7,1206.

10. Above n 8, at page note 243–4.

11. With this principle in mind in *Smithkline Beecham Corp v Apotex Inc* (2005) 403 F 3d 1331 Judge Gajarsa had raised the issue of patentable subject matter *sua sponte* (that is of his own volition) because in his words there was a 'significant public policy interest in removing invalid patents from the public arena'. According to Gajarsa, by effect of US Supreme Court authority 'established long ago', whether something 'is patentable or not is always open to the consideration of the court, whether the point is raised by the answer or not'.

12. *In re Bell* (1993) 991 F 2d 781: 'Bell does not claim all of the nucleic acids that might potentially code for IGF. Neither does Bell claim all nucleic acids coding for a protein having the biological activity of IGF. Rather, Bell claims only the human nucleic acid sequences coding for IGF. Absent anything in the cited prior art suggesting which of the possible sequences suggested by Rinderknecht corresponds to the IGF gene, the PTO has not met its burden of establishing that the prior art would have suggested the claimed sequences. This is not to say that a gene is never rendered obvious when the amino acid sequence of its coded protein is known. Bell concedes that in a case in which a known amino acid sequence is specified exclusively by unique codons, the gene might have been obvious. Such a case is not before us. Here, where Rinderknecht suggests a vast number of possible nucleic acid sequences, we conclude that the claimed human sequences would not have been obvious.'

13. *In re Deuel* (1995) 51 F 3d 1552: 'The redundancy of the genetic code precluded contemplation of or focus on the specific cDNA molecules of claims 5 and 7. Thus, one could not have conceived the subject matter of claims 5 and 7 based on the teachings in the cited prior art because, until the claimed molecules were actually isolated and purified, it would have been highly unlikely for one of ordinary skill in the art to contemplate what was ultimately obtained. What cannot be contemplated or conceived cannot be obvious. . . . A prior art disclosure of the amino acid sequence of a protein does not necessarily render particular DNA molecules encoding the protein obvious because the redundancy of the genetic code permits one to hypothesize an enormous number of DNA sequences coding for the protein. No particular one of these DNAs can be obvious unless there is something in the prior art to lead to the particular DNA and indicate that it should be prepared.'

14. US 4,769,238, granted 6 September 1988.

15. US 4,803,164, granted 7 February 1989.

16. See US 3,636,191 (18 January 1972) entitled 'Vaccine Against Viral Hepatitis and Process'. This patent did not however make any claim to the 'Australia antigen' in any form, but only to the use of the antigen in a process to make a vaccine and the vaccine itself.

17. 1925–; Nobel Prize, 1976. For a history of the discovery of hepatitis B, for which he was awarded the Nobel Prize see Blumberg, BS (1977), 'Australia Antigen and the Biology of Hepatitis B', *Science*, **197** (4298), 17–25, which is a copy of his Nobel lecture delivered on 13 December 1976.

18. 1923–.

19. Blumberg BS, AI Sutnick, WT London and I Millman (1970), 'Australia Antigen and Hepatitis', *New England Journal of Medicine*, **283** (7), 349–54.

20. *Chiron Corp v Organon & Others* [1994] FSR 202.

21. Since it was one of five viruses (HAV, HBV, HCV, human immunodeficiency virus (HIV) and human T-cell leukaemia virus (HTLV)) that would be screened on all human blood donations.

22. Bradley, DW et al (1979), 'Experimental Infection of Chimpanzees With Antihemophilic (Factor VIII) Materials: Recovery of Virus-Like Particles Associated with Non A, Non B Hepatitis', *Journal of Medical Virology*, 3, 253–69 and Bradley DW et al (1980), 'Non-A /Non-B Hepatitis in Experimentally Infected Chimpanzees: Cross Challenge and Electron Microscopic Studies', *Journal of Medical Virology*, 6, 185–201.

23. Australian Federal Court Transcript, NG 106/1994 *Murex Diagnostics Australia Pty Ltd v Chiron Corporation and Another*, 667.

24. Young, RA and EW Davis (1983), 'Efficient Isolation of Genes by Using Antibody Probes', *Proceedings of the National Academy of Sciences*, **80** (1), 1194–8.

25. First affidavit of Daniel Bradley, filed in *Murex Diagnostic Australia Pty Ltd v Chiron Corp* in the Federal Court of Australia, New South Wales District Registry, Action No NG 106 of 1994, para. 5.19.

26. Affidavit of Michael Houghton, ibid, para. 5.14.

27. Ibid, para. 4.1.

28. Ibid, para. 11.1.

29. Ibid, 11.7–11.

30. Affidavit of George Kuo, filed in ibid, para. 37.

31. Ibid, para. 41.

32. Ibid, 661–2.

33. Second affidavit of Daniel Bradley, filed in ibid, para. 35.

34. Ibid, para. 35.

35. Second affidavit of Gregory Reyes, filed in ibid, para. 15.

36. Ibid, 911.

37. Genelabs was subsequently acquired by Chiron Corporation on 10 March 1995. According to the press release Chiron and Genelabs 'jointly announced today the signing of a heads of agreement for a worldwide diagnostics alliance. The alliance is intended to capitalize on both companies' proprietary positions in hepatitis a large group of RNA viruses that includes the leukoviruses and lentiviruses; so called because they carry reverse transcriptase.'

38. 1931–; US Secretary of Health, Education, and Welfare 1977–9.

39. '2.3 After the effective date of this Agreement, CDC and Dr. Bradley will make Dr. Bradley and any supporting documents promptly and reasonably available to Chiron for the sole purpose of evaluating his claim to inventorship. After concluding such evaluation, Chiron may, at its discretion, (i) add Dr. Bradley to one or more Chiron Patents as an inventor if in Chiron's opinion Dr. Bradley is an inventor or (ii) submit any material information regarding inventorship to the U.S. Patent and Trademark Office. If Dr. Bradley is added as an inventor to one or more Chiron Patents, whether by Chiron or by any tribunal of competent jurisdiction, CDC and Dr. Bradley will cooperate fully with and without charge to Chiron, and execute any and all necessary and proper documents related to Chiron Patents and the assignment contained in paragraph 2.1.'

40. '2.1 CDC . . . the United States . . . and Dr. Bradley hereby forever release, discharge and assign to Chiron their entire right, title and interest in and to, any and all claims, actions and the like based in law or equity known or unknown, now existing or which might arise hereafter, (a) against Chiron or Chiron's employees (past or present), Chiron's directors (past or present) or licensees arising from actions occurring prior to the date of this Agreement and related to any collaboration among Dr. Bradley, CDC and Chiron; or (b) regarding the inventorship, ownership or control of Chiron Patents or foreign counterparts thereof. *CDC and Dr. Bradley hereby assign to Chiron any and all right title and interest in or to Chiron Patents and the inventions claimed therein*' (handwritten in italics).

41. Ibid, 667.

42. US District Court for the Northern District of California Action No. C-94-4342.

43. EP 0,318,216.

44. 'Recognizing the clinical implications of post-transfusion non-A, non-B hepatitis, physiochemically characterizing an agent not yet visualized, developing a novel approach to the molecular cloning and characterization of the genome of the causative agent of hepatitis C, and expressing virus-specific proteins that formed the basis for the first hepatitis C antibody test.'

45. Aldous J ruled: 'Chiron started work to produce a vaccine in 1989. By the middle of 1990, there were about 32 people working on the project and it became a major focus of Chiron. It has proceeded to the stage where a vaccine was tried on chimpanzees in January 1993. Up to that time, Dr Houghton estimates that something like 30 man years of qualified scientific work had been applied to the job. The tests on the chimpanzees look promising, but the trials are still continuing. Thus a vaccine may have been produced; but whether or not it will turn out to be sufficiently successful to be marketed has yet to be found out. The law requires the specification to be sufficiently detailed so that the skilled man can produce a vaccine without undue experimentation. If the description was sufficient, I would have expected a company with Chiron's expertise to be able to produce a trial vaccine without the need for 30 man years of qualified scientific work. The plaintiffs did not dispute that in normal cases the need to expend 30 man years of work would indicate that the description was insufficient, but submitted that this was an exceptional case where length of time was not an indication of insufficiency. I accept that in this case, a substantial time may be needed to test a vaccine, but 30 man years to achieve animal testing seems excessive.'

46. In 1999, Dr Michael Houghton, one of the 'inventors' of the HCV genetic products, admitted that after ten years of research there was no HCV vaccine. He said, 'There is no vaccine for HCV and the only available treatment, IFNalpha alone or in combination with ribavirin, has proven efficacious in less than 50% of patients. Given that approximately 200 million chronic HCV infections have been estimated worldwide, there is a pressing need to develop vaccination strategies aimed at preventing and possibly eradicating HCV infection. However, several major practical and scientific problems arise in designing an HCV vaccine. First, HCV is only readily detected as RNA by PCR. Second, the only species that can be infected by HCV are humans and chimpanzees. Third, the virus does not replicate efficiently in vitro. Fourth, some viral proteins have very high mutability. Last, there is little information on correlates of immunity. Although an ideal vaccine should protect from infection, in that it should elicit sterilizing immunity, this is quite an ambitious goal in the PCR era.' See Abrignani, S, M Houghton and HH Hsu (1999), 'Perspectives for a vaccine against hepatitis C virus' *Journal of Hepatology*, **31** Suppl (1), 259–63. There still is no vaccine for HCV.

47. Affidavit of Baruch S Blumberg, filed in *Murex Diagnostic Australia Pty Ltd v Chiron Corp* in the Federal Court of Australia, New South Wales District Registry, Action No NG 106 of 1994, para. 5.1.

48. EPO TBA decision T188/97 dated 8 February 2001.

49. *Genentech v Chiron Corp* (1997) 112 F 3d 495.

50. Novartis fully acquired Chiron on 20 April 2006.

51. *The Regents of the University of California v Eli Lilly & Co* (1995) US Dist LEXIS 19003.

52. The patent specification explained the distinction between human insulin, human proinsulin and human pre-proinsulin thus:
'Insulin consists of two polypeptide chains, known as the A and B chains, linked together by disulfide bridges. The A chain consists of 21 amino acids and the B chain consists of 30 amino acids. These chains are not synthesized independently in vivo but are derived from an immediate precursor, termed proinsulin: Proinsulin is a single polypeptide chain that contains a peptide, termed the C-peptide, which connects the A and B chains. See Steiner, D.F. et al., Science 157, 697 (1967). This C-peptide is excised during the packaging of insulin into the secretory granules of pancreatic B cells prior to secretion. See Tager, H.S. et al., Ann. Rev. Biochem. 43, 509 (1974). The current view of the function of the C-peptide is that it functions only in forming the three dimensional structure of the molecule. The amino acid sequence for human proinsulin, determined

by conventional techniques, is given in Table 1. In this table the B chain is amino acids 1–30, the C-peptide is amino acids 31–65 and the A chain is amino acids 66–86. . . . In the pancreatic B cells, the initial translation product is not proinsulin itself, but a pre-proinsulin that contains more than 20 additional amino acids on the amino terminus of proinsulin. See Cahn, S.J. et al., Proc. Nat. Acad. Sci. U.S.A. 73, 1964 (1976) and Lomedico, P.T. et al., Nucl. Acid Res. 3, 381 (1976). The additional amino acid sequence is termed the signal peptide. In human pre-proinsulin (see FIG. 2), the signal peptide has twenty-four amino acids and the sequence is ##STR9## The twenty-four amino acid sequence is thought to be a specific signal for the vectorial transport of the synthesized polypeptide into the endoplasmic reticulum of the B cell, and is cleaved away from proinsulin during this phase. See Blobel, G. et al., J. Cell. Biol. 67, 835 (1975).'

53. Oyer, PE, S Cho, JD Peterson and DF Steiner (1971), 'Studies on Human Proinsulin: Isolation and Amino Acid Sequences of the Human Pancreatic C-Peptide', *Journal of Biological Chemistry*, **246** (5), 1375–86.
54. 1932–; Nobel prize, 1980.
55. David Baltimore, Hebert Boyer, Stanley Cohen, Ronald Davis, David Hogness, Daniel Nathans, Richard Roblin, James Watson, Sherman Weissman and Norton Zinder.
56. Berg, P et al (1974), *Science*, **185** (4148), 303.
57. Wade, N (1977), *Science*, **197** (4311), 1342–5.
58. Ullrich, A, J Shine, J Chirgwin, R Pictet, E Tischer, WJ Rutter and H Goodman (1977), 'Rat Insulin Genes: Construction of Plasmids Containing the Coding Sequences', *Science*, New Series, **196** (4296), 1313–9.
59. Ibid, 1313.
60. *Science*, above n 57, 1345.
61. Above n 51, 19113–4.
62. *The Regents of the University of California v Eli Lilly & Co.* (1997) 119 F 3d 1559.
63. Ibid, 1571.
64. Skolnick, M (2007), 'Winning The Race to find BRCA 1', *Dolan DNA Learning Center*, available at http://www.dnai.org/text/mediashowcase/index2.html?id=316.
65. Ibid.
66. Miki, Y et al. (1994), 'A Strong Candidate for the Breast and Ovarian Cancer Susceptibility Gene BRCA 1', *Science*, New Series, **266** (5182), 66–71.
67. Futreal, PA et al (1994), *Science*, **266** (5182), 120–122.
68. Wooster, R et al (1994), *Science*, **265** (5181), 2088–2090.
69. Wooster, R et al (1995), 'Identification of the Breast Cancer Susceptibility Gene BRCA 2', *Nature*, **378**, 789–92 (addendum).
70. Tavtigian, SV et al (1996), 'The Complete BRCA 2 Gene and Mutations in Chromosome 13q-linked Kindreds', *Nature Genetics*, **12**, 333–7.
71. On 23 November 1995 they filed a British patent application (9523959.6) entitled 'Materials and Methods Relating to the Identification and Sequencing of the BRCA 2 Cancer Susceptibility Gene and Uses Thereof' Claim 1 defined the invention as '[a] nucleic acid molecule comprising a part of the BRCA 2 gene as set out in figures 1 and 2, or alleles thereof'.
72. European Society of Human Genetics press release issued on 15 June 2005.

10. Synthetic biology and a time for reflection

[A]n important priority for national initiatives . . . should be to push for placing as many of the DNA parts as possible in the public domain. This will encourage sharing of materials unshackled by IP licenses, reduce the cost and time of engineering and encourage the development of biological solutions to our most challenging problems. Most important, it will allow synthetic biology to reach its true power and potential.

Editorial, *Nature Biotechnology*, August 2007

One hundred years after Pasteur was granted a US patent for an improved beer-making process which included a claim to purified yeast,[1] Cohen and Boyer discovered that it was possible to cut DNA from the genome of one organism and splice it into the genome of another.[2] Their discovery, like Pasteur's discovery of 'pernicious germs', was so revolutionary that it changed scientific thinking for ever, contributing to a body of knowledge which finally enabled scientists to adapt nature's processes to manufacture biological materials in vast quantities and with a purity that was hitherto thought impossible. They were acknowledged as inventors on a US patent, although it was their university, not they, that received millions of dollars in royalties; but Stanford never exercised its patent rights to exclude others from using the 'invention' made possible by their discovery. Indeed the university's policy of non-exclusive licensing enabled Genentech, a company which Boyer co-founded, to patent the genetic material of the human gene which encoded human insulin, a natural substance that was made using genetic material that no one invented. Unchallenged, the patent proceeded to make both Boyer and Genentech rich, and their success sparked a new rush – not for gold but for genes.

Cohen and Boyer's discovery of how to use the cellular components of natural cells to express a protein encoded by foreign DNA was a scientific breakthrough; but imagine a situation in which cells have been constructed in a laboratory using amino acids. Imagine again that these cells have been engineered so that they contain genetic material which encodes for a human protein; and, further, that these cells have expressed that protein. Both the cell and the protein are artificial – both are synthetic.

According to Jonathan Tucker and Raymond Zilinskas,[3] '[t]he main difference between genetic engineering and synthetic biology is that whereas the former involves the transfer of individual genes from one species to another, the latter envisions the assembly of novel microbial genomes from a set of standardized genetic parts'. These standardized genetic parts are themselves products which enable the construction of a synthetic genome, much as other types of manufactured components enable the construction of machines. The implication here is that, like a machine, the synthetic genome, being the sum total of these genetic parts, is patentable subject matter, and that to the extent that these 'natural genes . . . have been redesigned to function more efficiently or . . . have been designed and synthesized from scratch', they meet the subsidiary thresholds of novelty and inventive step. Their analysis therefore suggests that these synthetic genomes are patentable inventions. Indeed the efficiency of synthetic genomes over genetically modified 'natural genes' to express proteins is supposedly an improvement that is useful in that it purports to improve cellular productivity, which in turn makes them valuable. Accordingly they *appear* to possess the attributes of things that have traditionally met the requirements of invention; but do they qualify?

On 25 January 2008 *The Independent*, a London newspaper, published an article written by Steve Connor, the science editor, carrying the headline, 'Playing God: the man who would create artificial life'. It was about Craig Venter, 'the controversial American scientific entrepreneur', who was described as such, no doubt, because his company, Celera Genomics, had not only managed to map the entire human genome, but had sought to patent it. The attempt raised such serious issues and public outrage at the time that it led US President Clinton and UK Prime Minister Blair to issue a joint statement in March 2000 condemning it and making it clear that the human genome belonged to no man; it was a resource that should be freely available to all researchers.

BOX 10.1   'CELERA TO QUIT SELLING GENOME INFORMATION'

'Celera Genomics, which raced with the publicly financed Human Genome Project to decipher the human DNA sequence, has decided to abandon the business of selling genetic information. The company said yesterday that it was discontinuing its genome database subscription business and putting the information into the public domain.'

Andrew Pollack, *New York Times*, 27 April 2005

Publicly rebuked and eventually removed by the Board as Celera's CEO, an undaunted Venter eventually turned his attention to Mycoplasma genitalium, a parasitic microbe which lives in the reproductive tract. Using the conventional cloning methods pioneered by Cohen and Boyer he developed a process in which sections of the genome of Mycoplasma genitalium were housed in 'cassettes' which when assembled in a laboratory produced the completed 'synthetic' genome. The sensational headline, no doubt designed to attract the public's attention, proclaimed that Venter's synthetic version of Mycoplasma genitalium meant that he had created 'artificial life', yet this was mere conjecture, and until such time as the synthetic genome is actually 'booted up' it will remain so. Yet Venter plans to try, and if he is successful he and his colleagues will probably claim to have created a synthetic life form made using synthetic biology. Their hypothesis is that these synthetic organisms will then replicate like natural organisms and, applying the protein synthesis idea first conceived of by Cohen and Boyer, they expect that they will synthesize proteins. Naturally this potential means, as with natural and genetically modified organisms, that these synthetic organisms have the potential to become new 'unnatural' pathogens. Unperturbed, Venter has allegedly modified the synthetic genome of Mycoplasma genitalium so that it contains, according to Connor, 'self-destruct mechanisms' which make it impossible to 'survive beyond the confines of a laboratory'. This of course implies that Venter knows all there is to know about how Mycoplasma genitalium will behave once the synthetic version is 'alive' and can guarantee that it will not mutate around this safeguard, but can he?[4] Moreover, the question remains: what have he and his co-inventors invented?

On 15 November 2007 patent application US 20070264688, modestly entitled 'Synthetic genomes', was filed by Venter and his co-inventors. The principal invention was defined as '[a] method for constructing a synthetic genome comprising: assembling nucleic acid cassettes that comprise portions of the synthetic genome, wherein at least one of the nucleic acid cassettes is constructed from nucleic acid components that have been chemically synthesized, or from copies of chemically synthesized nucleic acid components'. That is merely the beginning – the patent application makes it clear that the inventors contemplate that their method will be applied to construct all manner of genomes, including a 'eukaryotic cellular organelle'; 'a bacterial genome'; 'a minimal genome'; 'a minimal replicating genome'; anything that 'is substantially identical to a naturally occurring genome'; 'a non-naturally occurring genome'; 'a synthetic cellular genome' and '[a] synthetic genome'. The patent application also contains claims to cellular components such as 'nucleic acid[s] . . . that have been chemically synthesized or [made] from copies of the chemically synthesized nucleic acid components' and 'sequences that allow production of a product of interest'. Finally there are claims to products such as 'an energy source' (undefined in the patent specification other than by reference to 'hydrogen or ethanol'), and 'therapeutics and industrial polymers'.

The subject of this invention is 'a synthetic version of the Mycoplasma genitalium genome having 482 protein-coding genes and 43 RNA genes comprising a 580-kilobase circular chromosome'. Indeed the natural bacterium contains one of the smallest genomes of any known bacterium; clearly the reason Venter chose it to test his hypothesis. Accepting that the 'invention' is the method, one of its glaring deficiencies is its attempt to capture within the scope of the proposed patent monopoly *any* method of 'constructing a synthetic genome' using nucleic acid cassettes. Thus the product-by-process claims also seek patent monopolies over things such as a 'eukaryotic cellular organelle', constructed synthetically using any method employing nucleic acid cassettes.

The first problem with this approach, as previously discussed, is that the US Supreme Court ruled in *BASF* that this type of patenting is unacceptable. In this case the patent seeks to cover the technological field of making a synthetic genome, however this is performed. Even though it refers to 'cassettes', suggesting that the assembly will be completed using more than one cassette, it does not exclude the possibility that the synthetic genome can be assembled into one giant cassette. All that the patent application actually requires is that 'at least one of the nucleic acid cassettes' be constructed from nucleic acid components which have been 'chemically synthesized'. This means that if the entire genome can be chemically synthesized (that is made using conventional techniques) in a single operation then, the genome being in a 'nucleic acid cassette', any method which achieves this will come within the scope of the claim. Obviously Venter and his colleagues are not content to patent a specific method; their intention is to obtain a patent monopoly over all biological materials which are synthetically constructed, and the product-by-process claims will, theoretically, achieve this if the method claim is so understood. In this respect the patent monopoly of claim 32, which is for the 'synthetic genome' per se as a product, will automatically capture all methods of making it. Other claims tend to corroborate this conclusion; for instance claim 38, which is for '[a] method comprising: designing a synthetic genome; constructing the synthetic genome; introducing the synthetic genome into a biological system; and expressing the synthetic genome'.

The second problem is that neither Venter, nor anyone else, designed or created the genome of Mycoplasma genitalium. Apart from having been made in a laboratory, the truth is that the synthetic version is substantially identical to the natural. Perhaps, as Venter purports to have done, the genome has been tweaked so that it cannot infect humans but it is so closely related to the natural bacterium that it would be a misrepresentation to suggest that it is sufficiently different from the natural that it satisfies the thresholds established by the US Supreme Court in either *Brogdex* or *Chakrabarty*. The fact that it is incapable of infecting humans is not the kind of difference which would distinguish it in 'form, quality or property' (*Brogdex*), nor the kind of functionality that would be 'markedly different characteristics to any found in nature' (*Chakrabarty*). Consequently the patent specification merely provides particulars of a method that produces something which frankly is not patentable subject matter. That it is synthetic does not make it an invention (*BASF*).

The third problem is that, while the synthetic bacterium may provide the technical platform for the production of a synthetic 'energy source', the claims do not seek a patent monopoly over a form of synthetic hydrogen or ethanol which is in any way different from hydrogen or ethanol produced naturally or by any other methods (*BASF*; *Genentech*; *Kirin-Amgen*). Indeed nowhere in the patent application is there any information about how to make the synthetic 'energy source' made using the inventors' methods. Apart from describing a single method of constructing the bacterium, the patent specification appears to be completely devoid of anything that is inventive.

A week later, on 22 November 2007, Venter and his co-inventors filed US 20070269862 – a patent application entitled 'Installation of genomes or partial genomes into cells or cell-like systems'. The invention, acknowledged to have been 'made with government support', is defined as '[a] method for making a synthetic cell, the method comprising: obtaining a genome that is not within a cell; and introducing the genome into a cell or cell-like system'. Also claimed as an invention is '[a] synthetic cell produced by obtaining a genome that is not within a cell, and introducing the genome into a cell or cell-like system'. There was no claim to synthetic human insulin, but the patent specification states that 'insulin peptides' could be 'collected' from 'synthetic cells', clearly signalling that the inventors are contemplating that human insulin is one of the proteins that may be made using the invention.

If this patent application is granted in this form it would seem likely that the world will face the prospect of a new round of patents over the production of human insulin, erythropoietin and the myriad other proteins which are pharmaceutically useful. In the case of insulin, should this occur it will mean that since 1922 three different patent monopolies have controlled its production. The first, for purified insulin extracted from animal pancreases, was between 1922 and 1939; the second, for purified human insulin made using recombinant DNA, was between 1978 and 1995; and a third, for synthetic human insulin made using synthetic cells, although not yet a reality, is still a foreseeable possibility.

That said, some synthetic biologists are also proposing to modify nature's blueprints. The question is: will these modifications change the protein which the gene encodes or will they merely improve the production of natural proteins? This is an important distinction because, even if these genes are substantially different from natural genes and are enhanced, if the proteins which these synthetic cells express are identical to, or are substantially identical to, natural proteins then the proteins themselves are not *new*. The idea that 'anything under the sun made by man' is patentable subject matter suggests that artificiality is the key to invention, but there is, as has been argued here, much more to invention than that. Even putting to one side the patentability criteria of novelty, inventive step and industrial applicability and focusing on only the issue of patentable subject matter, it is undoubtedly the case that artificiality, while one of the necessary criteria of invention, is by no means the only criterion. The essence of invention is not mimicry but something 'new', and not in the sense of being novel but in the sense of being an 'invention' (*BASF; Brogdex; Chakbrabarty; Genentech*). Merely to replicate nature's protein products using natural genetic material, even if that material is synthetic and enhanced, is not to make something 'new' because the protein will be the same as the natural protein (*Kirin-Amgen*). Therefore while these synthetic cells are artificial and they incorporate into their genetic structure DNA which has been genetically modified from its natural equivalent, do the products which they produce 'display markedly different characteristics not found in nature'? Unless they do, these products are not patentable subject matter. Furthermore, to the extent that the processes employ synthetic genes which are substantially identical to natural genes, the processes will also not be patentable because they too are not new, or are *obvious*.

Even so there is still a long way to go. Despite all the hyperbole much of what synthetic biologists have achieved so far is to augment natural proteins with some unnatural amino acids; and, as fascinating as their research is, they have yet to produce anything that comes close to being a complete new protein which truly is an invention. For example Thomas Magliery from the Department of Molecular Biophysics and Biochemistry at Yale University writes[5] that synthetic biology has enabled the 'reprogramming of the templated synthesis of proteins'. While the paper describes how an 'unnatural amino acid'[6] has been incorporated into the genetic structure of a natural bacterium so that it 'does not require minimal medium for culturing [and] may be suitable for more ambitious organismal engineering projects', it still remains something which is substantially identical to the natural bacterium from which the vast majority of its amino acids are derived.

Nonetheless Magliery warns that this new science comes with 'the caveat that containment of the bacterium is exceedingly important'. Just as in the mid-1970s, when the NIH moved to regulate experiments that used genetically modified microorganisms,[7] caution needs to be exercised with synthetic biology. Perhaps even more so, for now scientists are not merely tinkering with the genomes of natural biological materials but are attempting to create biological materials which are potentially alien to nature. The consequences of such engineering must be fully understood; and it is clear that at the present time they are not.

Despite this risk progress in synthetic biology continues. As Jianming Xie and Peter Schultz, who is one of America's leading synthetic biologists, have explained,[8] 'although a 20-amino-acid code might be sufficient for life, it might not be optimal'. By this they mean that the use of non-natural amino acids may lead to the manufacture of therapeutically useful proteins which are significantly different from natural proteins and which perform *in vivo* in significantly different ways. They envisage, for example, the possibility of being able to produce proteins which exhibit an efficacy that is superior to that of natural proteins or which may provide new ways of protein drug delivery. They explain that at this stage in the science 'over 30 unnatural amino acids have been co-translationally incorporated into proteins with high fidelity using a unique codon and corresponding transfer-RNA:aminoacyl-tRNA-synthetase pair'.

Of course the synthesis of proteins still relies on natural microorganisms such as yeast and E. coli. This is confirmed by Wenshe Liu,[9] who has described experiments where protein synthesis is undertaken with the use of cells derived from Chinese hamsters, a mammalian cell line. He and his co-authors conclude that their method represents a further advance in synthetic biology because '[it] should facilitate cellular studies using biological probes [and ultimately] may allow the synthesis of therapeutic proteins containing unnatural amino acids in mammalian systems'.

Ambrx, the company co-founded by Schultz, has already applied for patents over human growth hormones (proteins that are produced naturally in humans) using this technology. In US 20050170404, entitled 'Modified human growth hormone polypeptides and their uses' and filed on 28 January 2005, the inventors Ho Sung Cho, Thomas Daniel, Richard DiMarchi, Troy Wilson, Bee-Cheng Sim and David Litzinger describe how they have modified natural human growth hormones so that their genetic architecture includes at least one unnatural amino acid. Their invention is '[a] hGH polypeptide comprising one or more non-naturally encoded amino acids' derived from the 'growth hormone (GH) supergene family'. It is defined to include 'growth hormone, prolactin, placental lactogen, erythropoietin, thrombopoietin, interleukin-2 to 13 and 15, oncostatin M, ciliary neurotrophic factor, leukemia inhibitory factor, alpha interferon, beta interferon, gamma interferon, omega interferon, tau interferon, epsilon interferon, granulocyte-colony stimulating factor, granulocyte-macrophage colony stimulating factor, macrophage colony stimulating factor and cardiotrophin-1'. Clearly the inventors suggest that the addition of unnatural amino acids enhances hGH polypeptides, but even so they are substantially the same and they will perform essentially the same function.

Their technology potentially applies to a number of human proteins which are already being therapeutically administered as drugs, such as human erythropoietin which will remain subject to patent protection in the United States until 2012. Amgen, as already discussed, is the world's largest producer of human erythropoietin (epoetin alfa), sold under the trade mark Epogen, and since September 2001 has been licensed by the FDA to manufacture and supply a modified form of erythropoietin (darbepoetin alfa). This new form of erythropoietin, sold under the trade mark Aranesp, is also subject to US and international patents but is distinct from Epogen as its therapeutic value is enhanced owing to its longer half-life, which means that its effects (to stimulate red blood cell production) last longer *in vivo* and patient dosage regimes are therefore lower. This is perhaps the kind of functional advantage[10] over human erythropoietin that satisfies the thresholds set by *Chakrabarty*, but the modification to its amino acid structure does not appear to be significant as it comprises only the addition of two N-glycosylation sites, bringing the total number to five (whereas human erythropoietin has three). In fact Aranesp could hardly be described as a protein that is so functionally different in 'form, quality or property' (*Brogdex*) that it could be considered to be an unnatural protein. The problem however is that Ambrx seeks to patent anything and everything that is made with the use of this technology, harking back to the 1870s when BASF attempted to do the very same in the context of processes for the manufacture of artificial alizarine; an attempt which the US Supreme Court ruled to be illegal (*BASF*).

Beyond the sheer breadth of the scope of such patent claims in terms of their potential use, other issues arise because of the terminology used to define the unnatural proteins. For instance in the International Preliminary Report of Patentability, published in accordance with the Patent Cooperation Treaty (PCT) on 24 May 2007, an objection to the patentability of Ambrx's patent was raised merely because the term 'non-naturally encoded amino acid' was 'unclear and could mean either an artificial amino acid or a naturally occurring amino acid substitution'. The report also questioned the novelty of the invention, citing an earlier US patent, namely US 6,608,183,[11] on the basis that it disclosed information about a human growth hormone which had also been genetically modified by a natural amino acid substitution. The effect of this substitution was to increase the 'stability and half-life' of this hormone, and consequently it cancelled out the only significant distinguishing feature in terms of its patentability.

MONOPOLIES IN THE AGE OF FREE TRADE

Despite the words of Cordell Hull and the establishment of the IMF, the World Bank and the United Nations – three of the world's most significant institutions – the world has not reached a state of economic détente. This failure, in part, explains why the world's patent systems have dramatically expanded their technological footprints, eroding more and more of the public domain in the process. Indeed since World War II the public domain has shrunk, in spite of the technological innovation and development that the world has witnessed. While it is true that significant inventions such as the steam engine, light bulb, telephone and radio were in themselves like superhighways which directed innovation at faster speeds and which took technologies into areas that were, prior to their development, thought impossible, the fact remains that alongside these advancements protectionist political and economic policies have played, and continue to play, an important role in encouraging the erosion of the public domain.

That patent systems were actually antithetical to free trade was well recognized in the UK and in Europe in the mid-nineteenth century; and, had it not been for a global recession in 1873 and the American promotion of patents, the future for patents would have seemed rather bleak. Believing in 'man's natural property in his own original ideas',[12] Americans perceived the 'many complaints and criticisms . . . directed against patent laws' to have been caused by a 'misapprehension of the true principles of the law'. Yet it was the protection of German industry which primarily motivated Bismarck to establish a national patent system in Germany, and it was, ironically, America's inability to foresee how Germany could exploit the US patent system that enabled Germany industry to suppress any indigenous chemical industry in the United States prior to World War I. Consequently, amid shortages of needed medicines, chemicals, dyes and other products, Americans learned how their own much-lauded patent system was used by German chemical companies during peacetime deliberately to undermine both their national security and economy during war. This was a powerful lesson, and Americans learnt that lesson well; and so began the use of their newly-found political and economic post-war power to develop policies which would protect their own nation and economy against all contingencies in the future. Their free trade rhetoric was used, much like German economist Friedrich List accused the British of doing in the nineteenth century, to mask their own protectionist objectives. The American withdrawal in 1950 of support for the International Trade Organization (ITO), the last piece in Cordell Hull's free trade paradigm, made that perfectly clear. An offensive strategy was henceforth built upon the premise of technological superiority – a superiority which would enable American companies, through the mutual recognition of patents and other intellectual property, to gain a competitive advantage. Intellectual property laws legitimated a policy of domestic protection by characterizing as unfair trade the manufactured goods made in countries which did not respect or enforce intellectual property to American standards. Naturally the implications of this strategy upon European manufacturers was understood by the EEC, which then set about meeting the American challenge. Much of the work of Kurt Haertel during the 1960s and early 1970s was focused on providing Europe with a centralized mechanism for the creation and enforcement of patents. The European Patent Convention thus provided Europe with the EPO, a substantial organization which could compete with the USPTO to generate European patents for Europeans. Clearly European policy-makers knew that they had to encourage their industries to patent as much technology as possible if Europe was to have any reasonable chance of beating the Americans at their own game. The competitiveness between these two substantial economic regions then laid the ground work for an economic war for technological supremacy. The lie, of course, was that this would be achieved in the spirit of free trade, and, with the GATT failing to acknowledge the role that intellectual property could play in erecting trade barriers, there was little that could be done to stop their proliferation. Inevitably Cohen and Boyer's breakthrough opened the doors to the exploitation of a new technology, but in the heat of this economic war, and with technological supremacy as their objective, the patent systems in the United States and Europe ignored a fundamental principle – that patents are about products of man and not products of nature.

The ability of a foreign patent owner to exercise absolute control over the use of a patented technology in any country which has a patent system is a conduit through which the economic policies of foreign countries can be implemented within the host country. Whether those policies are directed to encouraging skilled workers and artisans to emigrate from one country to another or create barriers to such emigration, as they did in the past, or whether they are directed towards protecting economies from the effects of 'unfair' competition as they are now, a case can be made that patents, rather than being the harbingers of innovation, are merely the instruments of a protectionist agenda. That inventors have benefited from patent monopolies is merely incidental to, and not a primary objective of, patent systems. Therefore patents facilitate extra-territorial control of technology in countries which are net importers of technology, and this is one of the reasons Switzerland in the nineteenth century repeatedly ignored Germany's demands that it adopt a national patent system, and why India in 1970 passed a patent law that specifically excluded 'substances intended for use, or capable of being used, as food or as medicine or drug'[13] as inventions. Indeed that is the very reason Germany did not allow the patenting of chemical substances between 1877 and 1968 and Italy did not allow patents for pharmaceutical substances (along with other European countries) until 1978. Moreover until 1978 the UK pursued a policy of compulsory licensing which could be applied in various ways, and between 1919 and 1949 also excluded the patenting of chemical substances.

This of course does not explain why countries which are net importers of technology have continued to embrace the patent system. Perhaps they believe that technological innovation needs to be encouraged; or that the costs imposed by the patent system are less than the benefits that it provides; or that they must retain it simply because, in the past, someone thought that granting monopoly rights was a good idea; or maybe they have accepted that without a patent system the markets of net exporting technology countries will be closed to them. Whatever the reason the current orthodoxy promotes the view that higher productive capacity and employment are generated by technological development – something to be encouraged. Of course there are many ways to encourage innovation. The fact that technological innovation occurred for thousands of years before anyone had heard of letters patent or *privilegi* may have simply been due to necessity. But as Eric Schiff's famous study on Switzerland and The Netherlands showed, the lack of a patent system did not stifle their industrialization during the late nineteenth century. Furthermore Christine MacLeod and Alessandro Nuvolari found that at the height of the UK's economic domination of world trade in the mid nineteenth century, about 40 per cent of significant inventions were not patented. In fact it was the appropriation of thousands of German and other 'enemy' patents, trade marks and copyrights by American governments in World War I and II that facilitated the establishment of key chemical, pharmaceutical and defence industries in the United States.

That patents continue to be part of the armoury which protects the American economy from 'unfair competition' is demonstrably clear. On 6 February 2008 a group of US trade unions which included the Communications Workers of America, the International Brotherhood of Teamsters, United Steelworkers and the Patent Office Professional

Association wrote to the US Senate expressing their 'deep concern' that the patent reform proposals contained in section 1145 of the Patent Reform Bill 2007 'could undermine the competitiveness of US industry and put our members' jobs at risk'. The proposed legislation sought to bring US patent law into line with the patent law of other countries, but, instead of supporting the creation of a level playing field, the trade unions complained that the legislation would increase 'the likelihood of American inventions being stolen by our international competitors' and this would have the negative effect of 'inhibiting sorely needed new investment in domestic manufacturing'. In rather an apocalyptic crescendo the trade unions' letter concluded that the legislation would only 'contribute' to the loss of American jobs, devastating 'scores of communities' across America.

Even prior to the trade unions' letter John Sullivan, the General Counsel of the US Department of Commerce, admitted that the first-to-file patent system, one of the proposed reforms which would bring the US patent system into line with the rest of the world, had 'potential benefits' for the United States. Yet in a letter to Howard Berman, the chairman of the Subcommittee on Courts, the Internet, and Intellectual Property

---

BOX 10.2   'END OF THE ROAD FOR US PATENT REFORM BILL'

Managing Intellectual Property, 12 May 2008

'The bill was added to the Senate calendar in January and was predicted to make it to the floor by April. However, the legislation has been stalled for some time due to a lack of agreement on key issues, such as reform of damages. The bill's demise appeared imminent last month when former USPTO solicitor John Whealan – who had been working closely with S1145's sponsor, Senator Patrick Leahy, for the past year – announced his resignation.

On April 10, Senator Leahy said in a statement: "I am disappointed that just a handful of words have stalled the Senate's debate on this important patent legislation. We have been working on these reforms for years. Thousands of hours have been spent in negotiations to address the concerns of 100 Senators, hundreds of Representatives, and dozens of stakeholders. This was a missed opportunity. I have said repeatedly that the time for patent reform is now. Unfortunately, some have yet to fully grasp this fact, and have stalled meaningful reform."'

Committee on the Judiciary in the House of Representatives, on 16 May 2007 he wrote that the Department did 'not support immediate conversion to first-to-file via this legislation'. One might have believed, judging by these letters, that the proposed legislation was detrimental to American competitiveness. In truth it was merely part of the process of internationalization of patent law which was initiated by the United States in 1873.

It would seem that the US trade unions were touting the same message as Pfizer and the American software industry in the 1970s,[14] that the so-called 'unprecedented decline' of the US international trade position was caused by the theft of 'American inventions by . . . international competitors'. Not only was this accusation now blatantly untrue and unfairly inculpatory, but it overlooked the fact that it is the sovereign right of all countries, subject to their own constitutions and to the international treaties to which they have subscribed, to make whatever laws they wish. In this respect it is a matter for their governments, subject to these caveats, to decide what is and what is not property or intellectual property within their sovereign domains. Indeed the unions ignored the fact that since 1995, when the World Trade Organization (WTO) was established, TRIPS, one of the core agreements of the WTO and now applicable in over 150 countries, has specifically provided minimum legal standards for the creation and enforcement of all forms of intellectual property, including patents. Thus for more than a decade these uniform standards, to which the US subscribes, have operated to counter the very threat that the trade unions were now afraid of. Since TRIPS, Free Trade Agreements which the United States has negotiated with many countries have raised these standards of intellectual property protections even more.

Moreover, the US trade unions in their letter overlooked a key issue: many American companies are no longer owned or controlled by Americans but have become subsidiaries or associates of multinational corporations headquartered in other countries. For instance Novartis and F Hoffmann-La Roche, both Swiss pharmaceutical giants, have been building significant business portfolios in the United States in the biotechnology, agriculture and pharmaceutical sectors.[15] Consequently many American subsidiaries, or associates of companies like them, owe no particular allegiance to the United States, let alone to US workers, particularly as their foreign-based managements are not predisposed to making investment and production decisions with the US economy or worker in mind. Predictably, and properly, their focus is on maximizing profits and, accordingly, their responsibility to shareholders means that if in order to achieve this objective the company is required to move production away from the United States to lower manufacturing cost countries, then this is precisely what happens. Put bluntly, at the time of their letter many significant 'American inventions' were probably no longer owned or controlled by Americans.

BOX 10.3 'AIRBUS PARENT BEATS BOEING FOR BIG US AIR FORCE CONTRACT'

International Herald Tribune, 1 March 2008

'The U.S. Air Force, in a stunning decision against Boeing, awarded a $40 billion contract for aerial refuelling tankers Friday to a partnership between Northrop Grumman and the European parent of Airbus, putting a critical military contract partly into the hands of a foreign company.

The contract, one of the largest at the Pentagon, has the potential to grow to $100 billion. It is also a sign of the growing influence of foreign suppliers within the Pentagon and breaks a decades long relationship with Boeing, which built the bulk of the existing tanker fleet and fought hard to land the new contract.

"This isn't an upset," said Loren Thompson, a military analyst at the Lexington Institute, a Washington-area research group. "It's an earthquake."

Under the contract, Northrop and the parent of Airbus, European Aeronautic Defense & Space, or EADS, would build a fleet of 179 planes, based on the existing Airbus 330, to provide in-air refueling to military aircraft, from fighter jets to cargo planes. It gives a huge lift to EADS, whose commercial aviation program has suffered a number of setbacks in recent years.

While final assembly of the craft would take place at an Airbus plant near Mobile, Alabama, parts would come from suppliers across the globe.

At a news conference, air force officials said the creation of domestic jobs was not a factor in the decision. In response to questions about possible negative reaction to the deal in Congress, General Arthur Lichte, head of the air force's air mobility command, said, "This will be an American tanker, flown by American airmen with an American flag on its tail and, every day, it will be saving American lives."

Reaction from some in Congress, however, was swift.

"We are outraged that this decision taps European Airbus and its foreign workers to provide a tanker to our American military," the delegation from Washington State said in a joint statement. Boeing planes are assembled outside Seattle. "This is a blow to the American aerospace industry, American workers and America's men and women in uniform."'

Finally, in accusing other countries of patent piracy, what the unions were clearly unaware of was the history of the actions of past US governments which led to the confiscation of the intellectual property and other property of foreigners which directly resulted in the advancement of the US economy; and while these foreigners were the nationals of countries that were considered to be enemies at the time, they were nonetheless private companies and individuals who were not directly involved in military hostilities against the United States. As a result, the rationale used by the United States to justify the confiscation of 'enemy' property appeared insincere and convenient in hindsight. Indeed if patents are personal property that belongs not to a State but to individuals, then on what possible basis could the US Government have justified the confiscation of that property? Surely a more appropriate response would have been to invalidate the US patents, thereby enabling anyone to work the technology or property which was previously subject to those patents? It may be that such legislative action would have been just as unfair and inequitable to the former patent owner as confiscation, but if the rationale for this action was to overcome the effects of war time shortages of essential medicines and commodities in the US, as indeed it was, then would it not have been better simply to open the market up, rather than transfer patent monopolies to fledgling American chemical companies?

Arguably the reason these US patents were not invalidated, but were confiscated to be kept intact and then sold on to Americans for prices well below their true value, was that the patent monopolies which came with them could then be used to inhibit the post war re-entry into the US market of the foreign companies and individuals. US policy-makers well knew that it was better to maintain these monopolies so that they could be used to protect their own post-war economy and their new owners, the American owners, in their home market. Furthermore the intention was then to use the US market and the anticipated productive capacity of the US economy as a springboard upon which to compete with the former owners in their previous international markets. In this respect the United States was not alone in acting in this capricious manner towards foreign 'enemies'. Other Allied powers used the Treaty of Versailles to confiscate patents, many of which were also ultimately transferred to US and UK companies. As a result the German chemical and pharmaceutical industries lost significant shares of their international markets to US or UK interests. One might argue that this was a form of wartime reparation, but the German companies involved did not start World War I, nor did they generally facilitate it.

However if one accepts that patents are not merely private property, but are also instruments of state-sanctioned economic war, then perhaps the Allied action was justified. In fact when one remembers that German chemical and pharmaceutical companies deliberately embarked upon a commercial strategy well before World War I that used US patent laws to suppress US production and employment, perhaps then the United States and other Allied Powers were arguably justified, on the grounds of national security alone, to do what they did.

Plainly the post-war American efforts to globalize its industries have produced economic and political policies which have favoured the freer movement of goods and services, especially useful when production is based in the United States or the technology is owned or controlled by the United States; but today the effects of these policies are starting to undermine American workers as more and more manufacturing (and also research and development) moves offshore. Unsurprisingly views within the United States are starting to shift away from the rhetoric of 'free trade' and back towards 'protectionism'. Gene Sperling, a former aide to US President William Clinton,[16] was quoted by the *Wall Street Journal* on 21 November 2007 as saying:

> Even those of us who are supportive of the open-market policies of the '90s have to take seriously that the large inflow of workers from China and India digesting American jobs is placing downward pressure on wages. That doesn't mean the answer is closing up shop in globalization, but it can't just mean business as usual either.

Globalization however is not as recent a phenomenon as Sperling suggests. Since World War II American policy-makers have understood that the United States has had much more to gain by exporting its domestic excess productive capacity. Not only did this bring employment to US workers, particularly in the early decades after World War II, but as US companies established factories in countries which had lower costs of production than in the United States, they were able to reduce prices of manufactured goods to American consumers while maximizing profits that were ultimately repatriated back to the United States to the benefit of American shareholders and taxpayers. In the drive for cheaper labour and production costs US industries have invested billions throughout the world, and in so doing have not only succeeded in meeting their own investment criteria but have, through these investments, significantly contributed to the industrialization of many developed and developing countries.

The change in emphasis in the United States away from manufacturing has, particularly since the 1990s, been facilitated with the help of various international trade agreements, such as the North American Free Trade Agreement (NAFTA) which came into effect on 1 January 1994. Through the effect of these kinds of agreements the United States has ensured that international intellectual property protections have been raised to acceptable US standards. Unfortunately this change in economic emphasis has also accelerated the redirection of capital away from traditional manufacturing industries in the United States towards both new technologies, such as biotechnology, and manufacturing in lower cost countries. These newer technologies are not as labour intensive as manufacturing, and the capital inflows into these industries have funded a closer, much more collaborative, relationship with American universities. Even by 1970 American policy-makers could anticipate this and the Bayh-Dole Act was one of the principal instruments through which this policy was eventually brought into effect.

Evidently, as America's internal capacity to generate income through manufacturing has diminished, it has been necessary to find a replacement source of income, and one way to do this has been through an economic rent charged on those who use American intellectual property. That rent, being income in the form of patent, trade mark and copyright royalties (in other words state sanctioned monopolies), is today absolutely vital to the US economy (just as it is to Japan and increasingly to members of the European Community). Of course it was foreseeable that without adequate rent collection measures this strategy would be undermined by counterfeiters; so by the late 1980s it had become essential that the world adopt minimum intellectual property protections – that is those acceptable to the United States, Japan and the European Community. This of course required the legal enforcement of those protections, and TRIPS, as previously discussed, was a result. Soon this economic rent will become significant to India and China as they are transformed from net producers of manufactured goods into net producers of new technology and other intellectual property.

Essentially what this means is that for the past 40 years American economic policy has deliberately sacrificed the traditional manufacturing working classes of the US mid to mid-west for a new paradigm – one which has significantly contributed to the income and wealth of the States of Washington and California in particular, where America's IT and biotechnology industries established themselves. While the benefits to these states and industries have been enormous, the cost in terms of social dislocation in the mid to mid-west has certainly been devastating. The result has seen a predictable political shift; on 4 October 2007 the *Wall Street Journal* reported, 'by a nearly two-to-one margin, Republican voters believe free trade is bad for the US economy'. That change in popular opinion among Republican voters has been encouraged in states like Ohio which have 'lost more than 200,000 manufacturing jobs . . . since NAFTA was implemented'.[17]

Perhaps hitherto this gamble has paid off for the United States, given lower levels of inflation and the inflows of foreign capital through its stock markets, but for the US workers who have been caught in the crossfire, other than through the lower prices that they have been paying for consumer goods made in other countries using or applying American owned intellectual property, the personal cost has been high.

The creation of more and more intellectual property has regrettably fuelled the idea that this new economic paradigm, assuming that a satisfactory enforcement system is in place internationally, is sustainable. And with dulled memories or deficient knowledge politicians and policymakers have accepted this, not only in the United States but throughout the world. Following the lead of the United States the Europeans and the Japanese have also adopted similar strategies, which explains for instance why patents for chemical substances were permitted in Germany in 1968 and why in 1978 Italy was forced, through its membership of the European Patent Convention, to remove the ban on the patenting of pharmaceuticals. Even India, which in 1970 passed a patent law which prohibited the patenting of pharmaceutical substances, complied with its obligations under TRIPS to remove this ban in 2005.

And this expansion of intellectual property is regrettable too because much of it has been created in biotechnology and IT through patents which do not deserve merit because they are not for 'inventions'. The expansion of the patent domain into these fields has often been made possible only by ignoring the historical fact that in 1623 the English Parliament acknowledged that it would be ultimately detrimental to the economy for monopolies to be allowed unless for a very limited time (14 years) and in respect of something that was an 'invention' (a manner of new manufacture). That the USPTO and the specialist patent appeals court, the CAFC, have aided and abetted the distortion of the patent system through the grant and enforcement of US patents for innovations which are not 'inventions', and that they have been supported in Europe and Japan and, ultimately, by many other countries in similar ways suggests that the time has come for the world to reconsider whether a patent system today is operating as it should be.

Currently the patent systems of the world are incapable of adequately assessing whether the patentability criteria which are set under Article 27.1 of TRIPS are being satisfied. The explosion in the number of patents has stretched the resources of patent offices everywhere. Many now struggle to employ the numbers of patent examiners needed to make these assessments properly. Moreover the cost of enforcement of patents is, as it has always been, incredibly high and inefficient. The economic cost of that inefficiency has been felt not only by patent owners who are trying to enforce their property claims around the world in different courts, but by the users of technology who may be paying an unnecessarily high price because no one can afford to challenge the validity of what is possibly an invalid patent. Often the breadth of the patent monopolies is so wide that they claim, as inventions, the speculative use of the technology that is the subject of the patent; for example patents which claim the use of isolated biological materials in vaccines, when all that the patent discloses is the genetic and amino acid sequence of that material and the use of that material in a rudimentary diagnostic assay. The impact of such overreaching and greedy activity is mostly unmeasured, but some would argue that intuitively it must be the case that it acts as a dampener on medical and scientific research, especially when the nexus between that research and commerce is as close as it is today. Surely it is obvious that if the ultimate objective of medical and scientific research is the achievement of a patent, then it must follow that if the field of research is already claimed by other patents the research that would have happened had that not been so *will now not happen*. Beyond these issues, today the vast majority of the world's patents are owned or controlled by companies that do not necessarily bear any allegiance to any particular country or any particular people. Fundamentally this was never the purpose of patents.

The assumption that without the world's patent systems the necessary investment in new technologies would evaporate or would be inadequate must be challenged; and if it is found that there is a need for some form of incentive then adequate measures should be put in place to ensure that these incentives are not abused. Frankly the time has come for the world, as a global community, seriously to question whether the patent system is all that it purports to be.

That the patent systems of the world are still facing the same sorts of criticisms that the English patent system faced in the 1850s and 1860s surely suggests that perhaps the world's patent systems are not and never can be optimal. After all, both Switzerland and The Netherlands survived very well without national patent systems, and most probably would have continued without them had it not been for the international pressure exerted upon them by Germany and the United States respectively. It cannot be ignored that Philips, a corporation which is now the world's largest single patent filer, started life in a country that did not have a patent law.

Winston Churchill said, 'the farther backward you can look, the farther forward you can see', and yet, as we seek solutions to the problems inherent in the workings of the world's modern patent systems, we seem unable to grasp this simple wisdom. If we cast our minds back to England 140 years ago, the British patent system was the subject of serious criticism; indeed by 1872 the House of Lords had passed a Bill that would, if the House of

Commons had followed suit, have reduced the patent term to seven years. The British Parliamentary Committee that scrutinized the British patent system between 1862 and 1864 examined a number of issues which are today, once more, the subject of the very same criticisms and concerns as were expressed at that time. First was the issue of patent quality, which was said to have led to patents of dubious validity. Second was the issue of the lack of a proper system of pre-grant patent examination, also contributing to dubious and overlapping patents. Third was the issue of the inefficiency and cost of the post-grant judicial scrutiny of granted patents which, it was believed, acted as a disincentive to the removal of invalid patents.

Nineteenth century Americans on the other hand believed that the US patent system, which had preliminary examination and 'less expensive' litigation, provided the right balance between the rights of the inventor to a patent monopoly and the rights of the State, which would be free to make use of the invention at the expiry of that monopoly. So it was the United States that was determined to arrest the trend which threatened Europe's patent systems. The process of internationalization encouraged further reforms in the British patent system and in other European countries, and slowly led to the establishment of the World Intellectual Property Organization and facilitated dialogue at an international level which also led to additional reforms and innovations within the patent systems of the world. The Patent Cooperation Treaty in particular was to provide inventors with a simple and efficient system of applying for patents around the world through a single patent application filed with the patent office of their choice; and today the unprecedented cooperation between patent offices is leading to the establishment of patent 'superhighways' in an attempt further to reduce the cost of patent examination and increase the productivity of the patent systems.[18] Whether this experiment will provide a permanent solution is yet to be seen.

In the meantime, in spite of all the developments, the patent communities are really no closer to resolving these presistent problems.[19] Whether this is because the patent system is a model that is fundamentally flawed or whether this is because, as those who believe in the patent system argue, it is merely a reflection of the fact that the process of reform has not yet reached its zenith is a debate or discussion that has yet to happen at an international level. So far all diplomatic efforts have proceeded on the assumptions that the patent system is a permanent reality; that there is no better system; that if only it could be 'improved' and made more 'efficient' then perhaps the issues of the lack of patent quality,[20] greater patent productivity[21] and less patent litigation and expense[22] – a patent utopia – would result.

The problem is that the present controversy over patent law reform in the United States, which has stalled, and the ad hoc discussions that have taken place across the globe about various aspects of patent law and patent administration have been blind to the fact that the world today is no longer a collection of feudal states which are so independent of each other that they can legitimately ignore the way in which their internal decisions impact on their neighbours. This is the point that Cordell Hull was making before the outbreak of World War II, and this is the point of having such organizations as the IMF, the World Bank, the United Nations and the World Trade Organization. The world no longer needs to operate under the illusion that the patent systems encourage innovation and improve economic opportunities. We now live in a global community which has been working towards true free trade for over 60 years, and although it is clear that the ultimate goal of no trade barriers of any kind has yet to be achieved, it is also clear that history does not support or justify the retention of the world's patent systems – systems that are one of the key instruments of economic protectionism. In a free trade world there is no place for such economic protections, and the global community needs to acknowledge that the patent system sits like the elephant of protectionism in the free trade room.

Watching how the patent system has ultimately intruded upon a field which until recently was sacrosanct, namely nature, only reinforces the strength of the argument against the retention of the world's patent systems. What this incursion has led to is a proliferation of patents over thousands of biological materials that are not and never were inventions; it has led to an explosion of patents that have reduced the productivity of patent offices throughout the world with respect to the prosecution of legitimate inventions; it has led to the misallocation of capital into the production of therapeutics and diagnostics over human illness and diseases, that are expensive and inefficient; it has contributed to undermining social and industrial reforms in the developing countries which have become the manufacturing centres for the owners of intellectual property; it has led to the growing reliance on technology to solve the world's problems by ignoring the problems that unregulated new technologies create; it has distorted the scientific spirit by encouraging scientists to be less open about their research and encouraged only by the promise of wealth; it has produced universities that are no longer citadels of independent research and learning, but components of a commercial world which justifies its actions solely on the basis of profit. Finally the patent system has contributed to the destruction of the generosity of past generations; generosity that had allowed people freely to borrow information about themselves, their cultures, their technologies and the world around them and contributed to that store of knowledge which the US Supreme Court described in *Funk Brothers* as being 'free to all men and reserved exclusively to none.'

A free culture has been our past, but it will only be our future if we change the path we are on right now.

Lawrence Lessig

NOTES

1. US 141,092 (22 July 1873), 'Improvement in the Manufacture of Beer and Yeast'.
2. Cohen SN, ACY Chang, HC Boyer and RB Helling (1973), 'Construction of Biologically Functional Bacterial Plasmids In Vitro', *Proceedings of the National Academy of Sciences of the United States of America*, **70** (11), 3240–44.
3. Tucker, JB and RA Zilinskas (2006), 'The Promise and Perils of Synthetic Biology', *The New Atlantis* 25–45.
4. One is reminded of Michael Crichton's novel *Jurassic Park* in which Dr Ian Malcolm, the mathematician, makes a dire prediction that inevitably the safety mechanisms employed on Isla Nublar by John Hammond's (the eccentric billionaire) company InGen, which clones dinosaurs from the DNA extracted from remnants preserved in Amber, would be overcome by nature.
5. Magliery, TJ (2005), 'Unnatural Protein Engineering: Producing Proteins with Unnatural Amino Acids', *Medical Chemistry Reviews-Online*, **2** (4), 303–23.
6. An artificial amino acid unknown in nature.
7. It will be recalled that Paul Berg, David Baltimore, Hebert Boyer, Stanley Cohen, Ronald Davis, David Hogness, Daniel Nathans, Richard Roblin, James Watson, Sherman Weissman and Norton Zinder, America's most distinguished molecular biologists of the day, had signed a letter entitled 'Potential Biohazards of Recombinant DNA Molecules': *Science*, New Series, **185** (4148), 303.
8. Xie, J and P Schultz (2006), 'A Chemical Toolkit for Proteins – an Expanded Genetics Code', *Molecular Cell Biology*, **7**, 778–82.
9. Liu, W, A Brock, S Chen, S Chen and P Schultz (2007), 'Genetic Incorporation of Unnatural Amino Acids into Proteins in Mammalian Cells', *Nature Methods*, **4** (3), 239–44.
10. Although the FDA has issued warnings over its use for cancer patients.
11. US 6,608,183 (19 August 2003), 'Derivatives of growth hormone and related proteins'.
12. Howson, H and C (1872), *A Brief Inquiry into the Principles, Effect. and Present State of the American Patent System* (Philadelphia: Sherman & Co) 9.
13. S. 5(1)(a) Patents Act 1970 (India).
14. Gorlin, JJ (1985), 'A Trade-Based Approach for the International Copyright Protection for Computer Software' (unpublished), provided to the author by Peter Drahos through private correspondence. According to Jacques Gorlin, 'There is mounting recognition that improved protection for software can be achieved by moving the IP (copyright) protection issue into the international trade regime. A number of trade associations have begun specifically to promote the inclusion of the issue in the MTN [Multinational Trade Negotiations]. These associations, in views already presented to the Office of the U.S. Trade Representative, seek: (1) *strengthen copyright enforcement in the developing countries* in order to deal with the piracy of computer software in such countries as Singapore, Taiwan, Korea and Brazil and in the Arab countries of the Persian Gulf. These LDCs are centers of piracy because they either do not have adequate copyright legislation that meets the minimal standards contained in Berne or Universal Copyright Conventions, or, if they do, do not undertake adequate enforcement measures that are generally found in the industrialised countries'.
15. Novartis fully acquired Chiron Corporation and La Roche holds a controlling interest in Genentech.
16. 1946 –, President of the United States, 1993–2001.

17. 'Candidates Rebuked For Attacks on NAFTA', *Financial Times*, 28 February 2008.

18. 'EPO and US speed up patent-granting process', *Managing Intellectual Property*, 17 March 2008.

19. Jaffe, AB and J Lerner (2004), *Innovations and Its Discontents: How Our Broken Patent System is Endangering Innovation and Progress, and What to do about it* (Princeton: Princeton University Press).

20. Staff Union of the European Patent Office (SUEPO) Position Paper, *Quality of Examination at the EPO*, May 2004. Also see US Government Accountability Office Report, *Hiring Efforts Are Not Sufficient to Reduce the Patent Application Backlog*, GAO-07-11-2, September 2007. This report states that the GAO undertook the report because of the 'increases in the volume and complexity of patent applications have lengthened the amount of time it takes the US Patent and Trademark Office to process them'.

21. EU Administrative Council Report to the Administrative Council Members of the EU, *Future workload*, CA/144/07, 23 November 2007. The Report states 'the pressure that follows from b) to h) translates itself into problems for the major patent offices in the world to cope with the ever increasing workload. These problems consist of growing backlogs and insufficient time and resources to examine applications with the necessary thoroughness.' p. 7 (para. 17). The problems b) to h) as listed are: b) dramatic growth of the number of patent applications; c) the complexity and volume of applications is increasing; c) much of the growth in patent activity comes from new and emerging technologies, like ICT, nanotechnology and others; e) international patent activity increases, and h) impact on the production. 3 (7) – 7 (16).

22. Statement of Mark B Myers, Senior Vice President, Corporate Research and Technology, Xerox Corporation (retired) to the US House of Representatives Subcommittee on Courts, the Internet, and Intellectual Property: Committee on the Judiciary, Intellectual Property Rights in the Knowledge-Based Economy, *A Patent System for the 21st Century*, 15 February 2007. He stated, 'Since 1980 a series of judicial, legislative, and administrative actions have extended patenting to new technologies (biotechnology) and to technologies previously without or subject to other forms of intellectual property protection (software and business methods), encouraged the emergence of new players (universities), strengthened the position of patent holders vis-à-vis infringers domestically and internationally, relaxed other restraints on the use of patents (antitrust enforcement), and extended their reach upstream from commercial products to scientific research tools and materials. As a result, patents are being more zealously sought, vigorously asserted, and aggressively enforced than ever before. There are many indications that firms in a variety of industries, as well as universities and public institutions, are attaching greater importance to patents and are willing to pay higher costs to acquire, exercise, and defend them. The workload of the U.S. Patent and Trademark Office has increased several-fold in the last few decades, to the point that it is issuing approximately 100 patents every working hour. Meanwhile, the costs of acquiring patents, promoting or securing licenses to patented technology, and prosecuting and defending against infringement allegations in the increasing number of patent suits are rising rapidly.'.

Bibliography

ARTICLES, BOOKS, SCIENTIFIC PAPERS

Abbott, F.M. (2005), 'The WTO Medicines Decision: World Pharmaceutical Trade and the Protection of Public Health', *The American Journal of International Law*, **99** (2), 317–58.

Abbott, K.W. (1990), 'United States-Section 337 of the Tariff Act of 1930, *The American Journal of International Law*, **84** (1), 274–80.

Abel, J.J. (1926), 'Crystalline Insulin', *Proceedings of the National Academy of Sciences of the United States of America*, **12** (2), 132–6.

Abel, J.J. (1927), 'Chemistry in Relation to Biology and Medicine with Especial Reference to Insulin and Other Hormones', *Science*, New Series, **66** (1711), 337–46.

Abelshausen, W. and W. von Hippel, J.A. Johnson, R.G. Stokes (2004), *German Industry and Global Enterprise, BASF: The History of a Company* (Cambridge: Cambridge, University Press).

Abrignani, S., M. Houghton and H.H. Hsu (1999), 'Perspectives for a Vaccine against Hepatitis C Virus', *Journal of Hepatology*, **31** Suppl 1, 259–63.

Achilladelis, B. (1993), 'The Dynamics of Technological Innovation: The Sector of Antibacterial Medicines', *Research Policy*, **22**, 279–308.

Allarakhia, M. and A. Wensley, (2005), 'Innovation and Intellectual Property Rights in Systems Biology', *Nature Biotechnology*, **23** (12), 1485–8.

Alston, P. (1993), 'Labor Rights Provisions in US Trade Law: "Aggressive Unilateralism"?', *Human Rights Quarterly,* **15** (1), 1–35.

Alto Charo, R. (2006), 'Body of Research – Ownership and Use of Human Tissue', *The New England Journal of Medicine*, **355** (15), 1517–19.

Andrews, L.B. (2005), 'Harnessing the Benefits of Biobanks', *Journal of Law, Medicine & Ethics* 22–30.

Angel, M. (2005), *The Truth About Drug Companies* (Carlton North, Australia: Scribe Publications).

Armitage, E. (2007), 'EU Industrial Property Policy for Patents', available at http://www.suepo.org/public/background/armitage_en.htm, 26 July.

Baader, G., S.E. Lederer, M. Low, F. Schmaltz and A.F. Schwerin (2005), 'Pathways to Human Experimentation, 1933–1945: Germany, Japan, and the United States', *Osiris*, 2nd Series, **20**, 205–31.

Balter, M. (2001), 'Transatlantic War over BRCA1 Patent', *Science*, New Series, **292** (5523), 1818.

Banting, F.G. (1937), 'Early Work on Insulin', *Science*, New Series, **85** (2217), 594–96.

Baptista R.J. and A.S. Travis (2006), 'I.G. Farben in America: The Technologies of General Aniline & Film', *History and Technology*, **22** (2), 187–224.

Barton, J.H. (2004), 'Emerging Patent Issues in Genomic Diagnostics', *Nature Biotechnology*, **24** (8), 939–41.

Baum, L. (1977), 'Judicial Specialization, Litigant Influence, and Substantive Policy: The Court of Customs and Patent Appeals', *Law & Society Review*, **11** (5), 823–50.

Baum, L., S. Goldman and A. Sarat (1981), 'The Evolution of Litigation in the Federal Courts of Appeals, 1895–1975', *Law & Society Review*, **16** (2), 291–310.

Bayh, B. (2004), Statement the National Institutes of Health, 25 May. Available at http://www.orpc.unh.edu/Bayhstatement.pdf.

Beckhart, B.H. (1944), 'The Bretton Woods Proposal for an International Monetary Fund', *Political Science Quarterly*, **59** (4), 489–528.

Beer, J.J. (1958), 'Coal Tar Dye Manufacture and the Origins of the Modern Industrial Research', *Isis*, **49** (2), 123–31.

Belfanti, C.M. (2004), 'Guilds, Patents, and the Circulation of Technical Knowledge', *Technology and Culture*, **45**, 569–89.

Bell, R. (1982), 'Testing the Open Door Thesis in Australia, 1941–1946', *The Pacific Historical Review,* **51** (3), 283–311.

Berg, P., D. Baltimore, H.W. Boyer, S.N. Cohen, R.W. Davis, D.S. Hogness, D. Nathans, R. Roblin, J.D. Watson, S. Weissman and N.D. Zinder (1974), 'Potential Biohazards of Recombinant DNA Molecules', *Science*, New Series, **185** (4148), 303.

Berman, H.A. (1945), 'Cartels and Enemy Property', *Law and Contemporary Problems*, **11** (1), 109–17.

Berman, H.J. (1994), 'The Origins of Historical Jurisprudence: Coke, Selden, Hale', *The Yale Law Journal*, **103** (7) 1651–738.

Bessen, J. and E. Maskin (2000), 'Sequential Innovation, Patents, and Imitation', Harvard University, Department of Economics, Working Paper Series, SSRN 206189.

Best, C.H. and D.A. Scott (1923), 'The Preparation of Insulin', *The Journal of Biological Chemistry*, 709–23.

Bhutkar, A. (2005), 'Synthetic Biology: Navigating the Challenges Ahead', *The Journal of Biolaw and Business*, **8** (2), 19–29.

Blackburn, R.P. (1999), 'Chiron's Licensing Policy', *Science*, New Series, **285** (5430), 1015.

Blackeney, M. (2003), 'The International Protection of Industrial Property from the Paris Convention to the TRIPS Agreement', *WIPO National Seminar on Intellectual Property*, Cairo, 17–19 February 2003, WIPO/IP/CAI/1/03/2.

Blinder, A.S. (2006), 'Offshoring: The Next Industrial Revolution?', *Foreign Affairs*, March/April.

Bliss, M. (1984), *The Discovery of Insulin* (Chicago: University of Chicago Press).

Bliss, M. (1986), 'Who Discovered Insulin?', *NIPS*, 31–6.

Bloxam, G.A. (1957), 'Letters Patent for Inventions: Their Use and Misuse', *The Journal of Industrial Economics*, **5** (3), 157–79.

Blumberg, B.S. (1977), 'Australia Antigen and the Biology of Hepatitis B', *Science*, **197** (4298), 17–25.

Blumberg, B.S., A.I. Sutnick, W.T. London and I. Millman (1970) 'Australia Antigen and Hepatitis', *New England Journal of Medicine*, **283** (7), 349–54.

Bohonos, N. and H.D. Piersma (1966), 'Natural Products in the Pharmaceutical Industry', *BioScience*, **16** (10), 706–14.

Borchard, E. (1943), 'Nationalization of Enemy Patents', *The American Journal of International Law*, **37**, 92–7.

Borchard, E. (1946), 'Protection of Foreign Investments', *Law and Contemporary Problems*, **11** (4), 835–47.

Borkin, J. and C.A. Welsh (1943), *Germany's Master Plan: The Story of Industrial Offensive* (New York: Duell, Sloan and Pearce).

Boucher, D.H. (1991), 'Cocaine and the Coca Plant', *BioScience*, **41** (2), 72–6.

Bowering, F. (2003), *Science, Seeds and Cyborgs: Biotechnology and the Appropriation of Life* (London: New York: Verso).

Boyer, R.J.F. (1944), 'Australia's Stake in World Organization', *Pacific Affairs*, **17** (4), 373–91.

Bradley, D.W. et al. (1979), 'Experimental Infection of Chimpanzees With Antihemophilic (Factor VIII) Materials: Recovery of Virus-Like Particles Associated with Non A, Non B Hepatitis', *Journal of Medical Virology*, **3**, 253–69.

Bradley, D.W. et al. (1980), 'Non-A /Non-B Hepatitis in Experimentally Infected Chimpanzees: Cross Challenge and Electron Microscopic Studies, *Journal of Medical Virology*, **6**, 185–201.

Braithwaite, J. (1984), *Corporate Crime in the Pharmaceutical Industry* (London: Routledge & Kegan Paul).

Bray, M.W. (1999), 'Trade as an Instrument of Dominance: The Latin American Experience', *Latin American Perspectives*, **26** (5), 55–74.

Brice, P. and S. Sanderson (2006), 'Pharmacogenetics: What are the Ethical and Economic Implications?', *The Pharmaceutical Journal*, **277**, 113–14.

Broughton, J. (2001), 'The Case against Harry Dexter White: Still Not Proven', *History of Political Economy*, **33** (2), 219–39.

Bugos, G.E. and D.J. Kevles (1992), 'Plants as Intellectual Property: American Practice, Law, and Policy in World Context, *Osiris*, 2nd Series, **7**, 74–104.

Burke, K. (1997), 'Loose-fitting Genes: The Inadequacies in Federal Regulation of Institutional Review Boards', *Boston University Journal of Science & Technology Law*, **3**, 10–46.

Butler, D. and S. Goodman (2001), 'French Researchers take a Stand against Gene Patent', *Nature*, **413**, 95–6.

Campbell, L.H. (1891), *The Patent System of the United States so Far as it Relates to the Granting of Patents* (Washington, DC: McGill and Wallace).

Caulfield, T., R. Cook-Deegan, F.S. Kieff and J.P. Walsh (2006), 'Evidence and Anecdotes: an Analysis of Human Gene Patenting Controversies', *Nature Biotechnology*, **24** (9), 1091–4.

Chain, E.B. (1963), 'Academic and Industrial Contributions to Drug Research', *Nature*, **200** (4905), 441–51.

Chan, S. and J. Harris (2006), 'The Ethics of Gene Therapy', *Current Opinion in Molecular Therapeutics*, **8** (5), 377–83.

Chandler, A.D. (1992), 'Organizational Capabilities and the Economic History of the Industrial Enterprise', *The Journal of Economic Perspectives*, **6** (3), 79–100.

Chappell, R.L. and W.H. Kenyon (1947), 'Patent Costs of Military Procurement in Wartime', *Law and Contemporary Problems*, **12**, 695–713.

Chaturvedi, K. and J. Chataway (2003), 'Policy and Technology Co-evolution in the Indian Pharmaceutical Industry', available at http://www.sussex.ac.uk/Units/spru/events/ocs/viewpaper.php?id=288.

Chaussivert, J. and M. Blackman (1987), *Louis Pasteur and the Pasteur Institute in Australia*, Occasion Monograph No 1, University of New South Wales, 4–5 September.

Choo, Q.L., G. Kuo, A.J. Weiner, L.R. Overby, D.W. Bradley and M. Houghton (1989), 'Isolation of a cDNA Clone Derived from a Blood-borne non-A, non-B Viral Hepatitis Genome', *Science*, New Series, **244**, 359–62.

Cipolla, C.M. (1952), 'The Decline of Italy: The Case of a Fully Matured Economy', *The Economic History Review*, **5** (2), 178–87.

Cipolla, C.M. (1963), 'Currency Depreciation in Medieval Europe', *The Economic History Review*, **15** (3), 413–22.

Cipolla, C.M. (1972), 'The Diffusions of Innovations in Early Modern Europe', *Comparative Studies in Society and History*, **14** (1), 46–52.

Clark, P. (1978), 'Thomas Scott and the Growth of Urban Opposition to the Early Stuart Regime', *The Historical Journal*, **21** (1), 1–26.

Cohen, J. (1999), 'The Scientific Challenge of Hepatitis C', *Science*, New Series, **285** (5424), 26–30.

Cohen, S.N., A.C.Y. Chang, H.C. Boyer and R.B. Helling (1973), 'Construction of Biologically Functional Bacterial Plasmids In Vitro', *Proceedings of the National Academy of Sciences of the United States of America*, **70** (11) 3240–44.

Coke, E. (1611), *The Reports of Sir Edward Coke*, Part 8, in Sheppard, S. (ed.) (2003), *The Selected Writings and Speeches of Sir Edward Coke, Vol. 1* (Indianapolis, Indiana: Liberty Fund).

Coke, E. (1615), *The Reports of Sir Edward Coke*, Part 11, in Sheppard, S. (ed.) (2003), *The Selected Writings and Speeches of Sir Edward Coke, Vol. 1* (Indianapolis, Indiana: Liberty Fund).

Coke, E. (1656), *The Reports of Sir Edward Coke*, Part 12, in Sheppard, S. (ed.) (2003), *The Selected Writings and Speeches of Sir Edward Coke, Vol. 1* (Indianapolis, Indiana: Liberty Fund).

Colclough, O.S. (1953), 'A New Patent Act – But the Same Basic Problem', *Journal of the Patent Office Society*, **35** (7), 501–11.

Connor, S. (2008), 'Playing God: the Man who would Create Artificial Life', *The Independent*, 25 January.

Cook, H.J. (1985), 'Against Common Right and Reason: The College of Physicians Versus Dr. Thomas Bonham', *American Journal of Legal History*, **29**, 301–22.

Cook-Deegan, R.M. and E. Marshall (1997), 'Insulin Gene Patent Litigation', *Science*, New Series, **278** (5338), 560–61.

Cooper, C.C. (1991), 'Making Inventions Patent', *Technology and Culture*, **32** (4), 837–45.

Cooper, C.C. (1991), 'Social Construction of Invention through Patent Management: Thomas Blanchard's Woodworking Machinery', *Technology and Culture*, **32** (4), 960–98.

Corley, T.A.B. (1999), 'The British Pharmaceutical Industry Since 1851', *Centre for International History, Working Paper Series, University of Reading*, available at http://www.rdg.ac.uk/Econ/Econ/working papers/emdp404.pdf, reproduced in Richmond, L., J. Stevenson and

A. Turton (2003), *The Pharmaceutical Industry: a Guide to Historical Records* (Aldershot: Ashgate Publishing Limited; Burlington: Ashgate Publishing Company).

Correa, C.M. (2006), 'Implications of Bilateral Free trade Agreements in Access to Medicines', *Bulletin of the World Health Organization*, **84**, 399–404.

Coscelli, A. (2000), 'The Importance of Doctors' and Patients' Preferences in the Prescription Decision', *The Journal of Industrial Economics*, **48** (3), 349–69.

Crespi, S. (1995), 'Biotechnology Patenting: The Wicked Animal Must Defend Itself', *European Intellectual Property Review*, **17** (9), 431–41.

Crespi, S. (2000), 'Patents on Genes: Can the Issues be Clarified?', *Bio-Science Law Review*, **3** (5), 199–204.

Crowell, M.W. (2006), 'Bayh-Dole at 25 Years: Where have We Been, and What Can We Expect?', Report on the International Patent Licensing Seminar 2006, available at http://www.ryutu.inpit.go.jp/seminar_a/2006/pdf/ps1_e.pdf.

Cuddly, K.J. (2003), 'Between the Lines: Crouching Tariffs, Hidden Protectionism', *Foreign Policy*, **134**, 74–5.

Dam, K.W. (2004), 'Cordell Hull, The Reciprocal Trade Agreement Act, and the WTO', *New York University Journal of Law and Business*, **1**, 709–30.

Daniel, E.M. (1884), *A Complete Treatise upon The New Law of Patents, Designs and Trade Marks Act, 1883* (London: Steven & Hayes).

Danzon, P.M. and L. Chao (2000), 'Does Regulation Drive out Competition in Pharmaceutical Markets?', *Journal of Law and Economics*, **43** (2), 311–57.

Davies, R.B. (1969), ' "Peacefully Working to Conquer the World:" The Singer Manufacturing Company in Foreign Markets, 1854–1889', *The Business History Review*, **43** (3), 299–325.

Davonport-Hines, R. (2007), 'Jephcott, Sir Harry', *Oxford Dictionary of National Biography*, available at http://www.oxforddnb.com.virtual.anu.edu.au/view/printable/31286.

de Berg, H. (1967), 'Transcript of Taped Interview with Lord Howard Florey', 5 April, National Library of Australia, Canberra.

de Carvalho, N.P. (2002), *The TRIPS Regime of Patent Rights* (New York: Kluwer Law International).

Demaine, L.J. and A.X. Fellmeth (2002), 'Reinventing the Double Helix: A Novel and Nonobvious Reconceptualization of the Biotechnology Patent', *Stanford Law Review*, **55**, 303–462.

Dickson, D. (1996), ' "Leak" Rumours Fuel Debate on Gene Patent', *Nature*, **379** (6566), 574.

Diggins, B. (1955), 'The Patent-Antitrust Problem', *Michigan Law Review*, **53** (8), 1093–1118.

Donnelly, J.F. (1986), 'Representations of Applied Science: Academics and Chemical Industry in Late Nineteenth-Century England', *Social Studies of Science*, **16** (2), 195–234.

Dood, K.J. (1991), 'Pursuing the Essence of Inventions: Reissuing Patents in the 19th Century', *Technology and Culture*, **32** (4), 999–1017.

Drahos, P. (1996), *A Philosophy of Intellectual Property* (Aldershot, Brookfield: Dartmouth).

Drahos, P. (1999), 'Biotechnology Patents, Markets and Morality', *European Intellectual Property Review*, **21** (9), 441–9.

Drahos, P. with J. Braithwaite (2002), *Information Feudalism* (London: Earthscan Publications Ltd).

Drahos, P. (ed.) (2005), *Death of Patents* (London: Lawtext Publishing and Queen Mary Intellectual Property Law Institute).

Dreyfuss, R.C. (1989), 'The Federal Circuit: A Case Study in Specialized Courts', *New York University Law Review*, **64**, 1.

Ducor, P.G. (1996), 'In Re Deuel: Biotechnology Industry v Patent Law', *European Intellectual Property Review*, **18** (1), 35–46.

Ducor, P.G. (1998), *Patenting the Recombinant Products of Biotechnology and Other Molecules* (London, Cambridge, US: Kluwer Law International).

Dukes, G. (2006), *The Law and Ethics of the Pharmaceutical Industry* (London, New York: Elsevier).

Dunford, R. (1987), 'The Suppression of Technology as a Strategy for Controlling Resource Dependence', *Administrative Science Quarterly*, **32** (4), 512–25.

Dunlavey, D.C. (1954), 'Can Artificially Created Isotopes of Chemical Elements Be Patented?', *California Law Review*, **42** (4), 676–89.

Dunner, D.R., J.M. Jakes and J.D. Karceski (1995), 'A Statistical Look at the Federal Circuit's Patent Decisions: 1982–1994,' *Federal Circuit Bar Journal*, **5**, 151–80.

Dunning, J.H. and H. Archer (1987), 'The Eclectic Paradigm and the Growth of UK Multinational Enterprise 1870–1983', *Business and Economic History*, **16** (2), 19–49.

Dutfield, G. (2003), *Intellectual Property Rights and the Life Sciences* (Hampstead: Ashgate Publishing Limited; Burlington: Ashgate Publishing Company).

Dutfield, G. (2007), 'Making TRIPS Work for Developing Countries', in G.P. Sampson and W. Bradnee Chambers (eds), *Developing Countries and the WTO: Policy Approaches* (New York: United Nations University Press).

Easterlin, R.A. (2000), 'The Worldwide Standard of Living since 1800', *The Journal of Economic Perspectives*, **14** (1), 7–26.

Eckes, A.E. (1973), 'Open Door Expansionism Reconsidered: The World War II Experience', *The Journal of American History*, **59** (4), 909–24.

Economist (The) (2002), 'Innovation's golden goose', **365** (8303), 3 (14 December).

Economist (The) (2004), 'Scholars for dollars; Patents', **373** (8405), 69 (11 December).

Economist (The) (2005), 'Baying for blood or Doling out cash?; Intellectual property', **377** (8458), 115 (24 December).

Economist (The) (2006), 'Life 2.0 – Synthetic biology', **380** (8493), 76 (2 September).

Economist (The) (2007), 'Patent pending; Artificial life', **383** (8533), 76 (16 June).

Economist (The) (2008), 'Nearly there artificial life', **386** (8564), (26 January 2008).

Eisenberg, R.S. (1987), 'Proprietary Rights and the Norms of Science in Biotechnology Research', *The Yale Law Journal*, **97** (2), 177–231.

Eisenberg, R.S. (1990), 'Patenting the Human Genome', *Emory Law Journal*, **39**, 721–45.

Eisenberg, R.S. (2000), 'Re-Examining the Role of Patents in Appropriating the Value of DNA Sequences', *Emory Law Journal*, **49**, 783–800.

Eisner, F.W. (1945), 'Administrative Machinery and Steps for the Lawyer', *Law and Contemporary Problems*, **11** (1), 61–75.

Ellsworth, P.T. (1949), ' The Havana Charter: Comment', *The American Economic Review*, **39** (6), 1268–73.

Eltis, K. (2007), 'Genetic Determinism and Discrimination: A Call to Re-orient Revailing Human Rights Discourse to Better Comport with the Public Implications of Individual Genetic Testing', *Journal of Law, Medicine & Ethics*, Summer, **35** (2), 281–194.

Fanning, L.J. and F. Shanahan (2000), 'The Hepatitis C Virus: Master of Diversity and Challenging Adversary', *Medscape General Medicine*, **2** (2), available at http://www.medscape.com/viewarticle/407947.

Favis, R. et al. (2000), 'Universal DNA Array Detection of Small Insertions and Deletions in BRCA 1 and BRCA 2', *Nature Biotechnology*, **18**, 561–4.

Feasby, W.B. (1958), 'The Discovery of Insulin', *Journal of the History of Medicine* 68–84.

Federico, P.J. (1937), 'Louis Pasteur's Patents', *Science*, New Series, **86** (2232), 327.

Federico, P.J. (1948), 'Compulsory Licensing in Other Countries', *Law and Contemporary Problems*, **13** (2), 295–319.

Federico, P.J. (1950), 'The Concept of Patentable Invention', *Journal of the Patent Office Society*, **32**, 118–22.

Federico, P.J. (1993), 'Commentary on the New Patent Act', *Journal of the Patent Office Society*, **75**, 162–231.

Feldenkirchen, W. (1987), 'Big Business in Interwar Germany: Organizational Innovation at Vereinigte Stahlwerke, IG Farben, and Siemens', *The Business History Review*, **61** (3), 417–51.

Feldenkirchen, W. (1999) 'Germany: The Invention of Intervention' in Foreman-Peck, J. and G. Federico (eds), *European Industrial Policy The Twentieth-Century Experience* (Oxford: Oxford University Press).

Fels, R. (1949), 'The Long-Wave Depression, 1873–97', *The Review of Economics and Statistics*, **31** (1), 69–73.

Ferguson, J.H. (1946), 'The Anglo-American Financial Agreement and Our Foreign Economic Policy, *The Yale Law Journal*, **55** (5), 1140–57.

Fink, C. and K.E. Maskus (eds) (2005), *Intellectual Property and Development* (New York: World Bank and Oxford University Press).

Fletcher Moulton, H. and J.H. Evans-Jackson (1920), *The Patents, Designs, and Trade Marks Acts* (London: Butterworth & Co).

Folk, G.E. (1948), 'The Relation of Patents to the Antitrust Laws', *Law and Contemporary Problems*, **13** (2), 278–94.

Fox, H.G. (1947), 'Patents in Relation to Monopoly: A Rejoinder', *The Canadian Journal of Economics and Political Science*, **13** (1), 68–80.

Fox, R. (1996), 'Thomas Edison's Parisian Campaign: Incandescent Lighting and the Hidden Face of Technology Transfer', *Annals of Science*, **53** (2), 157–93.

Fraser, J. (1860), *A Handy-Book of Patent and Copyright Law* (London: Sampson Low, Son, and Co.).

Frost, G.E. (1967), 'The 1967 Patent Law Debate: First-to-Invent vs. First-to-File', *Duke Law Journal*, **5**, 923–42.

Frumkin, M. (1945), 'The Origins of Patents', *Journal of the Patent Office Society*, **27** (3), 143–8.

Fulton, D. (1902), *The Law and Practice Relating to Patents, Trade Marks and Designs* (London: Jordan & Sons, Limited).

Fulton, D. (1905), *The Law and Practice Relating to Patents, Trade Marks and Designs* (3rd edn, London: Jordan & Sons, Limited).

Fulton, D. (1910), *The Law and Practice Relating to Patents, Trade Marks and Designs* (4th edn, London: Jordan & Sons, Limited).

Futreal, P.A. et al. (1994), 'BRCA 1 Mutations in Primary Breast and Ovarian Carcinomas', *Science,* New Series, **266** (5182), 120–22.

Ganslandt, M., K. Maskus and E. Wong (2001), 'Developing and Distributing Essential Medicines to Poor Countries: The *Defend* Proposal', *The Research Institute of Industrial Economics*, Working Paper No. 552, 2001, available at http://www.naringslivsforskning.se/Wfiles/wp/WP552.pdf.

Geison, G.L. (1978), 'Pasteur's Work on Rabies: Reexamining the Ethical Issues', *The Hastings Center Report*, **8** (2), 26–33.

Geison, G.L. (1995), *The Private Science of Louis Pasteur* (Princeton: Princeton University Press).

Gervais, D. (2003), *The TRIPS Agreement: Drafting History and Analysis* (2nd edn, London: Sweet & Maxwell).

Gervais, D. (ed.) (2007), *Intellectual Property, Trade and Development* (Oxford: Oxford University Press).

Gibbon, G. (1942), 'The Beveridge Report', *Journal of the Royal Statistical Society*, **105** (4), 336–40.

Gibbons, G.R. (1965), 'Price Fixing in Patent Licenses and the Antitrust Laws', *Virginia Law Review*, **51** (2), 273–304.

Gibson, D.G. et al. (2008), 'Complete Chemical Synthesis, Assembly, and Cloning of a Mycoplasma Genitalium Genome', *Science Express*, available at www.sciencexpress.org / 24 January 2008 / Page 1 / 10.1126/science.1151721.

Gilmour, J. (1978), 'Industrialization and Technological Backwardness: The Canadian Dilemma', *Canadian Public Policy*, **4** (1), 20–33.

Gispen, K. (2002), *Poems in Steel: National Socialism and the Politics of Inventing from Weimer to Bonn* (Oxford and New York: Berghahn Books).

Glaser-Schmidt, E. (1994), 'Foreign Trade Strategies after World War I', *Business and Economic Review*, **23** (1), 201–11.

Goldstein, J.A. and E. Golod (2002), 'Human Gene Patents', *Academic Medicine*, **77** (12), 1315–28.

Goldstone, J.R. (1983), 'Capitalist Origins of the English Revolution: Chasing a Chimera', *Theory and Society*, **12** (2) 143–80.

Goldsworthy, P. and A.C. McFarlane (2002), 'Howard Florey, Alexander Fleming and the Fairy Tale of Penicillin', *Medical Journal of Australia*, **176**, 178–80.

Gorlin, J.J. (1985), 'A Trade-based Approach for the International Copyright Protection for Computer Software' (unpublished).

Greenwood, H.L., H. Thorsteinsóttir, G. Perry, P. Renihan, P.A. Singer and A.S. Darr (2006), 'Regenerative Medicine: New Opportunities for Developing Countries', *International Journal of Biotechnology*, **1** (2), 60–76.

Hagedorn, H.C., B.N. Jensen, N.B. Karup and I. Wodstrup (1936), 'Protamine Insulinate', *Journal of the American Medical Association*, **106**, 177–80.

Hagen, A. (1997), 'Patents Legislation and German FDI in the British Chemical Industry before 1914', *The Business History Review*, **71** (3), 351–80.

Hager, W. (1944), 'Protectionism and Autonomy: How to Preserve Free Trade in Europe', *International Affairs (Royal Institute of International Affairs 1944–)*, **58** (3), 413–28.

Halewood, M. (1997), 'Regulating Patent Holders: Local Working Requirements and Compulsory Licences at International Law', *Osgoode Hall Law Journal*, **35** (2), 243–87.

Hansson, M.G., G. Helgesson, R. Wessman and R. Jaenisch (2007), 'Isolated Stem Cells – Patentable As Cultural Artifacts?', *Stem Cells*, 1–19.

Harris, J. (2007), Biography: Beveridge, William Henry, *Oxford Dictionary of National Biography*, available at http://www.oxforddnb.com/view/printable/31871.

Haugen, H.M. (2007), 'Patent Rights and Human Rights: Exploring their Relationships', *The Journal of World Intellectual Property*, **10** (2), 97–124.

Heiduk, G. (1982), 'Multinationalization in the Pharmaceutical Industry as a Response to National Health Policies', *Managerial and Decision Economics*, **3** (4), 194–204.

Heller, M. and R.S. Eisenberg (1998), 'Do Patents Deter Innovation? The Tragedy of the Anticommons in Biomedical Research', *Science*, New Series, **280** (5364), 698–701.

Henckels, C. (2006), 'GMOs in the WTO: A Critique of the Panel's Legal Reasoning in EC–Biotech', *Melbourne Journal of International Law*, **7**, 278–305.

Henderson, H. (1949), 'A Criticism of the Havana Charter', *The American Economic Review*, **39** (3), 605–17.

Hendrickson, T.L. (2003), 'Yielding at Stop Codons: Expanding the Genetic Code', *Chemistry & Biology*, **10**, 475–9.

Hendrickson, T.L. (2004), 'Incorporation of Nonnatural Amino Acids Into Proteins', *Annual Review of Biochemistry*, **73**, 147–76.

Henkel, J. and S.M. Maurer (2007), 'The Economics of Synthetic Biology', *Molecular Systems Biology*, **3** (117), 2–4.

Herder, M. (2006), 'Proliferating Patent Problems with Human Embryonic Stem Cell Research?', *Bioethical Inquiry*, **3**, 69–79.

Hilaire-Pérez, L. (1991), 'Invention and the State in 18th-Century France', *Technology and Culture*, **32** (4), Special Issue: Patents and Invention, 911–31.

Hill, C. (1981), 'Parliament and People in Seventeenth-Century England', *Past and Present*, **92**, 100–24.

Hoekman, B.M. (1993), 'New Issues in the Uruguay Round and Beyond', *The Economic Journal*, **103** (421), 1528–39.

Hopkins, M.M., S. Mahdi, S.M. Thomas and P. Patel (2006), *The Patenting of Human DNA: Global Trends in Public and Private Sector Activity*, Project Report, SPRU, Science and Technology Policy Research, University of Sussex.

Hoselitz, B.F. (1947), 'International Cartel Policy', *The Journal of Political Economy*, **55** (1), 1–27.

Howson, H. and C. (1872), *A Brief Inquiry into the Principles, Effect, and Present State of the American Patent System* (Philadelphia: Sherman & Co.).

Hughes S.S. (2001), 'Making Dollars out of DNA: The First Major Patent in Biotechnology and the Commercialization of Molecular Biology, 1974–1980', *Isis*, **92** (3), 541–75.

Hull, C. (1948), *The Memoirs of Cordell Hull* (New York: Macmillan Co.).

Hulme, H. (1956), 'The Winning of Freedom of Speech by the House of Commons', *The American Historical Review*, **61** (4), 825–53.

Hulsebosch, D.J. (2003), 'The English Constitution and the Expanding Empire: Sir Edward Coke's British Jurisprudence', *SSRN*, available at: http://ssrn.com/abstract=440461.

Ikenberry, G.J. (1992), 'A World Economy Restored: Expert Consensus and the Anglo-American Postwar Settlement', *International Organization*, **46** (1), 289–321.

Iliasu, A.A. (1971), 'The Cobden-Chevalier Commercial Treaty of 1860', *The Historical Journal*, **14** (1), 67–98.

Irminger-Finger, I. and C.E. Jefford (2006), 'Is there More to BARD1 than BRCA1?', *Cancer*, **6**, 382–91.

Israel, P. and R. Rosenberg (1991), 'Patent Office Records as a Historical Source: The Case of Thomas Edison', *Technology and Culture*, **32** (4), 1094–101.

Itakura, K., H. Tadaaki, R. Crea, A.D. Riggs, H.L. Heyneker, F. Bolivar and H.W. Boyer (1973), 'Expression in *Escherichia coli* of a Chemically Synthesized Gene for the Hormone Somatostatin', *Science*, **198** (4321), 1056–63.

Jaffe, A.B. and J. Lerner (2004), *Innovations and Its Discontents: How Our Broken Patent System is Endangering Innovation and Progress, and What to Do About It* (Princeton: Princeton University Press).

Jefferson, M. (1929), 'The Geographical Distribution of Inventiveness', *Geographical Review*, **19** (4), 649–61.

Jennings, J. (1992), 'The Declaration des droits de l'homme et du citoyen and Its Critics in France: Reaction and Ideologie', *The Historical Journal*, **35** (4), 839–59.

Jensen, K. and F. Murray (2005), 'Intellectual Property Landscape of the Human Genome', *Science*, **310** (5746), 238–40.

Jensen, M.F. and P. Gibbon (2007), 'Africa and the WTO Doha Round: An Overview', *Development Policy Review*, **25** (1), 5–24.

Jones, G. (1988), 'Foreign Multinationals and British Industry before 1945', *The Economic History Review*, **41** (3) 429–53.

Joslin, E.P. (1919), *A Diabetic Manual for the Mutual use of Doctor and Patient* (2nd edn, Philadelphia: Lea & Febiger).

Kaiser, J. (2007), 'Attempt to Patent Artificial Organism Draws a Protest', *Science*, New Series, **316** (5831), 1557.

Kamstra, G., M. Döring, N. Scott-Ram, A. Sheard and H. Wixon (2002), *Patents on Biotechnological Inventions: The E.C. Directive* (London: Sweet & Maxwell).

Kane, D.H. (1950), 'Patentable Invention and Our Political Economy', *Journal of the Patent Office Society*, **32**, 89–96.

Kane, E.M. (2007), 'Molecules and Conflict: Cancer, Patents, and Women's Health,' *Journal of Gender, Social Policy and The Law*, **15** (2), 311–41.

Kelves, D.J. (2002), 'A History of Patenting Life in the United States with Comparative Attention to Europe and Canada', *Office for Official Publication of the European Commission*.

Keynes, J.M. (1919), *The Economic Consequences of the Peace* (New York: BiblioBazaar (2007 edition)).

Kiga, D. et al. (2002), 'An Engineered Escherichia coli Tyrosyl-tRNA Synthetase for Site-Specific Incorporation of an Unnatural Amino Acid into Proteins in Eukaryotic Translation and Its Application in a Wheat Germ Cell-Free System', *Proceedings of the National Academy of Sciences of the United States of America*, **99** (15), 9715–20.

King, M., J.H. Marks and J.B. Mandell (2003), 'Breast and Ovarian Cancer Risks Due to Inherited Mutations in BRCA 1 and BRCA 2', *Science*, New Series, **302** (5645), 643–6.

Kloppenburg, J.R. Jr (1988), *First the Seed: The Political Economy of Plant Biotechnology: 1492–2000* (New York: Cambridge University Press).

Knorr, K. (1948), 'The Bretton Woods Institutions in Transition', *International Organization*, **2** (1), 19–38.

Knowles, S. and S. Adams (2001), 'Who Owns My DNA?: The National And International Intellectual Property Laws on Human Embryonic Tissue and Cloning', *Cumberland Law Review*, **32**, 475–86.

Krayenbühl, C. and T. Rosenberg (1946), 'Crystalline Protamine Insulin', *Reports of the Steno Memorial Hospital*, **1**, 60–73.

Kremer, M. (2002), 'Pharmaceuticals and the Developing World', *The Journal of Economic Perspectives*, **16** (4), 67–90.

Kronstein, H. (1942), 'The Dynamics of German Cartels and Patents. I', *The University of Chicago Law Review*, **9** (4), 643–71.

Kronstein, H. (1943), 'The Dynamics of German Cartels and Patents. II', *The University of Chicago Law Review*, **10** (1), 49–69.

Kronstein, H. (1952), 'Application of The Sherman Act to International Combinations', *The American Journal of Comparative Law*, **1** (1), 128–33.

Kronstein, H. (1952), 'The Nationality of International Enterprises', *Columbia Law Review*, **52** (8), 983–1002.

Kronstein, H. and I. Till (1947), 'A Reevaluation of the International Patent Convention', *Law and Contemporary Problems*, **12** (4), 765–81.

Krueger, A.O. (1999), 'Are Preferential Trading Arrangements Trade-liberalizing or Protectionist?', *The Journal of Economic Perspectives*, **13** (4), 105–24.

Lanoszka, A. (2003), 'The Global Politics of Intellectual Property Rights and Pharmaceutical Drug Policies in Developing Countries', *International Political Science Review*, **24** (2), 181–97.

Lartigue, C. et al. (2007), 'Genome Transplantation in Bacteria: Changing One Species to Another', *Science*, New Series, **317** (5838), 362–638.

Lasagna, L. (1969), 'The Pharmaceutical Revolution: Its Impact on Science and Society', *Science*, New Series, **166** (3910), 1227–33.

Law, S.D. (1870), *Copyright and Patent Laws of the United States, 1790 to 1870* (New York: Baker, Voorhis & Company).

Leaf, C. (2005), 'The Law of Unintended Consequences', *Fortune*, 19 September 2005, available at http://money.cnn.com/magazines/fortune/fortune_archive/2005/09/19/8272884/index.htm.

Leftwich, C. (2002), 'Patentable Subject [Anti]Matter', *Duke Law & Technology Review*, **27**, 22–34.

Leibovitz, J.S. (2002), 'Inventing a Nonexclusive Patent System', *The Yale Law Journal*, **111** (8), 2251–87.

Leonard, D.G.B. (2002), 'Medical Practice and Gene Patents: A Personal Perspective', *Academic Medicine*, **77** (12), 1388–91.

Lerner, J. (1995), 'Patenting in the Shadow of Competitors', *Journal of Law and Economics*, **38**, 463–95.

Letwin, W.L. (1954), 'The English Common Law concerning Monopolies', *The University of Chicago Law Review*, **21** (3), 355–85.

Li, A. (2003), *J.B. Collip and the Development of Medical Research in Canada* (Montreal; Canada: McGill-Queen's University Press).

Liebenau, J. (1987), 'The British Success with Penicillin', *Social Studies of Science*, **17** (1), 69–86.

Lipinski, T.A. and J.J. Britz (2000), 'Rethinking the Ownership of Information in the 21st Century: Ethical Implications', *Ethics and Information Technology*, **2**, 49–71.

Lippincott, I. (1919), 'Economic Factors in the Peace Settlement', *Annals of the American Academy of Political and Social Science*, **83**, 249–65.

List, F. (1841), *The National System of Political Economy* (translated by S.S. Lloyd MP, 1885 edn) (London: Longmans, Green & Co.).

Liu, W., A. Brock, S. Chen, S. Chen and P. Schultz (2007), 'Genetic Incorporation of Unnatural Amino Acids into Proteins in Mammalian Cells', *Nature Methods*, **4** (3), 239–44.

Lobell, S.E. (1999), 'Second Image Reversed Politics: Britain's Choice of Freer Trade or Imperial Preferences, 1903–1906, 1917–1923, 1930–1932', *International Studies Quarterly*, **43** (4), 671–93.

Long, P.O. (1991), 'Invention, Authorship, "Intellectual Property", and the Origin of Patents: Notes toward a Conceptual History', *Technology and Culture*, **32** (4), 846–84.

Lubar, S. (1991), 'The Transformation of Antebellum Patent Law', *Technology and Culture*, **32** (4), 932–59.

Lutz, K.B. (1953), 'The New 1952 Patent Statute', *Journal of the Patent Office Society*, **35** (3), 155–62.

Machlup, F. and E. Penrose (1950), 'The Patent Controversy in the Nineteenth Century', *The Journal of Economic History*, **10** (1), 1–29.

Machlup, F. (1961), 'Patents and Inventive Effort', *Science*, New Series, **133** (3463), 1463–6.

Maclaurin, W.R. (1953), 'The Sequence from Invention to Innovation and its Relation to Economic Growth', *The Quarterly Journal of Economics*, **67** (1), 97–111.

MacLeod, C. (1991), 'The Paradoxes of Patenting: Invention and Its Diffusion in 18th- and 19th-Century Britain, France, and North America', *Technology and Culture*, **32** (4), Special Issue: Patents and Invention, 885–910.

MacLeod, C. (1992), 'Strategies for Innovation: The Diffusion of New Technology in Nineteenth-Century British Industry', *The Economic History Review*, **45** (2), 285–307.

MacLeod, C., J. Tann, J. Andrew and J. Stein (2003), 'Evaluating Inventive Activity: the Cost of Nineteenth-century UK Patents and the Fallibility of Renewal Data', *The Economic History Review*, **46** (3), 537–62.

MacLeod, C. and A. Nuvolari (2006), 'The Pitfalls of Prosopography: Inventors in the Dictionary of National Biography', *Technology and Culture*, **47** (4), 757–76.

Madison, J.H. (1989), 'Manufacturing Pharmaceuticals: Eli Lilly and Company, 1876–1948', *Business and Economic History*, Second Series, **18**, 72–8.

Madrigal, A. (2008), 'Scientist Build First Man-made Genome; Synthetic Life Comes Next', *Wired*, 24 January, available at http://www.wired. com/print/science/discoveries/news/2008/01/synthetic_genome.

Magliery, T.J. (2005), 'Unnatural Protein Engineering: Producing Proteins with Unnatural Amino Acids', *Medical Chemistry Reviews-Online*, **2** (4), 303–23, available at http://www.ingentaconnect.com/content/ben/ mcro/2005/00000002/00000004/art00005.

Maier, C.S. (1977), 'The Politics of Productivity: Foundations of American International Economic Policy after World War II', *International Organization*, **31** (4), 607–33.

Malament, B. (1967), 'The "Economic Liberalism" of Sir Edward Coke', *Yale Law Journal*, **76** (7), 1321–58.

Managing Intellectual Property (2007), 'Drug maker hits back in Thai patent row' (1 March).

Managing Intellectual Property (2007), 'Why Thailand is at the centre of a patent storm' (March).

Managing Intellectual Property (2007), 'More drugs under threat in Thailand' (24 September).

Managing Intellectual Property (2008), 'EPO and US speed up patent-granting process' (17 March).

Managing Intellectual Property (2008), 'Federal Circuit seeks new patent-ability test in Bilski' (12 May).

Mandich, G. (1948), 'Venetian Patents (1450–1550)', *Journal of the Patent Office Society*, **30** (3), 166–224.

Mandich, G. (1960), 'Venetian Origins of Inventors' Rights', *Journal of the Patent Office Society*, **42**, 378–82.

Marshall, E. (1995), 'NIH Gets a Share of BRCA 1 Patent', *Science*, New Series, **267** (5201), 1086.

Marshall, E. (1996), 'Rifkin's Latest Target: Genetic Testing', *Science*, New Series, **272** (5265), 1094.

Marshall, E. (1997), 'Gene Tests Get Tested', *Science*, New Series, **275** (5301), 782.

Marshall, E. (1997), 'A Bitter Battle Over Insulin Gene', *Science*, New Series, **277** (5329), 1028–30.

Marshall, E. (1997), 'The Battle Over BRCA1 Goes to Court; BRCA2 May be Next', *Science*, New Series, **278** (5345), 1874.

Marshall, E. (2005), 'BRCA 2 Claim Faces New Challenge', *Science*, New Series, **308** (5730), 1851.

Marshall, E. (2005), 'Potentially More Lethal Variant Hits Migratory Birds in China', *Science*, New Series, **309** (5732), 231.

Maskel, G.S. (2006), 'Product-by-Process patent Claim Construction: Resolving the Federal Circuit's Conflicting Precedent', *Fordham*

Intellectual Property Media & Entertainment Law Journal, **17**, 115–52.

Maskus, K.E. (2000), 'Intellectual Property Rights and Economic Development', *Case Western Reserve Journal of International Law*, **32** (3), 471–506.

Maskus, K.E. (2004), 'The Globalization of Private Knowledge Goods and the Privatization of Global Public Goods' in K.E. Maskus and J.H. Riechman (eds), *International Public Goods & Transfer of Technology under a Globalized Intellectual Property Regime* (Cambridge: Cambridge University Press).

Maskus, K.E. (2006), 'Reforming US Patent Policy: Getting the Incentive Right', *Innovations*, **1** (4), 127–53.

Matthijs, G. (2006), 'The European Opposition Against the BRCA 1 Gene Patent', *Familial Cancer*, **5**, 95–102.

Maugh, T.H. (1981), 'FDA Approves Hepatitis B Vaccine', *Science*, New Series, **214** (4525), 1113.

May, C. (2002), 'The Venetian Movement: New Technologies, Legal Innovation and the Institutional Origins of Intellectual Property,' *Prometheus*, **20** (2), 159–79.

May, C. and S. Sell (2005), *Intellectual Property: A Critical History* (Boulder: Lynne Rienner Publishers).

Mayer, S. (2006), 'Declaration of Patent Applications as Financial Interests: a Survey of Practice among Authors of Papers on Molecular Biology in Nature', *Journal of Medical Ethics*, **32**, 658–61.

McKenna, S. (1996), 'Patentable Discovery?', *San Diego Law Review*, **33**, 1241–79.

McLean, D. (2006), 'From British Colony to American Satellite? Australia and the USA during the Cold War', *Australian Journal of Politics and History*, **52** (1), 64–79.

Mead, A.T.P. and S. Read (eds) (2007), *Pacific Genes & Life Patents* (Call of the Earth Llamado de la Tierra and The United Nations University Institute of Advanced Studies), available at http://www.earthcall.org/en/publications/index.html.

Meier, G.M. (1971), 'The Bretton Woods Agreement – Twenty-Five Years After', *Stanford Law Review*, **23** (2), 235–75.

Meinhardt, P. (1949), 'Patents and Inventions. Use by Crown', *Modern Law Review*, **12** (1), 112–4.

Merges, R.P. (1988), 'Commercial Success and Patent Standards: Economic Perspectives on Innovation', *California Law Review*, **76** (4), 803–76.

Merges, R.P. (2000), 'One Hundred Years of Solicitude: Intellectual Property Law, 1900–2000', *California Law Review*, **88** (6), 2187–240.

Merges, R.P. and R.R. Nelson (1990), 'On the Complex Economics of Patent Scope', *Columbia Law Review*, **90** (4), 839–916.

Mgbeoji, I. (2003), 'The Juridical Origins of the International Patent System: Towards a Historiography of the Role of Patents in Industrialization', *Journal of the History of International Law*, **5** (2), 403–22

Miki, Y. et al. (1994), 'A Strong Candidate for the Breast and Ovarian Cancer Susceptibility Gene BRCA 1', *Science*, New Series, **266** (5182), 66–71.

Miller, M.H. and J.E. Spencer (1977), 'The Static Economic Effects of the UK Joining the EEC: A General Equilibrium Approach', *The Review of Economic Studies*, **44** (1), 71–93.

Monbiot, G. (2003), 'Enslaved by Free Trade', *New Scientist*, **178** (2397), 25.

Morrow, J.F., S.N. Cohen, A.C.Y. Chang, H.W. Boyer, H.M. Goodman and R.B. Helling (1974), 'Replication and Transcription of Eukaryotic DNA in Escherichia coli', *Proceedings of the National Academy of Sciences of the United States of America*, **71** (5), 1743–7.

Mossoff, A. (2001), 'Rethinking the Development of Patents: An Intellectual History, 1550–1800', *Hastings Law Journal*, **52**, 1255, available at http://papers.ssrn.com/sol3/papers.cfm?abstract_id=863925.

Mowery, D.C. and B. Sampat (2004), 'The Bayh-Dole Act of 1980 and University–Industry Technology Transfer: A Model for Other OECD Governments?', *The Journal of Technology Transfer*, **30** (1–2), 115–27.

Murashige, K. (2002), 'Patents and Research – An Uneasy Alliance', *Academic Medicine*, **77** (12), 1320–38.

Murray, I. (1971), 'Paulesco and the Isolation of Insulin', *Journal of the History of Medicine*, April, 150–57.

Narod, S.A. and W.D. Foulkles (2004), 'BRCA 1 and BRCA 2: 1994 and Beyond', *Cancer*, **4**, 666–76.

Nathanson, K., R. Wooster and B.L. Webber (2001), 'Breast Cancer Genetics: What We Know and What We Need', *Nature Medicine*, **7** (5), 552–5.

Nature (editorial) (2007), 'Patenting the parts', *Nature*, **25** (8), 822.

Nayyer, D. (1992), 'The Dunkel Text: An Assessment', *Social Scientist*, **20** (1–2), 108–14.

Nelson, R.R. (2003), 'The Advance of Technology and the Scientific Commons', *Philosophical Transactions: Mathematical, Physical and Engineering Sciences*, **361** (1809), 1691–708.

Neumeyer, F. (1961), 'European Patent Legislation', *Modern Law Review*, **24**, 725–37.

Neushul, P. (1989), 'Seaweed for War: California's World War I Kelp Industry', *Technology & Culture*, **30** (3), 561–83.

Nolff, M. (2001), *TRIPS, PCT and Global Patent Procurement* (The Hague: Kluwer Law International).

Note: (1938), 'Lectureship in Honor of Dr. Julius Stieglitz', *Science*, New Series, **87** (2245), 9–10.

Note: (1939), 'Revocation of a Patent by Government Suit', *The Yale Law Journal*, **48** (6), 1095–101.

Note: (1947), 'Consent Decrees and Absent Cartel Participants', *The Yale Law Journal*, **56**, 396–402.

Note: (1950), 'Agreement between the Allied High Commission in Germany and the West German Federal Republic, Signed at Bonn, November 24, 1949', *International Organization*, **4** (1), 184–7.

Note: (1961), 'United States Participation in the General Agreement on Tariffs and Trade', *Columbia Law Review*, **61** (3), 505–69.

Notz, W. (1921), 'New Phases of Unfair Competition and Measures for Its Suppression: National and International', *The Yale Law Journal*, **30** (4), 384–94.

Nowak, R. (1994), 'Breast Cancer Gene Offers Surprises', *Science*, New Series, **265** (5180), 1796–9.

Nowak, R. (1994), 'NIH Danger of Losing Out on BRCA 1 Patent', *Science*, New Series, **266** (5183), 209.

Nye, J.V. (1991), 'The Myth of Free-trade Britain and Fortress France: Tariffs and Trade in the Nineteenth Century', *The Journal of Economic History*, **51** (1), 23–46.

Odek, J.O. (1994), 'The Kenya Patent Law: Promoting Local Inventiveness or Protecting Foreign Patentees?', *Journal of African Law*, **38** (2), 79–103.

Olson, D.S. (2006), 'Patentable Subject Matter: The Problem of the Absent Gatekeeper', *SSRN*, 933167.

Opie, R. (1957), 'Anglo-American Economic Relations in War-Time', *Oxford Economic Papers*, New Series, **9** (2), 115–51.

O'Reilly, D. (2006), 'Vesting GAF Corporation: The Roosevelt Administration's Decision to Americanise I.G. Farben's American Affiliates in World War II', *History and Technology*, **22** (2), 153–86.

Oudemans, G. (1963), *The Draft European Patent Convention* (London: Stevens & Sons Ltd; New York: Mathew Bender & Co. Inc.).

Owens, L. (1991), 'Patents, the "Frontiers" of American Invention, and the Monopoly Committee of 1939: Anatomy of a Discourse', *Technology and Culture*, **32** (4), 1076–93.

Oyer, P.E., S. Cho, J.D. Peterson and D.F. Steiner (1971), 'Studies on Human Proinsulin: Isolation and Amino Acid Sequences of the Human Pancreatic C-Peptide', *Journal of Biological Chemistry*, **246** (5), 1375–86.

Paine, T. (1791), *Rights of Man*, in M.D. Conway (ed.) (1894), *The Writings of Thomas Paine* (New York: G.P. Putnam's Sons).

Palombi, L. (2004), *The Patenting of Biological Materials in the Context of TRIPS*, PhD thesis, University of New South Wales, Sydney, Australia, available at http://cgkd.anu.edu.au/menus/PDFs/Palombi-PhD_Thesis.pdf.

Paradise, J., L. Andrews and T. Holbrook (2005), 'Patents on Human Genes: An Analysis of Scope and Claims', *Science*, **307** (5715), 1566–7.

Park, A. (2008) 'Scientist Creates Life – Almost', *Time*, 24 January.

Parry, C. (1941), 'The Trading with the Enemy Act and the Definition of an Enemy', *Modern Law Review*, **4** (3), 161–82.

Parry, J.P. (2001), 'The Impact of Napoleon III on British Politics, 1851–1880', *Transactions of the Royal Historical Society*, 6th Ser., **11**, 147–75.

Pattel, S. (1992), 'Statement to the Group of Ministers on Arthur Dunkel's Draft of the Final Act on Uruguay round of GATT Negotiations', *Social Scientist*, **20** (1–2), 99–107.

Pauwelyn, J. (2001), 'The Role of Public International Law in the WTO: How Far Can We Go?', *The American Journal of International Law*, **95** (3), 535–78.

Pennisi, E. (2005), 'Synthetic Biology Remakes Small Genomes', *Science*, New Series, **310** (5749), 769–70.

Pennisi, E. (2007), 'Replacement Genome Gives Microbe New Identity', *Science*, New Series, **316** (5833), 1827.

Ponder, B. (1994), 'Searches Begin and End', *Nature*, **371** (6495), 279.

Pottage, A. (2006), 'Too Much Ownership: Bio-prospecting in the Age of Synthetic Biology', *BioSocieties*, **1**, 137–58.

Powell, J. F. (1959), 'Patents: Standard of Invention: Effects of Sections 103 and 282 of Patent Act of 1952', *Michigan Law Review*, **57** (3), 426–9.

Prager, F.D. (1946), 'Brunelleschi's Patent', *Journal of the Patent Office Society*, **28** (2), 109–35.

Prager, F.D. (1952), 'Standards of Patentable Invention from 1474 to 1952', *The University of Chicago Law Review*, **20** (1), 69–95.

Prager, F.D. (1954), 'Proposals for the Patent Act of 1790', *Journal of the Patent Office Society*, **37** (3), 157–66.

Prager, F.D. (1961), 'The Influence of Mr. Justice Story on American Patent Law', *The American Journal of Legal History*, **5**, 254–64.

Prager, F.D. (1961), 'Historic Background and Foundation of American Patent Law', *The American Journal of Legal History*, **5**, 309–25.

Pratt, J.H. (1954), 'A Reappraisal of Researches leading to the Discovery of Insulin', *Journal of the History of Medicine*, July, 281–9.

Price, W.H. (2006), *The English Patents of Monopoly* (Clark, NJ: The Lawbook Exchange, Ltd).

Price, W.N. (2007), 'Patenting Race: The Problems of Ethnic Genetic Testing Patents', *The Columbia Science and Technology Law Review*, **8**, 119–46.

Prosser, R.B., M. Craven and S. Christian (2007), 'Lombe, Sir Thomas', *Oxford Dictionary of National Biography*, available at http://www.oxforddnb.com.virtual.anu.edu.au/view/printable/16956.

Rai, A. (2000), 'Addressing the Patent Gold Rush: The Role of Deference to PTO Patent Denials', USD School of Law, Public Working Paper No 5 and Law and Economics Research Paper 2, *SSRN*, 223758.

Rai, A. and J. Boyle (2007), 'Synthetic Biology: Caught between Property Rights, the Public Domain, and the Commons', *PloS Biology*, **5** (3), 389–93.

Rai, A. and S. Kumar (2007), 'Synthetic Biology: The Intellectual Property Puzzle', *Texas Law Review* **85**, 1745–68.

Re, E.D. (1953), 'United States: Dismissal of Suit for Failure to Produce Records; The "I.G. Chemie" Case', *The American Journal of Comparative Law*, **2** (4), 536–41.

Reeves, W.H. (1954), 'Is Confiscation of Enemy Assets in the National Interest of the United States?', *Virginia Law Review*, **40** (8), 1029–60.

Reingold, N. (1960), 'U.S. Patent Office Records as Sources for the History of Invention and Technological Property', *Technology and Culture*, **1** (2), 156–7.

Richards, D.G. (2004), *Intellectual Property Rights and Global Capitalism: The Political Economy of the TRIPS Agreement* (New York: M.E. Sharpe).

Rimmer, M. (2008), *Intellectual Property and Biotechnology* (Cheltenham, UK and Northhampton, MA, USA: Edward Elgar).

Ritter, D.S. (2004), 'Switzerland's Patent Law History', *Fordham Intellectual Property Media & Entertainment Law Journal*, **14**, 463–96.

Rosen, J.B. (1997), 'China, Emerging Economies, and the World Trade Order', *Duke Law Journal*, **46** (6), 1519–64.

Ross, E.J. (1945), 'Towards Postwar Social Cooperation', *The American Catholic Sociological Review*, **6** (2), 91–6.

Rossman, J. (1931), 'War and Invention', *The American Journal of Sociology*, **36** (4), 625–33.

Rostow, W.W. (1973), 'The Beginnings of Modern Growth in Europe: An Essay in Synthesis', *The Journal of Economic History*, **33** (3), 547–80.

Roth, J.K. (1980), 'Holocaust Business: Some Reflections on Arbeit Macht Frei,' *Annals of the American Academy of Political and Social Science*, **450**, 68–82.

Russell, A. (1999), 'Biotechnology as a Technological Paradigm in the Global Knowledge Structure', *Technology Analysis & Strategic Management*, **11** (2), 235–54.

Saalman, H. and P. Mattox (1985), 'The First Medici Palace', *The Journal of the Society of Architectural Historians*, **44** (4), 329–45.

Sandefur, T. (2002), 'The Common Law Right to Earn a Living', *The Independent Review*, **7** (1), 69–90.

Santoro, M.A. and T.M. Gorrie (eds) (2005), *Ethics and the Pharmaceutical Industry* (Cambridge: Cambridge University Press).

Safrin, S. (2004), 'Hyperownership in a Time of Biotechnological Promise: The International Conflict to Control the Building Blocks of Life', *The American Journal of International Law*, **98** (4), 641–85.

Salsman, R.M. (2004), 'The Cause and Consequences of the Great Depression, Part 1: What Made the Roaring '20s Roar', *The Intellectual Activist*, **18** (4), June, 16–24.

Sanger, F. (1958), 'The Chemistry of Insulin', *Nobel Lecture*, 11 December, 543–56.

Sayre, L.E. (1919), 'Patent Laws in Regard to the Protection of Chemical Industry', *Transactions of the Kansas Academy of Science*, **30**, 39–44.

Schatz, A.W. (1970), 'The Anglo-American Trade Agreement and Cordell Hull's Search for Peace 1936–1938', *The Journal of American History*, **57** (1), 85–103.

Scherer, F.M. (2000), 'The Pharmaceutical Industry and World Intellectual Property Standards', *Vanderbilt Law Review*, **53** (6), 2245–54.

Scherer, F.M. (2005), 'The Role of Patents in two US Monopolization Cases', *International Journal of the Economics of Business*, **12** (3), 297–305.

Scherer, F.M. (2006), 'The Political Economy of Patent Policy Reform in the United States', Harvard University, August, 1–58, available at, http://www.researchoninnovation.org/scherer/patpolic.pdf.

Schiff, E. (1971), *Industrialization without National Patents: The Netherlands, 1869–1912, Switzerland, 1850–1907* (Princeton, NJ: Princeton University Press).

Schröter, H.G. (1993), 'The German Question, the Unification of Europe, and the European Market Strategies of Germany's Chemical and Electrical Industries, 1900–1992', *The Business History Review*, **67** (3), 369–405.

Schurman, R.A. and D.D.T. Kelso (eds) (2003), *Engineering Trouble: Biotechnology and Its Discontents* (Berkeley and Los Angeles: University of California Press).

Schuster, E.J. (1913), 'Germany', *Journal of the Society of Comparative Legislation,* New Series, **13** (2), 302–3.

Schuster, G. (1909), 'The Patents and Designs Act, 1907', *The Economic Journal*, **19** (76), 538–51.

Scott, P. and T. Rooth (1999), 'Public Policy and Foreign-Based Enterprises in Britain Prior to the Second World War,' *The Historical Journal*, **42** (2), 495–515.

Scoville, W.C. (1952), 'The Huguenots and the Diffusion of Technology II', *The Journal of Political Economy*, **60** (5), 392–411.

Seckelmann, M. (2001), 'The Quest for Legal Stability: Patent Protection within the German Empire, 1871–1903', *EBHA Conference 2001*: Business and Knowledge: E2: Patents and Knowledge, available at http://web.bi.no/forskning/ebha2001:nsf/dd5cab6801f17235852564740 05327c8/a6cb7066ea59edu6c12567f30056ef4d/$FILE/E2%20-%20seck elmann%20ii.PDF.

Sell, S.K. (2003), *Private Power, Public Law: The Globalization of Intellectual Property Rights* (Cambridge: Cambridge University Press).

Sella, D. (1991), 'Coping with Famine: The Changing Demography of an Italian Village in the 1590s', *Sixteenth Century Journal*, **22** (2), 185–97.

Service, R.F. (2001), 'High-speed Biologists Search for Gold in Proteins', *Science*, New Series, **294** (5549), 2074–7.

Sevilla, C. et al. (2003), 'Impact of Gene Patents on the Cost-Effective Delivery of Care: The Case of BRCA1 Genetic Testing', *International Journal of Technology Assessment in Health Care*, **19** (2), 287–300.

Sherman, B. (1990), 'Patent Law in a Time of Change: Non-Obviousness and Biotechnology', *Oxford Journal of Legal Studies*, **10** (2), 278–87.

Shlaes, A. (2007), *The Forgotten Man: A New History of the Great Depression* (New York: Harper Collins).

Simmonds, K.R. (1961), 'The Interhandel Case', *The International and Comparative Law Quarterly*, **10** (3), 495–547.

Sims, A. (2007), 'The Case Against Patenting Methods Of Medical Treatment', *European Intellectual Property Review*, **29** (2), 43–51.

Sinding, C. (2002), 'Making the Unit of Insulin: Standards, Clinical Work, and Industry, 1920–1925', *Bulletin of the History of Medicine*, **76**, 231–70.

Skolnick, M. (2007), 'Winning The Race to find BRCA1, *Dolan DNA Learning Center*, available at http://www.dnai.org/text/mediashowcase/index2.html?id=316.

Slinn, J. (2001), 'Innovation in the UK Pharmaceutical Industry 1948–1978', EBHA Conference 2001: Business and Knowledge, available at http://web.bi.no/forskning/ebha2001.nsf/23e5e39594c064ee852564ae00 4fa010/a6cb7066ea59edu6c12567f30056ef4d/$FILE/D2%20-%20Slinn. PDF.

Slinn, J. (2005), 'Prescription Pharmaceuticals in the UK,' *Business History*, **47** (3), 352–66.

Sluyterman, K.E. and H.J. Winkelman (1993), 'The Dutch Family Firm Confronted with Chandler's Dynamics of Industrial Capitalism, 1890–1940', *Business History*, **35** (4), 152–83.

Smith, C. (1890), 'A Century of Patent Law', *The Quarterly Journal of Economics*, **5** (1), 44–69.

Sommerich, O.C. (1945), 'A Brief against Confiscation', *Law and Contemporary Problems*, **11** (1), 152–65.

Sommerich, O.C. (1955), 'Treatment by United States of World War I and II Enemy-Owned Patents and Copyrights', *The American Journal of Comparative Law*, **4** (4), 587–600.

Spencer, R. (1949), 'The German Patent Office', *Journal of the Patent Office Society*, **31** (2), 79–86.

Steele, H. (1964), 'Patent Restrictions and Price Competition in the Ethical Drugs Industry', *The Journal of Industrial Economics*, **12** (3), 198–223.

Steen, K. (2001), 'Patents, Patriotism, and "Skilled in the Art": USA v The Chemical Foundation, 1923–1926', *Isis*, **92**, 91–122.

Stein, E. (1964), 'Assimilation of National Laws as a Function of European Integration', *The American Journal of International Law*, **58** (1), 1–40.

Stranges, A.N. (1984), 'Friedrich Bergius and the Rise of the German Synthetic Fuel Industry', *Isis*, **75** (4), 642–67.

Streb, J., J. Baten and S. Yin (2006), 'Technological and Geographical Knowledge Spillover in the German Empire 1877–1918', *The Economic History Review*, **49**, 347–73.

Streiffer, R. (2006), 'Academic Freedom and Academic–Industry Relationships in Biotechnology', *Kennedy Institute of Ethics Journal*, June, 129–49.

Sulston, J. (2006), 'Staking Claims in the Biotechnology Klondike', *Bulletin of the World Health Organization*, **84** (5), 412–13.

Swan, K.R. (1908), *The Law and Commercial Usage of Patents, Designs and Trade Marks* (London: Archibald Constable & Co Ltd).

Swann, J.P. (1985), 'Arthur Tatum, Parke-Davis, and the Discovery of the Mapharsen as an Antisyphilitic Agent', *Journal of the History of Medicine*, **40**, 167–87.

Tavtigian, S.V. et al. (1996), 'The Complete BRCA 2 Gene and Mutations in Chromosome 13q-linked Kindreds', *Nature Genetics*, **12**, 333–7.

Taylor, T. (1949), 'The Nuremberg War Crimes Trials: An Appraisal', *Proceedings of the Academy of Political Science*, **23** (3), 19–34.

Teeling-Smith, G. (1980), 'Economic Misconceptions in the Pharmaceutical Industry', *Managerial and Decision Economics*, **1** (1), 37–41.

Temim, P. (1979), 'Technology, Regulation, and Market Structure in the Modern Pharmaceutical Industry', *The Bell Journal of Economics*, **10** (2), 429–46.

Templeman, S. (1998), 'Intellectual Property', *Journal of International Economic Law*, **1** (4), 585–602.

Thomas, E. (1927), 'An Outline of the Law of Chemical Patents', *Industrial and Engineering Chemistry*, February, 315–17.

Thompson, D. (1973), 'The Draft Convention for a European Patent', *The International and Comparative Law Quarterly*, **22** (1), 51–82.

Thorne, H.C. (1926–7), 'Relation of Patent Law to Natural Products', *Journal of the Patent Office Society*, **6**, 23–7.

Timberg, S. (1972), 'Antitrust in the Common Market: Innovation and Surprise', *Law and Contemporary Problems*, **37** (2), 329–40.

Tucker, J.B. and R.A. Zilinskas (2006), 'The Promise and Perils of Synthetic Biology', *The New Atlantis* 25–45.

Turner, S.S. (2005), 'Critical Junctures in Genetic Medicine: The Transformation of DNA Lab Science to Commercial Pharmacogenomics', *Journal of Business and Technical Communication*, **19**, 328–62.

Turner, T. (1851), *The Law of Patents and Registration of Invention and Designs in Manufacture* (London: John Crockford).

Ullrich, A., J. Shine, J. Chirgwin, R. Pictet, E. Tischer, W.J. Rutter and H. Goodman (1977), 'Rat Insulin Genes: Construction of Plasmids Containing the Coding Sequences', *Science*, New Series, **196** (4296), 1313–19.

Usselman, S.W. (1991), 'Patents Purloined: Railroads, Inventors, and the Diffusion of Innovation in 19th-Century America', *Technology and Culture*, **32** (4), 1047–75.

Vaughan, F.W. (1919), 'Suppression and Non-working of Patents, With Special Reference to the Dye and Chemical Industries', *The American Economic Review*, **9** (4), 693–700.

Verspagen, B. (1999), 'Large Firms and Knowledge Flows in the Dutch R&D System: A Case Study of Philips Electronics', *Technology Analysis & Strategic Management*, **11** (2), 211–33.

Victoria, M. (1978), 'The Patents Act, 1977', *Modern Law Review*, **41** (3), 328–9.

Wade, N. (1977), 'Recombinant DNA: NIH Rules Broken in Insulin Gene Project', Science, New Series, **197** (4311), 1342–5.

Wade, R.H. (2003), 'What Strategies are Viable for Developing Countries Today? The World Trade Organization and the Shrinking of "Development space"', *Review of International Political Economy*, **10** (4), 621–44.

Wadlow, C. (2006), 'The British Empire Patent 1901–1923: The "Global" Patent That Never Was', *Intellectual Property Quarterly*, **4**, 311–46.

Waller, J. (2002), *The Discovery of the Germ* (Cambridge: Icon Books).

Waller, S.W. (2004), 'The Antitrust Legacy of Thurman Arnold', *St John's Law Review*, **78**, 569–613.

Watkins, K. (2002), 'Is the WTO Legit?', *Foreign Policy*, **132**, 78–9.

Webb, J.M. (1957), 'Patents: The Changing Standard of Patentable Invention: Confusion Compounded', *Michigan Law Review*, **55** (7), 985–97.

Weber, M. (1976), Book Review: Pavel, I. (1976), *The Priority of N.C. Paulescu in the Discovery of Insulin*, Academy of the Socialist Republic of Romania, *The Journal of Historical Review*, **5** (1), 101–5.

Webster, T. (1844), *Reports and Notes and Cases on Letters Patent For Inventions* (London: Thomas Blenkarn).

Weesel, W. (1927), 'Dutch Patent Law and Chemical Inventions', *Industrial and Engineering Chemistry*, **19** (8), 956–7.

Westerlund, L. (2002), *Equivalence and Exclusions under European and U.S. Patent Law* (New York: Kluwer Law International).

Wigley, D.E. (2000), 'Evolution of the Concept of Non-obviousness of the Novel Invention: From a Flash of Genius to the Trilogy', *Arizona Law Review*, **42**, 581–605.

Williams, B. (2007), 'Sainsbury, Alan John', *Oxford Dictionary of National Biography*, available at http://www.oxforddnb.com.virtual.anu.edu.au/view/printable/71184.

Williams-Jones, B. (2002), 'History of a Gene Patent: Tracing the Development and Application of Commercial BRCA Testing', *Health Law Journal*, **10**, 123–46.

Wilson, C. (1954), *The History of Unilever: A Study in Economic Growth and Social Change* (London: Cassell & Company).

Wilson, C. (1965), 'Economy and Society in Late Victorian Britain', *The Economic History Review*, **18** (1), 183–98.

Wolfram, C.W. (1976), 'The Antibiotics Class Actions', *American Bar Foundation Research Journal*, **1** (1), 251–363.

Wolman L. (1943), 'The Beveridge Report', *Political Science Quarterly*, **58** (1), 1–10.

Wooster, R. et al. (1994), 'Localization of a Breast Cancer Susceptibility Gene, BRCA 2, to Chromosome 13q 12–13', *Science*, New Series, **265** (5181), 2088–90.

Wooster, R. et al. (1995), 'Identification of the Breast Cancer Susceptibility Gene BRCA 2', *Nature*, **378**, 789–92 (addendum).

Xie, J. and P. Schultz (2006), 'A Chemical Toolkit for Proteins – an Expanded Genetics Code', *Molecular Cell Biology*, **7**, 778–82.

Young, R.A. and E.W. Davis (1983), 'Efficient Isolation of Genes by Using Antibody Probes', *Proceedings of the National Academy of Sciences*, **80** (1), 1194–8.

Zebel, S.H. (1940), 'Fair Trade: An English Reaction to the Breakdown of the Cobden Treaty System', *The Journal of Modern History*, **12** (2), 161–85.

Zekos, G. (2006), 'Nanotechnology and Biotechnology Patents', *International Journal of Law and Information Technology*, **14**, 310–69.

REPORTS

Australia

National Health & Medical Research Council (1993), *Report on the Epidemiology, Natural History and Control of Hepatitis C*.

Denmark

Danish Council of Ethics (2004), *Report on Patenting Human Genes and Stem Cells*.

European Union

Administrative Council Report to the Administrative Council Members of the EU (2007), *Future workload*, CA/144/07, 23 November.

European Commission to the European Parliament and the Council (2002), *Development and Implications of Patent Law in the Field of Biotechnology and Genetic Engineering*.

European Commission to the European Parliament, The Council, The Economic and Social Committee and the Committee of the Regions (2002), *Life Sciences and Biotechnology – A Strategy for Europe*.

European Commission's Directorate-General for Internal Market (2004), *Study on Evaluating the Knowledge Economy: What are Patents Actually Worth?*

European Commission's Directorate-General for Research (2004), *Patenting DNA Sequences and Scope of Protection*.

European Commission's Directorate-General for Research (2006), *Europeans and Biotechnology in 2005: Patterns and Trends*.

European Commission's Joint Research Centre (2007), *Consequences, Opportunities and Challenges of Modern Biotechnology for Europe*.

European Group on Ethics in Science and New Technologies (2002), *A History of Patenting Life in the United States with Comparative Attention to Europe and Canada.*

India

Report of the Technical Expert Group (2006), *Patent Law Issues.*

United Kingdom

Board of Trade, C.H. Sargant (1931), *Report of the Departmental Committee on the Patents and Designs Acts and Practice of the Patent Office* [Cmd 3829].

Board of Trade, K.R. Swan (1945), *Patents and Designs Acts, First Interim Report of the Departmental Committee* [Cmd 6618].

Board of Trade, K.R. Swan (1946), *Patents and Designs Acts, Second Interim Report of the Departmental Committee* [Cmd 6789].

Board of Trade, K.R. Swan (1947), *Patents and Designs Acts, Final Report of the Departmental Committee* [Cmd 7206].

Board of Trade (1965), *United Kingdom Patent Law: the Effects of the Strasbourg Convention of 1963* [Cmd 2835].

Committee of Inquiry, Lord Sainsbury (1967), *Relationship of the Pharmaceutical Industry with the National Health Services* [Cmd 3410].

Committee of Inquiry, M.A.L. Banks (1970), *The British Patent System* [Cmd 4407].

Department of Health (2007), *The Path of Least Resistance.*

Department of Trade (1975), *Patent Law Reform* [Cmd 6000].

House of Lords Select Committee on The European Communities (1994), *Patent Protection For Biotechnological Inventions.*

Human Genetics Commission (2007), *More Genes Direct.*

Monopolies and Mergers Commission (1985), *Ford Motor Company Limited* [Cmd 9437].

Monopolies and Restrictive Practices Commission (1952), *Report on the Supply of Insulin.*

Monopolies and Restrictive Practices Commission (1973), *Report on the Supply of Chlordiazepoxide and Diazepam.*

Office of Fair Trading (2007), *The Pharmaceutical Price Regulation Scheme.*

Prime Minister (1983), *Intellectual Property Rights and Innovation* [Cmd 9117].

Royal Commission (1865), *Report of The Commissioners, Working of the Law Relating to Letters Patent for Inventions.*

Royal Pharmaceutical Society of Great Britain (2006), *Realising the Potential of Genomic Medicine.*

Royal Society (The) (2003), *Keeping Science Open: The Effects of Intellectual Property Policy on the Conduct of Science.*

United States of America

Alien Property Custodian (1919), *Alien Property Custodian Report 1918–1919*, Washington, DC: US Government Printing Office: reprinted 1977 (New York: Arno Press).

Department of Justice and The Fair Trade Commission (2007), *Antitrust Enforcement and Intellectual Property Rights: Promoting Innovation and Competition.*

Fair Trade Commission (2003), *To Promote Innovation: The Proper Balance of Competition and Patent Law and Policy.*

Government Accountability Office Report (2006), *Nutrigenetic Testing: Tests Purchased from Four Web Sites Mislead Consumers.*

Government Accountability Office Report (2007) *Hiring Efforts Are Not Sufficient to Reduce the Patent Application Backlog*, GAO-07-11-2, September.

House of Representatives, Judiciary Subcommittee on Courts and Intellectual Property (2000), *Gene Patents and Other Genomic Inventions*, 13 July.

House of Representatives Subcommittee on Courts, the Internet, and Intellectual Property: Committee on the Judiciary, Intellectual Property Rights in the Knowledge-Based Economy (2007), *A Patent System For The 21st Century*, 15 February.

Patent Office (1873), *Annual Report of the Commissioner of Patents for 1873.*

NGOs

Coalition for Patent Fairness (2007), *Patent Reform: Protecting Property Rights and the Marketplace of Ideas.*

Consumers International (2007), *Drugs, Doctors and Dinners, How drug companies influence health on the developing world.*

Greenpeace (2004), *The True Cost of Gene Patents*, available at http://web log.greenpeace.org/ge/archives/1study_True_Costs_Gene_Patents.pdf.

Nuffield Council on Bioethics (2002), *The Ethics of Patenting DNA: A Discussion Paper.*

National Research Council (2004), *A Patent System For The 21st Century*: http://www.nap.edu/html/patentsystem/0309089107.pdf.

Oxfam (2004), *Undermining Access to Medicines: Comparison of Five US FTA's.*

UN Agencies

WIPO (2007), *Patent Report Statistics on Worldwide Patent Activity.*
World Health Organization (2003), *Patent Applications for the SARS Virus and Genes.*

Others

Consumers International (2007), *Drugs, Doctors and Dinners, How drug companies influence health in the developing world.*
Ernst & Young (2007), *Final Report Benchmarking Project – Productivity of the EPO, UKIPO & DPMA.*
Price Waterhouse Coopers (2007), *Pharma 2020: The Vision: which Path will you Take?*
Staff Union of the European Patent Office (SUEPO) Position Paper (2004), *Quality of Examination at the EPO*, May.

PATENT APPLICATIONS AND PATENTS

Australia

AU 624, 105 (Effective from 18 November 1988), *NANBV diagnostics and vaccines.*

European Patents

EP 0,013,828 (25 March 1987), *Recombinant DNA, hosts transformed with it and processes for the preparation of polypeptides.*
EP 0,032,134 ((15 August 1984), *DNA sequences, recombinant DNA molecules and processes for producing human interferon-alpha like polypeptides.*
EP 0,077,670 (28 June 1989), *Human immune interferon.*
EP 0,083,286 (7 March 1990), *Modified vaccina virus and methods for making and using the same.*
EP 0,093,619 (13 September 1989), *Human tissue plasminogen activator, pharmaceutical compositions containing it, processes for making it, and DNA and transformed cell intermediates thereof.*
EP 0,096,430 (10 January 1990), *Cloning system for Kluyveromyces species.*

EP 0,112,149 (10 April 1991), *Molecular cloning and characterization of a further gene sequence coding for human relaxin.*

EP 0,122,791 (29 March 1989), *Plant gene expression.*

EP 0,148,605 (25 July 1990), *Production of erythropoietin.*

EP 0,159,418 (9 May 1990), *A process for the incorporation of foreign DNA into the genome of monocotyledonous plants.*

EP 0,182,442 (11 July 1990), *Recombinant DNA molecules and their method of production.*

EP 0,209,539 (20 May 1992), *Homogeneous Erythropoietin.*

EP 0,236,145 (27 March 1991), *Processes for the production of HCMV glycoproteins, antibodies thereto and HCMV vaccines, and recombinant vectors therefor.* [sic]

EP 0,318,216 (15 December 1993), *NANBV diagnostics.*

EP 0,411,678 (8 January 1992), *Method for the production of erythropoietin.*

EP 0,414,475 (10 December 1997), *Methods for culturing HCV in B- or T-lymphocyte cell lines.*

EP 0,450,931 (9 October 1991), *Combinations of hepatitis C virus (HCV) antigens for use in immunoassays for anti-HCV antibodies.*

EP 0,543,924 (18 June 1997), *NANBV diagnostics: polynucleotides useful for screening for hepatitis c virus.*

EP 0,693,687 (28 July 1999), *Combinations of hepatitis c virus (HCV) antigens for use in immunoassays for anti-HCV antibodies.*

EP 0,699,754 (10 January 2001), *Method for diagnosing a predisposition for breast and ovarian cancer.*

EP 0,705,902 (28 November 2001), *17q-linked breast and ovarian cancer susceptibility gene.*

EP 0,705,903 (23 May 2001), *17q-linked breast and ovarian cancer susceptibility gene.*

EP 0,785,216 (8 January 2003), *Chromosome 13-linked breast cancer susceptibility gene BRCA 2.*

EP 0,858,467 (11 February 2004), *Materials and methods relating to the identification and sequencing of the BRCA 2 cancer susceptibility gene and uses thereof.*

United Kingdom Patents

GB 0,747,779 (11 April 1956), *A new antibiotic tetracycline and salts thereof.*

GB 0,796,493 (11 June 1958), *Production of tetracycline by fermentation.*

GB 0,828,911 (24 February 1960), *Improvements in or relating to the purification and separation of tetracycline.*

GB 0,934,853 (21 August 1963), *Production of the antibiotic porfiromycin.*
GB 2,212,511 (22 January 1992), *Hepatitis C Virus.*
GB 2,257,784 (4 January 1995), *Combinations of hepatitis C virus (HCV) antigens for use in immunoassays for anti-HCV antibodies.*

United States Patents

US 0,095,465 (5 October 1869), '*Improved process of preparing alizarine.* (Reissued as: US 4,321 (4 April 1871) *Improvement in dyes or coloring matter from anthracine).*
US 0,135,245 (28 January 1873), *Improvement in Brewing Beer and Ale.*
US 0,141,092 (22 July 1873), *Improvement in the Manufacture of Beer and Yeast.*
US 0,153,536 (28 July 1874), *Improvement in the preparation of coloring matters from anthracene.*
US 0,644,077 (27 February 1900), *Acetly Salicylic Acid.*
US 1,018,502 (27 February 1912), *Incandescent Bodies For Electric Lamps.*
US 1,082,933 (30 December 1913), *Tungsten and methods of Making the same for use as Filaments of Incandescent Electric Lamps and for other purposes.*
US 1,469,994 (9 October 1923), *Extract Obtainable from the Mammalian Pancreas or from the Related Glands in Fishes, Useful in the Treatment of Diabetes Mellitus, and a Method of Preparing It.*
US 1,520,673 (23 December 1924), *Purified Antidiabetic Product and Process of Making It.*
US 2,442,141 (25 May 1948) *Method for production of penicillin.*
US 2,699,054 (11 January 1955), *Tetracycline.*
US 2,776,243 (1 January 1957), *Process for production of tetracycline.*
US 2,998,352 (29 August 1961), *Production of tetracyclines.*
US 3,420,810 (7 January 1969), *Process for Joining the A and B Chains of Insulin.*
US 3,591,574 (6 July 1971), *Tri-N-Phenylglycyl Derivatives of Insulin.*
US 3,636,191 (18 January 1972) *Vaccine Against Viral Hepatitis and Process.*
US 3,813,316 (28 May 1974), *Microorganisms having multiple compatible degradative energy-generating plasmids and preparation thereof.*
US 3,853,832 (10 December 1974), *Synthetic human pituitary growth hormone and method of producing it.*
US 3,872,225 (18 March 1975), *Process of viral diagnosis and reagent.*
US 3,903,068 (2 September 1975), *Facile synthesis of human insulin by modification of porcine insulin.*

US 4,007,196 (8 February 1977), *4-Phenylpiperidine compounds.*

US 4,029,642 (14 June 1977), *Process for the manufacture of human insulin.*

US 4,190,495 (26 February 1980), *Modified microorganisms and method of preparing and using same.*

US 4,237,224 (2 December 1980), *Process for producing biologically functional molecular chimeras.*

US 4,320,196 (16 March 1982), *Semi-synthesis of human insulin.*

US 4,332,892 (1 June 1982), *Protein synthesis.*

US 4,342,832 (3 August 1982), *Method of constructing a replicable cloning vehicle having quasi-synthetic genes.*

US 4,343,898 (10 August 1982), *Process for preparing esters of human insulin.*

US 4,356,270 (26 October 1982), *Recombinant DNA cloning vehicle.*

US 4,361,509 (30 November 1982), *Ultrapurification of factor VIII using monoclonal antibodies.* (Reissued as: US 32,011).

US 4,363,877 (14 December 1982), *Recombinant DNA transfer vectors.*

US 4,399,216 (16 August 1983), *Processes for inserting DNA into eucaryotic cells and for producing proteinaceous materials.*

US 4,421,685 (20 December 1983), *Process for producing an insulin.*

US 4,431,740 (14 February 1984), *DNA Transfer vector and transformed microorganism containing human proinsulin and pre-proinsulin genes.*

US 4,440,859 (3 April 1984), *Method for producing recombinant bacterial plasmids containing the coding sequences of higher organisms.*

US 4,565,785 (21 January 1986), *Recombinant DNA molecule.*

US 4,571,421 (18 February 1986), *Mammalian gene for microbial expression.*

US 4,601,980 (22 July 1986), *Microbial expression of a gene for human growth hormone.*

US 4,634,665 (6 January 1987), *Processes for inserting DNA into eucaryotic cells and for producing proteinaceous materials.*

US H245 (7 April 1987), *Plasmid for producing human insulin.*

US 4,652,525 (24 March 1987), *Recombinant bacterial plasmids containing the coding sequences of insulin genes.*

US 4,652,547 (24 March 1987), *Pharmaceutical formulations comprising human insulin and human proinsulin.*

US 4,673,575 (16 June 1987), *Composition, pharmaceutical preparation and method for treating viral hepatitis.*

US 4,674,204 (23 June 1987), *Shock absorbing innersole and method of preparing same.*

US 4,677,195 (30 June 1987), *Method for the purification of erythropoietin and erythropoietin compositions.*

US 4,703,008 (27 October 1987), *DNA sequences encoding erythropoietin.*

US 4,704,362 (3 November 1987), *Recombinant cloning vehicle microbial polypeptide expression.*

US 4,721,723 (26 January 1988), *Anti-depressant crystalline paroxetine hydrochloride hemihydrate.*

US 4,761,371 (2 August 1988), *Insulin receptor.*

US 4,769,238 (6 September 1988), *Synthesis of human virus antigens by yeast.*

US 4,803,164 (7 February, 1989), *Preparation of hepatitis b surface antigen in yeast.*

US 4,898,830 (6 February 1990), *Human growth hormone DNA.*

US 4,992,417 (12 February 1991), *Superactive human insulin analogues.*

US 5,179,017 (12 January 1993), *Processes for inserting DNA into eucaryotic cells and for producing proteinaceous materials.*

US 5,187,151 (16 February 1993), *Use of binding protein with IGF-I as an anabolic growth promoting agent.*

US 5,221,619 (22 June 1993), *Method and means for microbial polypeptide expression.*

US 5,242,900 (7 September 1993), *Treatment of diabetes using phosphorylated insulin.*

US 5,258,287 (2 November 1993), *DNA encoding and methods of production of insulin-like growth factor binding protein BP53.*

US 5,350,671 (27 September 1994), *HCV immunoassays employing C domain antigens.*

US 5,405,942, (11 April 1995), *Prepro insulin-like growth factors I and II.*

US 5,424,199 (13 June 1995), *Human growth hormone.*

US 5,583,013 (10 December 1996), *Method and means for microbial polypeptide expression.*

US 5,618,698 (8 April 1997), *Production of erythropoietin.*

US 5,621,080 (15 April 1997), *Production of erythropoietin.*

US 5,654,155 (5 August 1997), *Consensus sequence of the human BRCA 1 gene.*

US 5,693,473 (2 December 1997), *Linked breast and ovarian cancer susceptibility gene.*

US 5,710,001 (20 January 1998), *17q-linked breast and ovarian cancer susceptibility gene.*

US 5,712,088 (27 January 1998), *Methods for detecting Hepatitis C virus using polynucleotides specific for same.*

US 5,714,596 (3 February 1998), *NANBV diagnostics: polynucleotides useful for screening for hepatitis C virus.*

US 5,753,441 (19 May 1998), *170-linked breast and ovarian cancer susceptibility gene.*

US 5,811,266 (2 September 1998), *Methods for producing human insulin.*

US 5,837,492 (17 November 1998), *Chromosome 13-linked breast cancer susceptibility gene.*

US 5,854,018 (29 December 1998), *Expression of polypeptides in yeast.*

US 5,863,719 (26 January 1999), *Methods for detecting hepatitis C virus using polynucleotides specific for same.*

US 5,968,502 (19 October 1999), *Protein production and protein delivery.*

US 6,018,097 (25 January 2000), *Transgenic mice expressing human insulin.*

US 6,027,729 (22 February 2000), *NANBV Diagnostics and vaccines.*

US 6,033,857 (7 March, 2000), *Chromosome 13-linked breast cancer susceptibility gene.*

US 6,037,351 (14 March 2000), *Method of inhibiting hepatitis B virus.*

US 6,045,997 (4 April 2000), *Materials and methods relating to the identification and sequencing of the BRCA 2 cancer susceptibility gene and uses thereof.*

US 6,048,524 (11 April 2000), *In vivo production and delivery of erythropoietin for gene therapy.*

US 6,054,561 (25 April 2000), *Antigen-binding sites of antibody molecules specific for cancer antigens.*

US 6,074,816 (13 June 2000), *NANBV diagnostics: polynucleotides useful for screening for hepatitis C virus.*

US 6,113,944 (5 September 2000), *Paroxetine tablets and process to prepare them.*

US 6,124,104 (26 September 2000), *Chromosome 13-linked breast cancer susceptibility gene.*

US 6,331,414 (18 December 2001), *Preparation of human IGF via recombinant DNA technology.*

US 6,331,415 (18 December 2001), *Methods of producing immunoglobulins, vectors and transformed host cells for use therein.*

US 6,930,170 (16 August 2005), *PRO1184 polypeptides.*

US 6,989,265 (24 January 2006), *Bacteria with reduced genome.*

US 7,045,346 (16 May 2006), *Nucleic acid constructs useful for glucose regulated production of human insulin in somatic cell lines.*

US 7,105,315 (12 September 2006), *Method for making human insulin precursors.*

US 7,250,497 (31 July 2007), *Large deletions in human BRCA 1 gene and use thereof.*

United States Patent Applications

US 20030170663 (11 September 2003), *Nucleotide sequence of the Mycoplasma genitalium genome, fragments thereof, and uses thereof.*

US 20050170404 (28 January 2005), *Modified human growth hormone polypeptides and their uses.*

US 20050191316 (1 September 2005), *Neisseria genomic sequences and methods of their use.*

US 20070026021 (1 February 2007), *Neisseria meningitidis antigens and compositions.*

US 20070037165 (15 February 2007), *Polymorphisms in known genes associated with human disease, methods of detection and uses thereof.*

US 20070122826 (31 May 2007), *Minimal bacterial genome.*

US 20070264688 (15 November 2007), *Synthetic genomes.*

US 20070269862 (22 November 2007), *Installation of genomes or partial genomes into cells or cell-like systems.*

US 20080028478 (31 January 2008), *Method for Genetic Improvement of Terminal Boars.*

US 20080028482 (31 January 2008), *Corn Plant Mon88017 and Compositions and Methods for Detection Thereof.*

US 20080028491 (31 January 2008), *Hybrids of Exacum.*

US 20080028492 (31 January 2008), *Maize Cellulose Synthases and Uses Thereof.*

Index